Flood of Images

Flood of Images

MEDIA, MEMORY, AND
HURRICANE KATRINA

Bernie Cook

University of Texas Press   *Austin*

Requests for permission to reproduce material from this work should be
sent to:
   Permissions
   University of Texas Press
   P.O. Box 7819
   Austin, TX 78713-7819
   http://utpress.utexas.edu/index.php/rp-form

♾ The paper used in this book meets the minimum requirements of
ANSI/NISO Z39.48-1992 (R1997) (Permanence of Paper).

LIBRARY OF CONGRESS CATALOGING-IN-PUBLICATION DATA
Cook, Bernie, 1968–
   Flood of images : media, memory, and Hurricane Katrina /
by Bernie Cook. — First edition.
      pages   cm
   Includes bibliographical references and index.
   ISBN 978-0-292-77134-5 (cloth : alk. paper)
   ISBN 978-1-4773-0243-9 (pbk : alk. paper)
1. Hurricane Katrina, 2005—Press coverage.   2. Mass media—
Objectivity—United States.   3. Hurricane Katrina, 2005—Social
aspects.   4. United States—Social conditions—21st century.   I. Title.
   HV636 2005 .G85 C645   2015
   976'.044—dc23

                                             2014026619

doi:10.7560/771345

To my wife, Jen, and my children, Lucy and Emmett, my inspiration always. And to the people of New Orleans.

Contents

Preface

THIS BOOK IS A STUDY OF MEDIA REPRESENTATIONS of Hurricane Katrina and the flooding of New Orleans. Through examining the histories of production of Katrina media and through close analysis of specific textual strategies, I argue for the impact of Katrina media on understandings and memories of the storm and flood. Before I focus on media representations and collective memories, it is necessary to establish an understanding of the actual events that occurred in the profilmic world.

NOT THE STORM

On Monday, August 29, 2005, at 6:10 a.m., Hurricane Katrina made landfall at Buras, Louisiana. Though diminished from a Category 5 storm to a Category 3 storm, Katrina still pushed a twenty-one-foot storm surge onto shore, flooding Plaquemines Parish ("Flooded," *Times-Picayune*). Meteorologists had predicted that Katrina would strike New Orleans directly, but the storm jogged east before landfall, creating an even greater storm surge in Mississippi and flooding coastal towns Biloxi, Gulfport, and Bay St. Louis. New Orleans suffered wind damage from the storm, with windows at the downtown Hyatt Regency Hotel blown out, roofs torn off, and trees downed. But the greatest destruction to New Orleans, and the greatest loss of life, did not come directly from the storm.

Even before Katrina made landfall, parts of the greater New Orleans area began to flood. As early as 4:30 a.m., the Industrial Canal levees began to leak ("Flooded"). The levees along the Mississippi River Gulf Outlet (MR-GO) Canal failed, and St. Bernard Parish began to flood. By 6:30 a.m., the levees in New Orleans East failed, flooding thousands of homes. By 7:30 a.m., the levees on the west side of the Industrial Canal breached and the Upper Ninth Ward, Bywater, and Treme neighborhoods flooded. Shortly thereafter, the levees on the east side of the Industrial Canal failed, sending a wall of water into the Lower Ninth Ward and Arabi neighborhoods, pushing houses off foundations and tossing cars ("Flooded"). By 9:00 a.m., the surge overtopped the Orleans Avenue Canal, flooding City Park. By 9:30 a.m., the east wall of the London Avenue Canal breached, flooding the Gentilly neighborhood. By 9:45 a.m., the 17th Street Canal levees failed, flooding Lakeview, Midtown, and parts of Metairie. Katrina pushed water into MR-GO, Lake Borgne, Lake Pontchartrain, and the canal system, pouring water through multiple breaches in the levees constructed by the Army Corps of Engineers to protect the City of New Orleans from flooding due to a hurricane. Water continued to flow into the city from Lake Pontchartrain until Thursday, September 1, 2005, four days after Katrina's landfall. All told, 80 percent of the City of New Orleans flooded due to the failure of the federally constructed and maintained levee system. The Lower Ninth Ward, Arabi, Gentilly, Lakeview, and parts of New Orleans East were covered by more than ten feet of water.

The City of New Orleans was not completely drained of floodwater until the first week of October. Houses, buildings, and bodies remained in and under water for more than five weeks. A report by the Louisiana Department of Health and Hospitals estimated that 1,577 people died in Louisiana as a result of Katrina and the flooding. In the New Orleans area, 1,056 people died, including at least 700 who died in Orleans Parish. In Mississippi, 238 were estimated to have died. The Louisiana Department of Health and Hospitals report indicated that the elderly and the infirm made up the largest percentage of Katrina casualties (Warner, 2005). While people died in the largest numbers in the Lower Ninth Ward and in Gentilly, the report confirmed that people died across the city. Many of the bodies were not recovered for weeks. Some were discovered by family members months later.

Acknowledgments

I N RESEARCHING AND WRITING THIS BOOK, I HAVE BENE-
fitted from the assistance and support of many people. Like
Katrina media, Katrina scholarship is enriched by a diversity of perspectives and experiences. While the arguments (and any errors) in this book
are my own, the book is much richer for the contributions made by others.

I would like to thank Chester Gillis, dean of Georgetown College, for
his strong support of my scholarship, including providing a crucial research
leave early in the project.

I would like to thank Jim Burr, my editor at the University of Texas
Press. Jim was strongly supportive of this book from my earliest proposal.
I benefitted from his encouragement and insight throughout my writing
and editing. I also benefitted from the careful and thoughtful responses
from two outside readers.

I would like to thank the documentary filmmakers I interviewed for
this book. I learned so much from each interview, and these interviews
provided vital evidence for my research. Thanks to Tia Lessin, Carl Deal,
Dawn Logsdon, Lolis Elie, Luisa Dantas, Katherine Cecil, Leo Chiang, Jon
Siskel, Greg Jacobs, Nancy Biurski, and Phoebe Tooke. Special thanks to
Rebecca Snedeker for her insight and for introductions to other filmmakers.

I would like to thank the journalists I interviewed for this book. Miles
O'Brien and Kim Bondy provided considerable insight into television
news coverage of Katrina. A. C. Thompson discussed his long-form, long-
duration journalism and his collaboration on Katrina media.

I would like to thank David Simon and Eric Overmyer for insight into
the creation of the television series *Treme* and for broader insight into the
challenges of using fiction to respond to the flooding of New Orleans.

Thanks to Blake Leyh, who worked closely with Simon and Overmyer to pioneer new approaches to documenting musical performance in *Treme*.

I would like to thank Andy Horton, Caetlin Benson-Allott, and Jacob Brogan for joining me on a panel at the Society For Cinema and Media Studies Conference in New Orleans in 2011. The panel examined representations of New Orleans in film and media, and I presented the first version of my argument about mediation and memory of Katrina during this session.

I am deeply grateful to my colleagues in the College Dean's Office who supported my writing. Thanks to Anne Sullivan, Sue Lorenson, Keshia Woods, Ali Whitmer, and Ed Meyertholen. Special thanks to Robin Stanton for her help with my research and with the production of the manuscript.

I am also deeply indebted to my colleagues in Georgetown's Film and Media Studies Program. Lily Hughes provided support throughout, and Changa Bell provided special assistance with the selection and preparation of the illustrations. Heidi Ewing and Sky Sitney each offered important insights into the documentary process, and I learned a great deal from co-teaching *Social Justice Documentary* with them during the completion of this book. Caetlin Benson-Allott, Roberto Bocci, Anna Celenza, John Glavin, Ben Harbert, Brian Hochman, Miléna Santoro, Robynn Stillwell, Patricia Vieira, and Alejandro Yarza form a dynamic intellectual community of film and media scholars at Georgetown, enriching and inspiring my work.

Special thanks to my colleague Andrew Sobanet for his theorization of "documentary fiction" and for his support throughout my writing and editing.

I want to thank my students for responding to and for enriching aspects of my argument. Special thanks to Kylie Pienaar, Dan Thoenessen, and Sarah Moore for providing research assistance during the writing of this book.

I would like to thank my friends in New Orleans for supporting my work. Very special thanks to Sharon Courtney, generous friend and consummate host. I would also like to thank Terri Troncale and Margi Sunkel for their insights into the lived experience on the ground in New Orleans after the flood.

Finally, I would like to thank my family. I grew up on the West Bank of New Orleans, and my parents, Bernard and Rosemary, and my sister, Jennifer, have always supported my twin interests in media and in New Orleans culture. They strongly supported my work on this book. I would like to thank Margaret Drugay and David Horwitz for offering me a space in which to write and for supporting my work. Finally, I could not have written this book without the love and support of my children, Lucy and Emmett, and my wife, Jen. Together, they inspire everything that I do.

Where Y'at?

*W*HAT KATRINA MEANS, TEN YEARS LATER, DEPENDS on what you remember about the storm and flood. What you remember about Katrina depends on your location in relationship to the hurricane and the flooding of New Orleans. If you were in New Orleans or on the Gulf Coast during the storm, if you climbed into your attic in the Ninth Ward, or onto your roof in Chalmette, or up into a tree in Gulfport, Mississippi, to avoid the storm surge, you remember Katrina as life threatening and world changing. If you were far removed from New Orleans, watching events on a 24-hour cable news channel, you likely remember Katrina as disturbing, perhaps fascinating.

Location matters to the production and uses of memory as to the production and uses of media. The decision by television news networks to place resources in New Orleans's French Quarter and Central Business District had consequences for coverage of the failure of the federally built and maintained levees surrounding New Orleans. From the French Quarter and the lower Central Business District, which are located by the Mississippi River, near the original French settlement, television news could not see the flooding of New Orleans at first. Viewers watching at home, far from New Orleans, understood the hurricane to have largely spared the city because television news reported multiple versions of the "dodged the bullet" story.

If your primary source of information about Katrina was media, then your memories of Katrina, and your sense of what the hurricane meant in 2005, and what it means today, also were shaped by media—television news, documentary film, and fictional stories. As I argue in this book, the conditions of production of television news, of documentary film, and of fictional television shaped the versions of Katrina that were constructed and shared. Similarly, the conditions of reception of media shaped how viewers encountered, understood, and remembered how Katrina was represented in the national media.

Of course, the conditions of production of this book also shape what I am able to argue about Katrina, how Katrina was mediated, and how media representations shaped the possibilities for memory about Katrina. When the storm made landfall in the early hours of Monday, August 29, 2005, I was living in Alexandria, Virginia. I grew up on the West Bank of New Orleans, across the Mississippi River from the city, in the town of Gretna in Jefferson Parish. I remember Gretna as suburbia, full of ranch houses and strip malls, but many now remember the town because the Gretna police barricaded the Crescent City Connection bridge on Thursday, September 1, 2005, preventing fellow citizens from using the bridge to evacuate the flooded City of New Orleans for the largely unflooded West Bank. I moved away from New Orleans to attend college, and though I have often returned, I have not lived there since the mid-1980s.

On August 29, 2005, my parents were visiting from New Orleans for the Labor Day weekend. We stayed up late on Sunday, until the early hours of August 29, hoping to learn the fate of the city, even as we were distanced from the hurricane's immediate impact. As a film and media studies scholar, I was aware of Marita Sturken's 2001 work on the production of "weather citizens" by television news coverage of devastating storms, how television news hails viewers, encouraging continued viewing as a surrogate for implication and action. Mostly, however, I was worried about the status of my parents' home and about the safety of New Orleans residents who remained in the city. Later Monday morning, we watched television news reports that all was clear, and we used the newly unveiled Google Earth to find a satellite photograph confirming that my parents' house still stood. Even though we had deep-lived connections to New Orleans, we relied on visual technologies and media reports for information.

In *Old and New Media After Katrina* (2010), Diane Negra has argued that for most Americans, Katrina was a media event: "Katrina remains a cultural event strikingly difficult to access independent of its media" (5). Television and new media provided a sort of connection to the events in New Orleans, but both television news and new media technology also structured distance and disconnection. According to Sturken, distance and disconnection are central to the pleasures of weather citizenship. In our case, our lived connection to New Orleans worked against this structured distance, causing displeasure and frustration, as when we wanted television news to cover different parts of the city and to share different information. Our experience of Katrina involved negotiation and struggle with dominant media accounts. Our memories of Katrina are certainly shaped by television news coverage, but also by a sense of the problems and absences in that coverage. As a consequence, I have also sought out documentary and fictional representations of Katrina, both to continue to inform my understanding and memory of the storm and flood and to understand the implications of representational choices through comparative media analysis.

In "Rights and Return," Janet Walker discusses the importance (and some drawbacks) of "situated testimony" for understanding and remembering Katrina. In her analysis of Katrina media, from Spike Lee and Sam Pollard's *When the Levees Broke* (HBO 2006) to 2-Cent Media Collective's video *New Orleans for Sale* (2008), Walker examines interviews and observational scenes shot on location in New Orleans. She argues that documentary interviews and scenes can realize the materiality of testimony in the power of place (85). For Walker, situated testimony locates suffering and loss in space and history, providing testimony with the power to convey individual lived experience to others.

In this book, I undertake a form of situated scholarship. My own location vis-à-vis New Orleans, Katrina, media, and memory has shaped my research process, my arguments, and their expression. I interviewed television news producers and anchors, documentary filmmakers, and television show runners in order to understand, locate, and describe the modes of production that shaped Katrina media. As Peter Burke has argued, media is not evidence of history; rather, media is historical, shaped and created by practices that have their own histories (2001). Through interviews with Miles O'Brien, Tia Lessin, and David Simon, among many other media makers, I have sought to understand the implications for meaning and memory of how Katrina was represented.

In addition to conducting original research into the histories of production of Katrina media, I have located my analysis in close readings of media texts. Katrina media and memory were dominated initially by television news. The flood of images and sounds provided by 24-hour cable news networks CNN and Fox overwhelmed scholars as well as viewers. Negra notes "a mediathon of television coverage in September 2005," but neither she nor her contributors closely examine specific television news programs and reports (5). In "Failing Narratives, Initiating Technologies: Hurricane Katrina and the Production of a Weather Media Event," Nicole Fleetwood argues for "privilege given in public culture to the media coverage of the disaster" (767). Fleetwood promises to analyze "the news media archive of the storm and its aftermath," but she only references a single specific news report, a CNN story on an African American man identified as "Hardy Jackson," who lost his wife in the flood while saving his children (776). Fleetwood does not locate this report by date or context. My own review of CNN's coverage during the first week of the flood on *NewsNight with Aaron Brown* located this report as having been broadcast on Tuesday, August 30, 2005. While Fleetwood does not examine the form and structure of the report, I noted that this was one of the very few news reports on any network that identified a survivor by name. Moreover, CNN made a mistake in the report directly before the one cited by Fleetwood. In the preceding story, set in Mississippi, a white man in his early thirties is identified by a lower third title as "Hardy Jackson." After a few moments, CNN removed the title. Then, in the next report about the man from New Orleans, the network again applied the title "Hardy Jackson." Context suggests that the second man was Hardy Jackson and that the linkage of the name to the man in Mississippi was a mistake. Yet, this mistake reveals the tendency of television news to more readily identify white survivors by name and to interview African American survivors without identification or location. The mistaken doubling of "Hardy Jackson" raises questions about the identities of both men, and this rupture in television news convention raises questions about CNN's claim to represent real events with accuracy. Fleetwood states that "his face is etched in our collective memory," but a closer examination of the specifics of the report and its context reveals that viewers cannot even tell for sure which man is Jackson (776). I argue that close contextual analysis of television news is necessary to understand the impact of news coverage on collective memory about Katrina.

In *Flood of Images*, I closely examine the textually situated visual rhetorics through which television news reporting shaped versions of Katrina. Most Television Studies and Communications scholarship on television news uses transcripts of newscasts to analyze discourse. Drawing on Deborah Jaramillo's model in *Ugly War, Pretty Package* (2009) and building on my own approach to analyzing television news coverage of casualties in Vietnam (Cook, 2001), I examine specific news reports in detail in order to argue for the impact of visual rhetorics on representations of Katrina. Scholarship on television news has long privileged voice, how anchors and reporters address viewers, following television's own prioritization of spoken reporting to the "A roll" and visuals to the "B roll." In *Flood of Images*, I develop new approaches to the analysis of television news in order to understand the specific shapes and meanings of television news reporting on Katrina. I conduct this analysis in order to argue in specific ways about the terrain created by television news for the collective, public memory about Katrina.

I was able to apply close textual analysis to television news coverage of Katrina because the Vanderbilt Television News Archive has preserved and provides access to the nightly news programs on both the traditional broadcast networks and the cable news network. Thus, because of Vanderbilt's archival practices, I have focused on evening news coverage rather than on morning or daytime news programming about Katrina. Through Vanderbilt, I accessed full programs for the week of August 28 through September 4, 2005 (Sunday to Sunday, from apprehension over landfall to the final evacuation of the city): NBC *Nightly News* with Brian Williams, CNN's *NewsNight with Aaron Brown*, and *The Fox Report* with various studio anchors and Shepard Smith anchoring from the field in New Orleans.

I chose to focus on NBC, Fox, and CNN for several reasons. NBC was the most watched broadcast network during Katrina, averaging nearly 10.8 million viewers per night during the first week of the flood (Pew Research, March 13, 2006). Fox was the highest-rated cable news network, averaging 2.8 million viewers per night. CNN attracted 1.9 million viewers per night. According to the Pew Research Center, across all platforms, CNN attracted the most unique viewers of any news network, as many as 100 million over the first week. Thus, in terms of reach to audience, these three were the most significant television networks covering Katrina.

In addition, I chose to focus on NBC, Fox, and CNN because these networks provide a range of programming formats. NBC *Nightly News* was 30 minutes per night, broadcast nationally from 6:30 to 7:00 p.m. Eastern Standard Time. *The Fox Report* was 60 minutes, airing nightly from 7:00 to 8:00 p.m. EST. CNN's *NewsNight* was 120 minutes, airing nightly from 10:00 p.m. to midnight EST. Additionally, the three networks provided at least an ostensible range of ideological perspectives, with Fox explicitly addressing Republican and conservative viewers, while CNN and NBC addressed less differentiated audiences. While each claims editorial distinctiveness (for competitive advantage), the networks shared many common elements, approaches, and conclusions about Katrina-as-reported. I analyze distinctive reporting as well as the common approaches that created a television news supertext for Katrina. During the first week after the storm and flood, before the networks, and thus viewers, turned away from New Orleans, television news created the most extensive audiovisual representation of Katrina. This news archive fed the generation of collective national memories of Katrina.

The initial television news coverage of Katrina also served as source material for later mediations of the storm and flood. In particular, documentary filmmakers accessed the television news archive in order to visually represent aspects of the storm and flood. In the second section of this book, I follow the found footage, the link between television news and documentary film. If television news formed the broadest, most-watched set of representations of Katrina, documentary films were able to explore stories, witness events, and feature voices overlooked, neglected, or suppressed by television news. Where television news relentlessly chases the breaking story, documentary filmmaking proceeds at a slow, more deliberate pace (due to funding, access, and scheduling). Documentary practice is durational rather than reactive. Documentary often involves recovery of missing, lost, and underappreciated perspectives.

If television news established a baseline of understanding, a Katrina-as-reported, documentary films complicate and contest these broad understandings. Where television news reporting looked at and spoke about New Orleans residents, documentary film enabled survivors of the flood to speak and express their lived memories. In *They Must Be Represented*, Paula Rabinowitz's 1994 study of documentary and the relations between truth claims and political agency, she describes "the house of representation" as an alternative sphere in which those excluded from political representation can strive to be seen and heard (218). Rabinowitz imagines this metaphorical house as a political chamber, where those consigned to being documentary subjects might struggle for agency and self-representation. If television news flooded the house of representation with images and stories, documentary film offers perspective on those initial representations, changing what is known and remembered about Katrina.

Of course, as with any mediation, documentary involves the co-presence of perspectives, and filmmakers ultimately shape how viewers access, see, and hear their subjects. Thus, as with television news, I closely analyze moments of representation from key documentaries about Katrina. Documentaries examined include *Trouble the Water* (Tia Lessin and Carl Deal, 2008); *Faubourg Treme* (Dawn Logsdon and Lolis Elie, 2009); *A Village Called Versailles* (S. Leo Chiang, 2009); *Land of Opportunity* (Luisa Dantas, 2011); *Race* (Katherine Cecil, 2010); and Spike Lee and Sam Pollard's omnibus HBO documentaries *When the Levees Broke* (HBO 2006) and *If God Is Willing and Da Creek Don't Rise* (HBO 2010). In this section of the book, I propose that documentary film complicated and contested Katrina-as-remembered, not content to allow national television news to state what Katrina was and what it meant. While Nicole Fleetwood argues that television news visualized Achille Mbembe's theory of necropolitics, casting the survivors of Katrina as the already discounted and pre-dead, I argue that documentary films about Katrina offered what filmmaker Ricky Leacock called a "living cinema," countering necropolitics with portraits of life in the face of devastation, portraits inviting viewers to engage and to participate in the lives represented. Documentary provides survivors with access to the house of representation. Although television news coverage of Katrina reached much larger audiences, documentaries about Katrina continue to circulate and reach new audiences, in new contexts. Documentary films speaking from and of multiple perspectives form a crucial archive of the lived experience of the storm and flood.

Because the past, even the near past, is unavailable, film and media makers must find ways to render the inaccessible. Documentarians use found footage of past events, personal memories, archival documents, interviews, and other techniques to make the past present. Fictional media makers employ many of the same devices, but enjoy greater latitude to invent in order to access the inaccessible. Per John Grierson's definition, documentary can be understood as a creative treatment of actuality, but this same definition can be applied to fiction—at least fiction that aspires to treat the actual. In the third section of this book, I explore the importance of fiction for shaping Katrina-as-remembered. The key text in this final section is David Simon and Eric Overmyer's *Treme* (HBO 2010–2013). While documentaries often feature narratives, fictional narratives rarely attempt the same truth claim as documentary. *Treme* provides viewers with opportunities for accessing the points of view of characters whose experiences were built from careful research. As documentary fiction, *Treme* provides important understandings about Katrina, understandings connected explicitly to real events.

MEMORY PROJECT

As noted, Fleetwood asserts that Hardy Jackson's face had been "etched in our collective memory," but she does not define "collective memory" or how it might be constituted. In *On Collective Memory* (1992), Maurice Halbwachs argued that memory is social and that coherent and persistent memory takes place only in group contexts. Halbwachs understood collective memory to be produced by shared experiences: "crucial public events leave deep imprints on the minds of direct participants" (30). However, Katrina was marked by a paucity of experience and a surplus of mediation. Photographer and artist Aric Mayer has argued that Katrina was for most Americans a media event. Mayer traveled to New Orleans after Katrina and shot photographs from which he produced an exhibition called *Balance + Disorder: A Response to Hurricane Katrina and the Photographic Landscape*. In an article for *Public Culture* (2008), "Aesthetics of Catastrophe," Mayer notes that "to put the national Hurricane Katrina experience in perspective, fewer than several hundred thousand people witnessed the storm in person. For the other 99.8 percent of Americans, the disaster was a media experience with lasting implications for the public opinion and action" (178). According to Mayer, Katrina coverage left deep imprints on the minds of indirect participants, shaping public opinions and influencing action.

Any collective memory of Katrina is based more on mediation than on direct experience. In *Practices of Looking* (2009), Marita Sturken and Lisa Cartwright suggest that media can create a broader public by uniting people all watching the same things on different screens (156). As Mayer argues, 99.8 percent of Americans experienced Katrina as a media event. Per Halbwachs, the shared experience of watching the same mediations, especially in the case of television news coverage, could constitute a public and provide the ground for collective memory. Halbwachs drew a distinction between collective memory and two other forms of memory. He described the memory of events directly experienced as "autobiographical memory" (30). According to Mayer, only 0.2 percent of Americans experienced autobiographical memory of Katrina. Halbwachs suggested that collective memory was stronger and more lasting than autobiographical memory because collective memory involved minds working together in a society. If collective memory was formed via a process involving shared experience, Halbwachs defined "historical memory" as the end of the process of memory, when collective memory is hardened and fixed into official memory.

Official memory of Katrina involves exclusion and forgetting as much as remembering. Geoffrey Hartman is greatly concerned by the movement from collective memory to historical memory. In "Public Memory and Its Discontents" (1994), he contends that official history threatens public memory by seeking to fix the possibilities of memory into a unified account. Hartman considers official historical memory to be a form of "anti-memory" (6). He understands media as a tool for the production of official memory and is especially critical of television news, arguing that television news converts raw events and experience into stories and packages. By processing reality, television news produces distance, spectacle, exhaustion, and indifference (2). Hartman argues that the television apparatus creates two classes of people: those who suffer and those who watch the suffering of others. Applying Hartman's argument to Mayer's math, television news coverage of Katrina separated Americans into the 99.8 percent who watched the suffering of the 0.2 percent. Hartman draws a distinction between observing and witnessing, and he finds observing to lack the dimensions of connection and implication that invest witnessing with social responsibility and agency. Hartman warns that "memory is manipulated like news" (29).

Television news coverage influenced authoritative, official histories of Katrina. David Shayt's 2006 article, "Artifacts of Disaster," reveals the impact of television news coverage of Katrina on the possibilities for memory and history. Shayt is a curator in the Smithsonian's National Museum of American History, what Hartman describes as a "memory institution." In October 2005, after New Orleans was finally drained of floodwater, Shayt and colleagues went to the city to collect "the material record of that day" in order to create a "Katrina Collection" for use by future Smithsonian curators (357). Shayt relates, "We had made a big list of 'ghost artifacts' before we departed, things we thought belonged in an ideal material record of the storm" (357). These "ghost artifacts" included an axe used to chop through a roof, handmade "help!" signs, and Michael Brown's FEMA identification card. Shayt acknowledges that his approach to collecting material artifacts from New Orleans was shaped by his viewing of television news coverage. His sense of which objects counted as evidence for the future versions of the official historical memory of Katrina was already shaped and pre-determined by television news coverage. As Hartman notes, television news coverage is not disinterested. Thus, the values and decisions informing the television coverage of Katrina shaped the approaches of other memory institutions.

Where Hartman understands media to negatively influence public memory by shaping the conditions for memory according to particular conventions and values, Alison Landsberg argues for the progressive potential of media for memory (2004). Examining mass media and memory institutions in the twentieth century, Landsberg suggests that viewers of film and television and visitors to museums could experience "prosthetic memory," a process through which an individual could add virtual memories into one's "archive of experience." Landsberg defines prosthetic memory as a new form of memory that emerges at the interface of an individual and a historical narrative in an experiential setting (11). In a sense, Landsberg is arguing for the potential of media to enable viewers to form autobiographical memory through watching. Where Hartman argues that observing is a diminished form of witnessing, Landsberg argues that film and television offer the grounds not only for memory, but also for empathy. Building on the work of Jill Bennett, Landsberg draws historical distinctions between the concepts of sympathy and empathy. Landsberg considers sympathy to be the act of "pouring oneself into the other's place," of projecting oneself into the experience of another in a way that obscures the distance between self and other (149). In contrast, she argues that empathy is cognitive as well as affective. Empathy starts from a position of difference and is predicated on an understanding of things outside of the self (149).

Landsberg's concept of "prosthetic memory" suggests that Katrina media could convey experience in powerful and meaningful ways to viewers who lacked direct connection to the flooding of New Orleans. Even if television news reinforced official memory, documentary and (especially) fiction could provide viewers with opportunities to engage with the experiences of others, making new meanings and working toward empathy.

Hartman also offers an alternative to official memory, to the closing down of understanding. In contrast to collective memory, which Hartman finds to be too monolithic, he proposes the alternative of "collected memory." Hartman understands collected memory to be "active community memory" made up of "legends, poetry, symbols, dances, songs, festivals, and recitations" (6). Collected memory can be understood as an organic archive of multiple voices and perspectives: "by recording an experience collectively endured, by allowing anyone in the community a voice—that is, not focusing on an elite—a vernacular and many voiced dimension is caught" (11).

Katrina documentary can be understood as a form of collected memory of the storm and flood. Both individual documentaries, and the archive as a whole, speak to the experiences of Katrina with multiple voices, sharing distinct perspectives. In this way, documentary media on Katrina can serve as an alternative and corrective to the baseline for official memory produced by television news.

Jan Assman defines mnemohistory as the study of "the past as remembered" (1997). In *Flood of Images*, I examine the mnemohistory of Katrina through analysis of key representations in multiple modes. Assman argues that mnemohistory involves the "ongoing work of the reconstructive imagination" (9). Following Assman, I propose that the truth of Katrina may only be approached via the work of discovery, comparison, and analysis. Katrina is a twenty-first-century memory project. This is not a book about memory, but a book about a specific memory project. In *Flood of Images*, I examine Katrina media in order to use analysis to annotate memory.

WHERE Y'AT?

In New Orleans, the colloquial expression "where y'at?" is as much a greeting as an actual question. "Where y'at?" asks how you are doing as much as where you are located. The term "Yat," used to reference a native New Orleanian, is taken from this expression. As an inquiry about disposition and location, "where y'at?" is a necessary question to ask of the production of Katrina media, viewership of Katrina media, and scholarship about Katrina media. The location and disposition of the act of production, or reception, or analysis shapes the meanings produced and circulated. Distance from the flooding of New Orleans leaves viewers with only mediation to provide information about what happened. National media, especially television news, has strongly shaped collective memory about Katrina. In contrast, documentary and fiction have created opportunities to connect more closely to lived experience of the flooding of New Orleans. Through voice and situated testimony, documentary contributes collected memories about the storm and flood, memories that remain multivocal and unreduced. Through (re)creation and the construction of point of view, fiction provides viewers with access to versions of the lived experiences of survivors of Katrina. Both documentary and fiction create the grounds for empathy and thus implication and action.

In *Flood of Images*, I analyze the memory work around the representations of Katrina in various media and on various platforms, and the stakes involved for how Katrina is remembered. This book is itself an act of memory work. The critical act of analysis and argument itself contests the possible memories and meanings of Katrina. In this way, I offer *Flood of Images* as both analysis and intervention into the remembering and forgetting of Katrina and the flooding of New Orleans.

Flood of Images

Part One

TELEVISION NEWS

CHAPTER ONE

There Is No Wide Shot

TELEVISION NEWS AND COLLECTIVE MEMORY

*W*HEN CNN'S *NEWSNIGHT WITH AARON BROWN* WENT
on the air at 10:00 p.m. EST, August 29, 2005, sixteen
hours after Hurricane Katrina made landfall, the news network still did
not understand the extent or significance of the damage caused by the hurricane and the subsequent flooding of the City of New Orleans. Earlier that
evening, NBC *Nightly News* and *The Fox Report* had largely focused on the
storm's damage to the Mississippi Gulf Coast. Both NBC and Fox reported
that New Orleans had been spared catastrophic damage due to a slight eastern adjustment in the hurricane's path before landfall. At 7:00 p.m. Eastern
Standard Time, the story was that New Orleans had been spared. But by
10:00 p.m. EST, CNN admitted the limits of both its newsgathering and its
understanding of events on the ground.

News anchor Aaron Brown acknowledged and lamented the lack of a
comprehensive view of events.

> BROWN: There isn't what we refer to in the business as a wide shot.
> We can't get, authorities can't get . . . we can't give to those of
> you who are watching that wide picture of what these scenes are
> like.

Brown's statement is both intentionally and unintentionally revealing of
the processes by which television news usually constructs meaning. Unlike Brian Williams (NBC) or Shepard Smith (Fox), Brown regularly discusses on air CNN's technical approaches to producing news from events.
Brown employs terms like "wide shot" to educate his viewers about aspects of news production. Through this light reflexivity, Brown addresses

3

an audience sophisticated enough to understand that news is created, not "gathered."

However, Brown's statement, and the reports that provoked it, also reveal more than Brown's discourse about the relations between news and reality. Television news normatively produces wide shots, seemingly comprehensive and contained accounts of everything worth knowing about events. When television is working conventionally, wide shots construct understandings and arguments about the world that are largely persuasive. The construction of the wide shot is essential to television news's claim to report the real. Because the network lacked the images and information to construct a broad explanation of Katrina after sixteen hours, CNN was forced to acknowledge the limitations that are usually obscured by masterful, persuasive wide shots.

NBC also lacked a wide shot, but chose instead to focus on narrower views, reporting on relatively minimal damage in the French Quarter, while not yet recognizing or reporting on the breaching of levees and the flooding of the rest of the city. Fox provided a wider view of damage to the Mississippi Gulf Coast because the network had deployed significant resources to the state. Fox's reporting on New Orleans was partial and fragmented, and it too could not see or share the most important events occurring on Monday, August 29, 2005. Fox ended its broadcast with recently received aerial footage of the flooded city, but Shepard Smith indicated that the images were virtually a raw feed. He promised an edited package later, not yet recognizing the full significance of these images.

With a longer, two-hour format (ninety minutes longer than NBC, sixty minutes longer than Fox), CNN took different approaches to its coverage, presenting more live, real-time interaction between anchor Brown and reporters in the field. Toward the end of the first hour of *NewsNight* on Monday, August 29, 2005, CNN devoted more than twenty minutes to interviews by Brown with two colleagues: reporter Jeanne Meserve and cameraman Mark Biello. These segments were remarkable because of their length (NBC reports were typically 2:30, Fox slightly longer); format (interviews with staff rather than reports by staff); and, most crucially, the information revealed. In these segments, CNN first reported the extensive flooding caused by levee failures throughout New Orleans and the mortal threat caused by floodwaters to residents trapped in homes, especially in New Orleans East and in the Ninth Ward, but also in Arabi, Gentilly, Central City, and other neighborhoods.

Television news is a complex form of audiovisual communication and regularly conveys multiple messages, often articulating conflicting discourses. It communicates via recorded voices, images, sounds, sound effects, graphics, text on screen, and interstitial information, including promotions and commercials.

Television news advances the conceit that it is a form of journalism even as it is transformed into entertainment programming with commercial goals. It continues to draw upon the core claim of journalism to represent what is important to know about the world as it is. But television news takes events and elements of the real and converts those into "stories," short reports that follow familiar conventions and meet advertisers' and viewers' expectations of what is worth knowing about what is happening in the world. To watch television news is to accept the claim of the networks and channels that they are presenting the most important and valuable stories. In reality, the television news networks are presenting the stories they are prepared and ready to tell, based on choices of location, resource, technology, editorial perspective, and talent.

Television news works to produce stories from messy, raw, chaotic events, but it does so according to its own conventions, practices, values, and goals. In the process of converting reality into story, the news process itself becomes a primary focus. For example, in reporting during the first week after Katrina's landfall, NBC *Nightly News* would regularly focus on its *own* timeline of discovery, as if its process of creating news were reality itself. Similarly, on CNN, Aaron Brown talked during the week about what they had learned and reported, as if their learning curve was reality itself. As Negra and other scholars have argued, television news practice sought to convert Katrina into a media event, the reality of which existed in representation rather than in the world.

Television news is relentlessly focused forward. Broadcast network news (NBC) focuses on the news of the day, and cable network news (CNN, Fox) must feed a 24-hour cycle with content and thus focus on the news of the moment, chasing breaking stories and live reporting. Both models sacrifice significant, in-depth analysis, as stories are rushed onto screens. With only twenty-four minutes for nightly news stories, NBC's reporting is brief, with most segments only lasting two to three minutes. While cable news has more time and space, the emphasis on live-ness as guarantor of authenticity and significance also promotes speed over analysis. For these reasons, television news very rarely returns to revisit a report or to correct or clarify.

I have undertaken to reexamine television news reporting on Katrina and the flooding of New Orleans precisely because television news is usually ephemeral, made of voices and images that are presented and then superseded by the next stories, the next images. In its perpetual forward motion, television news approximates the analog process of interlacing by which television had created its images prior to the conversion to digital. Even lines, then odd lines, paint the screen, briefly sharing the frame before being replaced by the next images. Television news works against its own analysis since the text is constantly writing over itself.

By collecting the nightly news broadcasts of the major networks, Vanderbilt Television News Archive makes possible the close analysis of news broadcasts. I have undertaken this retrospective work seeking to determine the visual rhetorics by which television news shaped understandings of Katrina and the flooding of New Orleans. Television news has been a dominant contributor to the collective memory of Hurricane Katrina. By being first on the spot, with "live," breaking coverage, television news established the images and interpretations that would dominate understandings of the storm and flood, both during the week of August 28–September 4, 2005, and subsequently. Without the work of recovery and close analysis, however, we have only memories of fragments, images, and sounds, collected, traded, transformed. In a sense, without the sort of analysis I undertake in this book, we have only a rumor of the coverage of Katrina by television news. To understand what actually happened on the ground at the landfall of Katrina and after the failure of the levees protecting New Orleans, one must examine both the content of television news coverage and the perspectives and conventions guiding that coverage. To understand how we remember Katrina, we must examine how television news chose to cover the storm and flood.

Television news coverage of Katrina is significant for several reasons. First, due to failures in communications planning and infrastructure at all levels of government, FEMA, the military, and first responders depended on television news coverage for situational awareness (Fleetwood, 767). This coverage shaped official action on the ground. Second, television news shaped what national audiences saw and understood about the events in New Orleans. For national viewers without direct connection to the city, television news provided the dominant images and arguments about the flood. Third, television news coverage shaped the perspectives of the curators, archivists, and historians who would collect, preserve, and catalogue the material record of the storm, defining the possibilities for research into Katrina in the decades to come (see Shayt, 2006). In brief, television news

coverage affected real-time official response to the storm and flood, framed
collective memory of the storm for a national mass television audience,
and shaped the terms by which the storm could be researched and reexam-
ined over time. Because of its impact on all that we think we know about
Katrina, television news coverage of the storm must be closely analyzed
in order to argue for the significance of editorial choices and audiovisual
rhetoric. I analyze television news coverage to argue how and why we
know what we think we know about Katrina.

ELITE PANIC

Rebecca Solnit has argued that large-scale disasters often result in
differential responses (2010). Focusing on examples from Katrina to Haiti,
Solnit argues that people on the ground most often respond to disaster
by providing each other with mutual aid. She also notes that in response
to disaster, political, social, and media elites often panic, with significant
consequences.

Hurricanes disrupt communication. Katrina was especially disruptive of
communication on the ground in New Orleans, as landlines and cell phones
were unavailable or unreliable in the aftermath of the storm. The congressional panel investigating government response to Hurricane Katrina
concluded that inadequate emergency communications at the city, state,
and federal levels exacerbated the impact of the storm and flood, delaying
rescue and response and forestalling evacuation and aid (Select Bipartisan
Committee to Investigate Preparation and Response to Hurricane Katrina,
2007). In the absence of clear, consistent, and accurate official communication, government at all levels turned to television news for information.

Independent investigative journalist A. C. Thompson reported that
NOPD disaster communications failed on Tuesday, August 30, 2005; thereafter, police and responders were limited to short-range communication
(*Law & Disorder*, *Frontline*, 2010). In an interview for this book, Thompson noted that "policing is an information business." Without information,
rumor and panic fueled decisions by police. Katrina was marked by the
"CNN Effect," whereby television news coverage of events influenced official response to the events themselves. In the absence of official communication, television news regularly reported rumors as if they were facts.
Once reported, rumors took on their own status. For example, on Thursday, September 1, 2005, Shepard Smith shared explosive rumors without
reporting or verification.

SMITH: We are told someone opened fire on a rescue chopper. We are hearing reports of rapes at the Superdome and murders at the Convention Center.

Instead of providing images to support these assertions, Fox showed two shots of three white men, wearing bulletproof vests and holding shotguns. These men are not identified, and their status and affiliation is not revealed. These images do not show gunfire, rape, or murder. They do document an increased and insistent focus on armed response to New Orleans citizens who survived the storm and flood.

Despite greater efforts to report stories, NBC and CNN also regularly reported rumors without corroboration and did not return to correct or re-report on rumors that proved false. As a result, television news coverage of Katrina and the flooding of New Orleans picked up and extended confusion and panic on the ground; reported fears as facts; influenced decisions at the city, state, and federal levels; and contributed to decisions that yielded life-and-death consequences.

Television news networks also promoted elite panics at the national level. By reporting rumors of murders, rapes, and shootings, television news convinced many that the real threat in New Orleans was not the risk to survivors by floodwaters but the risk to reporters and responders posed by survivors themselves. On Monday, the networks were largely oblivious to the flooding of New Orleans. On Tuesday, they focused on the jeopardy faced by survivors. By Wednesday, the networks began to report on rumors of violence and on looting, pivoting from sympathy toward survivors toward distrust and fear. In turn, this demonization of New Orleans residents led to a shift in policy from focus on rescue and relief to a disastrous focus on security and control.

For example, on Tuesday, September 6, 2005, in an interview with Oprah Winfrey, New Orleans Police Commissioner Eddie Compass claimed that "some of the little babies (are) getting raped" in the Superdome. On the same broadcast, New Orleans Mayor Ray Nagin offered his own vision of apocalypse: "They have people standing out there, have been in that frickin' Superdome for five days watching dead bodies, watching hooligans killing people, raping people." Nagin concluded that New Orleans had descended into an "almost animalistic state" (Thevenot and Russell, 2005, 4). Though some have argued that racism guided the reporting on New Orleans after Katrina, Compass's and Nagin's performances suggest another dynamic at work: overwhelmed officials seeking to shift blame elsewhere.

The real horror of Katrina and the flood were the conditions experienced by the survivors. Americans expected their social contract with government to be honored, but city, state, and federal governments failed to protect, rescue, evacuate, and provide relief to citizens. Given this reality, efforts by local, state, and national officials to portray New Orleans citizens as violent, dangerous, and depraved suggest a desperate attempt to shift focus and blame from authorities to the survivors themselves.

Television news was complicit in this effort to demonize New Orleans residents. As subsidiaries of large media corporations, television news networks rarely mount substantive or sustained critiques of government. In the case of Katrina, television news often accepted and broadcast official perspectives without independent review, aiding authorities at all levels of government in efforts to shift responsibility. Television news also sought to apply familiar high-concept formulas, successful in attracting audiences during coverage of the U.S. wars in Iraq and Afghanistan (Jaramillo, 2009). Television news sensationalized events on the ground, drawing stark contrasts between authorities and citizens and offering justification for the increasing securitization of New Orleans. Finally, television news may have embraced the demonization of New Orleans residents as a relief from the overwhelming suffering dominating coverage on Tuesday, August 30. The television news networks responded to the panic and spin of officials and began focusing on the violence and depravity of New Orleans citizens as a way to defer fatigue in its audience.

RIGHT TIME, WRONG PLACE

The initial approach to covering Katrina employed what journalist Miles O'Brien described in an interview for this book as "the hurricane playbook," the predetermined moves that each network makes in response to a potential hurricane. That is, television news covers the storm track, interviews experts (National Hurricane Center), checks in on preparations, and interviews a few people. The hurricane playbook involves an anchor coordinating four or five correspondents, pivoting to weather and official experts. According to O'Brien, television news considers the reporter out in the storm ("the piñata in the storm") to be the most important visual. This visual is the "money shot" that confirms the danger posed by the storm, the live-ness of the coverage ("breaking news"), and the mastery of the television news apparatus to bring this managed danger to audiences. In turn, through this address, television news brings viewers into the status of "weather citizens," constructing a sense of watching from a distance as an obligation and a simulation of connection (Fleetwood, 2006; Sturken, 2001). The anchor must be shielded from the storm to guarantee the ability to broadcast: in the 24-hour news cycle of cable television, continuity of broadcast is paramount.

Until landfall, the television audience also included New Orleans residents, and some of the television news coverage was directed to New Orleans audiences (warnings to evacuate and to prepare). Pre-landfall coverage could not project as freely onto New Orleans as would later coverage because New Orleans residents were watching and could complain. As soon as Katrina hit land, and the Gulf Coast lost power, television news no longer addressed an audience that was directly affected. Instead, television news addressed a "weather disaster nation" hyped up to learn about the impact of the storm, but distanced from impact and implication.

"Weather citizens" enjoy the pleasurable apprehension of disaster from a mediated distance, able to view but not to feel the storm's impact (Sturken, 2001). Per Geoffrey Hartman's argument about television separating viewers into those who suffer and those who watch suffering, weather news viewers feel sympathy for New Orleanians, but not connection with them (1994, 2000). This logic depends on differentiation of "us" and "them" (with distinction in play as well: we would have left because we are sensible, and we are information junkies). A deeper, more political sense of empathy was not produced by television news because it emphasizes distance, difference, and disconnection. As long as television news crews had their own power generators, satellites, cameras, phones, food, and water, they were physically distinct from New Orleans even as they were reporting from it. The reporters and anchors were visually separated from survivors and used language to signify distinction ("can hardly believe this is America," "like a war zone," "refugees"). They controlled the televisual space, choosing whom to admit onto the screen, when to turn away and refocus, when to cut away. This distance, created by the apparatus of television news, further diminished the possibilities for connection and empathy, just as it diminished accuracy, completeness, insight, and perspective on those affected.

When New Orleanians lost power and were no longer part of the national television audience, coverage became further disconnected from the experience of residents and survivors on the ground. Coverage of the initial aftermath overemphasized tourists (standing in for national viewers) and reporters (standing in for actual residents). Reporters playing on TV's simulation of live-ness gained stature from location. Location lent immediacy and connection and a frisson of danger. But the self-imposed limitations on choice of location resulted in "coverage" rather than reporting: if it is not safe to send reporters, television news must hang out on dry land waiting for news to wash up out of the floodwaters.

What television produces as news is determined by logistics, finance, and past coverage. Television news is shaped to meet the perceived expectations of its audience. The early television news reporting on Katrina on all three networks was shaped by the location of news resources on the ground. By placing human (reporters, producers) and technological (satellite trucks, generators) resources in the French Quarter and the Central Business District (CBD), television news networks reported the impact of Katrina on these areas, with pre- and post-landfall stories about the state of the French Quarter featured on each network. Because the French Quarter and the lower CBD were among the few areas in the city not flooded by the multiple breaches in the levees, the television news networks initially did not see and did not report the actual story of the flooding of New Orleans (NBC's Martin Savidge, for example, reported on trees falling behind St. Louis Cathedral, sparing a statue of Jesus). Rather than send reporters out into the city, each network focused on immediate stories, extrapolating the consequences in one neighborhood in a way that proved terribly false: if the French Quarter had survived without flooding, the city must have, too. Of course, the French Quarter and CBD are the areas most familiar to tourists and thus to national viewing audiences, and these areas were familiar to television news from the broadcast of national sporting events staged at the Superdome in the CBD (including the National Football League's Super Bowl and the NCAA's Bowl Championship Series). For national television audiences, viewers addressed by the television news networks, the French Quarter *was* New Orleans. Visual overemphasis on this small part of the City of New Orleans contributed to the initial neglect by television news of representations of the much larger city, a neglect that had a real impact on response.

PSEUDO-WITNESSES

The anchors and anchor/reporters on the ground benefitted from their location and live-ness to produce forms of pseudo-witness of the events of Katrina. In this regard, Brian Williams of NBC and Shepard Smith of Fox enjoyed an advantage over Aaron Brown of CNN. While Brown reported exclusively from CNN's New York studio, Williams regularly anchored from Louisiana (New Orleans, Metairie, and Baton Rouge during the first week), and Smith served as anchor-on-the-ground and "reporter."

With a camera set up on the I-10 Expressway, showing the damaged Super-dome and New Orleans's CBD in the background, Williams proposed his own experience of the storm and flood as a form of witness to the lived experience of Katrina. Usually wardrobed in a long-sleeved chambray shirt with the sleeves rolled up, Williams visually conveyed the sense of anchor-as-disaster-zone-correspondent, using signifiers of dress and comportment to gain credibility and connection. Like other Fox talent in the field, Smith wore polo shirts and ball caps emblazoned with Fox logos and designs, serving as another form of visual branding.

By reporting from New Orleans, Williams and Smith proposed them-selves as witnesses of the destruction and lived impact of the city. Each personalized his discourse with references to what he had seen and experi-enced. Of course, Williams and Smith were not true witnesses to Katrina since they were present under very specific and controlled circumstances. As Miles O'Brien noted in an interview, the news networks sent consider-able resources into the field, including generators, food, and water to en-sure that their talent and crews had power and sustenance. Whereas New Orleanians left stranded at the Superdome or Convention Center had no food or shelter, television news crews retired to hotels, ate hot meals, and used indoor plumbing. The anchors and reporters sought, via dress and ref-erence, to associate themselves with the experience of survivors. However, the result was not true witness, but a professional facsimile. This process of replacement prevented real witness and permitted considerable construc-tion of reality via visual storytelling and rhetoric and reporting of rumor. This process ultimately shaped national understanding, with significant consequences for a national, collective memory. The collective memory of Katrina defined by television news enshrined projections, misunderstand-ings, and mistakes as the dominant national baseline of understanding for what Katrina was and what Katrina meant.

WITNESSES TO THE NOT-YET-VISIBLE

CNN was the first network to venture out from the safe, dry, famil-iar spaces to report on the actual conditions in the larger city. CNN pro-ducer and New Orleans native Kim Bondy had learned by phone from her mother and stepfather that her Gentilly neighborhood had begun to flood hours after Katrina's landfall (Bondy interview). Her awareness of rapidly rising floodwaters in parts of the city unseen from the French Quarter in-fluenced CNN's coverage. CNN was the first network to stop reporting that

New Orleans had been spared by Katrina's eastward "jog" and the first to seek more information about other areas of the city.

On Monday, August 29, 2005, CNN reporter Jeanne Meserve and cameraman Mark Biello left the CBD to seek information about possible flooding. First by car, and later by boat, they headed east into the Ninth Ward. Tellingly, the farther they moved from the centralized resources mobilized by CNN, the more they learned about the extent of flooding and the threat to the tens of thousands of residents trapped in their homes by rising floodwaters. Conversely, the closer they got to the story, the farther away they moved from technological resources. Meserve and Biello learned important details about the flooding of New Orleans on the day of landfall, but they were not able to supply a video report that Monday. Instead, they provided separate interviews to Aaron Brown via phone. These were played over images collected by other CNN colleagues or purchased from freelance videographers. The images shot by Biello were not available for broadcast until the Tuesday (August 30) broadcast of *NewsNight*, as Biello initially lacked access to a power source, necessary to transfer and send his images. Due to the limitations of news creation in the aftermath of a hurricane, CNN's reporting of Meserve and Biello's discoveries emphasized the power and importance of discourse, but also underscored the importance of images.

Lacking the typical stand-up shot of Meserve delivering her summary report to Brown, CNN instead put up a screen with still images and graphics under her voice-over report. Throughout coverage of Katrina, CNN typically featured a denser frame than either NBC or Fox. Under Meserve's report and interview, the CNN frame included a still file image of Meserve in the lower left corner. Below this still, but above the news crawl across the bottom of the frame, was the text "CNN: On the Phone: Jeanne Meserve." A map of Louisiana and Mississippi, with New Orleans identified as the locus of Meserve's voice, occupied the center and right portions of the frame. Unable to visually connect Meserve to the ground of her reporting, CNN had to provide a weaker visual claim to her authority, employing text and graphics to identify and locate her voice. While less persuasive visually than a stand-up shot, the CNN frame also included a small box in the upper left, above Meserve's image, that asserted a crucial claim to authority: a globe inside a grid bearing the word "Live." The live-ness of Meserve's report mitigated technical limitations, even converting the lack of images into a gain in immediacy—this report provided such breaking news that it would not wait for images. After a handoff by Brown, Meserve summarized what she and Biello had seen: massive, extensive flooding of residen-

Jeanne Meserve reporting by phone from the Lower Ninth Ward (CNN 8.29.05).

tial neighborhoods to the east of the French Quarter; rescue attempts by Coast Guard and local responders, but also the suspension of rescue efforts due to darkness; cries for help by multiple people trapped in their homes. Meserve's report was the first national television news broadcast that identified the extensiveness of flooding and the immediate peril faced by residents who had sheltered in their homes during the hurricane.

The lack of coverage kept viewers, including federal agencies that did not have communication on the ground, from understanding the dire situation until Tuesday. According to Jed Horne in *Breach of Faith*, small-scale search and rescue was suspended due to darkness and fears for the safety of responders working in the dark with exposed electrical wires and other hazards (2006). Since the extent of the threat to citizens had not been understood and reported by television news, and since communications on the ground were fragmented at best, the safety of responders was prioritized over the safety of residents. Thousands of New Orleanians faced death by drowning and exposure on Monday, August 29, 2005, in the hours after landfall and the breaching of the levees. Full resources for search and rescue were not employed until Friday, September 2, 2005, five days later, when tens of thousands of National Guard troops were finally deployed to New Orleans.

Recognizing the new information in Meserve's report, Brown interviewed her, attempting to draw out more detail in real time. The CNN reporting by Meserve and Biello was only partially scripted, departing from the television news tendency toward pre-production and editorial control. Significantly, Brown did not already know what Meserve and Biello would tell him. Usually, television news constructs a fiction of the anchor as all-knowing. Brown in particular created the impression of his control over the news broadcast by calling for changes in graphics, stopping reporters to ask questions, and at times demanding clarification. Brown's conversation with Meserve is notable because he was learning new information, much of it contradicting the network's previous reporting. For example, at the top of *NewsNight*, Brown declared: "Katrina, not quite the monster that everyone feared."

Importantly, Meserve's reporting focuses on the threat to New Orleans residents without judging them for staying in place. Fox and NBC took a different stance, blaming residents for "failing" to evacuate, suggesting that the survivors bore responsibility for their own jeopardy and, as a result, had waived claims to social status, even to citizenship. The early use by Brian Williams and Shepard Smith of the term "refugees" to describe New Orleans residents performs the discursive act of stripping rights and standing from fellow citizens. In contrast, Meserve emphasized shared humanity and context for the decision to remain.

> MESERVE: The area where I was, was a very poor neighborhood. Homes appeared one story high, with attic spaces above. These are people, I would guess, who did not have cars, did not have the option of driving or money for hotels.

Just as the deployment of overall network resources determines the stories observed and told, the placement of the camera in relation to people and places, and camera movement, especially changes in focal length, determine what the images selected by news editors can say about the lived experience of people who survived Katrina and who attempted to survive the subsequent flooding. Images produced from long distance, even images employing optical zooms and other techniques to simulate closeness, maintain a sense of disconnection from what is shown. For example, the next image in the sequence under Meserve's voice-over report shows what appear to be four African American men in a medium-long shot, only to zoom out to reveal that the image was taken from the remove of an expressway. The videographic apparatus allows for the simulation of proximity and connection, belying the actual distance involved in the creation of the images. This is especially significant in the television news reporting on Katrina, as the distance is meaningful between a cameraperson shooting from a dry concrete overpass and subjects wading through floodwaters

High-angle camera shot of survivors in floodwaters (CNN 8.29.05).

seeking safety. Response to the human disaster of the flooding of New Orleans was significantly impacted by the degree to which New Orleans residents were understood as American citizens, like the national viewers themselves. Television news coverage, in its production of images as well as in its scripting and delivery of language, produced opportunities for connection and disconnection with survivors in New Orleans that would influence local and national response in the days and weeks following landfall and would shape national memories of Katrina and its meanings in the years to follow.

BAGHDAD ON THE BAYOU

With conditions growing increasingly desperate in New Orleans as the week progressed and the arrival of large-scale federal help delayed through poor planning and communication, the television news networks presented increasingly sensational claims about violence and crime in the city. All three networks projected fears onto people they could not see, making claims of shootings, rapes, and murders without presenting evidence or direct testimony. Instead, they sought to represent New Orleans as "slipping deeper into violence and despair" (studio anchor Laurie Dhue led off *The Fox Report* on September 1, 2005, with this assertion).

The television news networks sought to apply aspects of their successful coverage of the U.S. invasion of Iraq to their coverage of New Orleans in the aftermath of Katrina. In *Ugly War, Pretty Package* (2009), Deborah Jaramillo argues that television news coverage of the two Gulf Wars sought to attract viewers by producing war coverage as blockbuster entertainment. Through computer graphics, theme music, and especially through storytelling and visual rhetorics, television news emphasized American military superiority and the righteousness of America's cause (161). Jaramillo identifies the attempt to produce blockbuster, high-concept news as a new phenomenon, driven in part by the collapse of divisions between news and entertainment and by the economic imperative to sell advertising during television news. The news networks sold the Iraq War in this way for economic more than for ideological reasons.

Jaramillo argues that Katrina did not fit into news networks' high-concept approach for three reasons: incomplete understandings of the causes and impacts of the storm, confusion on the ground, and a lack of clarity regarding protagonists and antagonists (212). However, there is evidence that television news repeatedly tried to push its coverage toward high concept, first by emphasizing search and rescue, then by devaluing and demonizing the citizens who survived the storm and struggled to survive the flood. It was not until Friday, September 2, and Saturday, September 3, that television news succeeded in temporarily converting Katrina into high concept through representations of a massive and belated federal response via the arrival of thousands of National Guard troops. In order to present a triumphalist arrival by the U.S. military, television news had to first convert American citizens into enemy resistance. In the logic of television news coverage, New Orleans first had to be represented as "lost" to non-citizens before it could be successfully retaken. New Orleans had to be converted into "Baghdad on the Bayou" before its citizens could be liberated from themselves.

All this demonization and recuperation served to distract television viewers from raising questions of responsibility. While the television news networks would occasionally offer criticism of delays in official response, the visual rhetoric of the broadcasts did not hold government officials responsible for the failure of planning, the failure of the levees, the failure of rescue, and the failure of relief. Instead, television news focused on the miserable conditions on the ground as disqualifying New Orleans from belonging to the United States. As Christiane Amanpour stated in her Sunday, September 4 report with Anderson Cooper, she approached reporting on Katrina as if she were reporting from a foreign war zone.

On NBC, as early as Monday, August 29, the day of Katrina's landfall, Brian Williams began referring to American citizens who survived the storm as "refugees." Other anchors and reporters also adopted the descriptor "refugees" based on previous models of reporting wars and global crises. As Henry Giroux and others have argued, this discursive recasting of American citizens as refugees in their own country stripped them of sovereignty, of rights and standing, and of the respect television news normally accords dead Americans. The representation of bodies in the coverage of Hurricane Katrina and the flooding of New Orleans involved visual constructions that prioritized some bodies over others. Reporters, responders, and officials were shown as having agency and cogency, while survivors were represented as victims, reduced, displaced, and weak.

In the effort by the television news networks to fit Katrina into high-concept schema, New Orleans residents were reduced in many of the same ways that Vietnamese, Iraqi, and Afghani men and women had been reduced before them. Unlike the wars in Vietnam, Iraq, or Afghanistan, Katrina was not easily, visually reduced into clear polarities of American virtue and power against others, figured as enemies and terrorists, in part because Katrina was understood initially as a natural disaster occurring on U.S. soil.

In each of the chapters that follow in the first section of *Flood of Images*, I analyze reports and stories broadcast by NBC, Fox, and CNN on each day of Katrina's first week, from the Sunday before landfall (August 28) until the following Sunday (September 4). In this way, I compare approaches by each network to similar news reporting. Moreover, by following the chronological development of television news coverage, I am able to argue for histories of production and for the progressive development of stories and themes over the course of the week. I begin with apprehension of the coming storm.

CHAPTER TWO

Weather Citizens

SUNDAY, AUGUST 28

M ARITA STURKEN AND NICOLE FLEETWOOD EACH AR-
gue that television's address of viewers before a major
storm or hurricane calls into being a viewing public united by a sense of
apprehension and excitement (Sturken, 2001; Fleetwood, 2006). Writing
about television coverage of the El Niño weather phenomenon in California, Sturken asserts that television news coverage constructs viewers as
"weather citizens," who feel connected to important events while remaining distanced. The perception of connection is forged by the production
of fear within the privileged and protective space of television viewership.
Viewers far from harm can feel pleasure through apprehension. Moreover,
according to Sturken, this pleasurable apprehension is connected to a sense
of politics divorced from agency. Weather citizens perform a facsimile of
duty by watching—consuming reporting, graphics, and advertisements—
without acting. In this formulation, the position of weather citizens depends on the double distance of mediation (the constructions of television
news coverage) and physical distance. To be in the path of the storm is
to remain embodied as an actual citizen, not to be freed to fantasies of
weather citizenship.

Building on Sturken's argument, Fleetwood applies the idea of weather
citizenship to Katrina. Television coverage in advance of landfall of Hurricane Katrina in the Gulf Coast created a public of anticipation, called into
being by the television news apparatus in response to a major storm. Television hails this public sense of anticipation to generate viewership numbers in order to drive up advertising rates. Informing the viewing public about a potential national natural or man-made disaster is both good
business and public service. As a consequence of the importance of storm

coverage for television's bottom line, networks and news producers employ business strategy, deploying resources and pre-producing stories according to the lessons of past practice (O'Brien's "hurricane playbook"). By following the conventions of past coverage, television networks minimize historical difference and maximize familiar and repeatable (consumable) stories. NBC, CNN, and Fox, by applying versions of strategic planning, shaped understandings of Hurricane Katrina and the flooding of New Orleans according to formula.

As a consequence, television news initially failed to understand and to report the actual impact of Hurricane Katrina on the federal levees. As Fleetwood argues, drawing from the final report of the House Select Committee to Investigate the Preparation and Response to Hurricane Katrina charged with investigating governmental response to Hurricane Katrina, early television news coverage of Katrina not only misinformed the viewing public, but also affected responses by first responders, who had lost communication and depended on media for situational information (767).

On Sunday night, August 28, 2005, NBC *Nightly News* broadcast 28.3 minutes of news and commercials as Hurricane Katrina moved toward landfall. John Seigenthaler served as weekend anchor from New York, and Brian Williams, moving into place to anchor coverage from New Orleans (or the Gulf) after the storm, reported by phone from Baton Rouge. Seigenthaler called on Williams to provide a sense of immediacy and proximity to the danger posed by the storm. According to producer Kim Bondy and anchor-reporter Miles O'Brien, both with CNN at the time, a signature trope of television news coverage of a storm is to position reporters in proximity to the storm's path as reminders of the potential human cost of the storm. At the same time, networks depend on star talent to anchor broadcasts and to introduce and coordinate reporting. Therefore, anchors remain in relative safety, near to sources of power and satellite communication. This is especially important in the case of cable news networks, which must fill hours of programming time with news shows. Thus, Williams was positioned close to, but protected from, the brunt of the storm, and O'Brien was kept out of New Orleans in advance of landfall.

In addition to teasing coverage to come via Williams's phone report ("stay tuned to NBC for up-to-the-minute coverage . . ."), Seigenthaler stoked viewer anxiety by discussing the storm's potential under a graphic labeled "Impact." Heralding that Katrina might be "the worst storm ever," Seigenthaler handed off to Martin Savidge, reporting from outside the Louisiana Superdome. Framed from a high angle, with light rain perceptible in the shot, Savidge reinforced the doomsday potential of the storm, stating that "a toxic gumbo" threatened to drown the city. After Katrina, the networks at times advanced the Bush administration's argument that no one could have anticipated or prepared for Katrina. However, before the storm, the networks trumpeted the direst possibilities, constructing and playing to a public of anticipation.

THE PARTY IS RELATIVELY OVER

The night before Katrina's landfall, CNN positioned reporter Dave Mattingly on Bourbon Street in the French Quarter. Fox similarly placed Shepard Smith at the Royal Sonesta Hotel on Royal Street, and NBC deployed Martin Savidge to French Quarter streets after the storm hit. The French Quarter is home to a small resident population, some of the city's oldest and most significant architecture, and many hotels, bars, and businesses catering to tourists. The French Quarter and nearby Central Business District (CBD) were familiar to the networks from previous news and sports productions. The National Football League and the Bowl Championship Series of college football regularly schedule championships in New Orleans because of its attractiveness to tourists as a site for revelry and debauchery. As a result, the networks had strategies in place for visualizing the French Quarter as a synecdoche for the city. These strategies involved projecting onto the city the qualities sought by tourists: New Orleans as playground, as "The Big Easy," as "The City That Care Forgot." In a conversation with Dave Mattingly, Aaron Brown characterized New Orleans as a "24-hour town" and "like Las Vegas without gambling" (although New Orleans has legalized gambling, brought in from Vegas) before cautioning that "the party is relatively over."

Mattingly's report begins with a long shot down a French Quarter street toward the CBD, cuts to a two-shot of two white men boarding up a business, and then shows a high-angle shot of details, from a neon bar sign and other advertisements to flags blowing in a breeze. Over these images, Mattingly reports that people remained in the French Quarter seeking a good time before the storm (in this regard, the tourists were not unlike cable news viewers enjoying the coverage before the storm).

As Mattingly continues reporting about restaurants and bars remaining open for visitors who want to "spend some money," the report cuts to an African American man in a white T-shirt, with a black cap, worn backwards, and black sunglasses. The man is riding a bicycle and carrying a white bag of carryout food in his right hand as he struggles to pedal forward against the stiffening breeze. The disjunction between this image and Mattingly's voice-over about tourists spending money suggests the dissonance between discursive meaning and visual argument in television news. While the first images in the sequence showed white tourists in the streets and white men protecting businesses, this image of a black man seems to suggest other narratives. The shot of the man pedaling against the wind suggests both struggle and resourcefulness. The fact that he is using a bike as transportation against pre-hurricane winds implies that he—like so many New Orleans residents who remained in the city in advance of the storm—lacked a car or other means of transportation to evacuate the city. He might have ended a shift in a French Quarter restaurant or bar, a member of the low-wage working class vital to New Orleans's tourist economy. Many New Orleanians could not leave in advance of Katrina for economic reasons: they had to remain and work in businesses catering to tourists. Because Katrina made landfall on Sunday at the end of the month of August, many residents remained, waiting for paychecks or Social Security checks. The man on the bike may have been taking food home from a final shift pre-storm. Where CNN's discourse remains focused on the perspectives of tourists (a comfortable position for viewers safely distant from the hurricane path, viewers whose interest in New Orleans might be stoked by the pleasures of its tourist economy), this shot of the man on the bike opens up other possibilities, referencing the larger number of residents (many black and poor, but certainly also many white residents) who remained in New Orleans in the neighborhoods outside the French Quarter and outside the familiar frame applied by CNN. This shot of the man on the bike references a New Orleans that the flooding would reveal, a world invisible to the usual representational strategies of television news and sports coverage.

NOT A LOT TO SHOW YOU AT THIS POINT

At the midpoint of CNN's extended two-hour *NewsNight* program on Sunday, August 28, 2005, anchor Aaron Brown acknowledged the different challenge facing 24-hour cable news networks covering Katrina. After Brown described the state of Louisiana's "contra flow" evacuation plan, which used all ten highway lanes to move cars from New Orleans to Baton Rouge, producers cut to a high-angle shot of cars on a highway. Described by Brown as "live footage of cars driving into Baton Rouge," this image is non-compelling: traffic is moving, albeit slowly. After a few seconds, Brown admits, "Not a lot to show you at this point." With four times more room for news than NBC and twice as much as Fox News, CNN explored questions with greater depth and was also forced to present (and repeat and recycle) relatively static images, like the long shot of traffic approaching Baton Rouge. This need to recycle made the production of anticipation more difficult.

Brown sought to alarm and excite viewers by citing historical precedent. He offered dark comparisons to Hurricanes Andrew (40 dead, billions in damages) and Camille (143 dead) before qualifying: "Just to remind you what we're doing here . . . this is no hype . . . this is a storm of historical proportions." By "covering" possibilities, Brown and CNN were trying to convince viewers to continue watching and not to switch the channel. As long as the damage and death would occur to other people and be experienced primarily as a screen phenomenon, not as a lived experience, viewers could be made excited about the storm and receptive to storm coverage. CNN's goal was to collect and keep eyeballs, to prevent viewers from looking away or turning off the television.

If television news did not know how to convert the failure of the federal levees and the flooding of New Orleans into high-concept news, the networks certainly knew how to sell anticipation as high concept. As noted, television news addressed viewers in advance of the storm with a sense of pleasurable anxiety over a storm that would not directly affect most of them. On CNN, this address began with the design of the elements in the frame, the creation and positioning of graphics, and the use of thematic music. Beginning on Sunday, August 28, and continuing on Monday, *NewsNight* broadcast introduced a screen with text, graphics, and images claiming for CNN the status of "Hurricane Headquarters." The screen featured a dark silhouette of seven palm trees blown from right to left by a strong wind, possibly images recycled from previous hurricane coverage in south Florida. Blue lines in the background suggested the technical production of images by the television apparatus. Across the screen was displayed "CNN" in red text and "Hurricane Katrina" in large white with blue letters. Beneath was "Headquarters" in smaller text, and below that, a second, smaller CNN logo in the lower left and a news crawl rolling from right to left. Over these visual details played a musical theme consisting of electronic keyboards, echo effects, and the sound of a ticking stopwatch. The music evoked a sense of anxiety about and anticipation of the storm, as did the image of the palm trees, which conveyed a sense of gathering force and potential destruction. However, these ominous elements were framed and contained by the graphic context that spoke to CNN's technological ability to "cover" the storm, converting raw, inchoate menace into stories, facts, and details for the consumption of its audience. Through this introduction, CNN presented "Katrina watching" as high-concept news.

Per Jaramillo, television news constructs high concept to generate the audience desired by advertisers. In commercial television, advertisements

Logo and graphics for Katrina coverage (CNN 8.29.05).

are part of the text, glossing the news coverage with additional meanings. Approximately twelve hours before Katrina's landfall on the Gulf Coast, NBC broadcast television commercials that underscored the news programming's construction of a public of anticipation and anxiety. The first commercial break in the half-hour news broadcast featured thirty- and sixty-second spots for Lipitor, Maalox, and Ambien. In the first spot, a man on a bike is chased downhill by a text graphic reading "270." He peddles furiously to escape the number, but he cannot get away. The voice-over suggests that he should use Lipitor to free himself from the number, representing his "bad cholesterol." An advertisement for Maalox illustrates how it can provide the relief of a "protective barrier," separating users from the raging forces of indigestion. The third spot sells Ambien, warning that "sleep does not come easy" without assistance from the sleep aid. Working with the television news text of reports and graphics on the potential destructiveness of the storm, these advertisements reinforce the play between apprehension and anxiety. Just as the television news text promises to answer the anxiety it produces by the reassurance of "coverage" and "live reporting," the commercial address promises better living through consumption. This palliative would not work for New Orleanians, who would soon need to escape floodwaters, toxic waste, failed levees, and destroyed homes. For New Orleanians, the failure of the levees ended the possibility and pleasures of weather citizenship.

CHAPTER THREE

These Are the First Pictures from the Air

MONDAY, AUGUST 29

*A*FTER PRODUCING SEGMENTS EMPHASIZING APPREHEN-
sion and excitement over the potential path and destructiveness of Hurricane Katrina on Sunday, August 28, 2005, the broadcast
and cable television news networks struggled to see and understand the
impact and aftermath of the storm on Monday, August 29.

It is important to note that CNN aired later in the evening (10:00 p.m.
to midnight Eastern Standard Time) than either NBC *Nightly News* (6:30
to 7:00 p.m. EST) or *The Fox Report* (7:00 to 8:00 p.m. EST). If CNN lacked
perspective and understanding at 10:00 p.m. on Monday, NBC and Fox had
even less time to produce reports and images. As a consequence, both NBC
and Fox initially reported that New Orleans had been spared the worst of
the hurricane.

WE WILL EDIT DOWN INTO A PACKAGE
THAT WILL LOOK A BIT CLEARER

Typical of the early reporting on Monday, *The Fox Report* featured a
title on screen, "Katrina Plows through LA, Largely Spares NO." Moreover,
the broadcast cut away from Katrina coverage to provide short reports on
Martha Stewart's release from prison for insider trading and the shooting
of hip-hop producer Suge Knight. Fox even reported on street flooding in
Santiago, Chile, showing a street covered by ten inches of water. Unaware
that whole neighborhoods in New Orleans were under ten to twenty feet
of water, Fox covered minor flooding in Chile (later in the week, Fox
would provide coverage of minor flooding in Denver, Colorado). Forty-
two minutes into the hour-long broadcast, in a moment revealing of the

process of producing television news, Shepard Smith introduced the "first aerials," high-angle, long shots from a helicopter, showing massive flooding throughout New Orleans. Characteristic of television news, Fox's process defined reality for its viewers. Until it had purchased freelance aerial footage (footage also shown by the other networks), Fox's representation of the reality of Katrina did not include massive flooding. At one point earlier in the hour, Smith asserted that "the levees were not breached. The levees held for the most part." If they could not see it, and could not show it, it did not exist.

Once it received the aerial footage, the Fox news team began to understand that they had been missing the reality on the ground. Unlike broadcast network news, 24-hour cable news would occasionally air breaking material without the usual editing and shaping. Smith seemed to be seeing the aerial images for the first time as he introduced them on air.

> SMITH: These are the first pictures from the air . . . just feeding in
> . . . we will edit down into a package that will look a bit clearer.

Not yet "edited down," the aerial footage provided information, rather than editorial perspective. This raw, minimally edited breaking footage was more document than documentary. Fox had not yet employed the usual process of converting footage into a tightly edited package, and thus this footage was more open to interpretation. Even as Smith and Fox struggled to understand that the levees had failed and that New Orleans was flooding, viewers began to see massive flooding and to ask questions.

MOTHER ON THE SECOND FLOOR

CNN producer Kim Bondy's personal and familial connections to New Orleans would influence CNN's coverage of Hurricane Katrina in significant ways, including an important early change in coverage on Monday, August 29 (Bondy interview). Both of Bondy's parents, who are divorced, and their spouses remained in New Orleans during the storm, and Bondy was able to contact her mother Ruby and stepfather via phone. Ruby and her husband were staying in Bondy's house on Elysian Fields Avenue in the Gentilly neighborhood, a house Bondy was restoring with the intention of eventually moving back to New Orleans from New York City. Bondy's brother owned the house next door and kept watch over her place. With the impending arrival of Katrina, her brother left with his small children, but her mother and stepfather stayed. Bondy's house had been built in the 1930s and had never before flooded. As Bondy returned to the CNN studio after a vacation, she learned from her mother that her backyard was flooding. In an interview for this book, Bondy indicated that this information was initially confusing since her expectation was that any floodwater would come from the front of her house on Elysian Fields. Instead, her mother reported that the water continued to rise from the back, soon flooding her sunroom. The London Avenue Canal is six blocks behind Bondy's house. She would later learn that the levee breach in this canal caused the flooding of her home and neighborhood. Not yet aware of the source of the flooding, Bondy's mother and stepfather went to the building's second floor as water continued to rise.

By 11:00 a.m., Bondy was certain that something significantly wrong was happening in New Orleans. Her brother called her in tears to share their mother's report that his house was completely under water. Indeed, her mother and stepfather were concerned that water might reach up into the second floor. After the call from her brother, Bondy called the CNN news desk and reported that New Orleans was flooding from unknown sources. As a result, CNN stopped reporting the all-clear and began to try to find out more information. As discussed in chapter 1, reporter Jeanne Meserve left downtown by boat to investigate and filed the first report (by phone) on the flooding of the Ninth Ward.

According to O'Brien, CNN had deployed more resources into the field to report on Katrina than the other networks, including hundreds of people deployed via convoy from Atlanta. Yet, despite these resources, CNN stuck to its pre-produced approach to hurricane coverage, finding it difficult to depart from the playbook in order to report actual conditions on the ground. Only after a senior producer reported personal information received by phone from her family did the network begin to revise its coverage.

CNN was the first to report about levee breaches and flooding, to Bondy's credit. Importantly, CNN sent reporters to the Ninth Ward to investigate. Jeanne Meserve's first phone reporting to Aaron Brown created immediacy and impact even without accompanying images. With voice and words, Meserve conveyed to Brown and the audience how desperate residents were trapped in houses and attics with floodwaters rising. In Meserve's initial reporting for CNN, her voice and reporting by phone were placed over other images from the day, some of them looped, due to the lack of synchronous images. Meserve's voice may have invested in the images resonance that they lacked on their own, the images may have suggested associatively what she was describing, or they may have weakened her reporting, distracting viewers.

Since cameraman Mark Biello's footage shot during Meserve's reporting was not yet available for broadcast, CNN used footage of flooding in New Orleans not explicitly linked to Meserve's voice-over during her segment. The sequence of images begins with a long shot of two African American men wading in the water next to a submerged car. The sequence then cuts to a high-angle image of Circle Foods, a familiar landmark in the city's Seventh Ward, submerged in water up to the entrance. This business, on the edge of the Treme neighborhood, would be more significant to local rather than national viewers, but, as an identifiable structure, this footage allowed the network and viewers to locate sites of flooding. The specificity of this shot points up the lack of specific location references in other footage on CNN.

The sequence then cuts from the high-angle long shot of Circle Foods to a medium long shot of two African American adults and a child wading through the water toward the camera as two young African American men walk in the other direction. Unlike the first shot, where the camera observes figures from a greater distance, this shot suggests relation between the camera and subjects. The image suggests that the subjects are aware of being filmed and thus implicates the camera and the television news broadcast in their situation. To CNN's credit, the image of the five people includes the zoom. The editor could have cut this shot with the zoomed-in, medium-long framing only, but instead includes the move, reminding viewers of the work of the production of visual images and implicating, if only briefly, the distance necessary for the production of television news.

In the next shot, for example, the distance is not underscored by inclusion of a change in focal length. After the zoom out, the sequence cuts to a high-angle, aerial shot of the roof of the Superdome, with wind damage clearly visible. Taken from a helicopter, the shot holds on the Superdome while the camera swings around 180 degrees to show the extent of damage. The Superdome is a more nationally identifiable landmark than Circle Foods, anchoring the camera's perspective in the geography of the city. However, given the distance and movement in the shot, this image speaks of the structure but not of the people who later sought shelter inside and who remained without power, sanitation, food, or water in Katrina's aftermath. Also, the shot of the Superdome alters the sequence, which had until this image been focused on New Orleanians escaping from floodwaters. Because of the dramatic shift in scale and location, the shot of the Superdome interrupts a visual argument about small group survival. It also reveals distance and disconnection between the sequence of images and Meserve's reporting on the conditions on the ground in the Ninth Ward and in New Orleans East. Where Meserve is talking about individual and family desperation and survival in the face of the levee breaches and the flood, the shot of the Superdome instead speaks to the impact of the hurricane on a well-known structure synonymous with the largest-scale national sporting events and television spectacle.

> MESERVE: Some people were able to use those axes and make holes in the roofs and stick their heads out or bodies out . . . others did not have (axes).

While the production rationale for the shot may have been a relative lack of images available for visual storytelling, and the need to carefully conserve images that were recycled throughout multiple reports, especially on Monday and Tuesday after landfall, the disjunction is typical of the visual rhetoric of television news reporting. The sequencing of images affects viewers' understanding of what Katrina means.

The next image in the sequence shows for the first time a scene of "rescue." In a medium-long framing, the shot shows a fishing boat piloted by a white man with what appear to be three African American men in the back, seemingly pulled from the floodwaters. Like the third shot of the sequence, this shot shows the figures moving toward the camera. Like the fourth shot, the camera zooms out to reveal its placement on an overpass. From the overpass, the camera shows the boats leaving the frame, as it moves underneath the structure. As in the fourth shot, by keeping the zoom, the editor reveals aspects of the production of the image.

The final three shots of the sequence show consequences of the flooding to things, rather than people, with the things symbolizing the missing residents: the seventh shot shows a truck submerged to its roof; the eighth shot shows a flooded street, with water up to the roofs of the houses; the ninth and final shot shows a car roof under water. Connected to Meserve's reporting about citizens trapped in their homes, trying to escape rising floodwaters, the eighth image of a street of flooded homes gains special significance. As Meserve noted, the Ninth Ward and New Orleans East were modest low- and middle-income areas with many one-story homes as well as some two-story homes. For New Orleanians unable to evacuate prior to Katrina, when floodwaters rose swiftly after the breaches to the Industrial Canal and the London Avenue Canal, the only option was to climb into attics. Since floodwaters rose higher than ten feet in many areas, waters rose above the level of the attic in many one-story homes. Residents who did not bring into their attics the means of breaking through roofs were

One of the sequence of images accompanying cameraman Mark Biello's reporting by phone from the Lower Ninth Ward (CNN 8.29.05).

trapped and drowned. Meserve's reporting and the image of submerged single-story homes began to reveal for the first time the large-scale loss of life happening in real time.

THE CAMERAMAN SPEAKS

After Brown concluded his interview with Meserve, he interviewed cameraman Mark Biello, also by phone. The Meserve and Biello interviews were unusual for several reasons. First, each interview was conducted in real time and not significantly pre-produced. As Brown interviewed Meserve and then Biello, his producer and editors brought up sequences of images. Since the conversations were not pre-structured, Brown controlled their length, with his team scrambling to add images. Each segment lasted more than ten minutes, much longer than a typical report and interview segment on CNN. Because the images used were recently received by the network and had not been pre-cut, they functioned more as documentary evidence than as pre-edited sequence (like the aerial footage used by Fox earlier the same evening). Where the sequence used with Meserve's interview (discussed above) was relatively short, the sequence accompanying Biello's was much more extensive, containing some seventy-two images, including several of the images also used under Meserve.

Second, this segment was unusual in that a cameraman was interviewed at all. Camera operators are almost always anonymous in television news, despite the fact that their choices in the field (made in concert with producers and sometimes with reporters) strongly shape the meanings available to editors, producers, and eventually, audiences. Biello was only interviewed because his footage was not yet available for broadcast. Because his images could not speak, CNN pressed him into service as amanuensis.

As discussed in chapter 4, when CNN returned to Meserve the next night, they replaced the images from the previous night with footage actually shot in the Ninth Ward. These two reports provide the closest access via television news to the experience of survivors and are thus unusual and significant. Further, they are more productive of empathy than sympathy because of Meserve's close ties to the story. The lack of images and the initial focus on her voice allows her reporting to avoid the visual construction of TV non-space typical of Brian Williams or Shepard Smith's stand-ups in New Orleans. By not creating a visual frame that selects mise-en-scène and excludes much of the real, Meserve's initial reporting via phone was more productive of connection, the grounds for empathy. Thus, the absences and gaps in television news coverage of Katrina on Monday, August 29, 2005, created by production decisions and technical challenges, generated not only misunderstandings, but also possibilities for connection.

CHAPTER FOUR

The Sort of Disaster Humans Cause

TUESDAY, AUGUST 30

*T*ELEVISION NEWS VERY RARELY RETURNS TO REVISIT A report or to correct or clarify. Thus, CNN's decision to return to Jeanne Meserve's reporting and Mark Biello's footage on Tuesday, August 30, 2005, underscores the significance of their initial reporting on the consequences of the flooding of New Orleans caused by the breaching of levees. It also reveals the investment by television news in controlling the combination of voice and image to shape story.

The significance of Meserve's reporting and Aaron Brown's cross-examination, and its status as "breaking news" (a coup for CNN), certainly influenced the network's decision to return to Meserve on the next night's broadcast. Moreover, since the network initially was unable to broadcast cameraman Mark Biello's images with Meserve's reporting, CNN had strong incentive to broadcast the images when available for the next night's program. The breakdown in the televisual apparatus, brought on by the exigencies of Katrina and the flood, resulted in a disjunction between voice and image that opened up "undesirable" space for viewer perspective and eroded the mastery of meaning preferred by television news. By re-reporting, CNN reasserted control over the apparatus and the story.

Brown was not coy about CNN's motivation, praising Meserve's reporting and indicating that the network had received more than six hundred e-mails praising her report. Providing an "encore" performance was good business as well as good television.

> BROWN: The humanity with which she reported that story. . . . I've never heard better.

In effect, on Tuesday night, CNN aired the report that it would have aired the night before, if time and technology had been available. On Monday night, Meserve and Biello were given ten minutes each to verbally report, but the re-report was edited down to a much tighter four minutes. The edited re-report drew from Meserve's original voice-over, but re-cut this over an edit of Biello's images. The resulting report gained in authority what it lost in immediacy. In the process, the juxtaposition of the two reports revealed the work by which television news is constructed and the specific process of generating stories from the chaotic experience of New Orleans as it flooded.

In the revised report on Tuesday, Biello's footage is much more powerful, direct, specific, and revealing than the more generic flood footage used by CNN on Monday night (generic in that it featured images from all over the city, not specifically from the Ninth Ward). The first image shows a responder using an axe to cut a hole in the roof of a home flooded to the eaves. The shot frames a middle-aged African American man wearing a denim shirt, jeans, and a floppy hat. He is chopping downward multiple times with an axe, cutting into a roof.

> RESPONDER: Make sure you keep your head away from the ceiling, OK?

Despite a lack of context, this first image reveals interesting and important information. Unlike the footage from Monday night, it captures the act of rescue. The dynamic movement of the man in the frame contrasts strongly with the very slow movement of figures struggling through flooded streets in the Monday footage. Whereas those shots suggest enormous forces (natural, man-made, systemic) challenging individuals, Biello's first shot frames agency, a New Orleanian acting to save other New Orleanians. Significantly, the figure is not wearing a uniform or any badge of office. Visually, he is represented as a responder, a rescuer, but not affiliated. Finally, perhaps most importantly, the Tuesday report includes the rescuer's own voice as he communicates to a trapped resident, whereas the Monday footage did not include any audio from subjects, instead depending on Meserve or Biello for explanation.

The second shot in the sequence shows the resolution of another rescue. The shot frames a middle-aged white man wearing a dirty white T-shirt, jeans, and a floppy hat. He is helping a young African American woman out of a hole in a roof. It may be that this is the same roof as the first shot, but the first man is not shown. What is clear is that CNN's revised report fea-

Biello's footage of a responder chopping through a roof (shot on 8.29.05).
(CNN 8.30.05).

turing Biello's footage presents images of rescue very differently than other footage used by NBC, Fox, and CNN that shows aerial rescues by the Coast Guard. These rescues were typically shot from a great distance, with the camera zoomed in, creating a facsimile of closeness that still possessed the vestiges of distance and remove. The second shot of the Tuesday re-report links Biello as cameraman and thus links the viewers to the rooftop on which the rescue took place. Again, the placement of the camera powerfully shaped the potential meanings, forging connection where other footage instantiated distance.

Next, the sequence cuts to the still image of Meserve with map and graphics, used on Monday night. Unlike Monday's report, the revised report remains only briefly on the identifying screen, before cutting to another image of rescue. In this fourth image, five men wearing partial uniforms load a family from a roof onto a flatbottom boat. They assist an African American woman into the boat and carry an older child and several small children. The footage is shot at night with flashlights for illumination.

The next shot demonstrates the work by which television news constructs authority. In her Monday report, Meserve had noted hearing dogs barking throughout the Ninth Ward. In the Tuesday report, the sequence cuts to a higher-angle shot over the roofs of several flooded houses, and while Meserve's comment is replayed, the audio track features sounds of dogs barking. By connecting voice, image, and sound, television news constructs the sense that it is representing the whole of reality. The difference between the two reports reveals the work involved in this production of authoritative wholeness.

The next two shots show additional flooded homes, with more dog sounds on the audio track. The eighth and ninth shots of the sequence are significant for complicating CNN's construction of who has been affected by the flooding. In the eighth shot, six male figures—two white and four African American, dressed in T-shirts indicating that they are NOPD officers—help a young white couple into a rescue boat and push off from a flooded home. The ninth shot reverses the angle, showing two men in the front of the boat using poles to feel under the surface of the floodwaters for submerged obstacles. The young couple is visible in the back of the boat. Unlike the footage from Monday night, this shot makes clear that the flooding threatened a broad range of New Orleanians, not only African Americans. In combination with the earlier images in the sequence showing African American and white responders working together to rescue citizens threatened by floodwater, this shot complicated the emerging consensus of television news that the impact of Katrina and the flooding of New Orleans was primarily about race.

Next, the sequence recycles one of the images from the Monday report. Shot in high angle from a bridge, this image shows a family being rescued on a fishing boat. Even with the strong new footage shot by Biello, CNN continued to draw from other images in order to tell specific stories. Again, this reuse of images suggests that all news reporting must be understood as representative, as allegorical but not as literally real. Rather than conveying reality, CNN's representation of the flooding of New Orleans after Katrina and the failure of the levees was constructed and produced.

The sequence then cuts to a shot of two men (one African American, one white), possibly the two from the first two shots in the sequence, talking to residents stranded on a roof and a submerged treetop. The shot underscores the difficulty in seeing and identifying residents trapped in flooded homes. From the boat, Biello's camera cannot quite make out the residents. Strikingly, in strong contrast to the roof and tree shot, the twelfth shot is a close-up of a gray-haired African American woman. Beginning with a close-up of her face, the camera then zooms out to reveal her rescuer, an African American male in a long white T-shirt. The woman's focus is on her rescuer, as if in recognition that he is her lifeline to safety.

The twentieth shot in the sequence also conveys a sense of the perspective of the rescued. The shot reveals another nighttime rescue, illuminating a scene via an on-camera light. An older African American man is being pulled, with difficulty, out of the dark water by two men. The man being

Biello's footage of survivor pulled through a hole in a roof (CNN 8.30.05).

rescued initially seems disoriented. A hand reaches into the frame to pat him on the left shoulder, encouraging him to "feel better." As the camera reframes both figures, the man pulled from the water reaches out to the second man, a younger African American in a black T-shirt and camouflage pants, with a gun strapped to his hip. The older man takes the younger man's hand, shaking it. When the younger man stops shaking, the older man continues to hold his rescuer's hand for several more seconds. The shot frames both men's hands (a yellow bracelet is visible on the rescuer's wrist) as the older man prolongs the moment, not releasing the younger man's hand per usual social convention. In the temporal economy of television news, this shot is held for a long time.

Biello's shot of the two hands strongly suggests the focalization of the older man, conveying powerfully his sense of relief, but also a sense of vulnerability and disorientation. The older man has been rescued, but after a significant amount of time in the water, in mortal jeopardy. The moment contains both ideas: rescue but also neglect. The shot's duration is as important as its graphic content. Whereas the very short cuts used under the Meserve audio on Monday's report gave some brief sense of the peril to human bodies, the greater length of the small scenes shot by Biello (and built by an editor between the Monday and Tuesday broadcasts) conveys much greater insight into the lived impact of the flood.

Unlike most television news coverage of Katrina, this particular shot begins to approach filmmaker Ricky Leacock's idea of "living cinema," a method employed by independent documentary to represent the human impact of Katrina and the flooding of New Orleans. By employing approaches used by documentarians—stretching duration and focusing on detail—CNN revealed more about the lived experience of the flooding of New Orleans in one shot than other networks revealed in whole broadcasts. CNN's decision to re-cut and re-report Meserve's story from Monday night enabled the creation of such moments, moments highly unusual in the regular practice of television news.

The twenty-third shot is a high-angle shot that pans from left to right over an African American man on a roof before zooming out to reveal the camera's extreme distance. The twenty-fourth shot shows the visual perspective of Biello's camera as he slowly floats in a boat at night past a house flooded to the eaves. The distance emphasized by the optical zoom in shot 23 emphasizes the closeness of camera (and cameraman) to the flooded home in shot 24. Over that shot, CNN plays Meserve's voice, as she discusses the difficulty in reporting on people trapped in flooded homes.

> MESERVE: When you stand in the dark and hear people yelling for
> help and you cannot get to them . . .

Meserve's voice-over articulates her emotional conflict over the play of closeness and disconnection inherent in television news reporting, a play

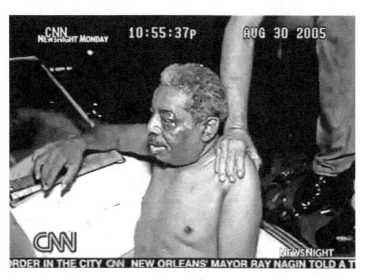

Biello's footage of a man pulled from the water and comforted by a rescuer
(CNN 8.30.05).

Biello's footage of a person trapped in an attic signaling with aluminum foil (CNN 8.30.05).

reinforced by the juxtaposition between the high-angle pan and zoom and the close shot from the boat. Meserve and Biello observed human suffering and death but, by the conventions of television journalism, could only report and recount, not intervene. As Meserve continues, Biello's camera frames a small movement. As the boat carrying the camera and cameraman floats past the house, the camera frames a piece of tinfoil pushed through a crack to catch the attention of potential rescuers. This image contains both the potential of the camera to see and record but also its inherent disconnection, condensing the conflict into a single image.

Unlike documentary, television news often does not identify subjects, especially citizens in crisis or disaster reporting. While television news always identifies public officials and paid consultants, citizen survivors are regularly represented without specification. Thus, the older man in the twentieth shot of the sequence is humanized but not identified. In a sense, human subjects are used like recycled footage: they are presented as representations to convey broad, allegorical understandings. While CNN's return to Meserve and Biello's reporting began to suggest some features of "living cinema," it still remained largely within the conventions of television news.

CNN's broadcast regularly featured multiple frames, and Meserve's voice-over and Biello's close observation were contained within a screen featuring other information, complicating viewers' access to the report and producing conflicting meanings. CNN's text crawl at the bottom of the screen summarizes news developments and official statements as the network's large frame features original reporting and images. The logic of the crawl supports the longer news reports: CNN's reporting can go into greater depth precisely because the network can simultaneously convey immediate information and breaking news. Of course, in the absence of truly breaking news, crawls often feature press releases and other official statements, often only minimally filtered. Textually, the crawl pulls at the viewer, bifurcating focus from the main story.

During Meserve's and Biello's combined voice-over and images, CNN featured a text crawl, running from left to right: BARBOUR SAYS THAT POLICE WILL BE "RUTHLESS" IN DEALING WITH LOOTERS, USING "WHATEVER MEANS NECESSARY" TO CONTROL THEM. In this case, the crawl features a statement by Mississippi Governor Haley Barbour threatening looters in his state with violent consequences. On one hand, the statement can be read as familiar political posturing. Appearing tough on crime in a crisis is usually good politics, and Louisiana Governor Kathleen Blanco issued very similar statements about crime and the use of deadly force by police and the National Guard in New Orleans. On the other hand, the juxtaposition of Barbour's statement with the image of the tinfoil and Meserve's voice-over creates a conflict over the meanings and dominant narratives in the first days after the storm. Barbour's statement frames the primary challenge posed by Katrina as the threat to property by looters. His solution is to shift resources to protect property with the threat of deadly force. However, Biello's image and Meserve's voice-over frame the primary challenge posed by Katrina as the mortal threat to residents trapped by floodwaters. The shot shows the viewer a human being desperately trying to attract the attention of potential rescuers while the audio track references people yelling for help in the dark.

Supported by television news coverage from the French Quarter and the Central Business District and focused first on minimal damage, then on threats to property, politicians at the local, state, and national level framed the Katrina crisis as primarily about property and "security." CNN's news report instead insisted that the crisis was about the peril faced by survivors and the need to emphasize rescue. By prioritizing property over people, "security" over succor, political leaders shifted the narrative from inadequate preparation and response by demonizing the survivors and diverting resources from search and rescue to property protection. The juxtaposition between the text crawl and the re-report of Meserve's story and Biello's images points up a central conflict in the struggle to understand, narrate, and control Katrina's meanings.

Other juxtapositions between text and image place meanings into conflict. In the same CNN report, another high-angle shot shows a tree that has fallen on the roof of a submerged house before zooming out to reveal two African American men sitting on the roof awaiting rescue (shot 17). Over this image, Meserve's voice relates that some New Orleans residents kept axes in their attics after Hurricane Betsy flooded the Ninth Ward and other parts of the city in 1969. Sound and image combine to suggest that the men escaped onto the roof of the house due to memory, planning, and action. Under this image, CNN's crawl reads: NATIONAL GUARD TROOPS MOVED INTO DOWNTOWN NEW ORLEANS BUSINESS DISTRICT. While the image argues that the greatest need is in the flooded neighborhoods, the crawl conveys official priorities: instead of protecting citizens, the National Guard is deployed to protect property and institutions from citizens.

Two shots later in the same sequence, the camera frames the same rescuers from the first two shots of the sequence: an African American man in a floppy hat and a white man with an axe. As the two men chop a hole in the roof of another submerged home, CNN's crawl continues: . . . AND STATE POLICE SQUADS BACKED BY SWAT TEAMS WERE SENT IN TO SCATTER LOOTERS AND RESTORE ORDER IN THE CITY. The juxtaposition again points up opposed meanings and the stakes involved. As with the National Guard, city and state resources were focused on threats to property, rather than on search and rescue. While CNN's images demonstrate that rescues were taking place, even after nightfall, the shot of the tinfoil and Meserve's reporting about the large numbers of people in dire need of rescue argue that the resources in play were insufficient. The crawl indicates a diversion of resources toward the protection of property, suggesting an official interpretation that has begun to demonize New Orleans residents, disqualifying survivors from the benefits of citizenship. When city, state, and national government failed to meet the social contract to protect and serve their citizens in the flooding after Katrina, officials could have acknowledged mistakes and addressed the urgent need. While some did, most authorities instead sought to demonize the New Orleanians who remained in the city before landfall (many lacking the means to leave when the city failed to provide buses, others unwilling to leave in any case), proposing that those citizens had violated the social contract by their choice to remain and were thus "on their own." As shown, many New Orleans residents responded to this abandonment by becoming their own first responders, saving themselves and others.

The tensions created between the meanings posed by reporting in the screen's main frame and text displayed across the bottom of the screen reveal some of the interests in play seeking to define how Katrina was understood in the immediate aftermath of the storm. These interests include government (local, state, and federal), citizens, television news networks, and national and international viewers. While the "official" argument that New Orleanians who stayed forfeited rights became dominant, with severe lived consequences, this interpretation was not monolithic. Importantly, reports like those of Meserve and Biello revealed the lived impact of the flooding, shaping understandings in real time. By presenting these different meanings within the same screen, CNN staged the conflict over Katrina's meanings as it was being waged. The network was hardly neutral, as it advanced its own agenda to win and keep viewers, satisfy advertisers, and burnish its reputation. However, unlike the other networks, CNN deployed its resources to report the story of the flooding of New Orleans at least a day before NBC and Fox. The fact of this reporting, and the specific choices in shooting, editing, and writing, shaped what viewers knew about the impact of Katrina on New Orleans. In turn, CNN's reporting influenced the emerging collective memory of television viewers about Katrina.

A BETTER VIEW OF THE WIDE SHOT

In the same Tuesday, August 30, 2005, broadcast that returned to Meserve's reporting combined with Biello's images, CNN also began to push stories of looting and crime in New Orleans. Thus, the network that most aggressively reported the flooding of New Orleans also became increasingly distracted by concerns about property and theft. Opening the two-hour broadcast, Aaron Brown references the confusion and lack of footage from Monday night's broadcast, reassuring viewers that CNN now understood more fully the situation in New Orleans. Framed in the self-referential discourse favored by television news, where story is more significant than reality, Brown confirms, "We have a better view of the wide shot."

CNN's wide shot on Tuesday looked significantly different from its presentation on Monday night. Then, closing with Meserve's reporting, CNN presented the story of failed levees, flooded homes, and trapped, mortally threatened residents. On Tuesday, likely in response to reporting by NBC and Fox in the hours before *NewsNight* aired, CNN presented a different view.

BROWN: (New Orleans) is not simply a natural disaster tonight.

Under Brown's voice-over, CNN showed a shot of an African American woman, wearing a white shirt and dark shorts and carrying two white trash bags. The camera zooms slightly, its interest drawn to the bags, although the shot does not reveal the contents. The next shot also featured an African American woman, wearing a red top, also carrying two bags. The third shot cut to an African American man, wearing a white T-shirt, carrying a bag and picking his way through rubble and detritus. (In my analysis of television news, I refer to specific details, such as the type and color of clothing, in order to locate historical individuals, countering the tendency of television news not to locate or name citizens.)

> BROWN (continuing): It has become the sort of disaster humans
> cause.

Based on CNN's own reporting from Monday, Brown seems at first to reference the failure of the levees and the problems with response and rescue. However, the image cuts to a high-angle shot, zoomed in from a remove, showing two African American teenaged boys and a younger boy climbing out of a broken door to a store on Canal Street. The boys drag bags, which do not appear to contain food or medicine.

> BROWN (continuing): There is looting and lawlessness, overwhelm-
> ing in some places the ability of police to keep order.

The first shots are challenging to read. The women and the man are carrying bags, but these bags might contain clothes or belongings salvaged from their flooded homes. The first three people seem to be seeking safety and shelter. Only Brown's voice-over suggests the possibility of theft, and since the television news apparatus is structured to provide the anchor with primary authority, Brown's perspective colors the viewers' ability to see other possibilities in the footage. The fourth shot more clearly argues that what it represents is criminal activity. The distance of the camera, suggested by the high angle and the zoom, indicates that the cameraperson filmed the boys from a remove. The shot suggests anxiety and surveillance and converts the boys into thieves and looters. Before Brown mentions "looting and lawlessness," the image has already established this idea.

After the shot of the three boys, the next image shows three African American men: the first in a white T-shirt and ball cap; the second, shirtless and pulling up his shorts; the third with his T-shirt pulled over his head.

The three men run from right to left across the frame, carrying clothing from a store. Like the shot of the boys, this image is also zoomed-in from a high angle.

Each of these shots looks at New Orleanians from a distance without much individuation. CNN's images reduce the particularity of these survivors, instead converting them into types, signs of criminality. The viewer cannot know from this report who they are, where they are from, what they have experienced, and what they need. Instead, the images begin to construct a sense of unease and danger, easily stoked into fear.

> BROWN (continuing): The more we see tonight, the more difficult it is to keep safe, the more desperate things appear.

The anchor's voice-over continues to overwrite the images. Brown performs a discursive slide between desperation and fear, and this slide reveals a significant shift in how television news understood and explained the meanings of Katrina and the flooding of New Orleans. All nine New Orleanians represented by CNN appear at risk, in need. They appear to need safety. But Brown's voice-over and the visual rhetoric of the images combine to frame these people as a threat to "public safety." Only twenty-four hours removed from Meserve's report of flooding in the Ninth Ward and New Orleans East, Brown begins CNN's telecast by demonizing the citizens who survived Katrina. Meserve's report was characterized by deep human concern about citizens trapped in flooded homes. These people were not kept safe by federal levees, were not evacuated by the City of New Orleans, and were not rescued by local, state, or federal responders. As Meserve's report made clear, these citizens were at risk. On Monday, the crisis was the safety of the trapped survivors.

By Tuesday, CNN and the other television news networks began to define the crisis as the threat to property posed by "refugees" who "looted." The images themselves do not represent a threat to human safety. Rather, they show nine people carrying bags of goods, some of which were taken from a store on Canal Street. The logic of the very early reporting on Monday, which focused on damage to property in the French Quarter by Hurricane Katrina, was now extended to the threat to property posed by citizens who survived the flood, but were without resources. On Tuesday, television news began to produce fear of the residents of New Orleans. As the week continued, this fear of the residents increasingly replaced fear for the plight of the residents. Television news was tapping into the same high-concept formula used to represent the approaching hurricane. This demonization of citizens of New Orleans had a profound and immediate impact on response to the storm. Responders began to fear the people they were to rescue, and security began to trump succor as the primary official priority. As a result, search and rescue was delayed, resources were diverted to the protection of property rather than to the rescue of people, and thousands of citizens who had escaped the flood were left stranded at the Superdome, the Convention Center, and on the city's elevated highways.

ONLY WHAT YOU KNOW, NOT WHAT YOU THINK YOU KNOW

Immediately after Brown suggested that the greatest threat facing New Orleans was looting by its surviving citizens, CNN shifted back to consider the causes of the flooding. From the shot of the three men carrying armfuls of clothes, CNN cut to a map graphic showing the New Orleans area and identifying points at which the levees breached: "Major breaches sent more water pouring into an already flooded city." In contrast to the first shots, in which citizens demonstrated mobility and agency (even as they were constructed as criminals), CNN here showed a shot of a man trapped on the roof of his house, waiting for rescue.

BROWN: It is now a race against time to find survivors.

CNN's stark contrast—demonstrating both fear of and concern for residents—reveals an internal conflict over the meanings of Katrina. Far from the wide shot promised by Brown, CNN instead showed a series of jarring juxtapositions, jump-cutting between demonization and concern (with only Meserve's report and Biello's images reaching the connection required for empathy). CNN's conflicted response to Katrina was demonstrated in Brown's interrogation from his New York studio of reporter Adaora Udoji, who reported on the conditions from New Orleans.

BROWN (beginning): How lawless is New Orleans tonight?
UDOJI: Police are trying to find out. Thousands of people have nowhere to go.

Unlike Brown, Udoji makes clear that she is reporting on expressed perspectives, not facts. She notes "reports" of looting on Canal Street and of shootings around the Superdome, but she does not assert that looting and shooting were taking place. Instead, Udoji suggests the consequences of misreading by authorities.

UDOJI: Police are riding in packs, fearing resistance.

Her careful phrasing documents the fears of the police without endorsing them. The turn in television news reporting on Tuesday seems to have been in response to the anxieties of authorities on the ground, compounded by the fears of reporters and producers in the field. As seen in the discussion of Brown's introductory segment, television news produced reports that reinforced, rather than questioned, these anxieties. In contrast, Udoji's response presents this fear not as a fact, but as a perception by police. Further, she suggests the implications of the police fearing their own citizens: a suspension of the social contract and neglect of those in greatest need.

In keeping with CNN's new focus, Udoji notes "reports" of looting, while CNN recycles some of the images from Brown's introduction.

BROWN: Are the dry streets safe?

Over these images constructing "looting" in the Central Business District (the "dry streets"), Udoji expresses concern about human misery, indicating that even those rescued from drowning are left stranded on highway overpasses.

UDOJI: You have all of these displaced people . . . (Brown tries to interrupt) . . . All of these people have nowhere to go, no info, no help.

BROWN: Is there a noticeable National Guard presence on the streets of New Orleans?

The disconnections in this exchange reveal the conflicting interpretations in play. While the image track replays the images of African Americans carrying bags in the streets of the CBD, Udoji's voice-over references rescue and relief. When Udoji focuses on the needs of those rescued and dumped, Brown asks about security. When she begins to answer, Brown cuts her off.

BROWN: Only what you know, not what you think you know, as we say around here.

Of course, Udoji was trying to report what she had learned on the ground, while Brown sought to impose what he thought he knew about New Orleans. This sequence makes visible the editorial shaping typically effaced in television news. The television news apparatus invests authority in the anchor, whose voice counts more than other voices. The exchange between Brown and Udoji is thus marked by television news convention, but also by gender and by race. The only female African American television news reporter on CNN was overridden by the white male anchor, and CNN's production headquarters in New York overwrote the reporting produced in the field. As a television news professional, Udoji enjoyed meals, electricity, and shelter. CNN provided not only for her safety, but also for her comfort. The final disconnection in television news is the experience of reporters and producers after the camera stops shooting. Their reality was entirely different from that faced by the survivors of the flood.

Not surprisingly, Brown reserves the last word for himself, combining the production of fear with a subtle, gendered patronization.

BROWN: Stay safe out there.

LOOTERS RAID STORES

The Fox Report on Tuesday, August 30th not only offered excuses for failures to protect the city and its residents, it also began a process of distancing national viewers from connection with New Orleans residents. Again, on the previous night's broadcast, *The Fox Report* had struggled to convey the scope and human impact of the flooding of New Orleans. On Tuesday, instead of focusing on search and rescue of survivors, Fox focused on portraying survivors as criminals. Through a trajectory of concern to blame to fear, Fox recast New Orleans residents as responsible for their own fate.

In a summary of top stories at the outset of the broadcast, Fox acknowledged the unfolding crisis. Shepard Smith related that water continued to pour into New Orleans "because of a broken levee," requiring "search and rescue by the thousands." But, rather than explore the threat posed to survivors by the rising floodwaters, or efforts to rescue those imperiled by floodwaters, Fox instead focused on looting. This focus initiated an emphasis that would continue over the next several nights, shifting how Fox understood and explained the meaning of the flooding, shaping national opinion about the surviving residents, and influencing local, state, and federal response. By converting survivors themselves into the greatest threat to "safety" and "security," Fox and the other television news networks contributed to the securitization of the flooding of New Orleans by authorities. As a consequence of the focus on "securing" the city from its own citizens, search and rescue was delayed and resources were diverted.

Triptych shows scenes of "looting" by surviving citizens (FOX 8.30.05).

The segmentation of Fox's screen emphasized looting as the biggest story of the August 30th newscast, larger than the drowning residents trapped in their homes. After mentioning the ongoing search and rescue, Smith warned of "rampant looting." The screen featured the title "looting" and divided into three boxes. In the upper left, three African Americans carried juice and water, a man and a woman walking toward the camera and another man walking away. In the upper right, an African American man carried a trash bag through water up to his waist. Below these two boxes, across the bottom of the frame, a larger box showed an African American man pulling a trash bag through floodwaters. In this example, Smith's voice, the on-screen titling, and the graphic organization of images in frames combine to overwrite the images themselves as representations of "looting." Solely on the basis of each image, the viewer cannot determine the contents of the trash bags or the origin of the water and juice. These images convey looting because of the authority of the anchor and the associative power of the television news screen, not because of the information in any of the three images. As with the controversial application of captions to still photos suggesting that African American residents "looted" goods and white residents "found" supplies, television news had to provide additional information to shape how viewers saw and understood images.

Even when images provided more information, they could not reveal motivation. While the first three images did not in themselves convey "looting," Fox's next image provided more information. The camera tilted up to reveal the entrance to a drugstore in the French Quarter. A white man handed out a trash bag to an African American man, while an older white woman walked out of the frame carrying water and sports drinks. The scene is strikingly calm, in contrast to Smith's verbal rhetoric, "amid the devastation, there is desperation." The three people do not seem desperate. Rather, they seem like they are requisitioning supplies in an emergency. Whereas in the first three images, Fox News captioned the images in order to convey the idea that these individuals were criminals, this image offers clear evidence that goods were removed from a store. But, this image fails to reveal the motivations of the "looters." By relying on images rather than on interviews, Fox sought to signify on these bodies rather than to allow them agency and perspective. In this sense, even the living are available for inscription by television news.

While this image conveyed people taking goods from a store, it did not suggest a strong sense of danger. The next image showed a young African American man in a white tank top and a young African American woman in a brown tank top running up a street toward the camera, both carrying trash bags. The youth and race of these figures, and their speed and motion, code them differently than the calm and order of the older, mixed race people in the first image.

> SMITH: Looters raiding abandoned stores, grabbing anything they
> can get their hands on, and making a run for it.

The next image further complicates the visual argument of the sequence. In this shot, an African American woman, wearing a pink tank top, holds a baby girl in her left arm, as two small girls, both under five years, hold her right hand and each other. A second African American woman, in a white T-shirt, holds the hand of a girl in a green dress and carries a white trash bag. Where the youth and motion of the two teens in the previous shot conveyed something of the idea of "making a run for it," the image of the women and girls contradicts Smith's assertion that "looters" are "grabbing anything" with the goal of theft.

Along with the first image of the older people, this image suggests family connection, mothers seeking sustenance for their children at a moment when the government at all levels has abandoned providing for those in need. This image resisted the overwriting attempted by Smith. It also contrasted with an on-screen graphic proclaiming, "Looters Raid Stores in New Orleans and Other Cities." Smith dismissed the possibility of sympathy and connection.

Mothers and daughters, described as "looters," wading in floodwater (FOX 8.30.05).

SMITH: One man asked for sympathy, saying, "Hey, we gotta eat";
   but, there are also signs of hope and survival.

Smith's "signs of hope and survival" refer to the next images of Coast Guard members loading an African American girl into a basket to be raised from a flooded roof. Typical of television news in general, *The Fox Report*'s early focus on looting provided multiple messages and was not completely coherent. The images contained other potential meanings than those over-written by Smith's discourse or Fox's graphics and titles. In order to convert survivors with legitimate claims into criminals able to be discarded, Fox had to emphasize blame first and then fear.

I AM DISAPPOINTED IN MYSELF

In addition to figuring New Orleanians as criminals rather than survivors, *The Fox Report* also implicated survivors as responsible for their own suffering. Reporting from Interstate 10, "three miles outside of the city," Anita Vogel narrated images of "survival." Vogel wears a white T-shirt and a Fox ball cap, with her hair pulled back. Unlike the survivors upon whom she would turn her crew's camera, Vogel appears clean and freshly clothed. Separated by her status as a professional TV reporter with access to supplies and shelter, Vogel is also separated by the television news apparatus that allows her to file her report from a remove, on an overpass, out of the water. Her professional mobility combines with the power of the apparatus to gather, edit, and present images in carefully constructed screen environments. She talks about survivors instead of interviewing survivors and allowing them to tell their stories. As Vogel talks, viewers see an image of five medics laboriously helping an older woman, who seems to cry out in pain. The image is stripped of audio, so that Vogel's voice can speak over the image. By removing the audio, Fox disallows the older woman's point of view. Viewers look at her without hearing her, the lack of her audio making her pain more distant and abstracted. As Geoffrey Hartman has argued, television news separates human beings into those who experience pain and those who look at others in pain (1994).

When Vogel's report does include the voice of a survivor, that voice is carefully controlled and framed. After a series of images—mostly of older African American and white women being evacuated by the Coast Guard—Vogel introduces a survivor who "learned a costly lesson." The report cuts to a medium shot of a middle-aged African American woman, clutching her purse in her right hand and holding onto a man's arm with her left hand. The woman is not introduced by name and does not receive a title on screen. In the hierarchy of television news, her voice is evidence for Vogel's argument, but her own history, the details of her life, are unimportant.

> WOMAN: I am disappointed that I did not follow directions about the evacuation out of the city, and I am angry with myself that my husband and I did not get out of here. We thought that we survived Hurricane Betsy back in '65, that we could survive anything. We were wrong.

Despite the depersonalization of her presentation by Fox, the woman does reveal aspects of her history. She and her husband (presumably the man holding her left arm) are long-time New Orleanians, and they had survived the last major hurricane to strike New Orleans and cause significant flooding in the Ninth Ward and other parts of the city. Her decision to remain with her husband and wait out Katrina was not arbitrary, but was based on history and past experience. Her conclusion is that she and her husband made a mistake in this case and that they would have been better off leaving the city before the storm. She blames herself because she knew better. At the same time, Fox seeks to locate responsibility for her suffering in her decision without considering the causes for the flooding or the delays in rescue and response. The woman seems to regret staying because government at all levels abandoned her and her husband. Fox instead blames survivors for surviving and for needing help, rather than blaming government for failing to build and maintain levees to protect citizens or to rescue those in peril. Vogel laments that "people thought they could stay home" and assumed that they would be safe. In conclusion, she argues that the survivors are responsible not only for their own danger and suffering, but also for endangering the lives of responders.

> VOGEL: It just becomes too dangerous for their men and women to be out in the dark.

In an amazing rhetorical slide, Vogel and Fox hold survivors responsible for their own plight, but argue that the safety of Coast Guard, National Guard, police, and other first responders should be prioritized. In *Breach of Faith* (2006), Jed Horne identifies this same argument as employed by National Guard troops who told doctors at Charity Hospital that they would not evacuate dying patients because they would put themselves at risk. Through Vogel's report, Fox extends and supports a logic whereby the safety and security of military and responders are figured as more valuable than the lives of citizens. This logic depends on an argument that the survivors are themselves to blame for their circumstances.

TERROR ALERT ELEVATED

The Fox Report on Tuesday, August 30, 2005, worked to push images of survivors as criminals looting private property; to excuse the government, the Army Corps, and responders for failing to protect and rescue those in peril; and to blame survivors for their own suffering by selecting sound bites indicating remorse. Through an hour-long broadcast, Fox began by showing concern for survivors, before assigning blame and excuses, and then finally projecting fear. In order for viewers to watch the suffering of American citizens without strong implication, and in order to excuse the government's massive neglect and abrogation of the social contract, Fox had to convert New Orleans residents from survivors into Others, disqualifying them from citizenship and making them seem dangerous, a threat.

Following Vogel's report, Smith introduces a report by Jeff Goldblatt. Offering a theme that would be expanded upon by Fox, NBC, and CNN on Wednesday and Thursday, Smith warns that "the city is slipping into crisis."

Goldblatt makes observations via camera phone from "up and down Poy-dras" in the Central Business District, noting that even the CBD had now received a couple of feet of water. A day earlier, from this location, which was favored by each of the three networks, the flooding was not visible. A day later, the flooding was inescapable. From Goldblatt's street-level view, he could see survivors.

Smith next introduces a more distanced view, images that correspond to his rhetorical conversion of survivors into non-citizens. The first image features a high-angle, extreme long shot looking down at the exterior of the Superdome. In this shot, people are visible, but reduced in scale to tiny dots. At the angle and distance of the shot, it is not possible to tell if the people are leaving or coming into the Superdome. The next image cuts to a mobile aerial view, rising above the lip of the Superdome, away from the people, showing the damage to the building's roof but losing the people from the frame.

> SMITH: At the Superdome, National Guard troops are bringing in refugees.

Fox was hardly alone in this misapplication of the term "refugee" to refer to American citizens who lost their homes due to the flooding after the levees failed. NBC and CNN also used the term freely and inaccurately. In this report, however, Fox provided a visual rhetoric that complemented the discursive act of stripping the survivors of their citizenship. The high-angle shot and the rising, aerial views abstracted and then framed out the people from the picture. In the same way, after blaming survivors for their own suffering and risk, Fox converted these individuals into non-citizens, offering further reason for government to treat them differently, to with-hold rights.

The slide from concern to blame to disenfranchisement to demoniza-tion was also enacted by a title crawl under the high-angle long shots of the Superdome. While the visual rhetoric removed the human scale, the title crawl announced, TERROR ALERT ELEVATED. By visually linking New Orleans citizens to the spectre of terrorism, Fox employed aspects of the high-concept presentation developed since September 11, 2001, and used during coverage of the U.S. invasion of Iraq and the war in Afghanistan. Fox's segment converts survivors via visual distance, rhetorical difference, and the suggestion of fear and danger.

As revealed in *Zeitoun* (2009), Dave Eggers's account of the experiences of Syrian immigrant and New Orleans small businessman Ahmed Zeitoun, the federal government invested significant resources on constructing a temporary jail in which to hold New Orleanians suspected of terrorism in the days after Katrina's landfall. After days of helping neighbors and delivering supplies, Zeitoun was arrested and detained without charges because his ethnicity implicated him as a terrorist. As *Zeitoun* reveals, the temporary Guantanamo was constructed outside the Amtrak station, next to the Superdome. Thus, if Fox had panned right during their aerial shot, the network might have revealed the construction of a prison at the same moment that Americans only blocks away lacked food, water, and medicine. Fox's crawl, TERROR ALERT ELEVATED, reveals the logic by which television news worked with the federal government to turn Americans into enemy combatants.

CITIZEN BRIEFING

Given the complexity and scale of the disaster of the flooding of New Orleans, television news reporting featured moments of rupture, even when sound, image, and voice worked together. These moments revealed other voices and other perspectives, complicating the official understandings circulated and reinforced by television news. In this way, very occasionally, television news provided moments that departed from the dominant, monolithic explanations of the meanings of Katrina and the flood. These moments resembled the approaches taken later by documentary filmmakers to feature multiple community voices in an effort to complicate and inform what was known and remembered about Katrina.

One example of such a departure from the script occurred in a report on CNN aired on Tuesday, August 30, 2005. In a pre-taped report, edited from footage produced by multiple crews in the field, anchor Aaron Brown sought to provide the "wide shot" he felt was missing. In voice-over, Brown confirmed the by-now-familiar interpretation that New Orleans had been abandoned and would soon erupt in violence.

BROWN: Supplies are running short, and so are tempers.

Surprisingly, the report cuts from Brown's warning to two African American women, both in the frame. A woman with red hair, wearing a white T-shirt, stands to the left. Another woman, wearing a red hat, stands to the right. The red-haired woman speaks to the camera, while the woman in the hat nods, fully engaged. This small moment within the report represents a rupture because Brown's voice stops and is (briefly) replaced by that of an actual survivor on the ground. While CNN was much more interested in interviewing survivors than NBC or Fox, the network would most often use a brief expression, usually a bite consisting of less than a sentence. This moment within an otherwise conventional segment is striking because the red-haired woman is allowed to speak at some length.

> RED-HAIRED WOMAN: The twin spans are down. The bridges are down. There is no electricity. Phone lines are down. Cellular phone lines are down. There is no way for us to get in touch with any family or friends or anybody that's left behind.

Strikingly, this citizen provides a more cogent briefing on conditions on the ground in New Orleans after the levees breached than any public official. She reports in a careful, systematic way on the reasons why she, her friend, and others who survived the hurricane and are surviving the flood cannot get out of the city. Rather than another glimpse of suffering, another quick cut to a mute and miserable survivor, this brief moment in this wholly typical report suggests that those on the ground possessed much greater agency and awareness than television news or authorities gave them credit for. She understands her situation in detail, has analyzed it, and has considered her options.

> RED-HAIRED WOMAN: We're gonna be here, whether we like it or not, because we can't take any road home.

Her evocation of "road home" suggests a deep investment in her community. This term would later be co-opted by the federally funded, state-run initiative Road Home Program. In a moment when most survivors would be thinking only of escape, this New Orleanian is already imagining how to overcome the barriers, natural and man-made, to her return home. The woman's comments to the camera resemble a documentary interview more than a television news bite. In her eloquence, she takes over the discourse of Brown's report and clearly communicates her perspective as a survivor and as a citizen.

However, as this moment is featured in a television news report and not a documentary, she is not identified by name (nor is her friend), and the report cuts away from the women and back to Brown's voice-over. He then introduces a more conventional "interview" in which an African American male, identified as Hardy Jackson (CNN mistakenly put a title on-screen earlier in Brown's report identifying a white Mississippi survivor as "Hardy Jackson"), tells a white female reporter about losing his wife to the flood.

JACKSON: She's gone. I held her hand as tight as I could . . . but I couldn't hold her. . . . I'm lost, that's all I had, that's all I had.

The young reporter cries in sympathy, and the report cuts back to Brown. By including only this bite, the report uses Jackson as a citation, a sign for suffering, rather than as a human being with a difficult story of loss. The contrast between the unnamed women and Jackson is striking. Where Jackson's story is fragmented and contained by the report, the red-haired woman's perspective challenges the report's claim to understand and to relate "the wide shot" to a national television audience. Embedded within traditional reporting, such moments of rupture suggest the sort of approaches to testimony and voice that would be used by documentarians attempting to understand the lived experience of the flood over the next several years.

CHAPTER FIVE

The Walking Dead

WEDNESDAY, AUGUST 31

*E*ARLY IN THE *FOX REPORT* NEWSCAST ON WEDNESDAY, August 31, 2005, Anita Vogel reported on hundreds of survivors stranded by the side of Interstate 10. Field anchor Shepard Smith opined, "New Orleans tonight is a dead city." Smith's assertion that New Orleans was a "dead city" followed a report on a large group of New Orleanians who were very much alive but in need of food, water, and shelter. Smith overwrote Vogel's report, providing an authoritative sounding conclusion that belied the visual evidence provided. New Orleans was a dead city because Smith said so.

This discursive transformation of living bodies into dead bodies recalls political theorist Achille Mbembe's theory of "necropolitics" (2003). In Mbembe's formulation, necropolitics determines different worth for different bodies, excluding some bodies from sovereignty, from rights, even from a claim to life. Many scholars and critics have accused the Bush administration (and neoliberalism more widely) of practicing necropolitics by politically, economically, and environmentally writing off whole populations as unworthy of rights to life and liberty. Henry Giroux (*Stormy Weather*, 2006) and Nicole Fleetwood (2006) each argue that the most vulnerable residents of New Orleans were already consigned to death by regulatory and political neglect in advance of Katrina's landfall. In this argument, the neglect of St. Bernard Parish, New Orleans East, and the Ninth Ward demonstrated an ecological necropolitics. By calling New Orleans "a dead city," Smith used the authority of voice as constructed by television news to convert the living into the dead.

Smith also worked a transformation of the living into the pre-dead in a rare field report aired on *The Fox Report* on August 31. After a hand-off from Laurie Dhue, the in-studio anchor, Smith introduced his own taped

Shepard Smith interviews survivors emerging from the floodwater
(FOX 8.31.05).

segment about New Orleanians coming out of the floodwaters onto an un-identified highway ramp.

As the segment begins, with his cameraman trailing, Smith approaches an African American man dressed in a white v-neck T-shirt and white ball cap, leading a little girl out of the water. Smith sticks out a microphone, as the camera frames Smith and the man.

> SMITH: You OK? Where have you been?
> MAN: I been pulling people out the water.
> SMITH: What's it like?
> MAN: I came from across the canal by Jackson Barracks. I was stuck in my attic. The water came up all at once.
> SMITH: Wow!

Unlike the undifferentiated survivors, framed en masse in Vogel's re-port, this man begins to reveal to Smith his specific history. He is from the Ninth Ward, or the other side of the Industrial Canal, by the Navy's Jack-son Barracks. He begins to tell his story of survival, of being trapped in his attic. He also makes clear that he has been actively attending to the needs of other survivors, "pulling people out the water." Yet, rather than pursue the man's story further, Smith turns from him, cutting him off in mid-story to accost two more men emerging from the water.

> SMITH: You OK? This the first time out?

Following Smith's direction, the camera swings around to frame the two new men. Smith's abandonment of the first man seems at first to be incredible, but the subservience of camera to Smith's voice and direction suggests that Smith was uncomfortable with the man's agency, his control of his story. By reframing on the two new men, Fox's camera makes the man in the cap disappear.

> GUY #1: Kicked out the window of a truck and swam.
> SMITH (to Guy #2): You OK?
> GUY #2 (angry): Yeah.
> SMITH: What do you need?
> GUY#2: I need somewhere to lay my head, food. We ain't had sleep or nothing . . .

Like the man in the cap, the two guys have specific stories of survival and need. But, as the second guy starts to itemize their need, Smith again turns away. Interrupting the second guy in mid-sentence, Smith points over the guy's shoulder, saying, "Look at this!" The cameraman instantly reframes, opening wider to follow Smith's direction, beginning to exclude the two guys from the frame. Again reasserting control over the news apparatus, Smith determines whose voice and story get "covered," whose stories get authorized by Fox.

> SMITH: Look at this! One after another come out of the water.

Smith interviews the first man out of the water (FOX 8.31.05).

Smith interrupts the first man to question the next man out of the water (FOX 8.31.05).

Man in the white hat provides mutual aid (Smith: "There is no one to rescue them") (FOX 8.31.05).

Smith's real attention is devoted to the camera and to the production of images for broadcast. As Smith walks away, the camera follows, trying to find frame. As it moves, the camera shows all three men, standing close together. Only framing and cutting have separated them. Disinterested in the stories of New Orleanians who survived the flood, Smith again overwrites with his editorial opinion.

SMITH: There is no one to rescue them. No one.

In the same way that the camera separated the men, Smith attempts to atomize the survivors. But, as Smith opines about the neglect faced by the survivors, the man in the white cap again enters the frame and wades back into the water to help the family approaching the highway ramp. Too busy imposing meaning, Smith and his camera miss this example of mutual aid. Indeed, Smith gestures to his right, pulling the camera away from the image of the man in the cap helping the family.

SMITH: They are everywhere.

As he says this, the camera zooms on distant figures, blocks away, struggling through the water toward the ramp. Smith ignores the men next to him or the man helping the family to his left. The spaces between Smith's verbal direction, the camera's response, and the images and voices of the survivors reveal the construction of editorial point of view. Smith actively works to overwrite the real and specific stories of the survivors, but this work is visible, revealing itself and eroding some of his authority. By focusing away from specific voices, Smith's report recasts survivors as the "Walking Dead," animated bodies of the already dead shuffling throughout a dead and damaged city. (Smith's line — "They are everywhere" — suggests the anxiety of human survivors in zombie media.) Clearly dehumanizing, this reporting transforms the living, excusing the lack of official rescue and response. While Smith's tone seems at first critical of the treatment of the survivors, his own disregard for their stories and voices, and his obliviousness to the real story of their mutual aid and support, perpetrates a secondary necropolitics.

But, the ruptures and gaps in the reporting provide space to recognize this work and to contest it. (This critical work may require close analysis and repeat viewings; possibly, viewers seeing the initial report might miss the ways in which Smith, through his control of the apparatus and frame, constructs the living survivors as the "Walking Dead.") For example, Smith stands to the side and narrates another act of mutual aid as a young African American man in a blue sleeveless T-shirt and a black ball cap helps a heavyset African American woman out of the water. Smith's disconnection from the plight of the survivors, his commitment to producing memorable sound bites and images rather than human stories, is apparent to the survivors. The young man turns to look at Smith, standing four feet from them, but separated by the television news apparatus. Inadvertently, the camera catches the young man's expression, which conveys awareness and the beginning of anger. The young man's look at the camera contests its presence and purpose, revealing a distinct and dissenting point of view and challenging the camera's claim to authority.

INCOHERENCE AND EDITORIAL VOICE

Smith's treatment of the survivors emerging from the floodwaters revealed the work of selection and prioritization involved in producing television news. Typically, Smith's report would have been cut down to excise the awkwardness of his quick dismissal of individual response. With more time, Fox might have left out these moments, instead suggesting that the faces and voices it chose to feature were the only ones available. The rush to get Smith's report on air resulted in the preservation of these revealing moments. The disregard of the individual experiences of flood survivors reveals much about the priorities of television news. In turn, this recognition reveals the limitations of basing understandings and collective memories about Katrina on television news reporting.

Smith ends the report by showing survivors gathering by the side of the elevated highway, waiting for transportation to shelter. Smith notes, "Here is where they end up, on a bridge." He notes their misery without observing or engaging, before offering an incipient critique of official response. Smith's camera shows a police car driving past the survivors. He asks the officer when and how these people will be helped, but the officer drives away without responding. Smith underscores the point: "Police cars drive past, without stopping." Earlier in this same broadcast, Smith had compared New Orleans to the Green Zone in Iraq, raising questions about the status and treatment of survivors and the allocation of national resources (National Guard troops deployed to Iraq were unavailable to help in Katrina). Of course, such comparisons—so tempting to reporters who had covered the U.S. invasion of Iraq—also work to convert U.S. citizens into enemy combatants, thus providing discursive support for the decision to treat New Orleans after Katrina like a military occupation rather than a rescue.

By criticizing police response, Smith implicates the various levels of government in the suffering resulting from Katrina and the flood, challenging the favored narrative of Katrina as a solely natural disaster. By questioning police response to suffering in New Orleans, especially by showing an officer ignoring survivors in need of aid, Smith creates the possibility of a critique of authorities. This critique was at odds with Fox's editorial policy that sought to reinforce the authority of the Bush administration (Brock and Rabin-Havt, 2012).

Smith's report is interrupted at this point. Studio anchor Laurie Dhue appears on screen, citing "technical difficulties" for "losing" Smith. Dhue then introduces new aerial footage of the 17th Street Canal (Fox was still arguing that the levees were overtopped by a massive, unprecedented storm surge, not that their structural integrity had failed). This is followed by a short segment on a shelter in Baton Rouge, where evacuees were being fed, emphasizing that survivors were taken care of. Finally, Dhue brings back Smith, but his tone is significantly changed. Before the "technical difficulties," Smith had criticized the individual officer and, by extension, the official response. In contrast, he now offers an excuse.

> SMITH: (There was) nothing he could do . . . not a knock on any-
> one, just an explanation of how enormous this task is . . .

In the three minutes he had been off air, Smith had changed his argument, replacing a critique with a version of the false inevitability excuse (the problem is so massive, so challenging, any response is impossible). As David Brock and Ari Rabin-Havt argue, Fox News has been characterized by strong editorial oversight promoting a clear ideological agenda.

The timing of the technical difficulty in Smith's reporting, and his strong reversal of his critique, suggest that Fox's editorial control extends to shaping reporting in real time. Seemingly, during a live broadcast, Fox News took a reporter off air due to his reporting and only returned him to air to repudiate his critique and adopt the company line that authorities could not have predicted or prepared for Katrina. In this instance, the incoherence of television news coverage of Katrina was the product of the collision between critique and support of a Republican presidential administration. Elsewhere, as in the disjunction between Smith's callous use of the images of survivors and his expression of sympathy for them and an incipient critique of authorities, the incoherence of television news coverage of Katrina indicated the clash between the television news apparatus, which relentlessly shapes reality into news story, and the lived perspective of an individual news professional who was moved to human response by reporting from New Orleans after Katrina.

CHAPTER SIX

Over My Drowned Body

THURSDAY, SEPTEMBER 1

*T*ELEVISION NEWS HAS ALWAYS HANDLED THE REPRESEN-
tation of dead bodies with great care. Historically, American
television news only shows dead bodies of those who matter less than the
bodies to whom the news is addressed. During the Vietnam War, American
television news carefully kept dead and dying American bodies out of the
frame. Some have argued that this practice was out of respect for the families of the wounded and dead, and one can certainly appreciate that no one
would want to see a loved one mortally wounded on television. However,
American television news would represent dead and dying Vietnamese
bodies with regularity. As I have argued elsewhere, given the absence of
representations of American bodies, American television news contributed to the idea of American military and bodily supremacy (Cook, 2001).
The representation of dead and dying Vietnamese offered cultural support
for the war effort, eroding the viewers' sense of the common humanity
of the Vietnamese, who were framed as smaller, weaker, devious, not us.
Long after Walter Cronkite said that the war in Vietnam was unwinnable,
CBS continued to broadcast images to offer visual argument that American
bodies were superior to Vietnamese bodies.

In *Believing Is Seeing* (2011), Errol Morris argues that the image of Sabrina Harman smiling with her thumb up, standing over the dead body of
Manadel al-Jamadi, is uniquely challenging to read because of the collision
of signifiers: dead Arabic male civilian and smiling white American female
soldier. Morris contends that Harman had nothing to do with al-Jamadi's
murder, which likely occurred during a CIA interrogation. However, her
pose over his body enacts a familiar practice in warfare: the inscription of
meaning on the bodies of the dead by the living. While the practice of ma-

nipulating dead bodies has been going on for centuries, audiovisual media in the twentieth and twenty-first centuries make this practice more pervasive and more widely disseminated. Regardless of Harman's intentions (whether to document a crime, to implicate her command in the crime, or, more generally, to document her time serving in Abu Ghraib prison in Iraq), her participation in one photo and her taking of a mirror image photo of fellow soldier Charles Graner both worked to use al-Jamadi's body for her own meanings. This process requires a devaluation of the humanity of the dead body in order to make it available for signification. In response to a question from Morris, Harman's answer implicates language in this transformation of person into body/sign: "If a soldier sees somebody dead, normally they'll take photos of it. I don't know why, maybe it's a curiosity thing, or if they see something odd, they take a photo of it" (99).

As Harman's answer suggests, in warfare and in other crisis situations, a body must be converted from a person into a thing (from a "him" to an "it") before it can be killed (either by action or by neglect). Relatedly, a human body must be made into an object in order to be shown and to be used as a sign for other meanings.

THE REALITY OF THE DISASTER ZONE

While television news broadcasts talked about death and dead bodies beginning on the evening of Monday, August 29, 2005, the networks did not show dead bodies until Thursday, September 1, 2005. On Monday on CNN, Jeanne Meserve had reported seeing dead bodies and hearing the cries of residents trapped in attics. But Mark Biello's footage from the Ninth Ward, when edited and broadcast with a re-edit of Meserve's report on Tuesday night, focused on living bodies pulled from homes by rescuers. However, by Thursday, with search and rescue still not mounted on a sufficient scale, Fox and NBC each aired reports showing dead bodies. As with American network coverage of the Vietnam War and as with the photograph of Harman from Abu Ghraib, the dead bodies of New Orleanians had to be converted for their use by television news.

As argued previously, Shepard Smith's reporting on Wednesday, August 31, had effectively rendered surviving New Orleans residents into the "Walking Dead": shambling, dis-individuated bodies slowly approaching the up ramp where he was positioned with his camera. On Thursday, Smith presented a taped report in which he introduced an actual dead body. He indicated the unusual nature of this report by prefacing the taped segment with a warning.

SMITH: The video you are about to see is disturbing.

Unlike the images of human suffering featured by Fox for days, these images, Smith signaled to his viewers, had heretofore been hidden from them.

SMITH: It is part of reality in the disaster zone.

While dead bodies had not been admitted previously to Fox's representation of "reality in the disaster zone," the network expanded its version of reality to include dead bodies as conditions worsened on the ground and as viewers became familiar with the images of suffering broadcast nightly. Fox was ready to up the ante representationally, both to suggest the cost of the flood in new ways and to compete with the representations of other networks.

Most of the report features a single shot with a significant amount of movement, both by the camera and by the reporter. Smith begins by addressing the camera from a highway overpass. He is wearing a blue T-shirt and a dark Fox baseball cap, looking more haggard than during his first few days of reporting from New Orleans. Smith gestures with his right hand at I-10 East behind him, where residents can be seen walking through the background of his frame.

SMITH: These are refugees making their way to the Superdome.

The camera swings right to left, moving away from Smith and into a low-angle shot, before zooming up on an African American man pushing a shopping cart, right to left through the frame. The man is walking on an elevated roadway above the camera's position. Without a cut, the camera pans back to Smith, moving left to right, and then past him, approaching the concrete railing to show a street of houses flooded to the roofs. The camera pans slowly past six houses, moving past 180 degrees and violating usual camera continuity. When the pan ends, Smith is again in front of the camera, having moved to reposition himself, opposite the position in which he began the report. He continues to talk about people who are suffering: "So many did not make it . . ." Then he turns toward his right shoulder, slightly away from the camera, to reveal the body of an African American male, face down on the ramp. Smith gestures with his left arm, then lets his arm drop to his right leg.

SMITH: This man is one of those.

Smith conceals the dead body behind him (FOX 9.1.05).

Smith reveals the dead body (FOX 9.1.05).

This report—consisting of a single, unedited shot—represents the most elaborate camerawork in any of Fox's reporting during the first week following Katrina. The shot seems to be extended, without editing, to certify the "reality" of the dead body it reveals, as if the lack of editing means a lack of artifice. The single shot shows the mortal consequences of the storm, "part of reality in the disaster zone."

However, in a different way, the shot is extremely artificial. The elaborate camera movements, and Smith's disappearance and reemergence, had to be choreographed in order to work. Both the camera and Smith had to end the move by hitting their marks in order for the dead body to be first concealed and then revealed. This shot would have had to be practiced, if not loosely storyboarded. Thus, the guarantor of the shot's authenticity—the lack of editing—is produced by elaborate artifice. Fox manufactured the "reality in the disaster zone."

The dual dance of Smith and camera around the dead body of a New Orleans resident also enacts a form of use (and abuse) of the dead. Like Sabrina Harman and Chuck Graner in Abu Ghraib, Smith and Fox are using a human body as a prop. Smith's big reveal is intended to shock and impress audiences—"The video you are about to see is disturbing"—but it does not tell viewers anything about the dead man. Who is he? How did he die? Why is he on the overpass? Where is his family? What will happen to him? All of the relevant questions are left unasked. His body is used by Fox News as a stand-in for the consequences of the flooding of New Orleans. Smith discursively uses the man as a symbol of his city.

SMITH: Left him dead in a city which died here with him.

Like his "Walking Dead" report, Smith's dance with the dead does not take seriously the individual humanity of flood survivors. His reporting converts reality into "story," reifying people into things signifying Fox's meanings.

Further undercutting the status of the report as a representation of

Smith uses the body to symbolize New Orleans as a "dead city" (FOX 9.1.05).

reality, Fox returned to Smith afterward, live from New Orleans. In contrast to his appearance in the report, Smith is now cleaned up, wearing a purple, short-sleeved, collared shirt over a black T-shirt and a black hat. He also offers a different discourse, a positive assessment of the ability of a "caring nation" to help rebuild New Orleans. The high contrast of this reporting underscores the lack of investment in the dead man. Fox used his body to make a point about the mortal cost of the flood, only to immediately undercut that point by arguing that "the nation's generosity" could make everything right. In this way, Fox advances a version of the Bush administration's neoliberal argument that the social contract has been replaced by sympathy and charity. Instead of figuring the federal government as responsible for saving its citizens from harm and rebuilding its cities from disaster, Fox adopts the administration's own argument that a smaller government cannot uphold the social contract. In this way, the impact of Katrina is the inevitable result of efforts to shrink government. The dead man demands justice, not charity. By signifying on and using his body to create its own meanings, Fox participates in the same dead body representational politics used during the coverage of wars and by the soldier photographers in Abu Ghraib.

THIS IS NOT IRAQ. THIS IS NOT SOMALIA. THIS IS HOME.

Like Fox, NBC offered a warning to viewers during its broadcast of Thursday, September 1, 2005.

> BRIAN WILLIAMS: We should warn you, already some of the scenes we saw, they are some of the most gruesome pictures so far in this crisis.

Williams's discourse performs a slide from profilmic reality to television representation, recalling Geoffrey Hartman's distinction between those who suffer and those who watch suffering (1994). Williams's warning to his viewers concerns images, not reality. By converting gruesome realities into "gruesome pictures," television news instantiates distance between its viewers and events, protecting not only the sensibilities of viewers, but also their implication. As Hartman maintains, such visual and verbal rhetorics generate the possibilities for sympathy, but not empathy. As Jill Bennett argues, where empathy demands connection and implication (and, potentially, action), sympathy places gentler demands on viewers (2005). They can look away from "gruesome pictures" or may even look at them and then quickly forget them. Representations that do not challenge and implicate viewers instead begin the conversion and erasure of the specifics of the lived experiences of Katrina and the flooding of New Orleans. "Gruesome pictures" replace gruesome realities.

As part of NBC *Nightly News* on September 1, Martin Savidge filed a report from the New Orleans Convention Center on the conditions on the ground for residents remaining in the flooded city. Savidge's report shares some features with Smith's dance with the dead report. Echoing Smith, Savidge extends the portentous discursive necropolitics that convert New Orleans into a "city of the dead" and New Orleans residents into the Walking Dead.

> SAVIDGE: But there is no life here. . . . Many honestly believe this is
> where they'll die.

And again:

> SAVIDGE: There are people here who barely seem alive.

However, unlike Smith's choreographed reveal of the body of a dead New Orleanian, Savidge's report focused more on the vulnerability of the living than on the sensational representation of a dead body on television news. Where Smith's report used a human body as a sign shorn of its history, Savidge's report located people in space, time, and circumstance.

Savidge's report begins with a medium-wide tracking shot from a car. The shot shows residents sitting on a curb outside the Riverwalk Mall complex, just above the Convention Center and next to the Hilton Hotel. As the camera moves from left to right, the frame shows a relatively sparse group of people sitting and waiting. From the remove of a car, at this speed and distance, the shot tells the viewer very little of the experience of these people. The report then cuts to another tracking shot, matching the movement in the first shot, this time closer and with tighter framing. The second shot shows people standing four or five deep outside the Convention Center. Unlike the people in the first shot, these people are aware of the camera, and they use it to address a national audience, chanting, "Help! Help!" A young African American man in a red shirt, wearing a backpack, pumps his arms, exhorting the crowd. These residents demonstrate agency, engaging with the apparatus to express their vulnerability and need.

This expression of subject point of view is immediately overwritten by Savidge's voice-over about "no life here." The contrast is striking. Both Fox and NBC seem invested in converting a damaged city with residents in mortal peril into a mausoleum. If New Orleans is already a dead city, officials (and television news networks) are no longer obliged to provide rescue and relief. However, unlike Smith's report on Fox, Savidge's report on NBC stages a conflict between discourse and rhetoric. While his voice-over seeks to convert the living into the already dead, the report's visual rhetoric emphasizes the continued struggle of the living. This tension reveals both the ideological work of television news and the contradictions that result in possibilities for other understandings.

From the second tracking shot, the report cuts to an image of the inside of the Convention Center. Breaking with the left-to-right movement of the first two shots, the third shot is handheld, moving in to explore the interior space. The camera tracks up to a white woman, with long, limp hair, sitting up on a blanket.

> MAN: This is my mother. She needs heart medication and she needs to get to the hospital immediately.

The camera moves into a close-up of the mother, who averts her eyes downward. The speaker is not shown, and neither the mother nor the son is identified.

The next shot shows an older African American woman in a light blue T-shirt, with a bandana over gray hair. The camera tilts up to show a younger African American woman in a dark shirt, also wearing a bandana.

> DAUGHTER: My mother suffers from congestive heart failure. I need to get her out of here.

The report then cuts to two African American men pushing a very old white woman on a gurney.

> SAVIDGE: This woman is over 100 years old, sitting amid the heat and chaos.

Again, none of the figures are identified, but as Savidge overwrites their experience, the camera, in close-up, shows a hand reach into the frame to smooth the hair on the one-hundred-year-old woman's brow. While national collective memory of Katrina, drawing heavily from television news coverage in the immediate aftermath of the storm and flood, figures the impact of the hurricane as divided along racial lines, this image suggests much more complicated relations on the ground. The visual rhetoric of Savidge's report strongly suggests that the impact of Katrina was based more on class than race.

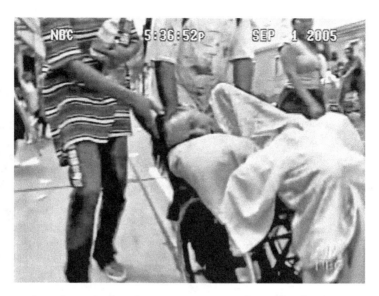

Evidence of mutual aid as African American men care for an older white woman (NBC 9.1.05).

After a cut to another older African American woman, with a younger woman to her right, the report cuts to a young white mother holding a limp baby in her arms. The mother is deeply worried, and she lifts her baby toward the camera, working to convey her situation via the television apparatus.

> MOM: Look how hot he is. He's not waking up very easy.

Briefly, the young mother directs the shot, creating a close-up by moving her baby closer to the camera lens. By forcing the camera to see her listless baby, the young mother addresses NBC's national audience. She destabilizes the distance inscribed by television's "story" and "images," reminding viewers of the pro-televisual, an actual mother desperately concerned about the survival of her child. For a brief instant, the young mother takes over the report's address, pushing viewers toward empathy rather than sympathy, replacing "gruesome images" with more troubling facts.

This brief moment of communication by the mother through the television apparatus is swiftly recuperated. Savidge's voice-over immediately reframes her specific experience as generally representative of suffering.

> SAVIDGE: There are people here who barely seem alive. Even children.

Evidence of mutual aid as a fellow survivor reaches into the frame to put a hat back on the head of a white woman with a sick baby (NBC 9.1.05).

Generalized suffering allows for the greater distance that is productive of sympathy, rather than the awareness of distance required for empathy. Again, however, verbal discourse and visual rhetoric are at odds. Even as Savidge generalizes, the frame shows an African American man's hand reach up to place a cap on the mother's head. Presumably, the cap fell off as she moved forward to address the camera. As with the shot of the hand smoothing the one-hundred-year-old's hair, this gesture strongly conveys solidarity and mutual aid.

Only at this point does the report show a dead human body. Unlike Smith's carefully planned reveal, Savidge's report simply cuts to a long shot, showing a body on the ground, covered by a white sheet, and another body in a wheelchair.

> SAVIDGE: Some have already died waiting . . . the elderly . . . the sick.

The camera zooms to frame the two bodies against a red wall, providing an aesthetic composition that begins to offer another form of relief, distancing the viewer. However, the camera continues to move, then cuts to another angle, showing the body in the wheelchair in a medium-close shot. Moving and zooming simultaneously, the camera frames in close-up a piece of paper placed in the dead woman's hand. Savidge explains that this is a "note for the next of kin." The close-up of the note, placed in the nonliving hand, suddenly reminds the viewer that this corpse was a person, a human being with a history, a context, a family (Spike Lee and Sam Pollard's *When the Levees Broke* reveals the body to be Ethel Freeman and the note to have been written by her son, Herbert Freeman Jr.). The NBC report is most revealing in its contradictions, as it struggles between documentary specificity and the editorial voice of television news, seeking to provide viewers with access, but not always with implication.

Both Fox and NBC sought to represent the human casualties of the flooding of New Orleans. But the differences in approach by each network yielded opposite meanings. Smith's choreographed reveal performed a visual equivalent of his verbal discourse. Smith argued that Katrina and the flooding had "killed" New Orleans, and his presentation of a dead body by the side of the expressway "proved" his argument. Because Smith and Fox provided no details about the dead man, he was easier to signify upon, a blank slate. Untroubled by history or context, Smith and Fox could contribute their own meanings to the corpse.

However, the baldness of the move also serves to undermine its authenticity. Indeed, the practiced nature of the camera movement to reveal the body raises the suspicion that the body itself may have been manipulated (a practice dating back to Alexander Gardner's 1863 Civil War photograph, *Sharpshooter in the Devil's Den*). In the case of Fox's report, the structure of the videography and Smith's performance to the camera suggest significant staging. In combination with the lack of information about the dead man, this staging raises questions for the viewer about the credibility of the information conveyed. Fox's ideological work to convert New Orleans into a dead city is revealed in its own production process. The stakes are significant: just like the man by the expressway, if New Orleans is already dead, it no longer requires immediate attention. If New Orleans is already dead, it need not be revived.

Like Fox, NBC also flirted with the dead city story line. As noted, Martin Savidge's voice-over employed language similar to Smith's. Importantly, the images and sounds accompanying Savidge's language make different arguments. Unlike the Fox report, where death has already come to the man and the city, NBC shows the living threatened by death. This distinction is extremely important. Fox provides viewers with no way of knowing how the man perished. In doing so, the network hides the real reasons for many of the casualties after Katrina. Fox's report extends the argument that Katrina was a large and deadly hurricane, without precedent, and that the storm could not have been predicted or prepared for. In Fox's formulation, Katrina was a killer storm.

In contrast, NBC's report showed the causes of death after the storm had passed. In Savidge's report, the very old, the very young, and the sick are dying from dehydration and lack of medical attention. While the storm created the context, Savidge's report reveals individuals imperiled by the neglect of their society, by the failure of response.

As in Smith's earlier report, Savidge confronts a New Orleans police officer on camera. The camera zooms in on a dark SUV, driving through the press of bodies outside the Convention Center. Honking to force people out of his path, the driver keeps the truck moving. Framed over his shoulder, Savidge leans toward the driver, a uniformed policeman. Dropping journalistic distance, Savidge instead advocates for the survivors.

> SAVIDGE: Excuse me, can you do anything to help these people?
> OFFICER: We have people coming to help.
> SAVIDGE: Who is coming?

Instead of responding, the officer accelerates and drives out of the frame. Like Smith, Savidge seems moved to empathy with the subjects of his news broadcast, and he attempts to use the apparatus to influence authority to provide relief. Whereas Smith was taken off the air immediately after his critique of authority, due to "technical difficulties," only to return minutes later to defang his critique, Savidge does not recant his criticism. Significantly, his report does not end with this critique. Instead, the report shows individuals responding to each other's need with mutual aid.

In contrast to this dominant representational work, some reports (mostly on CNN and NBC) demonstrated residents serving as their own first responders. As noted, Savidge's report featured moments of kindness and support, where survivors helped each other: an African American man smoothing the hair of a white woman, another African American man replacing the cap dropped by a white mother. Savidge's report ends with a segment on a nurse, who had sought shelter at the Convention Center, helping the most vulnerable. The camera shows a middle-aged white woman, wearing a gray T-shirt, her sleeves pushed up, her body drenched with sweat. Unlike the other subjects in the report, she is identified by name: Cindy Davis. While the previous images showed African Americans helping whites, this mini-story is about a white woman treating mostly African American survivors.

Davis is shown working with an African American man and his daughter, who is experiencing diabetic shock. Blending news with entertainment convention, Savidge builds suspense by introducing the "frantic family" and showing Davis's efforts to improvise a blood test. Davis calls

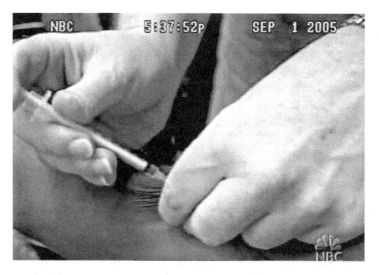

Insulin shot "appears" at the Convention Center as a citizen nurse tends to fellow survivors (NBC 9.1.05).

out for insulin, and, Savidge relates, "Amazingly, insulin appears." By failing to reveal the source of the insulin, the report suggests a miraculous Hollywood ending (and perhaps that the insulin was provided by NBC). Contra to NBC's suggestion of a miracle, the care provided by Davis and others to the girl underscores Rebecca Solnit's point about spontaneous networks forming in response to crises (2010). In the face of official neglect, the NBC reports shows survivors responding to each other.

Yet, the report does not end with this representation of mutual aid. Instead, in the final segment, Savidge underscores the suffering and anger of New Orleans residents. He is framed in a medium shot in front of a crowd of survivors. His proximity to the crowd lends authority to his reporting, especially given the evident tension.

SAVIDGE: They say it won't be long before this place explodes.

Whereas Fox worked to figure New Orleans as dead and gone, NBC concluded Savidge's report by acknowledging that citizens were alive and angry. While careful to frame his statement as a paraphrase, Savidge alludes to revolution as a response to the failure of the social contract. NBC's report suggests why revolution might be a necessary response to a necropolitics that has written off tens of thousands of New Orleanians. In a medium shot, Savidge notes that it has begun to rain and that the masses fear additional flooding. Following his direction, the camera whips and zooms to reveal an African American man in a white T-shirt striking a hotel window with a chair. The camera follows Savidge as he walks down the street, and his reporting become breathless, sacrificing his conventional masterful delivery. Surprisingly, instead of condemning the crowd for property damage, Savidge expresses sympathy and understanding: "What they are trying to do is to get to higher ground." Walking and talking, proximate if not implicated, Savidge makes clear the stakes involved.

> SAVIDGE: There is tremendous fear that with the rain will come
> more flooding, and with more flooding that they will be killed.

Behind Savidge, the man in the white T-shirt continues to try to break the window, but his blows have no discernible effect.

In contrast to Smith's "dead city" rhetoric, Savidge's report focuses on the living desperately struggling to avoid death. His report reveals that the conversion of New Orleans into a "dead city" following Katrina and the flood requires careful construction, framing out the living in order to focus on the dead. In the process, Smith's reporting conceals the causes of death and deflects questions of responsibility. Savidge's report shows particular groups at risk: the elderly, the young, the sick. As his report reveals, these citizens are being killed by neglect: lack of shelter, water, food, and medicine. New Orleans after Katrina is not a mausoleum. It is an abattoir.

The segment then cuts to a taped voice-over, calmed and assured now, reasserting mastery and control. Savidge clearly taped this part of the report after walking the street in front of the Convention Center. Given this relative distance from the events represented, his concluding remarks are especially interesting. Rather than recuperate the critique suggested by the report's visual rhetoric, Savidge expresses a (generalized) critique via language. Whereas Smith, and occasionally Williams, followed reporting on human suffering in New Orleans with a version of the false inevitability argument (unprecedented storm; no one could have anticipated; nothing could have been done), Savidge instead employs analogy to reinforce the argument of his images and sounds.

This final part of the segment begins with another dead body. As this body, covered by a sheet, is dragged away, the camera moves to keep the body in frame. This is the third dead body represented in the report, and the depiction of multiple bodies suggests the extensiveness of suffering and death (whereas Smith's focus on a single body allows for the use of that body as synecdoche for an already dead city). Importantly, underscoring the logic of Savidge's report, the end of the segment cuts from the dead to the living. A quick cut shows a middle-aged African American woman, wearing a black tank top and glasses, with her hands on her head, saying, "Oh, Jesus." Next, the report cuts to a young African American girl in a white tank top, bent over at the waist, being fanned from behind. The moment is desperate but also tender, and it offers further evidence of the pervasiveness of mutual aid in New Orleans. In contrast to much of the reporting on television news, New Orleanians, even while neglected by authorities, were not alone. Time and again, they helped each other. Intent on telling pre-produced stories, television news missed much of this mutual aid. As a consequence, it is preserved mostly in the background or in the corners of frames.

In voice-over, Savidge first takes a wrong step toward mystification: "These images are otherworldly." But, he quickly clarifies his meaning. These images are not from some fantastic dystopia. Rather, they are images with echoes of suffering usually seen outside the United States. A cut shows an African American man shouting down at another man, who is twisting in agony on the ground: "Breathe, man! Live!"

SAVIDGE: But this is not Iraq.

A dissolve reveals an African American woman carrying a little girl on her shoulders through the crowd in front of the Convention Center.

SAVIDGE: This is not Somalia.

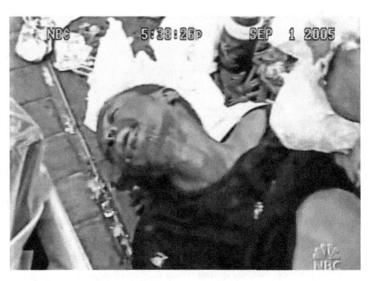

Man at the Convention Center collapses on the curb (NBC 9.1.05).

A cut shows two African American women walking. One of the women is pregnant. Another cut shows another African American woman, in a pink shirt, holding two babies, each wearing only a diaper. The woman speaks directly to the camera: "Help! Help! Help!"

SAVIDGE: This is home.

By linking New Orleans to Iraq and Somalia, Savidge seeks to convey to his viewers the desperate conditions faced by those on the ground in New Orleans after Katrina. He also seems to want to criticize the authorities who allowed this to happen at "home" by insufficient planning and response. But Savidge's linkage raises other troubling possibilities. If viewers of American television news can watch suffering in Iraq (caused by an American invasion) and Somalia (caused by a civil war) without implication, as per Jill Godmillow (1997) and Hartman (1994), they may also be able to watch suffering by New Orleanians without strong connection. Indeed, television news worked hard to construct survivors of Katrina and the flood as aberrant, not like "us." By describing citizens as "refugees," by blaming those who remained in New Orleans for their suffering, and by figuring survivors as violent criminals, television news reporting on Katrina and the flooding of New Orleans (on all three networks) produced the distance necessary to view suffering without strong implication. Whereas Savidge seems to critique the conditions on the ground in New Orleans as resembling a war zone in Africa or the Middle East, his logic also runs the other way: television news may take "home" and make it somewhere else ("otherworldly"), where other people suffer and "we" watch.

IN HIDING FROM PEOPLE THEY CAN'T EVEN SEE

On Thursday, September 1, 2005, NBC immediately followed Martin Savidge's report on conditions at the Convention Center with a report by Carl Quintanilla on a small group in very different circumstances. Bearing the title "Trapped," Quintanilla's segment focuses on ten white Americans, two Scottish tourists, and three dogs occupying a time-share condominium near the French Quarter. Quintanilla reports that the group had been "squatting" at a local hotel, but that the hotel prioritized evacuating its actual guests and left the group behind. A sympathetic hotel employee provided a key to the condominium, where the group had access to food and water, but "only half a bag of dog food."

The differences between the two reports are striking and revealing.

Whereas Savidge's report featured very large numbers of African Americans and a few white New Orleanians suffering from heat, neglect, and lack of food, water, and medicine, Quintanilla's report features only a dozen people, mostly tourists, who have food, water, and shelter. Yet, Quintanilla's report works to construct the tourists as neglected and imperiled. The contrast between their actual circumstances and Quintanilla's rhetoric, like the contrasts between the two reports, reveals both differential experiences of the impact of the flooding of New Orleans and differential coverage of those experiences. NBC *Nightly News* treats the tourists with respect and concern, individuating several by name, and interviews three people, allowing them to convey their perspectives to the camera. NBC also uses this report to manufacture a sense of threat and fear, perhaps in an effort to identify a high-concept approach appealing to viewers.

The twelve people featured in Quintanilla's report share qualities with NBC's national television audience. All but one are tourists, not residents of New Orleans. As tourists, they have a different relation to Katrina and the flooding of New Orleans. Once attracted to New Orleans, they want out after the storm and flood. They enjoy a mobility unavailable to the residents crowding the Superdome and Convention Center. They can leave New Orleans and go home. Similarly, NBC's audience is attracted to coverage of Katrina by fascination with New Orleans and the impact of the storm and flood. However, like the tourists in this report, NBC's viewers are not strongly tied to the implications of events on the ground. Home is elsewhere, and they can always change the channel. In "Trapped," NBC builds connections between subjects and audience, playing up the risks faced by the tourists in order to create suspense and identification. Whereas much of the reporting by NBC, CNN, and Fox on Wednesday and Thursday constructs New Orleans residents as not like viewers ("refugees," responsible for their own plight, violent and criminal), Quintanilla's report treats the tourists very differently.

The difference in mobility and status of the tourists is underscored by the visual rhetoric of the report. Savidge's segment ends with the frame crowded with African American bodies at street level, shouting "Help! Help! Help!" In contrast, Quintanilla's begins with a close-up of a white male, in his early thirties, before pulling back to show him looking down at the street. It is as if the white tourist was looking down at the masses in the streets below. But, from the distance of an upper-floor time-share, the tourists cannot hear, understand, or relate to the fellow survivors below. They are literally above it all and are shown repeatedly looking down at the streets below, framed within the frame by windows or the balcony railing, distanced from the cries for help.

"They are in hiding from people they can't even see" (NBC 9.1.05).

The spatial disconnection from residents below, amplified by the television news apparatus, creates room for the projection of fear. Rather than represent the group as safe, secure, and resourced, Quintanilla works to construct them as imperiled and under siege.

> QUINTANILLA: They wait for nightfall and hope no one comes knocking.

In combination with the high-angle long shots of the tourists looking down (but not seeing), Quintanilla's discourse disconnects them from their fellow survivors. Employing the language of the thriller, Quintanilla constructs a sense of threat, figuring the people in the streets, the African Americans and whites in Savidge's report, as menacing. In introducing the report, Quintanilla described the condominium as a "rooftop refuge from mayhem," without specifying the cause or nature of the "mayhem." The report excuses the conduct of the tourists, resisting judging them for "squatting."

> QUINTANILLA: This is not their house, but they believe it is safer than the violence in the streets.

Quintanilla cites "mayhem" and "violence" without providing any specific reference to actual events. Under Quintanilla's assertion about "violence in the streets," the screen shows four police cars and four unmarked cars driving through the street below the condominium. The image is opaque. Viewers do not know who is in the cars or where they might be going. Instead, Quintanilla's language overwrites the neutral image, captioning it to suggest an official response to an unspecified violent crime. The report shows one of the Scottish tourists, identified as Teresa Cherry, looking down.

CHERRY: I'm worried I am going to die here.

The disconnection between Cherry's fears and her circumstances reveals how elite panic involves projection and results in the further neglect of the truly vulnerable. As Savidge's report indicated, those at greatest risk in the aftermath of Katrina were the very old, the very young, and the sick. Cherry is young and in good health. She is not threatened by floodwaters, exposure, or want. For the moment, she is secure. She is also frightened.

QUINTANILLA: They are in hiding from people they can't even see.

In this remarkable statement, Quintanilla reveals the projective nature of Cherry's fear and the work of television news to stoke and promote fear as a reason for viewers to continue to watch coverage. Like a thriller, Quintanilla's report suggests that what is unseen, outside the frame, is a threat to the protagonists inside the frame. Even as he recognizes the limitations of the perspective of the tourists ("they can't even see"), Quintanilla conveys their fear without critique, accepting their affective expression of fear as real, despite the false assumptions driving the feeling.

Like Cherry's group, who fear those they cannot see and do not know, television news began on Wednesday to project criminality onto the New Orleans residents who survived Katrina and were struggling to survive the flood. At first, the focus was on looting and the threat to property. While excusing the tourists for taking spaces that were not theirs (and presumably food, water, clothing, and other resources), NBC News and the other networks criticized residents for taking supplies and goods. Next, television news reported rumors of violence and mayhem as fact, suggesting that New Orleans had descended into lawlessness and chaos. On Monday and Tuesday, CNN's Jeanne Meserve and Mark Biello had reported on the desperate conditions in the Ninth Ward and in New Orleans East. By Wednesday, television news coverage had begun to shift from figuring residents as survivors in need of rescue to blaming residents for staying and to understanding residents as looters and violent criminals.

While retrospective accounts of television news coverage of Katrina emphasize television news's opposition to government response to the disaster, the networks, rather than speak truth to power, often adopted official perspectives. This was especially true during the fourth and fifth days after landfall, when a focus on human suffering began to shift to a focus on rumors of violence and depravity by survivors. As noted, television news closely associated its perspective with that of NOPD officers on the ground. This embedding of point of view led the networks to demonstrate extreme credulity with significant consequences.

On Thursday, September 1, 2005, CNN anchor Aaron Brown presented footage from the Convention Center strongly overwritten by his voice-over and his perspective. The segment begins with a shot of crowds at street level outside the Convention Center. Like the shot that begins Martin Savidge's report on NBC, the shot that opens Brown's report was also taken from a car window, and the frame of the window and the movement of the car, in contrast to the stasis of the crowd, suggest visual disconnection. The report is presented visually from a perspective separate from those suffering at the Convention Center. Brown's report does not join the citizens at the curb, sharing their perspectives, but instead looks at them from a remove. The report cuts to an image of a young African American mother in a blue top holding an infant, wearing only a diaper. This image suggests vulnerability and the risk posed to the very young by exposure and lack of food and water. Brown's voice-over does not pick up on these possible meanings; instead, it focuses on police perspectives.

> BROWN: Eighty-eight police officers were sent to the Convention Center . . .

The report cuts from the young mother and child to show a long shot of four NOPD cars parked on the neutral ground on Tchoupitoulas Street. Five or six officers are visible, looking out of the frame in the direction of the Convention Center. The police cars are located near the Walmart where some NOPD officers participated in looting (Troncale interview).

> BROWN: . . . a mob beat them back, according to police.

With this, the report cuts to a medium-long shot with four figures prominent in the frame. Two older African American women, stooped and looking down, are framed on the left by a young African American woman in a dark bandana and on the right by a young African American man in a white ball cap. Each of the figures is slight, even skinny, and they convey no sense of threat.

BROWN: And inside, anarchy and death.

The report cuts to an extreme low-angle shot of the curb. The lower body of a person is visible, his legs stretched out from the curb into the street. Another man, only his legs visible, leans over the first, trying to help. As is the case with much television news reporting on Katrina, the image track contradicts the voice track. Brown speaks portentously about mobs resisting police and about anarchy and death, but the images make a different argument, focusing on peaceful citizens in acute need. The report provides no evidence of anarchy or violence; rather, it shows an act of mutual aid, as one survivor goes to the aid of another. Brown's report provides visual evidence to corroborate Solnit's argument about mutual aid, but it does not support the assertion by NOPD of violent resistance by citizens. Indeed, the shot of the four police cars and a small number of officers suggests that the NOPD story may have been an exaggeration or a distortion, produced to deflect responsibility for failing to respond with aid to citizens in need. New Orleans police feared their own citizens and pulled back to fortified defensive positions. The story of eighty-eight police officers being beaten back by a dangerous mob may have been created to justify such retrenchment.

UNIDENTIFIED VOICE-OVER: You got bodies in there.

The report included the voice of an actual citizen, but the speaker is not identified visually or by name. It also illustrates another challenge of Katrina coverage. CNN and the other television news networks struggled to make sense of the events in New Orleans. Their sources consisted of officials and sound bites taken from survivors. NOPD exaggerated and distorted events on the ground, sharing rumors with television news as if they were facts—if the rumors and distortions matched their own perspectives on events. Survivors also reported rumors and distortions to television journalists. *Times-Picayune* reporters Brian Thevenot and Gordon Russell demonstrated that many of the rumors of rape and murder at the Superdome and the Convention Center began with citizens, only to be picked up and amplified by police and public officials, and then to be reported and re-reported by television news and other media (2005).

In this case, the images correspond to and support the citizen's claim about dead bodies. Under his voice, the report cuts to a shot of white sheets by a red door. While not clear or definitive, the suggestion is that a body lies under the sheets. The next image shows a medium shot of an unmoving body in a wheelchair, the same body (Ethel Freeman) that appeared in Savidge's report on NBC, suggesting that the networks were circling each other to collect the same images of suffering and death. This is followed by a low-angle shot, in the style of the curb shot, looking up at the wheelchair. As with television news coverage of combat, some care is taken in the representation of dead bodies. The choices of framing and mise-en-scène (the sheets) seem meant to convey some respect for the dead; nevertheless, these bodies are considered available for some representation. This decision always reflects the ways in which bodies are valued by society and by television news.

> BROWN: It is hard to fathom some of what we report. The lootings and the carjackings not so much, but how do you explain snipers firing on a medevac helicopter trying to get people to safety?

Brown assumes the validity of his reporting and wonders about the possible motivations of snipers. Alternately, one might wonder about the validity of the reporting, given the outlandishness of the claims and the lack of evidence, visual or otherwise. Brown's final remarks are accompanied by shots of mothers with babies and of older women. These images speak to the pressing, acute need of survivors for medical attention and assistance. These images do not offer any evidence of alleged violence or "resistance."

The final image of the report shows an orange-and-white helicopter in daytime. The image begins in close-up, before zooming and pulling out, away from the helicopter. The helicopter is intact, operational, and not under fire. This image cannot stand as evidence of the assertion that snipers fired at rescue operations. The images of the young and old, exposed and neglected at the Convention Center, do stand as evidence that police and other responders failed to fulfill the social contract and offer aid to citizens. In order to fathom the credulity with which television news approached rumors and assertions, by police and survivors alike, one must consider that television news suffered its own form of elite panic, projecting fears onto the citizens who survived Katrina and influencing real-time response and how the meanings and impacts of Katrina would be understood over time.

CHAPTER SEVEN

Not Sure What Is the Truth or Rumor Anymore

FRIDAY, SEPTEMBER 2

F OX NEWS PROVIDES AN INTERESTING CASE STUDY OF the impact of the broadcasting of rumors of violence by New Orleans residents. On Friday, September 2, at the start of the second half of *The Fox Report*, field anchor Shepard Smith mentioned a large-scale hostage situation involving emergency responders. Beginning on Wednesday, all the television news networks had asserted that rescue workers and first responders had come under sniper fire by New Orleans residents. Most of these assertions lacked any contextualization or any evidence. Yet, despite the illogic of these reports (the question of why survivors might shoot at rescuers was never raised), the networks featured them at the end of the week. As Jed Horne notes in *Breach of Faith* (2006), one consequence of this reporting was a pulling back of emergency response. Rescue efforts would be halted at the first rumor of gunfire, and the security of responders was prioritized over the risks to those trapped in the flood. Unlike other networks, Fox conveyed some context to the rumors of sniper fire with Smith's assertion.

> SMITH: Late word that a rescue effort is underway today to rescue some 50–100 firefighters and families, apparently holed up in the Bell South Building in Chalmette.

In contrast to previous assertions of shootings and resistance, Smith related actual details of place and situation. He delivered this information in stand up, directly to camera, and did not introduce any images to support. Instead, Fox added a title in the lower third of the screen: "Firefighters & Families Under Fire in Gonzales, La." Thus, rather than provide visual "proof," Fox offered text as further assertion. Indeed, the specific text raised questions about the validity of the news story. Gonzales is a city in Ascension Parish, west of New Orleans, not in St. Bernard Parish, which is east of New Orleans, where Chalmette is located. The discrepancy between Smith's verbal report and the text on screen suggests a rush to broadcast a rumor before fact checking or actual reporting.

> SMITH: Snipers are picking off people as they try to leave Chalmette.

The rush to portray New Orleans as wracked by irrational violence served the same purpose as the earlier efforts to brand survivors as responsible for their own plight. These representations indemnified authorities, suggesting that the remaining population in New Orleans was always already lost even before the storm and the flood. In this context, the failure of governments to rescue citizens became recast as an impossible situation in which the government could not save people from their own stupidity and depravity. In these versions, the surviving citizens of New Orleans were themselves to blame for their predicament and had forfeited their rights as citizens because they did not rescue themselves and because they exhibited irrational violence. In this view, New Orleanians were their own worst enemies and also the enemies of the well-intentioned officials who sought to rescue them from their own depravity.

By assigning culpability to the poor, television news participated in and extended a necropolitics. By demonizing surviving citizens, television news went further, transforming residents into enemy combatants. The end result of this conversion of American citizens into enemies can be seen in incidents like the Danziger Bridge shooting, where police fired on unarmed civilians, killing two men.

> SMITH: We have word that SWAT teams are now being put together.

Fox's report garnered immediate attention on websites devoted to firefighters and responders. On www.firehouse.com, a website connected to *Firehouse* magazine, a community for fire service members and the industries who market products to firefighters, users took up and recirculated Fox's report. User RLFD14 responded to a thread on the website with a post dated 5:36 p.m. on September 2, indicating breaking news about firefighters held hostage in New Orleans: "Watching it right now." While the first response to RLFD14 expressed some caution (tfpd109: "RLFD14, let's hope your wrong . . . at this point I'd rather hear you were wrong on your post then for it to be correct"), other responses accepted RLFD14's assertion based on the Fox report.

> LEN1582: The reporter said a police officer may be dead and FF's and their families are being fired upon. The FF's are returning gunfire.

Fox's report and the response on firehouse.com document a rare example of real-time audience reception of television news. RLFD14 indicated Fox News as the source of his information, and Len1582 added details not shared by Smith on Fox. Either Len1582 was following a different news report, or he had begun the process of translation and circulation of interpretation that in social semiotics is understood as augmenting the text itself. Like Pierre Macherey's concept of incrustation, the rumor reported on Fox is taken up, extended, and altered by an online community (1978). In 2005, the year of the launch of YouTube and the year before the launch of Twitter, a version of social media took place on firehouse.com in response to the Fox newscast.

In addition to changing the details of the report, users of firehouse.com proposed solutions, many involving deadly force.

> LEN1582: I feel the military needs to be used, with the authority to use deadly force against these lowlifes and others that use deadly force against innocent civilians and emergency workers.

In Len1582's formulation, the alleged perpetrators of the alleged crime should be killed. Since the perpetrators were not visually identified, Len1582's argument could not distinguish between the "innocent civilians" and the "lowlifes."

Another user, stm4710 was even less measured.

> STM4710: Shoot the mother f u c king hostage takers. No warning shot. No mercy.

Another user, MemphisE34a, identified as Robert Kramer, a member of the Memphis Fire Department, again sounded a caution about the accuracy of news media.

> MEMPHISE34A: I just saw the report on Fox news as well. Hopefully, maybe they just have a bad report. The news has been known to screw stuff up. Hopefully that's the case here.

But, another user, cjennings, interpreted the lack of details as evidence that the events were so incendiary that they needed to be censored by the news media.

> CJENNINGS: I have been watching Fox for the last 15 minutes and have heard nothing. I almost wonder if there is some sort of media blackout in effect for certain things, I see post about police officers telling the situation that is more like a warzone that what is reported on TV. I hear on the net reports of many police officers dead, police snipers on the roofs and the police locking themselves up at night, bands of armed thugs in trucks etc etc. . . . But I see little on the news or main media outlets.

Cjennings makes an interesting distinction between user-generated reports online and television news. Lacking the standards and practices guiding television journalism, "the net" was a source of much unverified information about Katrina and the flooding of New Orleans. Instead of investing greater credence in television news, cjennings wondered whether television reporting was being censored. In fact, as the Fox case study reveals, television news was moving toward amateur Internet journalism in rushing to air stories based only on rumors. Interestingly, some of cjennings's posts seem to have partial basis in reality: in response to rumors of violence by New Orleans citizens, NOPD adopted a bunker mentality, fortifying police stations in advance of imagined attacks by their own citizens. Also, as A. C. Thompson later reported in ProPublica, armed groups of white vigilantes attacked black citizens in the Algiers Point neighborhood on the West Bank. Instead of digging deeper for facts and verification, cjennings concluded that anything being said on the web, but not being covered on television news, might have been censored. In this logic, events are more real for not being shown.

> CJENNINGS: Not sure what is truth or rumor any more.

In this argument, the lack of evidence suggests that reality is being censored. Rather than question the report, cjennings argues that the truth is what television news cannot report. It is interesting to note that the firehouse.com online community identified Fox News as the source of information about the St. Bernard firefighters. Fox News appears to have been the network of choice of this community, at least in this instance. The posts to firehouse.com may be read as revealing some of the expectations and perspectives of Fox News viewership: an eagerness for breaking information, even without verification; special interest in news about first responders, police, and military; readiness to apply the schema for understanding the U.S. invasion of Iraq and Afghanistan to a domestic disaster. This last point is worth amplifying: firehouse.com users who watched Fox News readily considered New Orleans residents as enemy combatants, without needing visual evidence or other corroboration. Deborah Jaramillo has identified Fox News as the most successful purveyor of high-concept coverage of the U.S. wars in the Middle East (2009). Firehouse.com users seemed to have been paying careful attention, ready to extend the formula of demonization as justification for deadly force to New Orleans.

A final post, by nmfire, at 8:00 p.m. on September 2, reveals the consequences of applying ways of reading television news coverage of Iraq and Afghanistan to New Orleans. Identified as writing from Maryland, nmfire has been a member of firehouse.com since 2002, and he is the most frequent poster among the responses analyzed here. His publicly available account information indicates that he has posted 5,741 times, more than ten times as many as RLFD14, who started the thread. Nmfire shared cjennings's concerns about the absence of follow-up coverage on Fox News. Like cjennings, he did not step back to question the veracity of the information. Instead, he provided some highly suggestive responses to the purported hostage situation.

> NMFIRE: I for one have had about enough of this crap. We need to cut the beurocratic bullshit that is making everything take so long and start doing what needs to be done when it needs to be done.

Like cjennings, nmfire is frustrated by the flow of information. He has already formed his interpretation of the situation, applying familiar frames through which to interpret events and through which to propose response.

> NMFIRE: We have thousands of MILITARY TROOPS with GUNS down the road. There should have been a detachment of blackhawks with god damn hellfire missiles and 50 caliber overhead at that location the moment word spread that it was happening.

For nmfire, the solution to the purported crisis was massive military force. As per Jaramillo, Fox News coverage of the U.S. wars in Iraq and Afghanistan focused on the representation of military technology applied in spectacular ways. Television broadcasts identified details of military technology and represented it in action, often from a distance, destroying "targets" and obscuring human casualties. In addition to the fetishization of military technology, television news's high-concept coverage of warfare provided simple narratives with clear identification of protagonists and antagonists.

> NMFIRE: We know where the good guys are. There are no inno-
> cent bystanders roaming the streets over there. It is good guys
> inside, bad guys hiding outside. Everything in the area is trashed
> already. We can formulate a strategic plan for 5 hours while they
> hide in the bushes and around corners sniping innocent res-
> cuers and families, or we can say enough is enough, lay down the
> smack down and take care of business. It is time to stop playing
> games and start blowing shit up as needed. There will be no mea-
> surable property loss and the only deaths will be domestic terror-
> ists holding these people hostage. No one is going to complain
> and no one is going to miss them.

Nmfire's reading of the situation recalls the affective response by the tourists in the time-share in the NBC report: he seems afraid of people he cannot see. Fox News did not share any images of firefighters and family members or of sniper fire. Rather, Smith related a rumor, and Fox began to post text on screen "reporting" the story. The Fox News tickers sent the following information crawling across the screen twice after Smith's initial mention: RESCUE EFFORTS UNDERWAY IN GONZALES, LA, IN EFFORT TO HELP 50–100 FIREFIGHTERS AND THEIR FAMILIES WHO ARE HOLED UP IN THE BELL SOUTH BUILDING IN CHALMETTE, LA; SNIPERS HAVE BEEN FIRING NEARBY, PREVENTING ANYONE FROM LEAVING THE BUILDING.

Without images or interviews, Fox could only assert that the events were happening. However, without any visual reference, nmfire proposed to identify and separate "good" from "bad" residents and to kill the "bad" residents. Like the white tourists, he seemed to be projecting his own fears on the event. He could see the antagonists clearly enough to target them for a "smack down." Without images, he could see the snipers hiding in the bushes, his reference to "bushes" suggesting racial undertones to his anxiety. Typical of high-concept presentation, nmfire's reading applies clear (if loaded) binaries: "good guys inside, bad guys hiding outside."

Nmfire's reading of the Fox story makes another important link. His reading of the New Orleans landscape suggests a war zone: "everything in the area is trashed already." His language suggests a reading of New Orleans as Baghdad, already "trashed" and thus a free-fire zone for aerial combat. But nmfire's reading goes further back, beyond Iraq, to September 11, 2001, and the terrorist attacks on U.S. soil. The September 11 attacks were mobilized by the Bush administration for justification of the invasion of Iraq and used as the excuse for a radical program of domestic surveillance and "homeland security." By labeling the supposed snipers as domestic terrorists, nmfire plays the ultimate post–September 11 card. Once labeled a "terrorist," a United States citizen can be stripped of his or her rights. In nmfire's formulation, he can divide the survivors of Katrina and the flooding of New Orleans into innocents and terrorists, sight unseen. And he can propose that the terrorists be killed: "no one is going to complain and no one is going to miss them."

Nmfire's response bears much in common with elite panic, even if his status as a member of a fire service community suggests middle-class, not elite, status. Without full information, on the basis of volatile rumors and projection, he read the situation in New Orleans and proposed a military response. According to Dave Eggers in *Zeitoun* (2009), the federal government began plans to construct a temporary prison for suspected domestic terrorists before Katrina made landfall, deploying fencing and barbed wire as early as Sunday, August 28. In this context, nmfire's response is not so much extreme as representative of perspectives shaping television news coverage and federal response. The consequence of reading Katrina as another September 11 or Iraq is to misunderstand the nature of the threat to citizens, to misdirect resources, and to authorize the use of violent military force to repress fellow U.S. citizens.

> NMFIRE: We should have done this with the hospital, the super-dome, the police station, and everywhere else having a rebel problem. If we see a known terrorist in Afghanistan, we can say the word and within 5 minutes, an F16 at 50,000 ft going 1000mph can hit the street and kill all the bad guys leaving the buildings untouched. WHY of god in heaven WHY can we not gain control of some hoodlams with guns they stole from WALMART!

Here, nmfire made the final slide from citizens to bad guys to terrorists to "rebels." Applying the frames developed watching Fox News high-concept coverage of the U.S. wars, he converted citizens into insurgents and called for air strikes on a major American city. Moreover, he interpolated the Pentagon argument, broadcast by television news, that "surgical strikes" with America's superior military technology could be undertaken without collateral damage. Television news footage of the flooding of New Orleans reveals the city itself to be collateral damage of congressional allocation and oversight of the Army Corps and the levee system. Reading nmfire's response, assessing his anxiety, it is easy to understand why both authorities and first responders on the ground in New Orleans became afraid of the very citizens they were trying to save. The application of aspects of high concept to the coverage of Katrina by Fox and NBC and CNN demonized citizens, fed panic, and affected emergency response. Reluctant responders may have missed opportunities to save dying citizens. The decision by those in command to halt rescue efforts at night, as documented in *Breach of Faith*, certainly resulted in continued exposure of citizens to life-threatening conditions.

Despite cjennings's concern about censorship, Fox News ultimately stopped reporting the story of snipers holding firefighters and family members hostage because the story was based on rumors that proved to be untrue. In a race to break a story before the other television news networks, and in an attempt to keep up with the speed of information circulated by nonprofessional online users, Fox reported a story without actually engaging in the work of reporting. As Michelle Mahl Buck indicates in her book, *The St. Bernard Fire Department in Hurricane Katrina*, no St. Bernard firefighters were held hostage by snipers in Chalmette or anywhere else (2008, 261). According to Buck, members of the New Orleans Fire Department went to the Bell South Building in downtown New Orleans to "fill the chillers," the stainless steel water storage tanks used for firefighting. The firefighters were stopped by Bell South security guards, resulting in a standoff between the two groups. This actual incident was the basis for the rumor about firefighters being held hostage.

As a cable news network with twenty-four hours to fill, Fox sought breaking stories of interest to its viewers. As noted, based on responses by the firehouse.com users to the Fox story about firefighters held hostage, Fox viewers were ready to believe that some New Orleans residents were capable of turning against first responders. Based on the high-concept presentation of the wars in Iraq and Afghanistan, these viewers were familiar with storylines featuring sympathetic service men and women threatened by menacing others. By reporting rumor, Fox News stoked fear of New Orleans residents and helped motivate calls for violent military response.

Fox News did not correct the story. Television news moves forward relentlessly, and networks very rarely return to re-report on previous stories. Unlike print newspapers, television news does not have a convention for airing corrections or retractions of previous stories. Instead, Fox News simply let the hostage story slip away, failing to acknowledge that they got the story wrong. Thus, Fox News allowed it to remain in the memory of viewers and to become part of the collective memory of New Orleans after

Katrina and the failure of the levees. With viewers like cjennings already suspecting that television news held back the "real story," Fox News gave reality to rumor by presenting the story of the firefighters under siege and, in the process, fueling interpretations of New Orleans as another Baghdad, a war zone requiring military response.

The impact of this approach to coverage and reception can be seen in footage of President Bush from the same September 2 Fox News broadcast. Shortly after presenting footage of Bush in Mobile, Alabama, uttering his now-infamous praise of FEMA director Michael Brown ("Brownie, you're doing a heck of a job"), Fox News showed Bush in Biloxi, grinning at the camera and saying, "The results are acceptable here in Mississippi." Instead of heading to New Orleans to address the greatest ongoing human misery, Bush was positioned by White House advisors Dan Bartlett and Karl Rove in two Republican states, praising state and local response to Katrina and its aftermath. Bush seemed to think differently about New Orleans: "We don't have enough security in New Orleans yet." Like nmfire and many of the posters on firehouse.com, President Bush seemed to draw a simple distinction between Mississippi/Alabama and New Orleans. The citizens of two conservative Republican states were acceptable. New Orleanians were a threat to be secured. Elite panic reached to the highest level.

FORT APACHE

On Friday, September 2, 2005, CNN's Christopher Lawrence reported to anchor Aaron Brown on the conditions inside the City of New Orleans. Aaron Brown introduced Lawrence by noting that he was reporting, "holed up on a rooftop of a police station." Lawrence's location is significant. By embedding with the NOPD, in a fortified police station, Lawrence's perspective is associated with the fearful attitudes of the police who perceived their own citizens as violent threats. From the roof of the police station, his range of vision was limited to the fearful and paranoid perspective of the police. Like the tourists squatting in the condo near the French Quarter, peering down from the roof, the police were afraid of people they could not even see.

Titled "A Night of Hell," Lawrence's report recounts a night spent with members of the NOPD on the roof of a police station. His report is remarkable in that it features the only broadcast evidence of alleged attacks against police by New Orleans citizens, although (as I argue) this evidence is neither clear nor unequivocal.

The sequence begins with a medium shot of a male police officer wear-

Chris Lawrence's report on "Fort Apache" (CNN 9.2.05).

ing a vest and carrying a shotgun, entering a damaged police station. With his movement, the camera tilts up to show a hole above the door and continues until it reveals a handmade sign, "Fort Apache."

The sign recalls the 1948 John Ford western but, more specifically, the reimagined western, *Fort Apache, The Bronx* (1981). In the latter, Paul Newman plays a police officer in a decaying station in a depressed part of the South Bronx. The police feel under siege by Puerto Rican immigrants, who are portrayed as violent Others, according to the conventions of the western.

LAWRENCE: They are prepared to defend their station.

Lawrence adopts the police perspective, figuring citizens as enemies, "Indians" according to the generic convention.

The sequence next shows a white male policeman, balding with a dark mustache, holding a shotgun, then cuts to a young, female African American officer, wearing braids and a camouflage hat backwards.

LAWRENCE: Officers are being shot at continuously. The same thing every day.

Up to this point, the report is typical, adopting police perspectives, offering assertions without proof or context. Lawrence does not stop to question if New Orleans residents were actually shooting at police or why they might do so. Instead, he accepts their assertion and reports it as fact.

The screen cuts to a flooded and smashed car, perhaps meant to suggest an unspecified threat, before panning to two undamaged NOPD cruisers. Seemingly, the police are better resourced and protected than the citizens they fear. An African American cop, in blue uniform, bald and unshaven, addresses the camera, criticizing police deserters. The sequence cuts to show a wide shot, panning right to left to reveal an exterior of the station, the Fort Apache sign clearly visible, police officers milling about, some in shorts and T-shirts, indistinguishable from civilians.

At this point, the sequence changes significantly. Night has fallen, and Lawrence and his cameraman have moved up to the roof of the station with a group of officers. A camera light illuminates the uniformed African American policeman. The camera then pans to reveal six police officers gathered around the rooftop, looking out. The female officer in braids and the camouflage hat whispers, "guys out there," to a white male officer.

At this, a sharp sound is heard, not loud but distinctive. The cameraman immediately kills his light and the frame goes black. Over the black frame, crunching sounds are heard as Lawrence, the cameraman, and the police officers crouch down on the roof.

POLICE OFFICER: We just heard a gun shot.

NOPD officer interviewed by Lawrence at "Fort Apache" (CNN 9.2.05).

When the cameraman turns his light back on, the viewer sees the officers peering over the sides of the roof. The police cannot see anything outside the small illuminated area on the roof of Fort Apache. Like the tourists, they cannot see what they fear and are left to imagine the context and intention of the threat. Moreover, the viewer could not see the flash from a muzzle. The camera missed it, and the sound had to be interpreted by a police officer.

The next part of the segment contained the only proof offered on television news of residents firing on police.

LAWRENCE: This was later.

The frame is black for a moment before four flashes are visible in the darkness and four reports are heard. As acknowledged by Lawrence, this sequence has been edited and condensed. Following the four flashes, the police officer in the vest speaks to camera.

POLICE OFFICER: I picked up the flash and put shots down there and quieted it down.

CNN showed the four flashes, but withheld images of the police firing from the roof into the surrounding neighborhoods. By altering the sequence and omitting the police response, CNN provided only partial, not fully contextualized evidence of the shooting. Following the prevailing logic of television news, Lawrence's report tells viewers what happened and what to think about it. The images are edited to support his narrative, closely connected to the narrative supplied to him by the police with whom he is embedded. In sum, Lawrence is able to assemble fragments of the experience of a night on the roof of the police station and combine these fragments with the anxiety felt by police toward citizens to create a sense of siege. Like homesteaders in a western, like Paul Newman in the South Bronx, the New Orleans Police Department perceived itself to be an outpost in hostile territory. Rather than respond to the pressing need of citizens for help, New Orleans police circled the wagons, presented arms, and fired weapons into the darkness at indistinct targets. Instead of questioning the police's anxiety, CNN created a report supporting the police and demonizing New Orleans residents, who remain off camera, out of frame, unable to offer perspective or challenge.

The segment ends with a chemical fire on the horizon, glowing green in the predawn light, providing visual confirmation of the report's "night of hell" motif. As the sun rises through the smoke, the camera shifts out of focus, providing a gauzy effect. This sort of aesthetic choice is unusual in television news, where images are usually subsidiary to words, further confirming the status of Lawrence's report as carefully produced and edited. Unlike much of the reporting rushed to air, evidence suggests that this report was carefully shot through the night and carefully edited in the hours before broadcast (the report may have been shot on Thursday, edited on Friday, and aired on Friday night). Lawrence's report seems aware of its status as some of the only evidence to support claims of violent unrest by New Orleans residents, claims being used to justify a focus on security and calls for military response to civilian suffering.

If the image of the chemical fire confirms the report's motif, the final interview moves beyond police paranoia to convey the perspective of a police officer about the future of her city. A white, middle-aged female officer, in uniform, speaks directly to camera about her concerns about New Orleans.

> FEMALE OFFICER: I think we are dealing with part two of Katrina, with the flooding, with the looting, with the killing, with the raping.

The officer recognizes connections between events. In its sensational focus on violent crime, television news had drifted from a focus on the continuing impact of Katrina. This officer understands what is happening as an effect and Katrina as the cause. Even as she continues to evince anxiety about widespread criminality by citizens, she offers a sense that what is happening is still part of Katrina.

> FEMALE OFFICER: Part three . . . what is going to happen to the city? Are we going to rebuild? We need to do more than survive, to live with faith, with hope and even with compassion for some of the people who did not have any for us.

Framed in a medium shot, the officer begins to break down as she speaks. Her questions offer a frame through which to question the logic of the "night of hell" report. Her recognition that mere survival is not enough can be read as a critique of the police's decision to circle the wagons at the station. Her call for faith and compassion, even for the citizens she and her colleagues fear, suggests the possibility of empathy and connection. While CNN's report did not to this point question the NOPD's anxiety and bunker mentality, instead adopting and presenting these perspectives, this final interview raises important questions about the perceived difference

NOPD officer on the roof at dawn (CNN 9.2.05).

between the police and the surviving citizens. Her questions are intercut with images of a military helicopter landing in the Central Business District and shots of smoke from other fires. The sequence ends with a daytime shot of Fort Apache, with cops moving back and forth in front of the station. This final image suggests that the female officer's call for connection is not widely shared. Even if the fog of anxiety has burned off a bit with the dawn, the police still seem mostly concerned with their own survival rather than with serving their citizens.

I SPENT THE NIGHT NEXT TO PATIENTS

Television news is capable of critical insight, as well as recuperation and obfuscation, often in response to the same subject matter. Both CNN and NBC produced reports on public health in New Orleans on Friday, September 2, 2005. The CNN report contained one of the most striking visual arguments in any of the television news coverage of Katrina. The NBC report offered one of the most sentimental stories, an effort to convert a reporter into a hero and to generate mild, warm emotion in viewers, rather than insight.

Following Christopher Lawrence's "Fort Apache" story, CNN broadcast a report by health correspondent Dr. Sanjay Gupta from Charity Hospital. For generations, Charity Hospital had served the poorest residents in

New Orleans, providing health care for those without the insurance or means to use private hospitals throughout the city. Mayor Ray Nagin delayed issuing a mandatory evacuation order until Sunday, August 28. As a result of this delay, city officials were unable to evacuate hospitals in advance of Katrina. After the storm, patients in critical condition were left in hospitals lacking power and necessary staff and resources. Gupta interviewed Dr. Ben DeBoisblanc and Dr. Kiersta Kurtz-Burke, both on staff at Charity, about conditions in the hospital after Katrina. DeBoisblanc and Kurtz-Burke each stated that on Tuesday the police and National Guard had promised that their patients would be evacuated. Three days later, Charity Hospital still awaited the promised evacuation, even as patients, doctors, and finally non-essential staff were evacuated from private university hospitals nearby. As is his habit, anchor Aaron Brown interviewed Gupta after his taped report, asking the doctor to confirm DeBoisblanc's and Kurtz-Burke's allegations.

> BROWN: I am sure there is an explanation for all this, but I cannot
> imagine what it is.

Despite Brown's half-hearted attempt to offer cover for authorities ("to be fair"), CNN presented critical visual arguments that evacuation efforts were benefitting private hospitals at the expense of Charity and its patients. This sequence marked a rare instance in which television news used camera work and editing to make an argument more powerful than verbal discourse. Where Brown equivocated, the images argued.

The first image in the sequence shows a low-angle shot of a helicopter landing on a roof. The next shot, a straight-on, medium-long shot, reveals the landing area to be the roof of Tulane University Hospital. Seven people board the helicopter without apparent difficulty. After tightening the frame to show that the people were Tulane Hospital staff members, the cameraperson used a whip pan and a rack focus to pull away from the Tulane roof and to reveal a gurney on the Charity Hospital roof, where the cameraperson was located. Two bare feet appear from beneath blankets, revealing an African American patient on the gurney. Eight figures, doctors and nurses surround the gurney, but are looking back to the Tulane roof, observing the evacuation of non-patient personnel. The camera move had inscribed the eyeline of the group on the Charity roof in reverse, tracing back from their view to their recognition. This sequence is remarkable in that it provides visual evidence to make a controversial point about injustice, a point that had merely been asserted earlier in the report. The editing of this short sequence, and especially the creative camera move, produced

Nonessential personnel evacuated from Tulane University Hospital (CNN 9.2.05).

a compelling visual argument about preferential treatment and neglect. This sequence was one of the most powerful and persuasive in all television news coverage of Katrina, demonstrating that television news possessed the tools for critical argument, if not the editorial will.

A report on NBC that same night demonstrated the more familiar recuperative work of television news. In strong contrast to the Gupta report on CNN, the NBC report, titled "Critical Care," sought to defuse any sense of injustice in the treatments of the most ill after Katrina. Instead of insight or outrage, the NBC report seemed to suggest that the network was not only covering events but was also itself a major actor on the ground. Instead of producing a critical argument, the NBC report produced sentiment.

On Friday, September 2, NBC aired "Critical Care." Anchor Brian Williams provided the hand-off to reporter Kerry Sanders, suggesting that NBC had no choice but to air the report.

> WILLIAMS: We are duty bound to show you another war zone
> tonight.

But, far from a war zone, the Sanders report is set at the New Orleans airport, which was converted into a large-scale emergency triage unit. The patients from Tulane and LSU Hospitals were evacuated to the airport. The patients at Charity were still waiting to be helicoptered from the hospital roof to the airport. Williams's attempt to associate medical attention with a war zone demonstrates just how far television news sought to stretch the war analogy in the pursuit of high concept.

> SANDERS: It is the largest medical event ever staged. I have never seen anything like this.

Sanders's slide from the unprovable assertion to the personal observation hints at the direction of the report. He intends to provide his own view of events, rather than interview patients, doctors, or authorities. By focusing on himself, and his personal observations and feelings, Sanders squanders the opportunity to make a critical argument. The raw material for a powerful argument is present. The camera observes bodies on stretchers everywhere, a thousand patients, many of them old and infirm. These images could serve as part of an analysis and critique of Katrina as a public health disaster, where inadequate planning and action doomed the most vulnerable citizens of New Orleans. One shot shows stretchers placed in baggage areas.

> SANDERS: The sick are stacked on luggage containers.

Here, Sanders's voice-over and the images begin to suggest the way in which the "largest medical event ever staged" was reifying human beings,

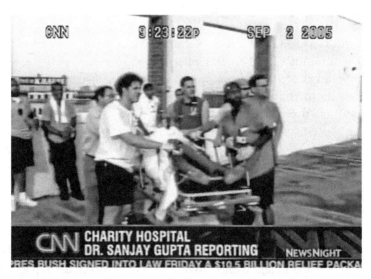

Whip pan reveals patients awaiting evacuation on the roof of Charity Hospital (CNN 9.2.05).

converting them into objects, like luggage, to be moved through a mechanized system. This potential argument reaches beyond CNN's specific critique of the unjust evacuation of patients to suggest that the entire relief effort was essentially inhumane, already complicit with a necropolitics that rendered particular bodies as always already dead, expendable and disposable.

Instead, Sanders tacked toward the sentimental and the personal, relieving viewers of implication and responsibility. In one sense, after the image suggesting the reification of the sick, the impulse to identify an individual makes sense. By interviewing a human being, and by telling his story, he could work against the tendency toward reification of the relief effort. Sanders could use television news to return an individual to personhood. Instead, he chose to focus on himself, effectively enacting another level of reification, using one of the sick for his own purposes.

SANDERS: Mark Juneau called out to me.

The camera shows Sanders approaching an elderly white man. After talking to him, Sanders begins to feed the man, dropping his performance as journalist and making himself part of the story. The camera shows Sanders settling in next to Juneau.

SANDERS: I spent the night next to patients. I woke up next to those who did not make it.

Rather than focus on the vulnerability of patients who had been rescued from flooded homes, transported to mobilization areas, and transported again to the airport, only to die awaiting final transport out of New Orleans to a hospital, Sanders focuses on his own experience of being near dead and dying citizens. A final shot of three stretchers with sheets pulled up contrasts with Sanders's first-person observations. They are dead, but he is not. Their dead bodies convey status and authenticity to Sanders's reporting.

WILLIAMS: Can it be this truly is bigger even than we know standing here tonight?

NBC's report constructs Sanders as a sympathetic hero journalist, comforter of the ill and witness to death. In the process, the report treats the sick as props, stage dressing. Apparently, the report connected with audiences. On the next night's NBC Nightly News, Sanders returned to report on

Mark Juneau, who had survived his night with the reporter. Viewers had expressed concern for Juneau after viewing "Critical Care." Sanders's act of feeding the elderly man had connected with viewers seeking moments of grace, however constructed, amid the suffering. In response, NBC made clear that Juneau had survived another night.

More than CNN or Fox, NBC resorted to stories intended to generate positive effect. In addition to "Critical Care," the network presented a series of reports by Campbell Brown on Charles Evans, a nine-year-old African American boy, waiting with his extended family to be evacuated from the Convention Center. As with Juneau, audience interest in Evans prompted NBC to follow his evacuation to Houston, where Brown again interviewed him in the Astrodome. Perhaps, NBC's status as a broadcast network, with the shortest time slot for news, prompted the network to produce a greater number of sentimental stories than the 24-hour cable networks (or, the cable networks diluted the impact of such stories by spreading them around the schedule). Williams's incoherent conclusion ("bigger even than we know") may have been an off-the-cuff response to his own program's attempt to reduce atrocity to sentiment. Significantly, NBC only serialized stories in order to reassure viewers about the fate of sympathetic characters. NBC returned to report on Mark Juneau and Charles Evans, but did not return to correct and clarify any reports on the shootings on the Danziger Bridge, as discussed in chapter 9.

CHAPTER EIGHT

A Big Corner Turned

SATURDAY, SEPTEMBER 3

IN LOLA VOLLEN AND CHRIS YING'S *VOICES FROM THE Storm* (2006), an oral history of survivors of Katrina and the flooding of New Orleans, poet and educator Kalamu Ya Salaam contends that the federal government held back the National Guard until Friday, September 2, five days after Katrina's landfall, so that the troops could enter New Orleans en masse, to "take the city back," like a conquering army (153). Salaam argues that this liberation of New Orleans from its own people was orchestrated for television news cameras. Even while acknowledging other reasons for delays in deployment (poor planning, poor communication, decision fatigue, massive troop deployments in the Middle East fighting two wars), when troops and resources arrived in New Orleans in large numbers beginning on Friday, the television news networks applied aspects of their high-concept approach to portraying the U.S. "liberation" of Iraq from Saddam Hussein.

THE NATIONAL GUARD POURS INTO A CITY IN FLAMES

After days of reporting on the suffering of New Orleans citizens, and after days of criminalizing New Orleanians for alleged violent depravity, the three television news networks were able to frame a feel-good story. *The Fox Report* on Friday opened with the title "Help is Here." Anchor Laurie Dhue heralded the arrival of National Guard troops with a combination of triumphalism and tone-deaf insensitivity.

> DHUE: Five days later, the National Guard pours into a city in flames to evacuate and feed the masses and to restore order.

104

Five days earlier, floodwaters had poured into New Orleans when the levees breached, flooding 80 percent of the city and drowning hundreds of citizens. Fox's choice to describe the belated arrival of aid as a sort of a flood suggests profound disconnection from the actual lived experience on the ground. This play of words winks at Fox's audience, who are figured as far away and unlike the wretched "refugees" left behind in New Orleans. Fox sought to connect its viewers to the National Guard troops rather than to the suffering citizens. After struggling all week to frame their coverage in a way that might connect their viewers to the stories of surviving New Orleanians, Fox (like NBC and CNN) began to construct New Orleanians as unlike the viewers of television news: New Orleanians were stubborn, foolish, ignorant, violent, and potentially enemies, if not terrorists. Built over Wednesday and Thursday, this construction excused the failures of authorities at the city, state, and national levels and blamed survivors for their own increasingly desperate situation. Only after demonizing and blaming residents could television news treat the long-delayed arrival of federal help as high concept.

Accompanying Dhue's voice-over, the newscast opened with a graphic of *The Fox Report*, a mobile, zooming trail following the program title. Next came an image of a burning building that had been converted into a black-and-white negative image. Blurring the line between presentation of visual evidence and the heavy stylization of content, the negative image of the burning building does not reveal much about actual events on the ground in New Orleans. The image then shifts from negative to positive as three boxes appear across the screen. On the left, a box shows a high-angle image of ten military trucks driving through several feet of water, with an overpass to the left. In the middle box is an image of the building on fire, which from context appears to be in the Central Business District. On the right, a box shows five military trucks, painted in camouflage, with thirty figures nearby (the location is unclear). In the next frame, gauzy borders are added to the three boxes, while an image of the New Orleans cityscape, filled with smoke, is visible underneath. Next, the title "Help Arrives" appears on screen, accompanied by two images. On the left, an African American man, skinny and weak, in a white T-shirt and a black cap, is being carried between two white men. On the right, a long shot of masses of people assembled outside the Superdome await aid and transportation. The speed of the editing does not allow for much to be read from these images in real time. The overall impression reinforces the title: help is seen arriving and responding to misery; National Guardsmen, most of them white, are seen helping residents, most of them African American. The specific images are subservient to the graphic design, and the overall presentation says more about Fox as a voice of news content than about New Orleans and its residents.

MALE VOICE-OVER: Live . . . from New Orleans.

While the voice asserts the live-ness so important to television news's claim to authority, the images under the voice are in fact taped and edited, as were those in the preceding sequence. The next image zooms out from a tight shot of a military truck rushing from left to right, laden with pallets full of supplies. This is followed by an image of a white National Guard soldier sitting on a camouflage truck and holding a machine gun. This is replaced by a high-angle image, from inside a helicopter, of sandbags being dropped into a breach in a levee. This shot is followed by an image of Shepard Smith, wearing a light blue shirt over a yellow T-shirt.

SMITH: Today, at last, convoys finally began to arrive.

The opening cuts away from Smith, as his voice continues, to show a zoom on the convoy of trucks featured in the left image in the opening triptych. This image is replaced by one of buses, which is followed by an image of two young Latinos and a group of African Americans with bags, waiting to board the busses.

SMITH: . . . To get people fed, to get people out, and to control unthinkable violence.

In sum, the opening title sequence and the introductory images show movement, activity, purpose, and progress by National Guard troops. Some of the images represent the suffering of survivors, but the pace of editing, and the graphics and framing, work against connection and empathy. Their suffering is shown largely as backdrop for the heroic work of the U.S. military. Per the high-concept playbook, the images focus on equipment, gear, and troops in action. The New Orleans residents play the role of the Iraqis or Afghanis, suffering, supplicant, and grateful. Even when Smith acknowledges suffering explicitly, he seems to be criticizing the survivors for their own condition.

SMITH: . . . Worst suffering imaginable, where corpses lie abandoned outside the building.

As elsewhere, the implication is that what happened in New Orleans is unimaginable, but that residents are somehow responsible for their own suffering (by not leaving, by looting, by shooting at responders). Here and elsewhere, Fox uses images and voice to distinguish between the imaginable America and the unimaginable America. Unlike the America from which viewers are watching, New Orleans is figured as another place—not because of the failure of local authorities and the neglect of federal authorities, but because of the nature and actions of the local populace. Fox argues that the "refugees" are suffering precisely because they are not like "us." Rather than promoting empathy and connection, Fox separates its viewers from the figures represented. As a consequence, viewers have a more difficult time recognizing the potential for what is happening in New Orleans to happen in their own communities. The choices in television news coverage strongly influenced viewers' memories of Katrina and the lessons they took away from that disaster.

Fox's broadcast ends with Shepard Smith interviewing National Guard troops about their impressions upon arriving in New Orleans. This segment is striking in that Fox rarely interviewed surviving residents about their perspectives (as noted, Fox typically presented its own anchors and reporters speaking, at times paraphrasing, interviews, but rarely allowing witnesses to take control of Fox's discourse). The end result of this final segment is to connect viewers to the perspective of the responders to ensure that viewer identification is with American troops "liberating" "refugees" (even from themselves).

> SMITH: For battle-hardened troops, back from Iraq, the scene is hard to believe.

At the conclusion of the broadcast, after more images of evacuation at the Superdome, Smith interviews an unnamed National Guard leader, an older African American, with a gray goatee and a black beret.

> NATIONAL GUARDSMAN: It reminds me of a movie set. It's just unbelievable.

Invoking the logic of high-concept news, Fox seeks to forge a connection between viewers and responders at the expense of a connection between viewers and survivors. Even a soldier who has seen conditions in Iraq and Afghanistan cannot recognize the scale of suffering in New Orleans post-Katrina. To say that New Orleans is like a disaster movie set is to de-realize the actual suffering and loss, to mark it as exclusive and unusual, and to brand the suffering citizens as not like "us." In Fox's coverage, suffering is seen as a disqualifier, much as poverty is figured elsewhere as a disqualifier:

the poor are not like the middle class; if they had middle class values and work ethic, they would pull themselves up. The implication is that by failing to rescue themselves (pull themselves up out of the floodwaters), New Orleanians deserve to suffer until they are delivered from themselves by the heroic U.S. military, which got there just as soon as it could.

HISTORIC AIRLIFT KICKS INTO HIGH GEAR

By Saturday, September 3, 2005, six days after Katrina made landfall and after the failure of the levees and the flooding of New Orleans, *The Fox Report* was trumpeting a high-concept story of U.S. military might responding to a national crisis. While Fox continued to reference the delays in federal response, and made a few references to continued suffering by survivors, the focus of the newscast was clearly signaled by the opening onscreen title: "Historic Airlift." Following a week of incoherent reporting, alternately criticizing federal response and arguing that delays were inevitable, Fox produced a clear, unequivocal story about federal military response as the triumphant and successful answer to the crisis in New Orleans.

In voice-over, anchor Kiran Chetry described "Operation Air Care" as an effort to evacuate more than ten thousand people from the flooded city. Under Chetry's voice-over, Fox opened with a low-angle image looking up at five hovering helicopters. This image cut to a medium-long shot of four African American men loading into a camouflage helicopter. This side-view shot then cut to a front-view shot of eight African American residents waiting to board a helicopter. The shots do not individuate any residents. Instead, their focus is on the helicopters and military rescue efforts. By focusing on the scale and difficulty of the airlift, *The Fox Report* does not raise important questions about the timing of the effort or the mortal consequences of the five-day delay.

> CHETRY: It is a mass exodus from New Orleans as delayed evacuation kicks into high gear.

Chetry delivers the word "delayed" in sotto voce, a performative de-emphasis that sets up the dominant idea of an evacuation kicking into high gear. *The Fox Report* highlights process, technology, and scale, overwhelming other questions. Even when acknowledging the challenge, the newscast focuses on changing viewers' impression of governmental neglect. *The Fox Report* is constructing a new interpretation of Katrina, in which the

High-concept, low-angle shot of "historic airlift" (FOX 9.3.05).

majesty of the technological response trumps accusations of mismanagement of federal response.

> CHETRY: While by all accounts they've turned a big corner in the relief effort, there is still much to be done.

Under Chetry's assertion of a new narrative ("they've turned a big corner"), *The Fox Report* showed a high-angle shot from a helicopter of another helicopter dropping boxes out of frame to people who are not shown. The shot reveals the effort involved in the production of its own image: the camera had to be placed on one helicopter in order to create the images of the other helicopter. The high-concept reporting on the "historic airlift" required significant production and expense. While Fox did not commit resources to reporting the levee failures and the flooding of the city, the television news network clearly committed significant resources to reporting the large-scale air rescue, ensuring the production of dramatic images showing a heroic federal response.

This shot demonstrates the military effort, but does not represent the citizens in need, the neglect they faced for nearly a week, or their perspectives. By focusing on air technology, Fox produced spectacular images that effaced human scale. While Chetry acknowledged that there remained "much to be done," Fox's camera did not show the need in specificity or from lived, human perspectives. Without the perspectives of actual survivors, Fox could reiterate the arguments of false inevitability marshaled to excuse delays in response by the federal government.

> CHETRY: Emergency workers have no choice but to drop supplies to people they have not been able to rescue yet.

By eliding the people from the high-angle long shots, Fox is able to present visual arguments for military superiority but simultaneously claim that the use of that technology was bound by inevitable limits, produced by the choices of survivors on the ground. Once again, the images accompanying the voice-over challenge the verbal discourse, demanding interpretation of visual rhetoric and opening up questions about the perspectives asserted.

> CHETRY: They are stuck in homes surrounded by filthy sewage-infested floodwaters that can spread disease.

Chetry's discourse is directly related to George W. Bush's statement to news cameras, while touring hurricane damage in Mississippi, that the federal government would "do its part." Rather than understand the social contract as obligating the government to provide safety and security for its citizens, the neoliberal argument for limited government contends that people are largely on their own. Due to specific choices in congressional appropriations and levee construction and maintenance, the levees failed in New Orleans. Due to specific choices in the funding and structuring of the Federal Emergency Management Agency post–September 11, FEMA was unprepared, underfunded, and poorly led. Due to a lack of leadership, preparation, poor communications, and nakedly partisan politics, the federal response was delayed by five days while American citizens drowned and died of exposure. The confluence of all of these specific and consequential decisions was that New Orleanians had no choice but to save themselves or die. By proposing false inevitability as an excuse for specific decisions, Fox News helped the federal government obscure the actual choices that yielded the flooding of New Orleans.

Following Chetry's voice-over, Fox cut to FEMA Director Mike Brown. Brown offers an odd and revealing locution to the camera.

> BROWN: There are still people who will present themselves and come to the Superdome, and we will continue that evacuation.

Brown makes clear that FEMA does not understand itself as responsible for rescuing American citizens at risk. "Its part" is much smaller, more circumscribed. Instead, citizens must rescue themselves from the floodwaters, swim to the Superdome, and "present themselves" to FEMA in order to be evacuated from New Orleans. Thus, even as the opening of *The Fox Report* presents a strong construction of a high-concept story line of mass evacuation by U.S. military technology, the report also contains visual and aural evidence of the work required to spin and shape the meanings of Katrina and the flooding of New Orleans. For high concept to replace government failure, television news must reframe, rename, and refigure events, in the process strongly shaping national and collective understandings of the meanings of the storm and flood.

CHAPTER NINE

A Violent Day

SUNDAY, SEPTEMBER 4

*B*RIAN THEVENOT AND GORDON RUSSELL DOCUMENTED a total of ten dead bodies recovered from the Superdome and the Convention Center, despite the fact that more than forty thousand people sought shelter in the two locations. Only one of the ten bodies recovered may have been the victim of a homicide. In contrast, the New Orleans *Times-Picayune* later reported that New Orleans police shot eleven people, all of them unarmed, six of them fatally, during Thursday to Sunday of the week after Katrina's landfall.

The deadliest incident of police violence occurred on Sunday, September 4, 2005, and an NBC news crew was close enough to film some of the event. At 9:00 a.m., a convoy of civilian rescue boats and construction workers, accompanied by an NOPD escort and an NBC news crew led by reporter Carl Quintanilla, crossed the I-10 high-rise heading east. On the bridge, the convoy was stopped by another group that claimed to have been fired upon by civilians. One of the officers escorting the boats and the NBC crew made a distress call asking for assistance. Her call seemed to suggest that a police officer was wounded under the Danziger Bridge, a smaller bridge parallel to the interstate. In response to this call, nine NOPD officers arrived at the Danziger Bridge in a Budget Rental truck, coming from the 7th District Station in eastern New Orleans. Even before stopping the truck, some officers opened fire on a group of civilians crossing the bridge from New Orleans East toward the Gentilly neighborhood. The Bartholomew family had been crossing the bridge seeking relief from the flooding in New Orleans East. James Brisette, a seventeen-year-old friend of the family, was shot more than ten times and died at the scene. Susan Bartholomew, thirty-eight years old, was shot five times, and her right arm was so badly injured that it had to be amputated. Leonard Bartholomew III was shot in the right knee and left upper back, and his head was struck by shotgun pellets. Lesha Bartholomew was shot three times, in her abdomen and her right and left legs. Nephew Jose Holmes was shot at least six times, including a point blank shot to the stomach. Leonard Bartholomew IV escaped the shots by jumping over the railing and fleeing under the bridge (Swenson, 2011; Maggi, 2011; Flaherty, 2010).

According to the *Times-Picayune*, as other civilians fled from the police bullets across the bridge toward Gentilly, NOPD officers Michael Hunter, Robert Gisevious, and Robert Faulcon, in an unmarked state police car, pursued brothers Lance and Ronald Madison. In court testimony, Hunter claimed that Faulcon shot Ronald Madison, a developmentally disabled forty-year old, in the back. He died at the scene. Lance was not shot, but was arrested and charged with eight counts of attempted murder (Swenson, 2011).

In the aftermath of the shootings, members of the New Orleans Police Department sought to cover up the crime, first claiming that the civilians had been armed and later lying about details of the attack. Witnesses also lied, attempting to exonerate the officers. District Attorney Eddie Jordan tried seven officers on murder and attempted murder charges, but a state court judge dismissed the case for prosecutorial misconduct in 2008. The U.S. Justice Department eventually indicted five officers for civil rights violations.

A VIOLENT DAY, WHICH WE WITNESSED FIRSTHAND

NBC's reporting on Sunday, September 4, 2005, was remarkable for the proximity of a news crew to the Danziger Bridge shootings but also for the failure of that crew to understand and to report what it saw and recorded. Weekend host John Seigenthaler anchored the broadcast from the Garden District in New Orleans. Dressed in a green, long-sleeved fishing shirt, Seigenthaler addresses the camera, with a flooded street visible behind him. NBC positioned Seigenthaler, like his colleague Brian Williams, in situ in order for him to gain authority by anchoring from the field. Fox used this technique to an even greater extent than NBC, as most of its "reporting" involved stand-ups to camera in which reporters verbally conveyed information and opinion without providing visual or other evidence (Fox used Shepard Smith as anchor in the field to gain authority for its stories). The image of Seigenthaler did not itself convey hardship or danger, so he attempted to emphasize verbally his proximity to devastation: "The smell of death and sewage is overwhelming." Of course, since television news cannot convey smell, viewers were left with his assertion without supporting or contradictory evidence.

For the first time in a week, NBC led off its newscast with a non-Katrina story on the death of Supreme Court Chief Justice William Rehnquist. Prior to the Rehnquist story, NBC teased an upcoming story with the title on screen, "Mean Streets." Seigenthaler promised a story about a "shootout amid all the chaos," as the screen showed a long shot of a group of men in plain clothes shooting along an expressway. The teaser did not locate the event or describe its context.

After the Rehnquist story, NBC returned to Seigenthaler in New Orleans, and he introduced a report by Carl Quintanilla, admitting that what would follow was "a developing story."

> SEIGENTHALER: We start with the eruption of more violence. It's a deadly shootout amid the chaos in New Orleans.

At this point, Seigenthaler gives way to Quintanilla, directly addressing the camera in a live introduction to a taped report. At first, Quintanilla does not reveal that he and his crew had been nearby at the time of the shooting. Instead, he bases the introduction of his report on information from other news sources.

> QUINTANILLA: According to the Associated Press, the Army Corps says some of its contractors were fired upon while they were crossing a bridge.

The report then cuts from Quintanilla to show a map graphic identifying Chef Menteur Highway crossing the Danziger Bridge and, parallel to the first bridge, Interstate 10 crossing the high-rise bridge. After initially projecting a generalized sense of violence and menace (Seigenthaler's "smell of death") as pervading the whole of New Orleans (constructed as a city in "chaos"), NBC begins to provide specific details of the actual incident.

> QUINTANILLA: The Associated Press reports that the police are saying they killed five or six of those gunmen. A violent day, which we witnessed firsthand.

At this point, NBC cuts to Quintanilla's taped report. The segment begins with an extreme long shot of men, not in uniform, shooting along an expressway ramp leading toward a bridge. This is the same shot used by NBC to tease this story at the top of the broadcast. From the distance of

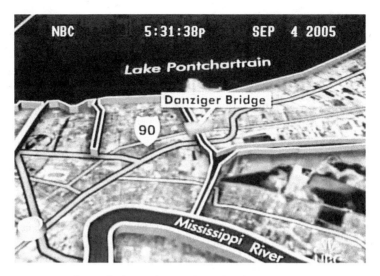

Danziger Bridge graphic locates shooting (NBC 9.4.05).

the shot, it is not possible to identify the men, their targets, or other de-tails. The audio track features popping sounds, presumably gunfire, famil-iar to viewers from similar extreme long shots of combat in Iraq and Af-ghanistan. Used twice, this shot is presumably the best footage captured by Quintanilla's cameraman. Given the limited information in the shot, Quintanilla provides an explanatory caption in voice-over.

> QUINTANILLA: Chasing these alleged suspects, police were forced to stop escorting a convoy of rescue boats.

The segment then shows a medium-long shot of a male police officer and a female police officer running away from the camera. The shift in perspective from the first extreme-long shot is confusing, and the viewer is destabilized, not clear on where Quintanilla and crew are located in re-lation to the shooting. NBC's footage was eventually admitted into evi-dence during the trial of the police officers accused of shooting civilians on the bridge. Court testimony confirmed that Quintanilla and crew had been driving with a convoy on the I-10 bridge and had stopped when their police escort had been hailed by another group. After Quintanilla's police escort had reported a shooting on the other bridge, the NBC crew wit-nessed the arrival of a group of NOPD officers in street clothes. The officers emerged from a Budget Rental truck and began firing. Based on this infor-mation, the camera distance of the first shots in the sequence suggests that the extreme-long shot was taken from the I-10 bridge of police shooting on the Danziger Bridge and that the medium-long shot was of Quintanilla's police escort reacting to the shooting from the I-10 bridge. By not immediately identifying the context in which Quintanilla and crew observed the events, NBC obscured the nature of the evidence it had collected. In court, both the prosecution and defense argued over interpretations of this footage. NBC did not provide its viewers with a clear opportunity to assess the footage and its potential meanings. Instead, continuing the logic of the opening, NBC chose to draw general rather than specific understandings from the shooting. This choice had significant consequences.

Without clearly revealing the reason for his proximity to the shooting, Quintanilla nevertheless frames the event from his own perspective.

> QUINTANILLA: It is this kind of urban warfare that makes life even more difficult for those trying to rescue and deliver relief. How are they supposed to rescue people if they have to go through gunfire on their way there?

Delivered breathlessly to the camera, Quintanilla's observations reveal the drawbacks of immediate interpretation in the field. As the shooting is going on, Quintanilla does not know what exactly is happening. Instead, he reports on his own experience of the event, which was to lose his police escort on the way to the intended story about construction workers creating holes in levees to allow water to drain from the city. Quintanilla seems surprisingly disinterested in the facts of the shooting. Instead of ascertaining who was shooting whom for what reason, he reports on his own situation, reiterating a familiar assertion that rescue work was being disrupted across the city by violent citizens shooting at responders.

> QUINTANILLA: Our police escort had to leave to respond to the firefight. We're stuck here in the middle.

The limitations of television news to understand and represent the impact of Katrina are on full display in this report. Quintanilla and crew were proximate to New Orleans police officers shooting and killing unarmed and innocent civilians, and they failed to see, understand, or show what happened. Moreover, instead of asking questions of their escorts, instead of using the camera and the television news apparatus to investigate the event as it was happened, Quintanilla personalized the story, elevating his inconvenience while failing to recognize police shooting unarmed civilians, even as it took place before his camera. In a response typical of television news,

Carl Quintanilla on the span across from Danziger Bridge (NBC 9.4.05).

he took the raw information of events and converted it into a pre-produced and familiar story: New Orleans was beset by senseless violence perpetrated by its own citizens against responders and rescue workers. By converting events into a familiar story, Quintanilla and NBC obscured the actual events, hiding the realities of the aftermath of Katrina. NBC's "Mean Streets" segment is an example of television news replacing reality with story.

This case also reveals the consequences of the closeness of television news and the police and other authorities. In coverage of the wars in Iraq and Afghanistan, the television networks depended upon the Pentagon to ensure access, information, and the safety and transportation of news crews. As a result, U.S. television networks often frame coverage of events in wartime from U.S. military perspectives. In Katrina, the television networks depended upon the NOPD and other authorities for access, information, and protection. By effectively embedding with police (see Christopher Lawrence's "Fort Apache" report, chapter 7), television news adopted the NOPD's view of New Orleans citizens as dangerous and out of control without raising important and necessary questions, on- or off-air. As a consequence, in this case, NBC failed to recognize or report on NOPD officers killing unarmed civilians in front of their own cameras.

> QUINTANILLA: One police officer, after the firefight, says he has
> seen five [firefights] since Katrina, but today's was the worst.

As was later revealed by investigative reporting by the *Times-Picayune* and by ProPublica, the event on the Danziger Bridge on Sunday, September 4, 2005, was not an example of "urban warfare" or of a "firefight." Rather, the Danziger Bridge shooting represented the execution of unarmed American citizens by heavily armed police officers, based on mistaken information, in the absence of all restraint. As reported by the *Times-Picayune* and ProPublica, on August 31, leadership of the NOPD changed the rules of engagement governing the use of deadly force and encouraged police to shoot citizens in an effort to "take back the city" (Shankman, et al., 2012). Television news took up the call by police for the use of deadly force to "take back the city," producing numerous reports that represented the citizens of New Orleans as dangerous and to be feared ("Fort Apache" and the tourists in the time-share are two examples). Television news contributed to the climate in which deadly force could be misapplied with disastrous consequences and failed to recognize or report on the killing of citizens, in part because of the closeness of television news and the police.

In sum, the consequences of misunderstanding the killings on the Danziger Bridge continue. As noted, television news moves constantly forward, on to the next breaking news, and rarely returns to correct or re-report a story. By misrepresenting the Danziger shootings, NBC created a false impression that was never corrected. Once broadcast, the "Mean Streets" report took on its own quasi-reality. If television news is a significant contributor to the collective memory of Katrina and the flooding of New Orleans, misrepresentations like "Mean Streets" enter into memory and gain purchase. Even when independent documentary media and fictional narrative attempt to dislodge the place of misreporting in the collective memory of Katrina, the reach and power of television news ensures some lingering power for these images. Once broadcast, television news is hard (if not impossible) to call back or undo.

CHAPTER TEN

99 Percent of It Is Bullshit

THE WEEKS AFTER

O N THE ONE HAND, PERVASIVE, SENSATIONAL RUMORS, uttered by authorities, were broadcast by television news networks, playing to the fears of audiences and substantiating the rumors in the process, giving them weight and consequence, if not truth. On the other hand, there were actual, verifiable experiences of people on the ground at the Superdome and the Convention Center in the week after Katrina made landfall. Surprisingly, even for those who were on the ground in New Orleans, the "truth" of Katrina is elusive.

Four weeks after landfall, *Times-Picayune* reporters Brian Thevenot and Gordon Russell intensively investigated the rumors of rape and murder at the Superdome and the Convention Center (2005). Louisiana National Guard Colonel Thomas Beron had served at the Superdome during the first five days after the storm, where as many as thirty thousand citizens had sought refuge after the storm. Beron confirmed that he handed over a total of six dead bodies to the Federal Emergency Management Agency. Four of the six had died of natural causes, one had died of a drug overdose, and another had committed suicide by jumping from an upper level of the building. FEMA doctors had expected more than two hundred bodies.

In the New Orleans Convention Center, only four bodies were recovered, "despite reports of corpses piled inside of the building" (Thevenot and Russell, 2005). Three were elderly and had died of natural causes, while the fourth may have been a homicide.

Despite this enormous discrepancy between fact and rumor, even those on the ground had difficulty sorting truth from fiction. Thevenot and Russell interviewed Doug Thornton, a regional vice president of the company that managed the Superdome. Thornton had remained at the Superdome with a staff of thirty-five employees. He inspected the facility each day and kept meticulous notes. Thornton confirmed that he did not see any evidence of violence and never felt threatened. Yet, despite his own experience and his collected evidence, Thornton expressed confusion about the actuality of the situation in the Superdome: "It's hard to determine what's real and what's not real" (Thevenot and Russell, 2005).

The reporters also interviewed New Orleans Police Department Captain Jeff Winn. Winn had led a twenty-member SWAT team into the Convention Center as many as ten times during the first week after landfall, responding to reports of shots being fired. Since the Convention Center was not designated an official shelter, it was not secured. This was in contrast to the Superdome, where National Guard troops secured the facility, searching citizens seeking shelter for weapons or contraband like alcohol or drugs. The ten thousand or more citizens in the Convention Center were not provided with any resources. As a result, many considered it to be an even more violent and dangerous place than the Superdome. Yet, Winn actually entered the building on multiple occasions and did not find evidence of violent crimes. Yet, like Thornton, he seemed uncertain about how to understand what was actually happening: "What's true and what's not, we don't really know" (Thevenot and Russell, 2005).

Thevenot and Russell attribute the reasons for such uncertainty, even in the face of firsthand experience and actual evidence, to "the fog of war–like conditions in Hurricane Katrina's aftermath." In *The Fog of War* (2003), filmmaker Erroll Morris, employing his interrotron technique of direct-to-camera filming, repeatedly interviews former U.S. Secretary of Defense Robert McNamara, seeking to create space for his viewers to understand McNamara's reasons for his interpretation of the Vietnam War. McNamara argues that, in the moment, causes and consequences are unclear and only become revealed over time, but Morris counters that McNamara and other architects of the war in Vietnam often manipulated perspectives to support favored interpretations and actions.

In the aftermath of Katrina, with communication disrupted and inadequate planning exposed, authorities and media had difficulty focusing on the central truth of the storm and flood: that as many as one hundred thousand citizens were at risk and in need of immediate aid. As Thevenot and Russell reported, when one thousand National Guard troops and police, in full battle gear, finally "secured" the Convention Center around noon on Friday, September 2, the soldiers met no resistance. Instead, they found "elderly people and infants near death without food, water, and medicine; crowds living in filth" (Thevenot and Russell, 2005). These same citizens are present in footage broadcast by television news networks (see chapter 6 for my analysis of Martin Savidge's report from the Convention Center on NBC), but as the story shifted from the desperate needs of the survivors to the rumors of violence committed by the survivors, the central truth of Katrina was obscured. The fog, generated by authorities and news networks, covered over the desperate, pressing needs of the survivors, changing events on the ground and affecting how mass television audiences nationwide and throughout the world understood the meanings of Katrina.

Sergeant 1st Class Jason Lachney, who had worked inside the Superdome throughout the week, providing humanitarian aid as well as security, assessed rumors and media coverage this way: "I think 99 percent of it is bullshit" (Thevenot and Russell, 2005). The fog had effectively hidden Katrina's core truth. Later, in response to the official and television news fog machine, documentary filmmakers, short and feature narrative filmmakers, and television show runners would attempt to cut through the fog to reveal aspects of the causes and impacts of Katrina and the flooding of New Orleans.

NO GOOD OR BAD NETWORKS

Analysis of television news coverage of Katrina and the flooding of New Orleans on NBC, Fox, and CNN reveals considerable incoherence and variation within the coverage on each network, rather than a clear spectrum of coverage from liberal to conservative, across the networks. Just as the flooding of New Orleans resisted conversion into simple binaries and opposition between good and bad residents, analysis of television news coverage does not reveal "good" and "bad" networks. The noted differences in editorial voice between Fox and CNN do not play out as might be expected in coverage of Katrina and the flood. While CNN may have been more critical of President Bush and the federal response to the flood, Fox also aired some criticism of federal response (even as the network provided favorable coverage of President Bush, providing him with relatively more opportunities to explain his response and more images of him responding with sympathy to those affected by the hurricane in Mississippi and Alabama). Fox was more critical of the New Orleanians who remained in the city before Katrina made landfall, but CNN and NBC also demonized New Orleans citizens who survived the storm and flood. Each of the three networks used the term "refugees" to discursively strip citizenship from survivors. Each of the three networks overemphasized the impact of property damage and crime by citizens and deemphasized the threat of the flood to the lives of New Orleans residents.

The clearest distinctions among the networks are based on format and investment in newsgathering. Of the three, CNN placed the most resources on the ground and most successfully reported on the storm and the flood. As noted, CNN's Kim Bondy and Jeanne Meserve helped break the story of the failure of the levees and the flooding of New Orleans. CNN's greater commitment to reporting yielded the most important information about the storm and flood. NBC also committed to reporting, but with only a thirty-minute nightly prime-time newscast (twenty-four minutes of news content plus six minutes of commercial content), NBC was limited in the stories it could report. *NewsNight with Aaron Brown* was four times longer than NBC *Nightly News* and twice as long as *The Fox Report*. Of the three networks, Fox was least committed to reporting, both in terms of resources for reporting and in terms of presenting original evidence on its nightly broadcast. Fox most often employed reporters, standing in front of and directly addressing the camera, telling what they had seen (or what others had seen) instead of showing viewers original images. This tendency made Fox relatively more vulnerable to reporting rumor, as reporters and anchors were often forced to report what others had (allegedly) seen. In sum, as news operations within larger media companies within diversified conglomerates, NBC, Fox, and CNN had much in common in their coverage of Katrina and the flood. There were no "good" and "bad" television news networks reporting on Katrina and the flooding of New Orleans. There were just networks reporting the news according to their own conventions, editorial perspectives and policies, and the possibilities and limitations of the commercial television apparatus.

Part Two

DOCUMENTARY

CHAPTER ELEVEN

Familiar from Television

DOCUMENTARY AS COLLECTED MEMORY

IN HIS *NEW YORK TIMES* REVIEW OF SPIKE LEE AND SAM
Pollard's *When the Levees Broke: A Requiem in Four Acts* (2006),
critic Stephen Holden suggests that a shared, national memory existed regarding Katrina and the flooding of New Orleans. For Holden, television
news coverage provided the common memory of Katrina that viewers
would bring to their viewing of *When the Levees Broke*: "The sights, familiar
from television, are as shocking as ever." In the days after landfall on August
29, 2005, national and international viewers of broadcast and cable news
viewed common, shocking images. They retained these shocking images
as the raw material for memory of the storm. According to Holden, viewers' memories may have been of discrete images or of longer moments or
events: "Most of the events in the first two hours will be familiar to anyone
who watched television news in the disaster's early weeks" (Holden, 2006).

Importantly, following Holden, television viewers would remember
television news coverage of events, rather than the events themselves.
Viewers not directly impacted by the storm (i.e., viewers outside of the
Gulf Coast region), without independent sources of information about
the storm and flood (from family, friends, connections), would remember
the images selected and stories shaped and edited by television news. Thus,
Holden's collective memory is the memory of viewing television, not the
memory of events themselves.

While television news formed the foundation for the memory and
understanding of Katrina, documentary film and video both built upon
that foundation and attempted to destabilize it by offering contrasting information and interpretation. If audiences approached a documentary like
Lee and Pollard's *When the Levees Broke* through the frame of television
news coverage, the filmmakers themselves were also informed by the

evidence and perspectives provided by television news. Filmmakers do not exist outside the frameworks of interpretation inhabited by viewers. Moreover, many documentary filmmakers, especially those working in the immediate aftermath of Katrina, accessed and used television news footage as archival material in their own films. Even as filmmakers edited and re-contextualized television news footage, the footage also brought into their films some of its own meanings and valences, established at the moment of initial broadcast. Again, television news coverage was the experience of Katrina for most Americans. Per Alison Landsberg, many Americans brought television news representations into their own perspectives, making these manufactured stories into a form of collective memory (2004). As a result, all documentary filmmakers must position their audio-visual arguments against existing interpretations, most especially in the case of films using significant amounts of archival footage from networks. Some filmmakers sought out amateur or alternative representations of the storm and flood in order to complicate and contrast dominant images and sounds (see Tia Lessin and Carl Deals's *Trouble the Water*, Neil Alexander's *An Eye in the Storm*, Jon Siskel and Greg Jacobs's *Witness: Katrina*, among others).

THE CONDITIONS OF PRODUCTION OF DOCUMENTARY

Television news always moves relentlessly forward, producing new story lines, very rarely stopping to consider a subject or question with any depth. It is about immediacy, and it works to construct "live-ness" as a source of authority. As a result, television news prioritizes the moment and the future over the past.

Documentary approaches to representing Katrina and the flooding of New Orleans benefitted from a production process distinctly different from that of television news. If television news followed a hurricane playbook and then struggled to construct a flood playbook, documentary filmmakers also followed a set of conventions in approaching the challenge of representing the storm and flood. Documentary film is usually financed independently, via grants and foundation support. Public media in the United States will provide some funding to promising projects late in post-production, but most productions must raise initial and sustaining funding in order to pre-produce and produce documentary content. The Independent Television and Video Service (ITVS) funds certain projects with particular parameters (underserved voices), but in general, the Corporation for Public Broadcasting and the Public Broadcasting Service do not provide financing for documentary production. As a consequence, unless filmmakers build a business to sustain their work by producing commercial work as well as documentary features (for example, Heidi Ewing and Rachel Grady's Loki Films), most documentarians work project to project and must spend as much time fund-raising and applying for grants as pre-producing and shooting documentary material. As a result, the production process of independent documentary takes exponentially longer than television news. Documentary cannot manufacture the immediacy of television news, but the longer duration of documentary work allows for greater depth of exploration and consideration (for example, see Harry Shearer's investigation of levee failures in *The Big Uneasy* [2010]). Television news gets there first, establishing a national baseline of understanding. Documentary must position itself against these already established understandings, working with, complicating, or refuting them.

Television news also features very conventional and constrained formats that do not allow for depth of exploration or reporting, for long interviews or examination. Traditional broadcast news networks maintain the thirty-minute nightly format almost fifty years after the expansion of evening news from fifteen minutes. In a news "half-hour," at least six minutes are devoted to commercial content and additional time is taken for credits and "bumps," text, and music signaling shifts to and from commercials. On NBC, twenty-four minutes of news time might only allow for eight two-and-a-half minute "stories." Cable television news has departed from the formats used by the broadcast networks. *The Fox Report* aired for sixty minutes per night during and after Katrina. CNN's *NewsNight* aired for one hundred and twenty minutes during and after Katrina. These more expansive formats allowed for more flexible story structures. Aaron Brown's interview with reporter Jeanne Meserve on Monday, August 29, in which she reported by phone on the flooding in the Ninth Ward, lasts ten minutes, almost five times as long as the usual NBC story format. The dominant format for television news prioritizes immediate, arresting, visual content and strong, authorial voices.

Long-form documentary typically follows either the feature film format (70–120 minutes) or the television hour, depending upon the method of distribution. Even short-form documentary (10–30 minutes) offers longer formats than television news. As a result, documentary can explore topics in much greater detail. Instead of focusing relentlessly on the present and future, documentaries are often deeply interested in historical questions. Many documentaries use archival footage to connect an exploration of the present with representations and arguments about the past. Documentary can also feature several stories, questions, or characters. Documentaries typically feature greater narrative and structural complexity than television news. With longer formats allowing for greater nuance and complexity of argument, documentaries also may question some of their own claims and perspectives. Where television news seeks easy access to the authority produced by the claims of newsmaking, documentary can be reflexive. While many documentaries seek to produce rather than problematize their own authority, the documentary format allows for the production of authority through questioning and critical work by its audience. In contrast, television news most often seeks to produce authority through assertion. Television news is true because it says it is.

While documentary does not "report," in the sense of television news, it does seek and shape evidence of events and understandings in the real world. Crucially, documentary features human voice in a very different way than television news. Where television news features a few voices that dominate and assert meaning and truth, documentary features multiple voices, offering multiple perspectives, some at odds with each other. Truth in documentary is sought by viewers, not provided by filmmakers. To forge understanding, viewers must weigh and compare voices and perspectives. While documentaries use experts—at times relying on expert assertion in ways similar to television news's reliance on anchors and reporters—they also feature the voices and perspectives of ordinary citizens. In general terms, documentary is more poly-vocal than television news. If television news contributes to the formation of collective memory, documentary can create a form of collected memory, gathering and shaping an array of perspectives, and provide a more prismatic understanding of events. As Geoffrey Hartman argues, collected memory can be a form of active community memory, where the relation between the present and the past is organic and in play (1994, 30).

Furthermore, like television news, documentary also may use forms of immediacy in order to support claims to truth. The several forms of observational documentary claim in different ways to show what actually happened with minimal construction. Whereas television news gains from claiming that it is showing events as they happen, documentary always has a retrospective dimension. The documentary production process inevitably means that time has passed since the events featured in the documentary occurred. This different relation to temporality allows documentary to have a different relation to the production of history.

Because television news reaches many more viewers, even though it explores events in much less depth with less sophistication, it arguably has a wider impact than documentary. Then again, documentary may accrue more viewers over time, through multiple forms of distribution (for example, theatrical, broadcast, DVD, on demand, rebroadcast, and educational). In this way, documentaries may eventually build a significantly large cumulative audience, even though initial numbers are significantly smaller than television news. In the case of a documentary produced by a highly recognized filmmaker, that audience is even more substantial over time.

CHAPTER TWELVE

A Requiem in Four Acts

WHEN THE LEVEES BROKE

S PIKE LEE AND SAM POLLARD'S *WHEN THE LEVEES BROKE* (2006) is unlike other documentaries about Katrina and the flooding of New Orleans in that Lee is both a celebrated filmmaker and a media celebrity. He has cultivated an auteur persona and status as a sports fan, Nike spokesman, and occasional cultural commentator. Lee associated himself with the politics of reparation by naming his production company 40 Acres and a Mule Filmworks. Earlier in his career, he focused on making films about the African American experience for mixed audiences. More recently, he has alternated between making more personal films about his home borough Brooklyn and directing genre films. Lee brings an audience to projects, and his audience approaches his filmmaking through intertextual frames, informed by his entire body of work.

As a premium cable service, HBO bases its business model on subscriptions. Viewers pay to add this service to a basic cable package, and HBO retains a generous cut of this fee (usually $17 to $20 per month). Since the cable network is more concerned with adding and retaining subscribers, it claims not to be focused on television ratings, the metric employed by the industry to project viewership. HBO is in the business of attracting interest and prestige. Unlike other premium cable channels, it finances and programs documentary content and features a regular broadcast window on Monday nights. Attracted to Lee, the occasional documentarian, because of his fame, his persona, and his prominent, if not always consistent, point of view, HBO provided financing for *When the Levees Broke*, hoping to leverage the director's celebrity and audience to generate critical press attention.

*Commentary on television news coverage, posted in the Ninth Ward (*When the Levees Broke*, frame capture).*

NOT AS SEEN ON TV

Forty-nine minutes into Act 3, *Levees* features a shot of a cardboard sign, spray-painted red with white, stenciled letters: "Not as Seen on TV." The sign is attached to a telephone pole in the Lower Ninth Ward, with the Florida Avenue bridge visible in the left background. The shot involves a slight left to right tracking movement, as the camera finds and frames the sign. This shot follows a long sequence in which jazz trumpeter and composer Terence Blanchard takes his mother Wilhelmina to visit the remains of her home in the Gentilly Woods neighborhood. The shot of the sign punctuates the scene of return, speaking directly and reflexively to viewers about the documentary's difference from other representations, especially television news, of Katrina. *Levees* picks up on the critique offered by the sign's creator that television news failed to represent the actual experience of the storm and flood. The documentary extends this critique by placing the shot after a sequence in which Terence and Wilhelmina Blanchard return to her flooded home and by extending the time in which the image remains on screen.

In many ways, *Levees* was conceived as a counter to the limitations of television news. The documentary enjoyed a relatively much greater time in production and certainly much more space in format. At a running time of 256 minutes, *Levees* is approximately eight times longer than a full NBC *Nightly News* report (including commercial content). Cablecast over two nights, with two acts per night, *Levees* is much longer than even the longest of television news formats. Lee negotiated this format with HBO based on the amount of material he and his collaborators had shot and could edit, and Sheila Nevins, president of HBO Documentary Films, gave him a second night (O'Connell, 2013). Unlike television news, which chooses content to fit preexisting formats, *Levees* pioneered a new and unusual format to fit its content. Typical HBO documentaries are between sixty and ninety minutes and broadcast on Monday nights.

Levees enjoyed much longer time in production than television news. With a broadcast deadline of August 2006, the one-year anniversary of Katrina, Lee and Pollard began shooting in the months after the storm and flood, and they continued to gather material until late in post-production. *Levees* was created within the conventions of practice, but Lee's stature, and his standing with HBO, enabled him to extend and stretch the conventions of documentary production.

Levees differs not only from television news, but also from other documentary films about Katrina. With Lee's celebrity and HBO's money, it was one of the first documentaries about Katrina to reach a national audience, with a broadcast on August 21 and 22, 2006, just before the first anniversary of the storm and flood. As noted, HBO's economic model is to attract and retain subscribers able to afford a premium charge on a monthly cable bill. As a consequence, as Deborah Jaramillo has argued, HBO focuses on creating a sense of quality programming that allows its audience to feel distinguished from average viewers (2002). HBO markets itself as something other than television as usual: "It's not television. It's HBO."

With the goal of distinction and differentiation from other television content, HBO was willing to spend more money on production. Documentarian Heidi Ewing indicated in an interview that a standard HBO budget is $750,000 to $1 million for a single documentary film. *When the Levees Broke* was budgeted at $2 million, proportionally appropriate by HBO standards, but significantly better funded than other Katrina documentary projects (O'Connell, 2013). By this metric, *Levees* was not only the first documentary on Katrina to be broadcast nationally, it was also the highest budgeted documentary about Katrina to date.

HBO could justify the budget because of the potential prestige and attention the project would generate. *Levees* screened in competition at the 2006 Venice Film Festival, winning the Premio Orrizonti prize for documentary, which was highly unusual for an HBO project. At broadcast, it was widely and favorably reviewed. Since HBO publicly expresses disinterest in ratings, the success of *Levees*, from the network's point of view, can best be assessed by the ways in which the documentary fulfilled the needs of the network for prestige and of subscribers for distinction. HBO bet that its viewers would be interested in a well-reviewed, prestigious documentary film by a recognized, celebrity filmmaker. Its subscribers have as much (and arguably more) interest in connection to cultural signifiers as in the consequences of Katrina on New Orleans.

DESTROY THIS MEMORY

Late in Act 3, immediately following the shot of the "Not as Seen on TV" sign, *Levees* cuts to a shot of a red brick, one-story house. One window is visible. To the left of the window, a green shutter hangs. To the right, the paired shutter is missing. In the window, a set of blinds has fallen down, with slats sticking out like the ribs of a small animal. Above and to the left of the window, written with chalk, in cursive, appear the words, "Destroy this Memory." As with the preceding shot, this shot speaks to viewers about the documentary's overarching project. The shot is positioned between the scene of the Blanchards' return and the final scene of Act 3, in which Kimberly Polk tells the camera about the drowning of her daughter, Serena. "Not as Seen on TV" suggests that documentary media may be able to show some things that television news did not or could not. If television news presented false versions of Katrina, per the argument of the first sign, those versions affected memory, both for those distanced from the lived impact of the storm and flood and for those caught up in events on the ground. (For example, responders pulled back rescue efforts in the face of television news reporting about snipers shooting at rescuers.) The use of "Not as Seen on TV" suggests that documentary can show what television would not, but also that documentary enjoys a privileged relation to memory. If television news created and disseminated false memories, documentary could collect and share authentic memories.

"Destroy this Memory" is more ambiguous. Wilhelmina Blanchard understands Katrina as an attack on memory, crying out upon her return home when she sees her ruined china cabinet in a different room from what she remembers. The flooding of New Orleans destroyed many touchstones of memory, photographs, material objects. It also destroyed the possibility of creating new memories with loved ones who died, as the loss of Serena Polk denied Kimberly the opportunity to say goodbye to her daughter. Clearly, Katrina threatened these aspects of memory as human interaction with the lived past.

Katrina also produced traumatic memory. Survivors of the storm and flood bore memories of rising water, peril, and lost loved ones. Responders bore memories of finding dead bodies in attics and floating in floodwaters. New Orleanians returning to the city, like the Blanchards, faced

*Commentary on flooded home (*When the Levees Broke*, frame capture).*

new memories of seeing their homes destroyed by flooding. Faced with traumatic memory, survivors might well wish to destroy these new and painful memories. In this sense, forgetting could be understood as a form of coping, as a short-term strategy for survival.

THIS FILM IS A REMEMBRANCE

When the Levees Broke begins with the sound of drums over a black screen. After a few seconds, white text appears, crawling from the bottom of the frame to the top: "This film is a remembrance of all the Hurricane Katrina victims." Before the documentary's first image appears on screen, the film positions itself as remembrance, a calling into memory. As a counter to forgetting, remembrance has political valence. As a form of remembrance, documentary works to counter the destruction of memory.

As noted, Alison Landsberg (2004) has theorized the potential of media, among other processes of representation, for producing "prosthetic memory." For Landsberg, prosthetic memories serve the important progressive function of providing access to important events and experiences that one did not live through. She links prosthetic memory to the generation of empathy, a stronger bond of connection between viewer and "subject" than mere sympathy. Following Landsberg, a documentary film could provide viewers with prosthetic memories of Katrina. The intent of Lee and Pollard, it seems, is to bring into being important memories about Katrina not seen on television news. Of course, if television news could create and "implant" false memories of Katrina, such as the rumor about snipers holding firefighters and their families hostage in St. Bernard, then documentary film could also create false memory. Thus, prosthetic memory contains both positive and negative potential. Since it provides memory that was not personally experienced, it could educate and inform, but it could also manipulate and misinform. Documentary film has the potential to counter misapprehension, but also to create misunderstanding, so specific documentaries must be carefully and closely analyzed in order to determine the specific memory work undertaken by each text. Because documentary can "destroy this memory," correcting or replacing, good or bad, it must be analyzed and its work and relation to memory considered.

DO YOU KNOW WHAT IT MEANS?

When the Levees Broke opens with the sound of drums over a black screen with a crawl of text from the bottom to the top of the frame. As noted, this text proclaims the film's goal to offer a "remembrance," bringing past events into active memory. After the end of the crawl, and a fade-up from black, *Levees* performs remembrance through editing in an opening montage. The sequence begins with an extreme-long aerial shot of the City of New Orleans from the east. This first shot establishes New Orleans visually, but also creates a tension between sunlight reflecting on distant downtown buildings and the dark water visible in the streets below.

Over this first image, Eddie DeLange and Lee Alter's song, "Do You Know What It Means to Miss New Orleans?" performed by New Orleans

*Aerial shot of New Orleans from opening (*When the Levees Broke, *frame capture).*

*Tracking shot down a street in the Lower Ninth Ward (*When the Levees Broke, *frame capture).*

native Louis Armstrong, plays on the soundtrack. DeLange and Alter had written the song for the musical *New Orleans* (United Artists 1947), starring Armstrong and Billie Holiday. In the film, Holiday sings the song over Armstrong's accompaniment, but *Levees* employs the more familiar version with Armstrong on vocals. In combination with the lyric, the first shot suggests an elegy, or perhaps the requiem promised by the DVD packaging. However, the first shot immediately gives way to a tighter, but still long shot, moving from right to left, of three houses flooded up to their eaves. The shot seems to have been taken from a bridge.

Whereas the opening aerial shot is bright with golden light, the second image is darker and immediate, suggesting events unfolding rather than retrospective melancholy. The second image suggests that the film will bring viewers back from the aftermath to expose the events themselves. The third shot is a forward tracking shot down a street with debris from destroyed houses piled five feet high on either side. Where the first shot was light and the second dark, the third shot is blanched, drained of color and suggestive of dust and dirt after the floodwaters receded. Played over the first three images, Armstrong's performance of regret and longing takes on the new valence of the loss of New Orleans itself. The problem is no longer that the singer, long gone from New Orleans, cannot get back to the city, but that New Orleans may itself be gone.

The opening montage suggests the fatal cost of the failure of the levees and the flooding of New Orleans by including shots of X symbols and messages by search-and-rescue teams, spray-painted onto homes, indicating "dead body inside." The bodies referenced in spray paint remain hidden, and *Levees* only suggests, but does not yet show the deadly consequences of the flood. Late in Act 1, *Levees* returns to consider those killed by the flood and by the conditions in the aftermath, beginning to tell the stories behind the spray paint.

On Thursday, September 1, 2005, NBC *Nightly News* aired a report by correspondent Martin Savidge on conditions at the New Orleans Convention Center. Savidge reported that the suffering he witnessed in New Orleans reminded him of conditions in war zones in Somalia and Iraq. To illustrate this point, the report showed footage of three dead bodies left at the Convention Center. One body, an elderly woman in a wheelchair, covered by a sheet, has a note placed in her hand. Savidge uses the image of the woman's body to stand in for the costs of Katrina. He does not identify the body, even though the note seems to contain information about her and her next of kin. Instead, the report cuts away, and Savidge continues his voice-over, lamenting the conditions. NBC uses the image of the woman's dead body, along with two other bodies covered in sheets, to represent the consequences of Katrina. In this way, these dead body images are signs, much like the spray-painted X's used by search teams, standing in for other meanings.

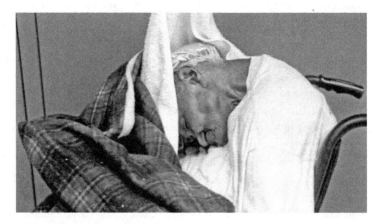

*Ethel Freeman's body, outside the Convention Center (*When the Levees Broke, *frame capture).*

*Note with Herbert Freeman Jr.'s contact information, which he left with his mother's body (*When the Levees Broke*, frame capture).*

In contrast, *Levees* identifies the dead woman as Ethel Freeman, and Lee interviews her son, Herbert Freeman Jr., to determine who she was and how she died. Freeman reveals that he and his ninety-year-old mother sought shelter at the Convention Center after the flooding of the city. Mother and son waited to be evacuated for days in punishing heat, without adequate supplies. In an interview to camera, Freeman relates that before any buses arrived, he discovered that his mother had died. In the absence of police or other authorities, Freeman consulted with other survivors and decided to wheel his mother outside the building and place her body next to another dead body. His hope was that authorities would collect both bodies. When buses finally arrived, Freeman appealed to a National Guardsman, only to be told that he could not bring his mother's body onto a bus. Freeman was given the choice of leaving her or staying in the city with her body. Freeman wrote a note, with her name, his name and relationship, and his telephone number, placing it in his mother's hand. He then boarded a bus to be evacuated.

The interview ends with news footage of Ethel Freeman's body, in her wheelchair, outside the Convention Center, next to another body. She wears a light blue shower cap, and her head is bent down upon her chest. Freeman wrapped his mother's body in a poncho and a blanket, but the image shows the poncho open at her left shoulder, revealing her face, as if a cameraperson had peeled the covering back to expose her face for filming. The image zooms on her before cutting to a handheld tracking shot up to the note in her hand, containing the information written by her son.

In this sequence, *Levees* works to construct Herbert Freeman Jr. as sympathetic and to condemn authorities for neglecting his mother and forcing her son to leave her. Freeman is taciturn and contains his emotions during this interview. To counter his low affect, *Levees* brings up Terence Blanchard's score. Trumpet and piano are heard loudly, overwriting emotion not expressed to the camera by Freeman. This is only partially effective, and viewers may wonder if Freeman reached his decision to leave his mother's body with similar seeming dispassion. Despite this challenge in working with Freeman's interview, *Levees* does what NBC did not: the documentary identifies Ethel Freeman and returns her body to history and specificity. While it uses her story to convey the suffering and death caused by Katrina's aftermath, it does not reduce her body to a symbol, as television news had done. By making the effort to identify her and to find and interview her son, *Levees* changes the viewer's relationship to the footage of her dead body. In so doing, *Levees* demonstrates a crucial difference between television news and documentary: where television news abstracts, documentary deals in details. By identifying Ethel Freeman, *Levees* argues that the consequences of Katrina were individual, not general. In this sequence, the documentary argues that each of the 1,056 New Orleanians killed by Katrina and the flood had a history.

Act 3 ends with an interview with Kimberly Polk, whose five-year-old daughter Serena drowned during the flooding of the Ninth Ward. Lee interviews Polk on a bench by the Mississippi River, and she is positioned to address the camera over her left shoulder, a contorted position created in order to allow for a composition with the river, the Central Business District (CBD), and the Crescent City Connection bridge visible in the back-

*Kimberly Polk holding a photograph of daughter Serena Polk (*When the Levees Broke, *frame capture).*

ground. The interview is sympathetic to her loss, but Polk's positioning and framing remind viewers that Lee and Pollard are documentary filmmakers taking and using the grief and memories of survivors. As with all documentary films, *Levees* uses lived memories as building blocks for story and argument. Polk describes to Lee's camera how she learned of Serena's death when her daughter's body was discovered, weeks after the flood, in a house on Tennessee Street, where Serena was staying with her father. The interview is followed by a short observational scene of Serena's funeral, shot at a church in the country.

> POLK: I did not want to have the service in New Orleans because I blame New Orleans for her death.

In Act 4, Lee interviews Paris Ervin, a student at the University of New Orleans, about his mother's death. Unlike Freeman's mother, Ervin's mother was not featured on television news. For weeks after the storm and flood, Ervin was unable to contact her. When he returned to the home they shared not far from UNO's campus, Ervin noted spray paint indicating that the house had been searched and that no bodies had been found. When he entered the house to examine the damage, he found his mother's dead body in the kitchen. She had drowned during the flooding. In an interview to camera, Ervin describes his emotion at finding his mother's body. He seems most angry at the fact that she died alone and that her death was unaccounted for by the inconsistent search efforts after the storm. His story deepens the exploration of loss and the cost of the storm, and it also speaks to the duration of impact, as relatives continued to discover dead bodies of loved ones for weeks and months after the floodwaters had receded.

Even when the documentary does not identify a dead body by name, *Levees* provides some context for the dead. For example, in Act 1, following Herbert Freeman Jr.'s interview, *Levees* features a short sequence built from a British television news broadcast. The British reporter tells the story of a group of five children—the oldest twelve years old and the youngest an infant—whose mother had died in the days after Katrina. The reporter emphasizes the children's plight before the camera moves toward the doorway to the mother's bedroom. Visible through the doorframe, the mother's body lies on the bed, face up. She is wearing boxer shorts, and her belly is exposed and distended. Her feet are bare. The camera looks in from the front room, approximating the point of view of the children, checking on their dead mother. The reporter narrates that his crew evacuated the children on their boat. He does not mention the fate of the mother's body.

Presumably, she was left behind, like Ethel Freeman, as the exigency of the living took precedence over the care of the dead.

HIS NAME WAS EDDIE

By following Ethel Freeman's story with the re-cut footage from British television, *Levees* moves from the largely obscured body of Freeman to the exposed body of the dead mother. In Act 2, *Levees* becomes more explicit in the representation of death. In the second major montage sequence of the documentary, *Levees* creates a thirty-shot sequence of escalating and intentionally discomforting explicitness. The dead body montage follows a sequence focused on Mayor Ray Nagin—in which Nagin congratulates himself for speaking truth to power, but in which he also reveals that he enjoyed a long, hot shower on *Air Force One*—and underscores the cost to New Orleans residents of the failures of all elected officials. After documenting the post-Katrina blame game, in which city, state, and federal officials sought to deflect responsibility, *Levees* features a montage that cuts through political discourse to remind viewers about the consequences of failed preparation, failed protection, and failed rescue in the starkest terms. While the dead body montage does not locate each person individually within history, it does argue collectively for the moral failings of government and the mortal consequences of policy choices. I describe each body image in detail in order to provide markers for the potential identification and recovery for history of each human being.

The second montage begins with the testimony of a surviving citizen, Michael Knight, interviewed outside his ruined house in the Lower Ninth Ward. Taking a break from gutting his flooded home, Knight talks to Lee's camera about friends and neighbors who died.

> KNIGHT: A lot of dead people was floating in the water. My buddy around the corner, over by the gate. He swole up this big, man (arms wide). His name was Eddie.

As Knight names his friend, the frame cuts to a large African-American man, face down against a gate. He is bald and wears dark pants and a dirty white T-shirt. Unlike Savidge's NBC report on the dead outside the Convention Center or Smith's dance with the dead on FOX, *Levees* carefully connects an image of a dead body with a story, naming the dead, locating loss in place and history. As with Ethel Freeman, *Levees* reverses visual reification typical of television news coverage of combat and disaster, where bodies are rendered as things, available for signification. Here, *Levees* insists that the dead body is a person named Eddie. It is not any body.

As the montage continues, *Levees* cannot continue to identify bodies. Yet, having identified Ethel and Eddie, the documentary has made the point that each body is the remains of a human being. Even when unable to convey the identity of other bodies, *Levees* informs how the viewer sees and interprets other dead bodies.

The image of Eddie's body is followed by an image of another body, an African American, face down, next to a yellow fire hydrant. This body wears a pink shirt, with legs spread wide. This image cuts to an image of a body under a blue tarp in shallow water, near a curb, among storm debris. This image cuts to a close-up of a white tennis shoe sticking out from the blue tarp. The close-up of the shoe is followed by a tracking shot, from a boat, moving right to left, observing the dead body of an African American male on top of a partially submerged car. The man's body is face down, his arms hanging over the passenger windows and his legs hanging over the rear window. This moving image cuts to a still image of an African American male on his back, without a shirt, his body swollen and waterlogged. This is followed by a high-angle photograph of a male body under a blue tarp. The sequence cuts to the body of another African American man, face down in shallow water. The Circle Foods store (1522 St. Bernard Avenue, in the Seventh Ward) is visible in the background of the image. The sequence next cuts to a body under a sheet in a gas station parking lot. No water is visible in the frame. The next image cuts to a close-up of a shoe, sticking out from under the sheet, continuing the symbolism of feet and shoes representing the personhood of dead bodies (reminding the viewer that human bodies are never only things). In the fifteenth shot of the sequence, another still image shows the body of an African American woman, face down in water, wearing blue shorts, with her top riding up, exposing her bare back.

The next shot is a still image of two dogs eating the dead body of an African American male. The body is torn and bones are exposed. This is the sixteenth shot in the sequence, and the image follows many explicit and disturbing shots, but it shocks and disrupts viewers because of the representation of a human body being consumed by animals. As a still photo, this image freezes the action of the animals, challenging viewers, but also sparing the horror of a time-based representation. Placed in the middle of the sequence, this image intends to shock viewers out of any level of comfort with the overall sequence, jarring viewers out of a pattern.

The shot of the dogs and the dead body is followed by video of the body of an African American male on his back on the neutral ground, water visible on the street behind. Rigor mortis has set in, and the body is rigid. This is followed by a photographic image of a body wearing a yellow T-shirt, a zoom on another body under a white sheet, and a photograph of a body against a fence. This last image may be of Michael Knight's friend Eddie.

The final ten shots of the montage continue to show dead bodies, alternating between video and still images. All the bodies appear to be African American and male. The twenty-fifth shot is a high-angle photograph looking down at a body trapped against a gate in a chain-link fence. This may be another shot of Eddie. This shot is followed by another still image of a body of an African-American man face down on the ground. These still images are followed by two video shots. The first shows an older African American man face down in shallow water. The second shows another African American man floating face up, also in shallow water. The final two shots show homemade memorials, shifting back from direct to oblique representation of the dead. By alternating between still and video images, and by constructing patterns of bodies facing the camera and turned away from the camera, Lee and Pollard employed a visual poetics to represent the costs of Katrina and the flooding of New Orleans. By shaping this material in this way, they provide viewers with a way through these images, another way to process the inherent challenge of viewing dead human beings. Each discrete image poses a series of ethical questions, some directed toward the filmmakers, others toward the viewer.

Images of dead bodies challenge signification. They do not represent death as much as the absence of life, what remains after life has ended. As Vivian Sobchack has argued in "Inscribing Ethical Space — 10 Propositions on Death, Representation, and Documentary" (1984), an image of a dead body raises fundamental questions about the production of the image and about its reception by viewers. Viewers of *Levees* might question the sources of the images combined into a montage of dead bodies and the decision to combine these images in this way. The images seem to be documentary in nature, created as a record of the human cost of the flood. Yet, the viewer may wonder if some of the images were created with other motives, to shock and sensationalize, or if the images respect or exploit the dead.

Television news has long cited a concern with respect for the dead and consideration of living relatives when deciding not to represent dead Americans in combat. However, in the interest of respecting the dead, this representational practice instead edits the dead out of the scene, hiding the consequences of warfare, obscuring histories. Additionally, all representational practices involve exploitation insofar as they enact uneven power dynamics. The dead did not give consent to be photographed or shot. They did not consent to be included in a montage with other images of other dead bodies. While the montage may make a strong argument about the extensiveness of the human cost of the flood by linking together images of dead people, it also reduces the particularity of each life, creating a visual trope. As noted, the exception here is Michael Knight's identification of his friend Eddie. By naming one of the dead, Knight counters the visual equivalence produced by the montage. By including Knight's remembrance, Lee and Pollard change the viewer's relationship to the overall montage, providing a necessary reminder that these bodies were individual people with names, families, histories.

The dead body montage in Act 2 of *Levees* challenges viewers, who are trained by television news to expect death to be concealed, framed out. *Levees* insists that they must look at and attend to images of the dead. The length and form of the montage force viewers to engage with its images. They cannot easily look away as the sequence continues. When viewing on DVD, they could jump ahead to the next scene. But, to do so, viewers must actively decide to avoid engaging with the representation of those killed by the failure of the levees and the flooding of New Orleans. Otherwise, if viewers continue to look, they must engage in a complex process of ethical engagement with the film. Ultimately, the dead body montage is not easily consumed or avoided. As a result, the montage challenges viewers to reflect on their own implication in events and on their response to the filmmakers' choices.

Lee and Pollard choose to focus exclusively on dead African Americans in this sequence, and most of the images they selected represent male bodies. Brunkhard, Namulanda, and Ratard (2008) conclude that 51 percent of those who died in Katrina and the flood were African American and that 53 percent of the victims were male. In this montage, Lee and Pollard focus on the impact of Katrina on African American males, and this choice shapes how the viewer sees and understands the impact of the storm. Perhaps, Lee and Pollard chose to focus this montage on dead African American males to counter the tendency of television to figure the living African American male body as a site of threat, as in the television news footage of "looting." Lee and Pollard's montage challenges viewers' relations to representations of those killed by the flooding of New Orleans, but the montage may also provide a false memory, in Landsberg's sense, strongly suggesting that African American males suffered disproportionately the fatal consequences of the flood, an argument disproved by demographic research into the casualties of Katrina.

By placing the montage at the end of Act 2, near the midpoint of the four-hour documentary, Lee and Pollard position it as an interpretive key for viewers. The montage serves as the pivot between the early focus on documenting the events of Katrina and the flood and the shift toward the impact of those events on survivors. The montage of the dead punctuates *Levees*'s representation of the cost of Katrina.

LOOTERS WILL BE SHOT

At the beginning of Act 2, after a short, five-shot montage to reset the documentary's second hour, *Levees* raises the issue of "elite panic" as fuel for official and unofficial violence. Disaster sociologists argue that elite panics occur when authorities perceive themselves to have lost their customary control over a society. With the failure of infrastructure and communications after Katrina, due to poor planning, authorities panicked, projecting fear generated by their loss of control onto their own citizens who were figured as dangerous and out of control. As discussed in detail earlier, television news picked up and amplified this elite panic, reporting rumor as fact and extending fear mongering with deadly results. The initial focus of television news coverage on Monday, August 29, and Tuesday, August 30, was on search and rescue of those trapped and imperiled by floodwaters. However, once NOPD lost communications on Tuesday, August 30, officials began to panic, basing responses on rumors of violence by citizens against responders. After learning about the shooting of a police officer, and in response to reports of widespread looting, Mayor Ray Nagin shifted focus away from rescue toward the protection of property. Chief of Police Eddie Compass voiced alarmist rumors on television news, which he later repeated on Oprah Winfrey's syndicated talk show, claiming that babies were being raped at the Superdome. *Levees* includes footage from a Wednesday, August 31, press conference in which Louisiana Governor Kathleen Blanco encouraged National Guard troops to use deadly violence in order to "restore law and order."

> BLANCO: These troops know how to shoot and kill and they are more than willing to do so if necessary. And I expect that they will.

Lost in Blanco's focus on "law and order" is the fact that the violence she endorses would be directed at her own citizens. In the aftermath of Katrina, authorities at the federal, state, and local level abandoned the social contract with their citizens. By failing to provide adequate infrastructure, planning, or response, authorities failed to uphold order. However, after the failure of the state to provide for its citizens, when citizens took food and clothing, the state focused on the violent restoration of order, defined as the protection of private property, not the protection of living citizens.

Elite panic also fueled paranoia on the ground. In *Levees*, Lee interviews white Ninth Ward resident Emile Dumesnil about his actions after Katrina. Dumesnil relates that he armed himself upon returning to New Orleans and that he stockpiled weapons at his home against unspecified threats. Lee makes a joke in response to Dumesnil's description of his weapons (multiple rifles and handguns), pointing out the disproportion between Dumesnil's actual situation and his weaponry.

LEE: Yo, were you looking for bin Laden?

The West Bank of New Orleans, across the Mississippi River from the Central Business District and the French Quarter, was not flooded by Katrina or by the failure of the levees. Yet, while the West Bank was spared, authorities and citizens nevertheless panicked in the aftermath of Katrina. Most famously, police from the City of Gretna and Jefferson Parish barricaded the Crescent City Connection, the bridge linking the East Bank to the West Bank of New Orleans. Citizens who had survived the flooding attempted to evacuate on foot across to the unflooded West Bank, only to be blocked by police from the West Bank. Instead of welcoming fellow citizens out of the floodwaters, some West Bank authorities (most white) feared that their fellow citizens (many African American) would damage property and loot goods.

At the same time, some white residents in the Algiers Point neighborhood constructed barricades, seeking to control access to and movement through their neighborhood. According to the *Times-Picayune* reporting of A. C. Thompson and Brendan McCarthy, small groups of white men targeted African American men attempting to pass through the neighborhood.

Donnell Herrington, an African American male in his twenties, was looking for an opportunity to evacuate the West Bank of New Orleans, which, although unflooded, lacked power and services. Walking through the Algiers Point neighborhood with his cousin and friend, heading toward the ferry terminal on the point that had been designated an evacuation site, Herrington was shot twice.

Unlike the dead bodies in the montage, which required others to speak for them, either in voice-over (like Knight) or via editing (like Lee and

Pollard in constructing the sequence), Herrington tells his story directly to Lee and Pollard's camera, speaking for himself, but also being shaped by the filmmakers' formal choices. The sequence begins with a shot of a sign identifying the site of the shooting: "Welcome to Old Algiers, founded in 1719, New Orleans' Best Kept Secret." Herrington's voice begins over the image of the sign, relating the story of his shooting. As he continues, the sequence cuts to a shot of Herrington on the Algiers levee, in bright daylight. Herrington is framed so that the French Quarter and the CBD are visible in the background, and a ship passes through the frame behind him as he relates this story. Through this framing, *Levees* reminds viewers of the spatial dimensions of Herrington's story, near the city and the Convention Center, but separated by the river (and the lack of flooding). Herrington wears a tan sweatshirt and a white T-shirt, and the camera zooms on him as he talks, making visible a prominent scar on the left side of his neck, the mark of the violence enacted on his body.

HERRINGTON: Before you know it, I heard a boom, a blast.

This memory triggers an audio effect re-creating the sound of a shotgun blast and the frame cuts to show two shots of plywood signs, spray-painted with warnings of violence: "Shooting with no questions" and "Looters will be shot." Over these images, Herrington relates that his body was lifted into the air by the shotgun blast. The images then synchronize with Herrington, zooming on him as he concludes the memory to camera: "and I hit the ground." While the audio effect suggests something of Herrington's focalization, potentially bringing the viewer into his experience, the shots of the handmade signs make an argument directed outward toward the viewer about panic, perception, and violence.

To emphasize the point, the sequence cuts to two more shots of warning signs, "Beware! We shoot looters" and "Trespassers will be shot!!!" The discourse of the signs echoes Blanco's exhortation for the violent re-instantiation of order. The official position valuing property rights over civil and human rights was expressed at street level in Algiers Point. The sequence cuts back to Herrington, in synch, telling about how a white man with a shotgun approached him as he lay bleeding on the ground. After the man reloaded, Herrington relates that he "heard another bang." Again, the sequence employs a sound effect of a gunshot. Herrington's memory of trauma maintains the structure of his experience. His version of the experience is somatic. Herrington describes the impact of events on his body, not attempting to rewrite his experience from a master perspective. His knowledge of events was seen, heard, and felt.

The filmmakers constructed the sequence after interviewing Herrington. *Levees* uses Herrington's story as an example of the costs of Katrina on the surviving citizens, partially exploiting his experience for the film's argument, but also giving Herrington voice and the opportunity to document his experience. This last role is especially important given that NOPD neglected to investigate the shooting (and other crimes by citizens against citizens). For Herrington, his participation in *Levees* is existential: he is asserting that his life, and near death, have significance despite official disinterest.

The sequence seeks to convey Herrington's somatic experience by showing the marks of violence on his body. In a medium shot, the camera frames Herrington's head and shoulders. As he lifts his shirt, the camera pans down to show his torso, where more than twenty scars from shotgun pellets are visible. The camera moves down his body, reframing on his stomach, until he lets his shirt fall. The camera then moves up to his neck, focusing on a four-inch-long pink scar, where surgeons from West Jefferson Hospital repaired his torn jugular vein, saving his life. While Herrington continues in voice-over, the images testify to the violence enacted by fellow citizens, who projected fears onto his body.

PERFORMANCE OF PLEASURE

The third goal of *Levees*, after establishing what happened and who suffered, is to represent the performance of culture. Beginning in Act 1, and continuing throughout the other three acts, performance is the most consistent element of the multi-part documentary film. When examined as a whole, rather than as four distinct films, *Levees* is structured so that performance answers the pain and suffering of loss and trauma. The documentary argues that the performance of culture is what distinguished New Orleans before Katrina: jazz funerals; second lines; Mardi Gras Indians costuming, singing, and parading; Social Aid and Pleasure Clubs and stepping clubs; and cooking and eating.

Les Blank's 1978 documentary *Always for Pleasure* is a key intertext for *When the Levees Broke*, just as it is for David Simon and Eric Overmyer's *Treme*. Blank studied at Tulane University in New Orleans and experienced the performance of culture firsthand. In *Always for Pleasure*, building on the model of Ricky Leacock and D. A. Pennebaker, Blank uses a handheld camera to observe the production of culture up close. As with these Direct Cinema filmmakers, Blank employs an immersive approach. He places his camera at street level, within a second line or group of steppers, so that he can show viewers an approximation of culture from the inside out. As a Californian who learned about traditions and folkways through living in New Orleans, Blank created in *Always for Pleasure* a primer on New Orleans culture for non-natives. Lee and Pollard draw heavily on *Always for Pleasure*'s approach to documenting culture. For example, Blank introduces the jazz funeral and second line traditions via interviews with Preservation Hall Jazz Band member Kid Thomas Valentine and musician and producer Allen Toussaint. Valentine summarizes the worldview of the jazz funeral tradition.

VALENTINE: You be here today, gone tomorrow.

Blank works to show the consequence of this belief through close observation of a march to the cemetery to lay a community member to rest and of the exuberant second line returning from the burial. Again, Blank positions his camera to observe details of individual performance: the slow, dignified shuffle of a marshal leading the funeral procession and the stepping and laying back of a mourner celebrating the life of the deceased on the way back. These shots are largely handheld, with mobile framing following individuals as they move. For Blank, New Orleans culture is summed up in the journey from funeral to celebration, from the copresence of loss and remembrance, of suffering and pleasure.

Blank structures his documentary to focus on the ways in which New Orleanians invest in the "here today" as answer to the inevitability of "gone tomorrow." After establishing the oppositions of death and life, Blank moves on to food and foodways. He interviews singer Irma Thomas as she cooks a pot of red beans. One of the most important soul and rhythm and blues singers in New Orleans, Thomas was famous for cooking for her patrons at her Lion's Den Lounge. As Thomas demonstrates the process of creating "a gorgeous pot of red beans," Blank brings his camera to the rim of the pot, peering into the bubbling beans. He creates texture through proximity and movement. His immersive approach to documenting culture established a strong model for later work.

After showing the process of boiling crawfish at Frankie & Johnny's restaurant in uptown New Orleans, Blank shifts his attention to street parades, first St. Patrick's Day and then Mardi Gras. Here, Blank's approach shifts from observation to participation. In order to represent the experience of a parade, Blank takes his camera into the parade itself, marching with walking krewes, showing the perspective of the walkers, steppers, and marchers. Blank makes the point that parading is inherently participatory by joining the parade. In the process, he creates and shares images that structure viewers into the act of performance.

In this way, Blank develops a form of what Ricky Leacock described as "living cinema." As Blank makes clear, the performance of culture in New Orleans is exuberant but not manic. For Blank, cooking, parading, making music are all answers to the inevitability of death and the likelihood of suffering, especially in a city in the American South without strong economic and educational opportunities. The film's title is taken from a banner used by a group of steppers in a parade. Blank posits that this sentiment is essential to survival in New Orleans. Rather than a call to hedonism, "always for pleasure" is an affirmation of life in the face of suffering and death. If television news participates in a necropolitics that renders some bodies (some neighborhoods) as already dead, writing off the living as unimportant, documentary can enact a living cinema that insists on the continued vitality of the people and the community. In this sense, Blank's version of living cinema stands against the broader project of media necropolitics.

Drawing on *Always for Pleasure* as a key intertext, *Levees* argues for culture as a way home, a way back to life. *Levees* maintains that performance can constitute a New Orleans that cannot be flooded or destroyed. Culture is produced by community, by people handing down traditions and practices. Before Katrina, New Orleans culture was under threat by economic forces—including a tourist economy, depressed wages, poor public education, and gentrification—that threatened the brass band, second line, and Mardi Gras Indian traditions. The storm and flood fractured community, killing the elders who bore the deepest lived knowledge of tradition (Brunkhard, Namulanda, and Ratard found that 49 percent of those who died were seventy-five and older). The evacuation of the city created a diaspora, involuntarily dropping survivors all over the country. The loss of public housing by federal and local decision, the difficulty in securing resources to gut and rebuild homes, the problems with insurance and FEMA, the rise in rent and the loss of income kept many community members from being able to return. Even as *Levees* posits culture as a partial answer to Katrina, the documentary acknowledges some of the forces working against the continuance and renewal of culture.

IT'S BEEN DAMNED GOOD TO KNOW YOU

In the third act, *Levees* uses interviews with musician Wynton Marsalis and activist Gralen Banks to explain the jazz funeral and second line traditions. These interviews, like Blank's interviews in *Always for Pleasure*, prepare non–New Orleanians to understand and potentially participate in the performance of culture. Marsalis explains the history of the practice, explaining the distinction between the first line (the hearse and the brass band) and the second line (the mourners following behind). As a prominent jazz trumpeter, composer, and bandleader, Marsalis explains the difference between the songs played at the start of a jazz funeral march and those played at the end. As a community member, Banks explains the affective meaning of the jazz funeral.

> BANKS: Yeah, I'm sad you're gone, but it's been damned good to know you.

Per Banks, the jazz funeral recognizes what is lost, but also celebrates what abides: shared memories and shared traditions. In a sense, Spike Lee and Sam Pollard structure *When the Levees Broke* as a four-hour jazz funeral. The film documents what was damaged and lost, mourns those who are gone, and celebrates what unites and animates many of the citizens of New Orleans. Importantly, *Levees* offers itself as a performance, a vehicle for mourning, remembering, and recovering.

In Act 3, *Levees* stages a performance that functions like a jazz funeral. In this sequence, trumpeter Terence Blanchard marches by himself through the streets of Gentilly Woods, the New Orleans neighborhood in which he grew up. Blanchard plays the traditional gospel song "Just a Closer Walk with Thee." A frequent collaborator with Lee, Blanchard created and performed the soundtracks for *Jungle Fever*, *Malcolm X*, *25th Hour*, *Four Little Girls*, and *The Inside Man*, among other films. He is also the composer for *When the Levees Broke*. By performing for the camera, within the frame, Blanchard unites diegetic with extra-diegetic sound, bridging the gap between sound and image.

The sequence begins with Blanchard performing "Just a Closer Walk with Thee" on solo trumpet on the soundtrack. The song begins over a medium close-up of six wooden crosses, some with beads strung on them, and a piece of concrete with "Lower 9 RIP" sprayed on it. As the song continues, the first shot dissolves into a high-angled, handheld shot of more wooden crosses (at least ten are visible). The third shot locates Blanchard within the frame. He wears a black coat and pants, glasses, and an earring in his left ear. He holds a trumpet to his mouth, playing the song, providing a visual anchor for the sounds on the audio track. As he plays, Blanchard walks slowly down a dead-end street, away from train tracks, with train cars visible in the background.

The sequence is more neo-realist than realist, a staged performance located within the ruins of New Orleans. By uniting the soundtrack with the anchoring image of Blanchard playing the trumpet, the sequence demonstrates the power of cinema to structure performance. The sequence replaces the synchronous sounds of Blanchard's actual performance with a carefully produced and engineered studio performance on the soundtrack. This moment represents in microcosm the film's larger project: to take the lived performance of New Orleans culture and to amplify and shape that lived performance into cinematic performance. In this sense, Lee and Pollard perform in this sequence as much as Blanchard, and the meaning of the sequence is more about their ambitions for *Levees* than about Blanchard's experience of playing a funeral march for his neighborhood. The sequence continues the documentary's structuring conceit of a jazz funeral, rather than the performance of an actual funeral. In this way, the sequence is like the trumpeter's return with his mother Wilhemina Blanchard to her flooded home. While Blanchard and his mother would have returned independent of the production of the documentary, their participation in the documentary transforms actual experience into a scene designed to convey that experience to camera, through editing, to audience.

As Blanchard walks toward the camera, the camera tracks backward with his movement, holding him in the frame. The next shot cuts to a side view, slightly in front of him, as he moves right to left in front of a five-foot pile of debris torn from a gutted house. The sequence then cuts to interview footage.

> BLANCHARD: Man, it was rough. This was the first time I've been
> back.

Next, the sequence cuts to a right-to-left tracking shot past houses with piles of debris at the curb, seemingly approximating Blanchard's perspective. As if to confirm, the next shot looks at Blanchard from the side, tracking with him as he slowly marches, watching him playing and looking. Over this image and the music, the viewer hears Blanchard's voice.

> BLANCHARD: Man, you gotta prepare yourself.

With this, the sequence cuts to a wide-angle shot, panning from right to left from a destroyed house spray-painted with an *X* to a barge, washed onto land. Like the crane shot that ends the opening montage in Act 1, this shot is somewhat ostentatious, exceeding the requirements of documentation and shading into formalism. The next image shows a porch with the word "Jesus" painted on the eaves, a reminder that "Just a Closer Walk with Thee" is a gospel song and that much of New Orleans culture is intertwined with Catholicism. The next shot shows in close-up the word "Jesus" painted on a white rocking chair. Over these shots, the viewer hears more from Blanchard.

> BLANCHARD: The camera can't really tell you the level of devastation you are going to see.

Under this, the sequence cuts to a high-angle shot looking up at the word "Jesus," painted on the eaves. Alternating between small details and wider panorama, the sequence cuts to a 180-degree pan over destroyed houses. The shift in perspective seems to respond to Blanchard's observation about seeing and showing. As with Dziga Vertov's concept of *kino-glaz*, or film-eye, Lee uses cinema to show perspectives unavailable to the individual. Only *Levees* can move from the close-up to the wide shot in a single cut. If the camera cannot show us what Blanchard saw, it also shows more than he could see.

As if to emphasize this disjunction between Blanchard seeing and being seen, the sequence cuts to a slightly high-angle medium shot that shows him performing, framing his head and shoulders. The viewer sees Blanchard rather than seeing through him. Instead, his music focalizes his perspective, the mournful trumpet channeling his point of view. We hear what he saw—or rather how he felt about what he saw—rather than see it. What we see is Lee and Pollard's cinematic performance. We see what the apparatus can show us.

> BLANCHARD: I was trying to prepare myself.

The next shot cuts to another view of Blanchard, this time in front of him, to his right, as he marches slowly toward the camera. The next image shows a boat propped against a house, and the following shows a house completely collapsed onto itself.

> BLANCHARD: I'm looking at a place where I grew up, homes I used to frequent.

With this, the sequence cuts to an extreme high-angle shot of a house moved off its foundation. In voice-over, Blanchard is narrating his personal memory of return, an experience felt by all who fled New Orleans ahead of Katrina. Whether as a function of Lee and Pollard's editing of his interview, or as a reflection of the structure of memory itself, Blanchard presents a mix of temporalities. He talks about anticipating and preparing for return, about his impressions upon first seeing his old neighborhood, and about the inadequacy of the cinematic apparatus to approximate his perspective. The viewer is shown something very different, a performance of Blanchard enacting a one-man jazz funeral for his neighborhood, his city. This performance is intercut with visual perspectives only available to cinema, with jumps and shifts between the intimate and the distant, between angles and positions unavailable to embodied human beings. In this way, this sequence functions like memory. Rather than showing experience, it processes experience, combining the lived with images and information from multiple sources, creating a supertext. This supertext conveys something of Blanchard's feelings upon his return, but only after being processed and shaped, as with the process of performing the song "Just a Closer Walk with Thee," or blocking and shooting a scene of Blanchard marching through the Gentilly Woods neighborhood. The sequence is an answer to experience, a response to the feelings Blanchard recalls in voice-over. The sequence is a requiem, a calling to memory, just like the march to the cemetery in a jazz funeral.

The sequence continues with a long shot of Blanchard marching, the camera positioned twenty yards ahead. Next, for the first time, the sequence cuts to a perspective other than Blanchard's. Tulane engineering professor Calvin Mackie describes the cityscape post-flood.

MACKIE: It was like a nuclear bomb went off.

Here the sequence works to connect Blanchard's experience to the experiences of others, suggesting shared dimensions of experience among those who returned. The sequence cuts to a left-to-right pan of stairs and a railing leading to a bare slab, a foundation without a house, confirming Mackie's vision of vaporization. A shot of Mt. Carmel Church, struck by the sun, is followed by an image of two cars, one atop the other, like two bodies in a final embrace. The image of the church supports the conceit of the funeral march, while the cars stand in for human cost.

Returning to Blanchard, the sequence shows a front view of him in a tighter long shot, continuing to march toward the camera. This image is followed by a high-angle tracking shot from right to left over a destroyed car. Over this, community member Gina Montana's voice offers another conceptualization of the flood's damage.

MONTANA: It was like a time warp, and I was in Europe after a bombing in World War II.

Both Mackie and Montana reference the consequences of global conflict to explain the devastation of New Orleans, rejecting natural causes and instead suggesting human responsibility for Katrina's devastation.

Under Montana's statement, the sequence shows downed power lines crossing the frame, with a destroyed house in the background of the shot. This is replaced by an image of a light blue car, upside down in the mud, and another image of the corpse of a dog by a brick house.

> MONTANA (continuing): Everything was gray, no green, no flowers, no birds, no dogs, no kids.

Under this, the sequence cuts to a close-up of a white plastic tricycle, upside down against a chain-link fence, recalling the image of Eddie's dead body trapped against a similar fence. Unlike the dead body montage in Act 2, the "Just a Closer Walk with Thee" montage avoids showing dead human beings. Instead, the sequence suggests, but does not show, the human costs. The next shot shows a plastic Barbie doll in dark mud, followed by a low-angle look up at a swing set, which is replaced by an image of a small yellow boat atop a sports utility vehicle and a truck.

Next, the sequence shows Tanya Harris, a Ninth Ward resident and a volunteer for the Association of Community Organizations for Reform Now. She is wearing a red ACORN shirt and a black headscarf. This is followed by a left-to-right tracking shot of a wooden house listing, about to collapse, as Harris's voice-over describes seeing her own house moved off its foundation.

> HARRIS: Oh my God! We had to stop taking pictures.

The sequence then zooms out to show a street sign (Derbigny), continuing to reveal a boat sitting on the curb. The next shot shows a house sitting on a car, the car's front end sticking out, and then an extreme close-up of the front of the car from the left side. While the sequence has not shown Blanchard over the last fourteen shots, he continues to perform "Just a Closer Walk with Thee," his trumpet keening over high notes.

> HARRIS: Because when I saw the Lower Nine, when I saw my neighborhood, it was like a friend who had been disfigured.

Under this, a left-to-right tracking shot shows a house collapsed in on itself, before cutting to a close-up of a skull painted on a piece of wood, another visual substitution for the human cost conveyed in the interviews.

HARRIS: You just don't recognize them.

Harris makes clear that Katrina presented a challenge to memory. Like a friend scarred in an accident, the Lower Ninth was rendered unrecognizable by the levees breaching and the flooding. Or, rather, the damage created a conflict between the remembered and the present, between what is known and what is seen. Harris attempts to use technology to enhance memory, but the challenge to memory overwhelmed the apparatus: "we had to stop taking pictures." This long sequence seeks both to demonstrate the problem and to intervene, offering documentary as (partial) answer to the impact of trauma on memory. Unlike photography, documentary combines images with voice, using testimony and oral history to contextualize and challenge images and images to spark and interrogate memories.

Here the sequence returns to Blanchard, zooming on him as he blows his horn, moving toward the song's climax. Blanchard is positioned in the right portion of the frame, with his trumpet filling the leading space. The zoom collapses space and centers Blanchard, completing his musical performance. As he plays the final notes, the sequence cuts to local newsman Garland Robinette, who connects New Orleans to other global cities devastated by disasters, environmental, economic, and political.

ROBINETTE: We are destroyed.

The sequence shows a tattered American flag, flying in front of a damaged home. The door of the house is barred. This image locates Katrina as an American disaster, even as Robinette links New Orleans to other cities, other suffering. Even as the flag might suggest a common national experience of the storm, metal bars on the door suggest division, separation. The bars hint at histories of poverty and crime and at "security" as solution. This image condenses the larger problem of local, state, and federal response to the flooding of New Orleans. The barred door recalls Gretna police turning away residents seeking to cross the Crescent City Connection bridge to the unflooded West Bank. The image recalls responders and news crews eating in a chow line at Harrah's Casino, while blocks away at the New Orleans Convention Center, ten thousand citizens went without food and water. New Orleanians were separated by barriers before the flood. After the flood, new forms of apartheid were quickly established. In the context of the image, Robinette's remark speaks as much to response as to the flood itself.

ROBINETTE: I've seen Beirut.

As Robinette continues in voice-over, the camera moves in a tracking shot, right to left over foundations and debris. The Industrial Canal can be seen in the background, locating the footage in the Lower Ninth Ward. A bulldozer is visible in the frame, temporally identifying the footage as shot in the weeks after the water receded. The bulldozer suggests the work of demolition and debris removal that overwhelmed the city.

> ROBINETTE: I've seen Calcutta, downtown Jakarta. I've seen Aceh.
> They have nothing on us.

Robinette's reference to Aceh picks up on a criticism that the U.S. government responded more quickly and decisively with aid to tsunami victims across the world than to the citizens of a poor, Democratic, Southern city. Many in New Orleans and around the country argued that the Bush administration did not respond more swiftly and effectively because the site of crisis was New Orleans. In this reading, the swift flow of aid to neighboring Mississippi, whose governor, Haley Barbour, was a key Republican fundraiser, indicated that federal aid had been politicized. The Mississippi Gulf Coast was devastated by Katrina's storm surge. A wall of water pulverized coastal towns like Biloxi, Gulfport, and Pass Christian. Mississippi needed immediate aid, as did New Orleans. The key difference was the failure of the levees in New Orleans. Most of the damage to Mississippi was wrought by Katrina itself. Most of the damage to New Orleans was due to flooding in the days after landfall. In this context, slow and uneven federal response imperiled lives in New Orleans, lives threatened by floodwaters in the twenty-four to forty-eight hours after Katrina had passed.

As Robinette connects New Orleans to other cities wracked by poverty and suffering, the camera zooms on the bulldozer. Again, this image suggests the necessity of tearing down and disposing of much of the housing stock, vernacular architecture, and familial and individual touchstones of New Orleans. It also speaks to the different resources available in America. New Orleans may be like Calcutta, Jakarta, or Aceh in some ways, but it is not those cities. The bulldozer also suggests the need and will to rebuild. To emphasize this will to rebuild and return, the penultimate image in the sequence shows a close-up on a wooden board spray-painted with the words "Restore us, O Lord God of Hosts."

One scene that dominates documentary and fictional representations of Katrina is the trope of return. Citizens with resources and foresight left New Orleans in advance of Katrina. Those without resources, or who chose to stay due to history and habit, were eventually evacuated from New Orleans. Because New Orleans lacked utilities and services, even the 20 percent of the city that did not flood was eventually evacuated. Thus, leaving the city and eventually returning was a common experience for all New Orleanians in the face of Katrina. Documentary and fictional representations of the storm and flood have sought to convey to broad audiences of non-natives this signature experience.

The sequence of Blanchard's performance of "Just a Closer Walk with Thee" in *Levees* ends with a shot of a black wrought-iron sign reading "Gentilly Woods" in white letters. Over this image, the viewer hears a female voice saying, "Look at this!" The voice-over conveys personal urgency, commanding the viewer to pay attention, marking off what follows as especially meaningful.

The scene that follows shows Blanchard taking his mother to see her house for the first time after the flooding of New Orleans. As the most prominent scene in *Levees*, the Blanchards' return was shot by a professional crew, and the crew interacts with and shapes the Blanchards' experience of return. As noted, the scene begins with an aural bridge from Blanchard's performance of "Just a Closer Walk with Thee."

WILHELMINA: Look at this! I'm telling you.

Before revealing the source of this comment, *Levees* shows her perspective, focalizing the image of the Gentilly Woods sign through her perspective, connecting voice to image. Then a cut shows the inside of a van moving past the sign. Three figures are in the frame, identified by a lower third title: Terence Blanchard, Wilhelmina Blanchard, and a friend, Alice Douglas.

WILHELMINA: Nothing but destruction, everywhere you look.

After initially anchoring the image to Wilhelmina's perspective, the camera now examines her, in close-up, as she looks to her left, out of frame right. She is revealed to be an African American woman in her seventies, with curled gray hair, her face flecked with freckles and birthmarks. The sequence then cuts to an angle approximating her perspective on the destruction. In a left-to-right tracking shot, moving with the motion of the van, the image shows debris, chairs, parts of tables, bedroom furniture, window treatments, all disgorged in a tangle at the curb, four or five feet tall. The sequence cuts back to Wilhelmina in close-up, her mouth open. From this reaction shot, the sequence cuts back to the three shot, reinforcing her relationship to her famous son. When Blanchard is excluded from the frame, the naturalism of Wilhelmina's reaction is heightened. When Blanchard is shown with his mother, the viewer is reminded that this scene of return has been staged for the film, that it exists because she is the mother of the composer, Lee's partner.

WILHELMINA: This is strange.

This comment follows another shot of tall piles of debris at the curb, a Bobcat backhoe visible in front of a house, number 2308. As Wilhelmina notes the strangeness of the scene, the camera zooms on her, collapsing screen space, creating a simulation of the strangeness she is feeling. The sequence cuts again to show muddy yards and construction material under a tarp. While Wilhelmina sees destruction, the frame contains evidence of demolition, the precondition for reconstruction. Unlike other neighborhoods that remained devastated and untouched, Gentilly Woods is being gutted. The backhoe and construction material suggest resources for rebuilding, marking the neighborhood as middle class.

WILHELMINA: I knew I was going to see my house for the first time, and not knowing what I was going to see. I am just at a loss.

She makes this statement directly to the camera, weakening the illusion that the viewer was receiving privileged access to her point of view. As she acknowledges verbally, and her look at the camera underscores visually, this sequence is constructed for the film by the camera and by postproduction. This tension between her actual experience and the film's presentation of her experience continues as the next shot shows an exterior of an image of the van, now parked, as Alice emerges, looking to her right, out of the left side of the frame and then back to the camera. The sequence withholds revealing what she sees. The next shot shows Blanchard, in a medium shot, from behind, helping his mother out of the van. Both son and mother have masks around their necks. The camera swings around to Wilhelmina as she reacts to the scene outside of the frame, raising her hand to cover her mouth.

BLANCHARD: Take your time.

As he seeks to soothe his mother, the sequence cuts to a wider shot of the three figures. Blanchard rubs her back as she starts to cry. The focus of the sequence remains on her and her reaction, as the image of her home remains out of frame. These shots seem to promote sentiment and sympathy for her. Suddenly, Wilhelmina sneaks a look up at the camera, indicating her dual awareness: she is not only breaking down, she is breaking down on camera. This double consciousness infuses the scene. Instead of sympathy, the weaker condition of connection, easily put on or sloughed off, her look and her awareness promote empathy, the deeper, more fraught condition of understanding the difference between her experience and that of the viewers. Indeed, Wilhelmina recognizes the difference between her experience and the appearance of her experience.

BLANCHARD: You're OK. This is all stuff that can be rebuilt.

He begins to lead her forward as he says this, and the camera tracks with them from the right side. The cameraperson had been shooting handheld in the van, in order to make quick movements in the contained space, but the impact of the handheld framing and movement is fully felt as the son leads his mother forward toward her house. Finally, the sequence reveals the house, in a long shot, as Alice stands by the door, with Blanchard and Wilhelmina approaching from the left of frame. As Alice opens the door, the handheld camera moves into a medium close-up, watching Wilhelmina, as her son puts his arm around her. The next cut places the camera in reverse position, observing mother and son from in front as they enter the door.

WILHELMINA: What is all of this?

Again, the camera jumps, now positioned inside to observe first Blanchard and then Wilhelmina enter the house. They are both wearing masks to protect against mold and contaminants. The inside of the house is dark, with the only light coming in through moldy curtains. It is possible to see that the front room is in great disarray. A refrigerator is visible, upended.

WILHELMINA: Look, this thing is way over here.

The camera follows her statement, looking over her shoulder at the room. The cameraperson has turned on a light to better illuminate the dark interior of the house. The added illumination reminds that the documentary image is shaped by the encounter of the apparatus with the event.

*Terence and Wilhelmina Blanchard in her flooded home in Gentilly Woods (*When the Levees Broke, *frame capture).*

WILHELMINA: What is that?
BLANCHARD: That looks . . . that looks like your china closet.
WILHELMINA: The china closet don't have no business being over there. It's over in the den.

Wilhelmina sets herself against the destruction of the flood, asserting her memory against the new information of her senses. She seems to be seeing double, remembering how her house looked, how she had arranged it, and also seeing how the floodwaters had dis-arranged her furniture, her belongings. Through this scene, *Levees* stages the conflict between memory and evidence that is the meaning of return to New Orleans after Katrina. Wilhelmina's experience of return suggests the psychoanalytic concept of the uncanny. Everything she sees is familiar, yet different. Her home is her home, yet it is not. Blanchard's stout assurance that everything can be re-built, a promise revealing the resources available to a star jazz musician and film composer, does not yet comprehend the damage done by the flood to Wilhelmina's relation to the things that have been lost and destroyed. The difference represented by the uncanny is deeply disruptive and disturbing. In the face of the evidence of rebuilding in Gentilly Woods, the sequence of Wilhelmina's return suggests that rebuilding will not only be about the rehabilitation of space, but also about the embodied relation of person to place that represents the affective construct of home.

After observing Blanchard and Wilhelmina through a doorframe dur-ing their exchange about the china closet, the camera cuts to a point-of-view shot, suggesting her view of furniture and photographs lying on the floor. The image then reverses, showing mother and son, as Wilhelmina looks down, beginning to cry, and turns away from the room and from the camera, holding onto Blanchard. After comforting his mother, Blanchard reaches down with a handkerchief to pick up a ruined object, an artifact of memory.

BLANCHARD: Today, going into the house was really hard.

Blanchard's voice-over emphasizes the constructedness of the documentary scene. This moment combines images shot at one time with an interview shot later. Blanchard is already reflecting on the experience of return, an experience the film is showing viewers for the first time. This disjunction in temporality reveals that the film is pursuing documentary truth, real insight as produced through the creation and combination of sound and image, rather than the profilmic real.

In order to understand the meaning of this pivotal scene for the larger film—and this short scene is one of the most important in the four-plus hours of *Levees*—one must consider the status of the scene of return. As noted, this sequence shifts between suggesting the point of view of characters and revealing the work involved in constructing point of view. Just as Wilhelmina's reaction involves a tension between memory and evidence, the sequence stages tension between actual return and an observational documentary scene of return. The sequence is between the actual and the creative, recalling John Grierson's foundational conceptualization of documentary itself as a creative treatment of actuality. Lee and Pollard staged the scene of return in order to create an observational scene for their film. Because of its difference in style from much of the rest of *Levees* and because of its creative treatment of the moment of return, a pivotal part of the experience of the flooding of New Orleans for citizens, this scene is one of the most often mentioned in criticism of the documentary. The blocking of the camera and the use of editing to create foreshadowing and suspense in the scene create an experience for viewers different from actually being at the house for the mother and son's return. Moreover, Wilhelmina acknowledges the constructedness of the scene by looking at the camera, by addressing the camera, and by performing with awareness of the camera's presence. Careful viewers understand the status of the scene as about the experience of making a documentary scene, but a scene also resonant with actual emotion and feeling, conveyed via careful artifice. Documentary can no more convey actual reality than can television news or dramatic fictional television series. At moments, *Levees* creates access to experience and perspective, access built through the documentary apparatus that brings viewers closer to understanding and meaning. Like the scene of Irving Trevigne's return in *Faubourg Treme* (see chapter 14), the impact of which is earned through the careful construction of Trevigne's character, the scene of Wilhelmina and Terence Blanchard's return in *When the Levees Broke* reveals to viewers what it feels like to lose home.

THE SECOND LINE

The final act of *Levees* opens by staging a jazz funeral. Like Blanchard's performance of "Just a Closer Walk with Thee," this jazz funeral is performed for the camera. The scene opens with a high-angle shot, up from black, of a marshal, wearing a white sash, marching in front of a traditional brass band, wearing the traditional white shirts and dark caps. As the marshal slowly moves forward, the camera zooms slowly toward him, bringing the viewer into closer proximity. The scene cuts to a high-angle, medium-close shot of the marshal's feet and shadow. The next shot zooms out into a long shot, showing the whole band, playing and moving forward. The fourth shot moves ahead of the funeral procession, tracking backward slowly as they move forward. The next shot individuates the tuba player in a side view, then moves around to observe him playing. The sixth shot again broadens the frame, showing a side view of a horse-drawn hearse with a cardboard sign reading "Katrina," confirming the shift from actual to symbolic funeral. Rather than burying individual victims of the failed evacuation and failed levees, the film seeks to bury the hurricane itself, to stage the triumph of culture over loss. The next shot zooms on the band, individuating the clarinet player and revealing the drummer to be Uncle Lionel Batiste, a long-time member of the Treme Brass Band.

At this point, the scene shifts from the funeral to a shot of a young African American male in the left portion of the frame, standing near a sign for N. Claiborne Street. Several shots later, the young man is identified as Dinneral "Dick" Shavers. Shavers gestures with his left arm at the damaged homes visible behind him.

> SHAVERS: This is what's left. Your whole history is just somewhere under a pile of rubble.

Under Shavers's voice-over, the next two shots show ruined houses and destroyed cars, the camera moving from left to right. The scene then cuts back to the wide, high-angle shot of the funeral process, same as the first and fourth shots. By moving away from the jazz funeral to bring in

Shavers's testimony, *Levees* again plays with artifice and actuality. The jazz funeral that opens the final act might seem overly constructed, an attempt by New York-based filmmakers to use tradition as metaphor. By intercutting the funeral with Shavers's perspective, the film locates the jazz funeral performance as linked to the struggle of survivors to reconcile themselves with what has been lost.

The camera follows Shavers as he walks in his neighborhood, the Florida Avenue bridge visible in the background, locating him in the Ninth Ward.

> SHAVERS: No landmarks or nothing to help you remember where you are at.

With this, the image shows a straight-on medium shot of a small red brick church. Spray-painted on the door is the message "dog inside." The camera then zooms out to locate the church in the neighborhood. Next, the image cuts back to Shavers. As he gestures to the left, the camera swings around to show what he is seeing. This linkage of camera and point of view recalls Shepard Smith's control of the camera in the Fox News coverage of the storm and flood. However, where Smith came to New Orleans as a news professional and imposed his meanings onto the people (men and women emerging from the water; the dance with the dead body), Shavers speaks as a resident, not only of New Orleans but also of the Ninth Ward.

> SHAVERS: This is a good neighborhood that's just gone, gone.

The sequence cuts back to a straight-on shot of a hearse, driven by an African American man in a top hat and bow tie. On the soundtrack, a male voice sings a gospel song, "A World of Suffering and Pain." The image cuts to reveal the singer to be Glen David Andrews, a local musician, member of the Treme Brass Band, and cousin to fellow musicians James Andrews and Troy "Trombone Shorty" Andrews. The next shot begins high and wide, but moves in on Andrews as he sings, "suffering, oh, and pain." This is followed by a low-angle shot of the hearse passing the camera, the "Katrina" sign prominently visible. The sequence continues to frame Andrews as he sings and then plays the trombone with the band. Then, the sequence cuts to a framing familiar from Acts 1 and 2 of *Levees*. In a straight-on, wide shot, the marshal marches down a street, toward the camera, between large piles of debris burying both curbs. *Levees* uses a version of this shot, without the jazz funeral, in the opening montage of Act 1. By returning at the opening of the final act, and by locating a jazz funeral for Katrina in this space, the film transforms the earlier tracking shot. Where that shot had tracked in between the debris, down the street, this shot performs a jazz funeral, staging a retaking of space through the performance of culture.

The sequence cuts to Shavers, as he also walks the neighborhood, right to left. Without the self-conscious symbolism of the funeral march, Shavers's walk through his neighborhood enacts an individual reassertion of history. The markers of his life are either gone or buried, but Shavers remembers a history that cannot be clearly seen. By walking and describing, Shavers reinscribes place, filling in gaps and absences with memory. As with the Blanchards' return to Gentilly Woods, similarly staged for the camera, Shavers's return to the Ninth Ward involves a contest of absence and presence, what is and what was.

SHAVERS: They still finding dead people, man.

The image shows a white house. Shavers, sunstruck, pauses in front, before moving around to get a closer look, the camera following his movement, keeping him in close-up. Then the camera leaves Shavers, zooming out into a high-angle shot, panning left to right over the devastation before fading to black. This shot connects Shavers's experience of Katrina with others in the neighborhood, and the Ninth Ward with the rest of the city. The sequence ends with the fade to black, Shavers's testimony given prominence over the jazz funeral performance. But, by not resolving the funeral, *Levees* also sets up the return of the funeral as second line at the end of the film.

Shavers's presence in *Levees* has taken on different meaning due to subsequent events. Shavers, a founding member of the Hot 8 Brass Band, was featured in Act 3 performing in New York with the group. At the time he was filmed and interviewed in early 2006, Shavers was twenty-five years old. In addition to performing, he had also begun teaching music in a local school program. On December 28, 2006, four months after *Levees* premiered on HBO, Shavers was shot and killed by a teenager who was targeting Shavers's stepson. Shavers's murder had a deep impact on New Orleans. Violent crime had long been a scourge in the city, often exacerbated by a corrupt and violent police department. In the immediate aftermath of Katrina, violent crime dropped significantly, due in part to the diaspora of residents and to the presence of the National Guard. By 2006, violent crime was again on the rise. Just a few weeks after Shavers's murder, local filmmaker Helen Hill was shot to death by an intruder inside her home in the Marigny neighborhood. The violent murders of Shavers and Hill shook New Orleans, but were felt most acutely by fellow musicians and artists.

*Second line staged in Lower Ninth Ward (*When the Levees Broke, *frame capture).*

*Hot 8 Brass Band and snare drummer Dinneral Shavers in Times Square (*When the Levees Broke, *frame capture).*

Their murders suggested that efforts to rebuild New Orleans after Katrina required more than gutting and restoring homes and property, and the murders of artists challenged the hope that culture could answer injustice. Their murders inspired a wide-scale march and demonstration against violence on January 11, 2007 (Simon and Overmyer restage Shavers's funeral and the Stop The Violence March in Season 2, Episode 5 of *Treme*).

After Shavers's murder, his presence in the opening sequence of Act 4 of *Levees* takes on additional meaning. Shavers's recognition that the destroyed landscape of his neighborhood contains human remains offers a strong challenge to Lee and Pollard's use of the neighborhood as the site for their staged funeral. The use of images of destruction in photography and documentary is ethically fraught. Both Jill Godmillow and Geoffrey Hartman have cautioned against the ways in which documentary can render the pain of others into something easily represented and consumed. In this interview, and in leading the camera through his neighborhood, Shavers reminds viewers that what he sees is different from what they see. He challenges viewers to remember that the ruined landscape of New Orleans represents painful death, grievous loss, and continual struggle with grief and recovery.

Lee and Pollard do not go as far as Heidi Ewing and Rachel Grady, who interrogate the visual fascination with "ruin porn" in their film *Detropia* (2012). *Detropia* examines the human costs of the failure of another American city, Detroit, and offers an instructive contrast to *Levees*. *Detropia* interviews artists who come from outside Detroit to make culture in the ruins, where the cost of living is minimal and the landscape seemingly available. In this way, Ewing and Grady acknowledge their own presence as artists making culture out of the ruins of Detroit. *Levees* does not demonstrate similar self-consciousness about its own relation to New Orleans. The film seems confident that it is saying important things about Katrina and the flooding of New Orleans and that it is making important analogies. However, moments like Shavers's testimony enable viewers to find perspective on *Levees* itself, articulating questions about the appropriateness of documenting the experience of disaster.

As Brian Nobles says in Tia Lessin and Carl Deal's *Trouble the Water*, "Katrina is still going on." The storm and flood made worse inequities and injustices that had developed for decades in New Orleans. Shavers testifies to the losses and hardships wrought by the failed evacuation and the failed levees. His murder testifies to other failures: of economic opportunity, of education, of policing, and of gun control. Just as with any cultural text, *When the Levees Broke* takes on additional meanings in changed context. Through documentary interview and observational footage, Shavers continues to testify to the lived impact of Katrina years after his own death.

THE WAY BACK

As Gralen Banks and Wynton Marsalis explain in Act 3, the concept of the second line refers to the mourners who follow the deceased and the band during a jazz funeral. The hearse, marshal, and band form the first line. Everyone else follows behind in the second line. After the burial, when the procession reforms and heads back, the second line dances to the brass band music in an expression of celebration of the life of the deceased, and of life itself. As noted, the first part of a jazz funeral is about mourning and grief. The second part is about celebration and remembrance. Banks summarized the twinned sentiments.

BANKS: Yeah, I'm sad you're gone, but damn it sure was nice to know you.

When the Levees Broke concludes with the performance of a second line celebration, the second half of the funeral march that began Act 4. Following Phyllis Montana-Leblanc's performance to camera of her poem, "Not Only the Levees Broke," the film cuts to a high-angle wide shot of the Treme Brass Band starting up the gospel standard "I'll Fly Away." The image cuts to a side view of the hearse, reminding viewers that the funeral is for Katrina, the goal to bury the storm and move on. Next, the sequence shows an extreme close-up on the marshal's left foot as he hops to the music. This is followed by four mock pallbearers stepping and carrying a coffin. The next shot shows the second line from the side, destroyed buildings and a damaged playground visible in the background behind the marchers. The marshal sinks into a crouch, his knees flexing. In the next shot, Glen David Andrews is visible singing, then playing the trumpet. The marshal doffs his hat in a high-angle shot, then a medium shot shows the tuba player moving in front of the playground sign. The image cuts to a wider shot of the band, before finding and framing Andrews. The next image is of the marshal's feet and shadow, as he dances forward, pulling the funeral and the second line with him. A cut shows him from the side, and another shows the pallbearers dancing around the coffin. The next shot is a close-up of the coffin with the "Katrina" sign. The pallbearers' feet are visible moving around the coffin. The sequence then breaks the emerging alternation of wide and tight shots by cutting to a crane shot that moves up and over the dancers. This is followed by images of the marshal and pallbearers dancing, the clarinetist playing, and Andrews singing. This pattern of images is altered by the appearance of Gralen Banks, dressed in a suit with a white ball cap, holding a sign reading "Katrina." As the group lifts the coffin in time with the music, Banks is heard in voice-over.

BANKS: We are born in this.

The return of Banks recalls his earlier lesson about the nature and purpose of the second line. By bringing him back and placing him with the second line in the jazz funeral for Katrina, Lee and Pollard connect *Levees'*

*Dancing over "Katrina" coffin (*When the Levees Broke*, frame capture).*

earlier emphases on the impact and cost of Katrina and the flooding of New Orleans. Banks is a lifelong New Orleanian, culture bearer, and a member of a Social Aid and Pleasure Club. He was also working security at the Hyatt Regency, next to the Superdome, during and after the storm. As noted in the first half of *Levees*, Banks collaborated with the National Guard to ensure the orderly evacuation of citizens from the Superdome. By placing Banks in the final second line, Lee and Pollard make clear the importance of the jazz funeral and second line as answer to Katrina.

After showing Banks dancing, from a low angle, the sequence dissolves to the Causeway, the long man-made bridge leading across Lake Pontchartrain, away from New Orleans. The camera is located in a car driving away from the city. As Andrews continues to sing, his voice echoing, the image dissolves again to show a right-to-left tracking shot over open water. The image is placid, not turbulent, and open to interpretation: it could be seen as the storm moving out and away from New Orleans, or it could be understood as the filmmakers, who came to New Orleans from New York to make a long, multipart documentary for HBO, taking their leave and returning home. With Andrews fading out, the image fades to black, ending the 256 minutes of *Levees*.

The first minute of *When the Levees Broke* begins with an aerial shot of New Orleans from the east. The last minute concludes with an aerial shot over water as the camera seems to head east away from New Orleans. Even as the second line for Katrina heads back from the mock funeral, celebrating survival more than the storm, the film itself seems to fly away. While New Orleans residents stake themselves on the continuance of culture as a continuance of place, the filmmakers seem to take their meanings and head back north. The length and pedigree of the documentary also convey the sense of famous filmmakers, and a premium cable network, coming to New Orleans, taking images and voices, and leaving again to craft a documentary clearly striving for importance, directed toward a national audience with more interest in than knowledge about New Orleans and Katrina.

This is an inherent dilemma in documentary film. Filmmakers frequently come to subjects, characters, and situations from outside, employing techniques developed in parallel fields like ethnography to observe, listen, and record expression and data. With an airdate around Katrina's first anniversary in August 2006, *Levees* was made relatively quickly, over a period of approximately ten months. Films made quickly by filmmakers from outside a subject run the risk of misunderstanding context, nuance, and meaning and of getting as much wrong as right. *Levees* leveraged speed against resources and ambition. While made quickly, the film enjoyed a significant budget from HBO ($2 million), allowing for a large team and crew. By conceiving of *Levees* as a two-night, four-act film, Lee and Pollard were able to use scope to capture more voices, perspectives, and stories. The voices are crucial to what the film is able to say about Katrina and the flooding of New Orleans. Lee and Pollard learn from their interviews, and the shape and arguments of the film emerge from the interviews.

Certainly, Lee and Pollard bring their own hardly dispassionate or neutral perspectives to the film. They seem to have been attracted initially by the apparently disproportionate impact of Katrina and the flooding of New Orleans on African Americans. TV news showed more African Americans waiting at the Convention Center and at the Superdome, fueling Kanye West's unscripted accusation that "George Bush doesn't care about black people," made during a Katrina fundraiser on the NBC networks. Lee and Pollard are critical of the Bush administration's response, but they were unable to include any significant interviews with administration personnel. In their follow-up film, *If God Is Willing and Da Creek Don't Rise*, they interview Michael Brown, head of FEMA during Katrina. However, they allow Brown to mount justifications of his actions, not judging him as harshly as they did in *Levees*. Lee and Pollard go much easier on Ray Nagin, who seems to have charmed the filmmakers. Like many African Americans in New Orleans, Lee and Pollard seem to have decided not to criticize Nagin strongly on his actions or politics because of his race.

On August 23 and 24, 2010, a week before the fifth anniversary of Katrina and the flooding of New Orleans, HBO aired *If God Is Willing and Da Creek Don't Rise*, Lee and Pollard's sequel to *When the Levees Broke*

(2006). Much like Paul Almond and Michael Apted's television documentary series *Seven Up!* (1968), Lee and Pollard revisit many of the characters originally introduced in *Levees* in order to understand their lives in the years after Katrina and, by extension, to understand the status of New Orleans. In order to introduce segments on the status of characters five years after Katrina, *Creek* replays footage from the earlier documentary, with on-screen titles indicating that the material originated in *Levees*. For example, *Creek* shows footage of Terence and Wilhelmina Blanchard's visit to her home in Gentilly Woods, a pivotal scene in *Levees*, in order to introduce a new scene showing Wilhelmina's restored home. In a sense, *Creek* is a literally derivative work.

Even in a four-hour format, aired over two nights, *Creek* did not develop subtopics in great depth, but instead used a digest format, introducing multiple issues affecting New Orleans after Katrina: a spike in violence and crime, including NOPD officers shooting civilians; the loss of housing and the challenges of rebuilding; the massive infrastructural damage to an already failing public education system, the rise of charter schools, and the takeover of Orleans Parish schools by the state of Louisiana; the increase of physical and mental health problems and the lack of hospitals and treatment, especially for the poor; the arrival of new immigrants, seeking opportunity via low-wage jobs rebuilding New Orleans, and the hostility of locals toward new immigrants. In contrast, Lee and Pollard propose the New Orleans Saints victory in Super Bowl XLIV (February 2010), the first professional sports championship in the city's history, as a symbol of the resurgence of New Orleans after Katrina.

The most original element in the new documentary is the attention to the British Petroleum oil spill in the Gulf of Mexico. The Deepwater Horizon rig exploded on April 20, 2010, as Lee and Pollard were in production on *Creek*. In response, they devoted a significant portion of the final hour of the film to the disaster. Lee and Pollard record reactions from some of their main characters, including Calvin Mackie, a Tulane engineering professor, and Ivor Van Heerden, an expert on hurricanes, levees, and wetlands restoration. In this way, *Creek* works to connect the BP spill to Katrina, understanding both disasters to have been man-made, produced by neglect and by the discounting of human and natural life as acceptable losses.

If God Is Willing and Da Creek Don't Rise is a less sure, more conflicted film, derivative of *When the Levees Broke* and other documentaries about aspects of Katrina. *Creek* provides a digest of ongoing concerns and an update on the personal histories of characters introduced in the first film, adding four hours to Lee and Pollard's documentary work on New Orleans. In total, the eight hours form a mega-text about Katrina, dominating criticism about Katrina documentary and influencing the memories of HBO viewers.

In sum, *When the Levees Broke* was the first large-scale, big-budget documentary about Katrina to be aired on U.S. cable television. HBO promoted the broadcast of *When the Levees Broke* as an event, and the film was widely reviewed and commented upon. As the first major national documentary on Katrina, *Levees* provided viewers with the first opportunity since the initial television news coverage to (re)consider the storm and flood via images and sounds. The film combined extensive interviews with found footage drawn from television news. It also featured carefully constructed montages that used the power of the cinematic apparatus to argue for particular understandings of Katrina. Finally, the film created observational scenes (like the Blanchards' return to Gentilly Woods) and a series of performances (like Blanchard's performance of "Just a Closer Walk with Thee" and the Treme Brass Band's performance of "I'll Fly Away"). *Levees* structures its four acts to educate viewers about the events of the storm and the failure of the levees, to convey the cost of the storm and flood, and, finally, to argue that the survival of the people of New Orleans depends upon the continued production of culture: music, food, Mardi Gras Indians, jazz funerals, and second lines. By listening closely to residents talk about what happened, to whom, with what consequences, *Levees* provides a more comprehensive and nuanced take on Katrina than did television news, which was pre-produced, hurried, and reactive. Moreover, rather than only lament who and what was lost and rather than fall into the theme of New Orleans as a dead city, *Levees* observes, celebrates, and tries to approximate the creation of culture as response to disaster, injustice, and oppression.

CHAPTER THIRTEEN

Ain't Nobody Got What I Got

TROUBLE THE WATER

*I*N THE FIRST SCENE IN TIA LESSIN AND CARL DEAL'S documentary *Trouble the Water* (2008), the viewer can see one film ending and another being born. The first shot is a handheld tracking shot, moving past a small group of volunteers and a police officer toward the glass doors of a medium-sized sports arena. While not apparent initially, the camera follows ten paces behind an African American woman, wearing a tan T-shirt and camouflage pants, as she walks up to and through the doors. The scene then cuts to inside the arena. The second shot is a handheld pan, from left to right, finding and framing Jeff, a white man in a Red Cross vest. As the frame holds the Red Cross volunteer, we hear Deal speaking off camera.

> DEAL: Hey, Jeff, we're ready for the interview. Do you have time right now?

As Jeff begins to respond affirmatively, the African American woman, seen entering the building in the first shot, interrupts from off camera. Because the crew is focused on Jeff, with the boom mic pointing toward him, and because Deal is speaking with him, it is difficult at first to understand what the woman is saying. Deal's response to the woman is clearly audible.

> DEAL: Can we hook up with you in like fifteen minutes?

With this, the camera quickly pans to the left, leaving Jeff, moving past an African American man and young girl, and finding the woman. Deal's arm enters the frame gesturing toward a possible meeting spot, and the woman nods. At this, Jeff tries to reassert authority, and the camera swings back to frame him.

> JEFF: What you need to do, if you could, you need to meet out front, if you don't mind.

With Jeff's request, the camera seems caught between the two figures, uncertain about which visual information is important, which story is unfolding. The handheld camera shakes, moves past another African American male, leaves Jeff, and points down at the floor. By placing the camera in a waiting position, the cameraperson seems to have decided to wait for the interview with Jeff to begin, determining that the Red Cross is the story. Instead, the woman, who is named Kimberly Roberts, speaks again from off camera.

> ROBERTS: I want to tell people what I've been through. Yeah man, what I've got . . . whoo!

This time she can be heard clearly, and her words change the course of the film, ending one focus and introducing another. The camera comes back up, framing the woman, and Deal enters the frame as well.

> ROBERTS: I'm not going to give it to nobody local. This needs to be worldwide.

Jeff is framed out and will not be seen again in the film. Deal consciously steps out of the frame, leaving the woman the sole focus.

> ROBERTS: All the footage I've seen on TV, ain't nobody got what I've got.

The camera has steadied on the woman. She smiles at the camera, alone in the frame.

> ROBERTS: I was right there in the hurricane.

With this, she makes a framing gesture with both hands, suggesting how she used a camera to represent what happened to her in the hurricane. She pantomimes shooting video.

At this point, *Trouble the Water* cuts to a two-shot of the woman and her

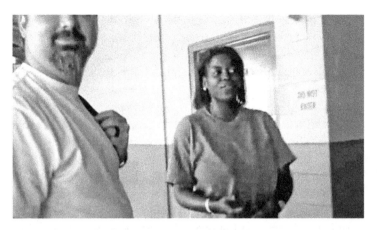

*Kimberly and Scott Roberts interrupt Carl Deal's interview with shelter officials in Alexandria, LA (*Trouble the Water, *frame capture).*

husband, seen earlier in a panning shot, a typical documentary introduction shot. Deal is heard off camera, directing them.

> DEAL: Into the camera, please.

The man and woman introduce themselves.

> SCOTT: My name is Scott Michael Roberts . . .
> ROBERTS: (interjecting) And I'm Kimberly Roberts.
> SCOTT: (continuing) . . . and this is my wife, Kimberly Roberts.
> DEAL: Where are you from?
> SCOTT: We're from the Ninth Ward, New Orleans. Underwater.

Kimberly Roberts nods to the camera and then the scene fades to black.

This first scene of *Trouble the Water* reveals much about the process of documentary production and about the construction of documentary subjects. Deal and Lessin were experienced documentary producers, but *Trouble* was their first feature documentary. Lessin had directed and produced the hour-long social justice documentary *Behind the Labels* (2001), and she had served as supervising producer on Michael Moore's *Bowling for Columbine* (2002) and *Fahrenheit 9/11* (2004), two of the highest-grossing documentary films of all time. Deal had worked as an investigative journalist, and he served as archival producer on *Columbine* and as field and archival producer on *Fahrenheit*.

In 2005, Lessin and Deal were seeking to develop a feature documentary about National Guard troops from Louisiana. According to Lessin, their initial concept focused on the experiences of National Guard troops serving in Iraq and on the difficulties and dislocations experienced by ordinary citizens called up to serve (Lessin interview). After having shot some footage of National Guard troops in Iraq, Lessin and Deal identified Alexandria, Louisiana, as a location where they could shoot the return of National Guard troops and attempt to develop documentary subjects to follow.

When Katrina hit, they decided to head to Alexandria with co-producer Amir Bar-Lev. They planned to film the crisis in Louisiana in order to make the point that the National Guard troops deployed to Iraq were needed to respond to Katrina in Louisiana. Further, they wanted to emphasize the losses experienced at home by Louisiana National Guard troops.

Lessin, Deal, Bar-Lev, and crew were at the Rapides Parish Coliseum, a Red Cross shelter in Alexandria, Louisiana, two weeks after Katrina and the flooding of New Orleans. They intended to interview Red Cross staffers like Jeff about the impact of the storm and flood on National Guard families. Drawing on their work with Moore, Lessin and Deal conceived of their documentary as a critique of decisions by the Bush White House regarding open-ended troop deployment in Iraq and Afghanistan. They were strongly committed to this concept and had pre-produced the Alexandria shoot to yield footage to develop their concept.

Instead, Lessin and Deal met Kimberly and Scott Roberts, and they pivoted from their first concept toward a new and uncertain direction. Unlike fictional narrative, documentary film production—especially productions employing observational approaches—involves an openness to changing circumstances. While Lessin and Deal had researched and written treatments for their Louisiana National Guard film, they were not following a script. This approach to production enabled them to respond to Roberts's presence and to the promise of the footage she claimed to have shot of Katrina and the flooding of the Ninth Ward.

I CAME HOME FROM WAR

While Lessin and Deal shifted the focus of their feature documentary, Amir Bar-Lev made a documentary short called *New Orleans Furlough* (2006), developed from the initial focus on the Louisiana National Guard and produced by Lessin and Deal. Prior to working with Lessin and Deal, Bar-Lev had directed the documentary feature *The Fighter* (2000), about two friends returning to the site of Terezin (Theresienstadt) concentration camp in the Czech Republic. Bar-Lev raises questions of memory and meaning by having his subjects interrogate each other about their experiences. After *New Orleans Furlough*, Bar-Lev produced and directed *My Kid Could Paint That* (2007) and *The Tillman Story* (2010). Both films question the reliability of representation and the challenge of determining truth.

New Orleans Furlough opens with a scene of National Guard troops returning to Louisiana after a tour of duty in Iraq. One by one, the soldiers are met by loved ones. One man remains, waiting. In voice-over, this young, white soldier asserts that he is done with war and that he looks forward to seeing his "old lady." Bar-Lev's camera isolates him as he smokes and waits. Eventually, his fiancée shows up, but she does not demonstrate much emotion. The film continues to follow this soldier, providing viewers with access to his thoughts via voice-over interview. Despite his protest that he is done with war and is ready to get married, the soldier has trouble sleeping and longs for the "rush" he experienced in combat. After his fiancée decides that she is not ready to get married, he heads home to New Orleans to check on the status of the apartment he shares with his mother. He finds the lock broken, but he cannot determine if anything has been stolen. Having watched news reports about looting and crime in the city, the soldier projects his experience in Iraq onto New Orleans.

SOLDIER: I came home from war, and I get another one.

This misreading of New Orleans as war zone is fueled by post-traumatic stress, racism, and television news coverage. Like a twenty-first-century Travis Bickle, he arms himself, starts drinking, and begins to project his fears and anxiety onto others. In one shot, the camera frames him standing in front of a strip joint, holding a shotgun in one hand, a beer and a cigarette in the other. A sign reading "love acts" is visible behind him. But, unable to make a love connection with his fiancée, he focuses on hate and seeks violence. Sensing trouble, a New Orleans police officer confiscates his shotgun shells. Stumbling around the French Quarter, the soldier does not find the enemy combatants he expected.

SOLDIER: Obviously, it is not as dangerous as I thought it would be.

He eventually decides to leave New Orleans and return to his National Guard post. As he is driving out of the French Quarter, he passes a film crew in production, emphasizing the difference between the actuality of New Orleans after Katrina and media representations and individual projections. Unable to imagine options, the soldier decides to return to Iraq. The film ends where it began, with a shot of National Guard troops exiting a bus and reuniting with families. In the final shot, one soldier is alone in the frame, waiting for connection.

Through following an off-duty soldier back from Iraq to New Orleans, *Furlough* reveals one of the consequences of deploying active duty National Guard troops in New Orleans after Katrina. Drawing upon their experiences in Iraq, many National Guard troops misunderstood New Orleans as a war zone and American citizens as enemy combatants. In Iraq, lack of language skill, of cultural and political understanding, and of accurate information from their government led troops to profoundly misunderstand their environment and misread the intentions of Iraqi citizens. In New Orleans, troops projected many of the same misunderstandings onto their fellow citizens. In Lee and Pollard's *If God Is Willing and Da Creek Don't Rise*, an interview with Lt. General Russel Honoré, commander of Joint Task Force Katrina, underscores the extent of this reading of Iraq onto New Orleans. As National Guard troops finally entered New Orleans on Friday, September 2, 2005, they were on high alert and targeted fellow citizens as hostiles. While Honoré was able to intervene in one case, which was captured by television news and reedited by Pollard, in many other instances, troops focused on security rather than relief and stripped fellow Americans of their shared citizenship by treating them as enemies. *Furlough* shows one example of how a soldier could return from Iraq and fundamentally misunderstand his own city.

Furlough also demonstrates the different experience of those who remained in New Orleans and experienced the flood versus those who were outside the city (because of resources or chance) and avoided the flood. In *Furlough*, the soldier's misreading of New Orleans is only possible because he does not connect with other people and cannot understand other perspectives. As David Grossman has argued, in order for soldiers to kill in wartime, they must discount the humanity of their enemies (1995). Successful warfare depends on dehumanization (via culture, discourse, and technology) and demonization of others. According to Grossman, soldiers have difficulty killing others to whom they feel connected by common experience. By choosing to follow Kimberly and Scott Roberts, Lessin and Deal construct a film about the lived experience of survivors of the flooding of New Orleans. *Trouble the Water* offers an answer to *Furlough*'s soldier, forging connection with human experience.

Lessin and Deal's decision to construct *Trouble*'s first scene from the chance encounter with Roberts was both necessary and revealing of their approach to documentary. Instead of simply introducing Roberts, this scene also introduces the birth of a documentary idea. Deal and camera initially bracket out Roberts, excluding her from the frame and asking her to meet them at another location. But, as Roberts persists, the camera moves away from Jeff to find her. In near real time, we see the filmmakers decide that the shelter is not the story of the scene, that Jeff is not as important as Roberts, and that their film has begun to change. Once Roberts reveals that she has video footage of her experience of the flooding in the Ninth Ward, *Trouble the Water* is born as a story about a native New Orleanian's unique perspective on the flood.

As New York-based filmmakers, Lessin and Deal need Roberts's perspective to make a film about the flooding of New Orleans. They brought to the project experience in helping make feature documentaries in which the filmmaker is a prominent character onscreen. However, despite working closely with Michael Moore on his feature documentaries and on his television show, *The Awful Truth* (Bravo, 1999–2000), Lessin and Deal do not adopt his method. They decline to place themselves at the center of their film. Instead, they choose to include their voices or images only when the inclusion reveals important information about the construction of their documentary film. Thus, Deal's voice and image are present in the first scene because the filmmakers wish to show how they first met Kimberly Roberts and how their idea for a documentary changed. Later in the film, Lessin is heard on a phone call with Roberts, discussing a missing check from FEMA, and Deal is heard in voice-over asking Scott about their motivations for moving to Memphis. As with all documentarians, Lessin and Deal are present in their film through their choices. At times, they make viewers aware of some of these choices. They do so in order to make their film more reflexive, so that viewers can understand how the filmmakers interacted with their main character to construct a film about Kimberly's experience of Katrina and about their experience of making a film about Kimberly.

Lessin and Deal also avoid the trap into which filmmakers Ed Pincus and Lucia Small place themselves. Pincus and Small co-directed and co-produced *The Axe in the Attic* (2007), another documentary made by Northeasterners about the impact of Katrina on New Orleans. Pincus had shot documentaries about the civil rights movement in the South in the 1960s and 1970s, but he left filmmaking in the early 1980s. Small directed her first documentary, *My Father, the Genius*, in 2002. Like most Americans, Pincus and Small watched television news coverage of Katrina and the flooding of New Orleans. Unlike most Americans, they decided to make a documentary about a place and an experience about which they knew very little. Moreover, without strong connections on the ground in New Orleans and without significant resources or support, Pincus and Small decided to place themselves at the center of their film. *The Axe in the Attic* became less about the experience of New Orleanians, and more about Pincus and Small's efforts to get to New Orleans and to understand what happened. Their lack of knowledge and connection became the film's focus. Moreover, much of the film is devoted to how they feel about the challenge of making the film. Unlike Lessin and Deal, Pincus and Small unapologetically offer narration and place themselves in front of the camera.

> PINCUS: Staying behind the camera just does not seem an option.

Initially, this feels like a reflexive move, and viewers expect the filmmakers to address the limitations of their knowledge and of the documentary apparatus itself. Pincus and Small might have approximated James Agee and his lacerating self-doubt in *Let Us Now Praise Famous Men*. Instead, they seem self-indulgent and lost.

> SMALL: I'm stressed out. We don't have a map. I missed a turn. We're lost.

Small and Pincus might have used their getting lost as an opportunity to examine their standing to make a film about Katrina. Instead, Small focuses not so much on being lost as on how the experience is stressful to her. Compared to the stress experienced by Kimberly Polk, whose daughter was drowned in the Ninth Ward, or by Kimberly and Scott Roberts, trying to lead thirty people out of New Orleans, the stress of a filmmaker trying to find her way into New Orleans after Katrina seems inconsequential.

Pincus and Small also rely too heavily on television news as a source of information and orientation. As with many other documentaries on Katrina, *The Axe in the Attic* uses and re-cuts network footage to approximate the experiences related by survivors, without acknowledging that those television reports were strongly pre-produced, shaped by ideas, values, and conventions brought to New Orleans by national news networks. Documentaries informed by and based on this partial, interested, and significantly flawed record build arguments on unsafe foundations. Alternative voices, images, and versions that challenge and complicate television news are desperately needed if the historical record and collective memory are to understand Katrina in all of its dimensions.

Lessin and Deal avoid the pitfalls of Pincus and Small by including themselves in *Trouble* only when their presence increases the viewer's understanding of how the documentary makes meaning. Otherwise, they keep their focus on Kimberly Roberts. While Lee and Pollard seek to provide a panoramic view of Katrina by including many interviews and voices in *Levees* (and by returning to many in *Creek*), Lessin and Deal instead choose to focus their story on one woman's experience of the storm and flood. Of course, in the case of *Trouble*, the main character also brings to the film unique video footage and dynamic perspective.

BREAKING IT DOWN FOR THE '05 DOCUMENTARY

The single most unique element of *Trouble the Water* is Kimberly Roberts's video footage. Indeed, her footage is unique among all representations of Katrina for showing the first-person perspectives of a resident of the Ninth Ward before, during, and after Katrina and the failure of the levees.

Jon Siskel and Greg Jacobs's *Witness: Katrina* (2010) is a compilation documentary created from multiple sources of video. Siskel and Jacobs had previously created *102 Minutes That Changed America* (2008), a near real-time retelling of the September 11, 2001, attacks on the World Trade Center and the collapse of both towers. To tell the unfolding story of that morning, Siskel and Jacobs compiled amateur and professional footage from a wide array of sources. *102 Minutes* provides new, unseen perspectives on September 11. In *Witness: Katrina*, New Orleans filmmaker and producer Rebecca Snedeker worked as a combination field and archival producer for the Chicago-based Siskel (nephew of the late film critic Gene Siskel) and Jacobs, finding and licensing first-person amateur footage of the storm and flood. Together with professional documentary footage and television news footage, the amateur footage found by Snedeker for *Witness: Katrina* is at times as immediate and revealing as Kimberly Roberts's footage.

However, Roberts's footage is the product of one shooter and one consistent voice. This consistency of perspective distinguishes her footage from the multiple perspectives collected by Snedeker and shaped by Siskel and Jacobs. *Witness: Katrina* presents a mosaic approach to Katrina, offering many views from many perspectives, where *Trouble the Water* uses Roberts's footage to offer the lived perspective of one person in one place. The focus of *Witness: Katrina* is on the hurricane and its aftermath. The focus of *Trouble the Water* is on Roberts's experience of the hurricane and flood, and her efforts to put her life back together in the aftermath.

After their initial encounter at the Red Cross shelter in Alexandria, Louisiana, Roberts agreed to allow Lessin and Deal to make a copy of her footage. Recognizing Roberts's potential as a documentary subject, Lessin and Deal offered to bring her, Scott Roberts, and their friend Brian Nobles (also visible in the scene at the shelter) back into New Orleans to visit their neighborhood. Lessin, Deal, Bar-Lev, two cinematographers, and a sound person accompanied Kimberly, Scott, and Nobles back to the Ninth Ward, shooting footage of the trip and of the New Orleanians' reactions to the devastation wrought by the flood. In this footage, Roberts directs their camera, explaining places of significance, reading the landscape for the filmmakers. She provides the professional documentarians with a way of seeing the impact and cost of the flooding of New Orleans.

Lessin and Deal did not review Roberts's footage until they returned to New York. They discovered that Roberts had shot approximately forty-five minutes of video over a three-day period, from Sunday, August 28, through Tuesday, August 30. In the days before Katrina, Roberts had purchased a secondhand Sony Handycam High-8 video camera. She shot her neighbors preparing for the storm, the experience of her family during the hurricane, and their efforts to escape swiftly rising flood waters. Over the three days, Kimberly's shooting was constrained by her available battery power and by the need to put down the camera to help herself and others to safety.

Roberts's footage demonstrates all the marks of amateur video. Lacking a tripod, she shot mostly handheld, and as a result her frame frequently moves, creating shaky images. As a novice cinematographer, she does not hold her shots, consistently panning and tilting and moving the frame, not always sure of her visual focus. Apparently, she used manual exposure because the quality of the image does not vary with changes to the lighting environment, and, as a consequence, some of her footage is over- or underexposed. All these factors mark her footage as unlike professional news or documentary footage of Katrina. These factors can make her footage difficult to watch, but they also provide a strong sense of immediacy. Roberts's offhand framing captures images and perspectives that would have been missed by a professional shooter. Her footage and her perspective are unique among Katrina media.

Working with editor T. Woody Richman, Lessin and Deal had to find ways to make Roberts's footage usable in their film. According to Lessin, the filmmakers were immediately struck by the unique access and strong images. Roberts's footage was a wholly unique element, justifying their impulse to follow her story. Yet, of the total forty-five minutes, the film-makers identified fewer than twenty minutes of usable material. From the larger footage, Lessin, Deal, and Richman worked to identify unifying elements and to build scenes.

The filmmakers use Roberts's footage extensively during the first third of the documentary. After the initial scene of their encounter with her and Scott, Lessin and Deal create their first scene from Roberts's footage. After Kimberly and Scott introduce themselves to camera and state that they are from the Ninth Ward, the film fades to black. A title appears on screen: "two weeks earlier." The image fades up on an extreme close-up of a television screen showing a weather report. Graphics on screen indicate that the temperature is 88 degrees and that skies are mostly cloudy. Underneath, a crawl moves from right to left, warning ALERT!! HURRICANE. A burn-in code is visible in the lower right of the frame, indicating the date as August 28, 2005. Over this image, Kimberly speaks to the camera mic.

ROBERTS: We got this hurricane Katrina coming.

The camera pans right of the television screen, then swings right to left to show Roberts, wearing a white T-shirt, addressing the camera.

ROBERTS: You know me, I'm still me, Kimberly Rivers.

Though the movement of the camera suggests that she does not have much experience shooting video, Roberts's introduction of herself demonstrates a sophisticated understanding of media presentation. Throughout her footage, Roberts uses the apparatus to address an audience and to shape messages. Even without clear plans for how to use or distribute her footage, she is already thinking about her self-presentation. Interestingly, she uses "Rivers," her maiden name, whereas elsewhere she describes herself as Kimberly Roberts. This moment suggests that Roberts is using the process of creating a video of Katrina as a process of self-expression, self-definition, and, given the ominous warning on the television weather report, self-preservation.

ROBERTS: Breaking it down for the '05 documentary, how it really is, starting right now.

Roberts makes clear that she intends not merely to create footage or home movies. From the jump, "starting right now," she conceives of her project as a documentary. Moreover, she reflects on the nature of documentary media by acknowledging an inherent truth claim. Roberts promises to show her viewer "how it really is." She seems to understand that what she lacks as a media professional will be offset by her direct experience and ability to break down what is happening to her and to her city.

As she speaks in synch to camera, Roberts frames herself from a slight high angle. Because she is holding the camera in one hand, toward herself, the image shakes. She then turns toward the room, her hand briefly covering the lens. Lessin, Deal, and Richman use moments like this to cut Roberts's footage. Where she shot in long, continuous takes, Lessin, Deal, and Richman create the impression of continuous action, while extracting less important or more visually distracting moments.

The scene continues with a handheld shot moving through the house, past a table and a gray-and-white cat, into the kitchen. Roberts indicates their preparedness by showing a bag of charcoal and some condiments. The image whips to the freezer, where she shows bags of ice and packages of hot dogs. The scene continues as the camera tracks to the rear screen door, looks out, and moves through the door into the backyard. Here, the images tilt down from a high angle to observe two dogs; one of the dogs leaps up at the lens. The image then turns, right to left, to show a chain-link fence. Through the fence, the camera observes five National Guard trucks speeding past. Here, Lessin, Deal, and Richman cut again, taking advantage of another whip pan to jump to an African American man packing a wheelchair into a pickup truck. From off camera, Roberts addresses her neighbor.

> ROBERTS: Y'all getting out of here? Ain't nothing wrong with that. If I had wheels, I'd be gone too.

By showing the mundane visual details of Kimberly and Scott's home, *Trouble* substantiates what was lost to the flood. Where other representations—on television news or in other documentaries—showed the aftermath of the flood, *Trouble* uses Roberts's footage to show how New Orleanians lived prior to Katrina. Food, pets, furniture are seen unspoiled, whole, alive. These images connect the more familiar shots of disgorged contents of homes and lives back to the people themselves.

In addition, this scene answers the assertion that New Orleans citizens who did not evacuate were themselves responsible for their fate. *Trouble* clearly indicates that Mayor Ray Nagin's mandatory evacuation order on Sunday, August 28, 2005, came too late for many citizens. An on-screen title informs viewers that the New Orleans government did not provide buses to evacuate citizens. By failing to provide emergency transportation,

Nagin and the city government effectively abandoned the most vulnerable citizens. As *Trouble* demonstrates, and as Roberts articulates, those who had transportation left. Like Roberts, those without transportation were left behind to save themselves.

Trouble is careful not to construct Roberts as a saint. As the scene continues, the image cuts as Roberts approaches a red car. The camera looks down at the car in an extreme close-up, and Kimberly and Scott are visible only as reflections in the car's surface.

DRIVER: You got weed?

Roberts answers obliquely, but the exchange makes clear that she and Scott deal drugs.

ROBERTS: Hey, I'm gonna have to shut it off, bra, cause I don't know when I'm going to get some in. I'm trying to hold down for the fucking storm.

Her choice to create the unusual framing on the car might have been to protect the identity of her client. Lessin and Deal include this moment in the film so that their viewers will understand that Roberts deals drugs. For Lessin and Deal, this information not only complicates Kimberly and Scott, but it also reveals their limited economic options in pre-Katrina New Orleans. This brief moment speaks to the struggles Kimberly and Scott faced before Katrina.

Lessin and Deal end their scene with Roberts's own sign-off to camera. As she speaks, she tilts the camera up to frame her face. As with her self-introduction, Roberts's use of a sign-off demonstrates her awareness of the conventions of television news and documentary media. She is self-consciously referencing and playing with convention in order to create her own representation of her experience and the experience of her neighbors in the Ninth Ward.

ROBERTS: Anyhoo, signing off, off top, it's me, Kold Madina. 'Til later.

Roberts's images are unconventional and revealing, her mistakes providing perspective that a professional cameraperson would not think to attempt. For example, her representation of a potential drug deal provides proximity to the exchange but also conceals details that might yield consequences. Roberts's video is also marked by her strong and unique address.

*Kimberly Roberts reporting as "Kold Madina" (*Trouble the Water, *frame capture).*

Here, she signs off using a pseudonym, "Kold Madina." Lessin and Deal reveal later that Roberts is an aspiring hip-hop artist who self-produced a CD prior to Katrina. Roberts raps as Black Kold Madina, seemingly a reference to Tone Loc's hit song "Funky Cold Medina" (1989). She brings the bold assertion of rap to her performance to and off camera. Her verbal expressiveness and play with language and media convention draw on the practices of the hip-hop MC. Roberts's rapping and her media creation share the goal of creatively expressing details of her life and experience. Both her music and her video speak to her unique experience and individual value as a person. Through her creation, Roberts makes an argument against necropolitics, against being categorized as unimportant, expendable, already dead.

YOU GOT ME ON CAMERA

After determining that no more than twenty of the forty-five minutes shot by Roberts were usable in *Trouble the Water,* Lessin and Deal worked with Richman to determine how best to employ the usable footage. About eight minutes of this footage focused on Sunday, August 28, before Katrina made landfall. Lessin, Deal, and Richman created three scenes from this footage, including the scene analyzed above. Approximately six minutes of footage focused on Katrina, the failure of the levees, and the flooding of the Ninth Ward. They shaped this material into eight scene fragments, between a half-minute and a minute-and-a-half long. Lessin, Deal, and Richman used these moments, intercut with television news and other found footage, to tell the story of Kimberly and Scott's experience during the storm and their escape from the flood. About two minutes of footage focused on the immediate aftermath of the storm, as Kimberly, Scott, and a few neighbors moved from the Roberts house to a taller building across the street. Lessin, Deal, and Richman organized this material into three short pieces. In all, they used a little more than sixteen minutes of Roberts's footage in *Trouble the Water*, about 17 percent of the film's total running time of ninety-three minutes. Roberts herself appears in almost every scene in the film, excepting the found footage and a short scene of Scott working for a building contractor a year and a half after Katrina.

In the third pre-Katrina scene constructed from Roberts's footage, Lessin and Deal explore the competing urges to prepare and to party. For many New Orleanians, hurricane preparation was as much about anticipation and a break with usual routines as about actual consequences. At a little more than five minutes, this is the longest pre-Katrina scene, and it contains some of Roberts's most striking images. Since the viewer knows that Katrina is coming and that the New Orleans levee system failed, flooding 80 percent of the city, the attitudes and choices of the citizens who could not evacuate become loaded with significance. Even for viewers who had not seen *When The Levees Broke*, the dark knowledge communicated by the dead body montage hangs over Roberts's footage. Some of the neighbors she filmed died in the storm and flood.

The third scene begins with a shot looking down at the silver handlebars of a bike as Roberts pedals through her neighborhood. Her knees, clad in blue jeans, come into the frames with each revolution of the pedals. As she approaches a stop sign, Roberts brings the camera up, only to let it fall again as she picks up speed. The angle is distinctive. Where a professional might use a bike to create a low-tech tracking shot, or where an amateur might attach a camera to the handlebars facing forward, Roberts makes the unorthodox choice to shoot while also riding her bike. Lessin and Deal keep the shot because it is formally striking, because Roberts talks about her neighborhood as she bikes, and because the shot establishes the next location for the scene, the K&M Super Market, Super Meat Market. The bike shot does convey a strong sense of the exhilaration of movement. After the tighter interior shots, this footage feels free, conveying formally the upside to the anticipation of hurricanes. While many residents of New Orleans have evacuated, Roberts's Ninth Ward neighborhood is still full of people on Sunday afternoon.

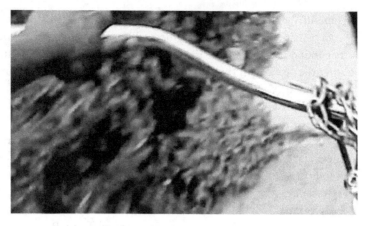

*Roberts's first-person shooting while riding a bike through the Ninth Ward (*Trouble the Water*, frame capture).*

Lessin, Deal, and Richman cut to Roberts's arrival at the local market and butcher shop. With a quick tilt, the camera creates an establishing shot of the market's signage, painted on its exterior wall: "K & M Super Market, Super Meat Market." They cut again as Roberts enters. Her purpose is to shop and to shoot, and she asks a young African American man if he intends to stay.

YOUNG MAN: Yeah, man. I'm going to be here.

The image then pans left to right, and back through the store, observing the rows of goods and the counter.

ROBERTS: In case it's all gone.

Roberts is making a record of her neighborhood, the ways she and her people lived. The mundane act of biking to the store takes on special significance due to looming events. While she and her interview subjects do not seem to take the threat of the hurricane too seriously, her proposition was borne out. The store and all of its contents would be destroyed by floodwaters within twenty-four hours.

But Roberts and her footage are not portentous. She is not at the K & M only to make a social historical record. She is also there to shop.

ROBERTS: Look, let me get a pound of smoked neck bones. Cut 'em up for me.

The camera pans left to right, looking at the meat counter, as she places her order. Smoked neck bones are slow cooked and used in various dishes, including greens and white beans. Presumably, Roberts intended to cook a pot of beans or greens, hurricane preparedness Ninth Ward–style. Lessin, Deal, and Richman cut to a shot of two African American men behind the counter. Next to them stands a white man, with a mustache, glasses, and a cap worn backward. The white man glares at the camera, but Roberts maintains her framing, keeping the focus on him.

ROBERTS: What you looking at? You got me on camera. Shit.

Not only is Roberts conversant in the conventions of television news and documentary, she also understands intimately the use of video for surveillance and control. Here, she turns her consumer video camera on K&M's proprietor, challenging his right to take security video of his customers. Her look back at him is measured, but insistent. Roberts is using media to reverse the direction of surveillance, to assert the right of a customer to record the property owner, a black woman using the apparatus to reverse the usual power dynamic in which the white male owner can look and record. Lessin and Deal use this moment in *Trouble* to reveal Roberts's sophistication and her critical use of video. For viewers of television news coverage of Katrina, Roberts's reversal of the usual dynamic of property over people takes on additional importance after the official shift of resources from search and rescue to protection of property. In a crisis zone, military and civil authorities can requisition property. When the federal government suspended the social contract after Katrina, deciding not to provide for the needs of all American citizens, survivors in New Orleans took food and water out of necessity. As shaped by Lessin and Deal after Katrina, this moment reads as a challenge to the prioritization of property.

Trouble next cuts outside the K&M, as Roberts interacts with three men drinking beer. The camera frames a thin older African American man in a close-up. He is wearing wraparound sunglasses, a camouflage hat turned backward, gold earrings, a white shell necklace over a clean white T-shirt, and a messenger bag over his shoulder. He is visibly drunk. Roberts addresses him as her uncle.

UNCLE: I went to work. They were closed. I ain't never been so happy.

His friend, wearing a Detroit T-shirt, enters the frame and pretends to fight with her uncle.

"What you looking at? You got me on camera. Shit" (Trouble the Water, *frame capture*).

> ROBERTS: The police ain't gonna come, cause they got to wait for
> the hurricane.

This comment breaks up the three men. The third man, wearing a stained Rocawear jersey, reaches to dap the hand holding the camera, creating an unusual moment of intimacy and connection between camera and subject. The man's gesture causes the frame to move, producing a visual record of his profilmic presence. Again, recalling Lee and Pollard's montage of dead bodies, most of them African American men, this scene is both funny and freighted. While Roberts prepares for the storm by getting food and ice, her uncle and friends celebrate the freedom from work by getting drunk.

The image then pans over to a small group of women and boys on a stoop across from K&M. Roberts engages them, underscoring, with humor, the potential stakes for her media making.

> ROBERTS: It's going to be a day to remember. That's why I'm
> recording. Hey, if this really hits, I'll be having something to
> show my children. If I get some exciting shit, I might could sell
> it to them white folks.

Roberts understands the value of her footage. Her footage is a personal record, an enhancement for her own memory and the memories of her family. Here, Roberts acknowledges Katrina as a threat not only to homes and to bodies, but also to memory and community. Roberts shot video in order to preserve the everyday social history of her neighborhood, for herself and her people.

She also understands her footage to have value to others, including the national media, whom she perspicaciously identifies as "white folks." Even before Katrina, and coverage by the television news networks, Roberts understands that no one else would have thought to make a record of how life was lived in her neighborhood. She understands that in the worst case, if New Orleans were destroyed, her footage would become newsworthy, important to others far distant from the Ninth Ward. Roberts understands that her amateur video could become part of the historical record.

Of course, Lessin and Deal are also white folks interested in Roberts's footage. They chose to use this moment in order to acknowledge their own relationship to Roberts's footage. They want and need her "exciting shit" in order to make a documentary about her experience of Katrina. Rather than pay her outright, as a television network would, they enter into a partnership with her. Beginning at the Red Cross shelter, Roberts becomes a collaborator with Lessin and Deal, even as she becomes the main character of their film. Roberts is self-authored to a significant degree. Lessin and Deal can work with her, but they cannot ultimately use her. By choosing to develop *Trouble* as a participatory documentary, Lessin, Deal, and Kimberly Roberts collaborate to create one of the most revealing mediations in response to Katrina.

LOOK AT THIS GUY

Lessin and Deal conclude their third scene built from Roberts's footage with her encounter with her uncle, now passed out. The image again shows a mobile tracking shot as Roberts bikes through the Ninth Ward. The image cuts as she stops, throwing down her bike. A young boy is visible, standing over his own bike. The soundtrack features wind noise, louder now than earlier in the scene. This use of wind noise as foreshadowing is an example of the work done by Lessin, Deal, and Richman on Roberts's footage. The filmmakers minimize the impression of shaping, while actually sweetening the footage with audio enhancements and precise cutting. Here, they add additional wind sound in order to underscore the coming storm and its rising effects. Under the sound of wind, the camera looks down at a shingle, blown off a nearby roof. The camera tracks with the boy as he stoops to pick up the shingle. Without the wind sound, this gesture would not signify. On the boy's movement, Richman cuts to a tracking shot up to Roberts's uncle, finding and framing him passed out on a stoop.

> ROBERTS: Look at this guy. Let's walk over here to this guy, see what he's going to be doing on the day of the hurricane.

Under this, the camera tracks into an extreme close-up on her uncle. This move produces an unusual image of her uncle's face. It shows him in the familiar vertical orientation of the documentary interview, but, to create this framing, Roberts must stand over him, turning the camera, as he is lying across a step. She adjusts what would be a canted framing, producing a conventional framing, but conveying some sense of the labor involved in the production of the image. In so doing, Roberts's shot individuates and emphasizes her uncle and also reveals the conditions of production of the image.

At first, Roberts plays with the conventions of the television news interview. She narrates to camera her intention to approach and observe him, inviting the viewer to join her in her observation. She frames her interest in terms of information gathering. She even pretends not to know him, addressing him several times as "sir."

Once she frames him in the extreme close-up, Roberts drops her performance as reporter, warning the boy not to emulate her uncle when he is grown. Then she leans down to address her uncle directly.

> ROBERTS: Nat! Get your ass up. Hurricane's gonna take you away from here.

With this, Uncle Nat rouses himself. Standing, he looks around, before staggering off, out of the frame. Roberts pans slightly to watch him. Her hand crosses the frame, as if waving goodbye. Like the moment at K&M, where her uncle's friend reached out to bump her hand, causing the camera to move, Roberts's gesture into the frame is personal, not professional. Lessin, Deal, and Richman keep this frame in their film in order to further demonstrate the complexity of Roberts's roles and her relation to her footage. In this brief moment at the end of a longer scene, Roberts is both reporter and concerned niece.

The discovery of Uncle Nat is surprising as Roberts had seemingly left him back at the K&M, drinking with his friends. By including her discovery of Nat, Lessin and Deal reveal that their editing of the footage is manipulating time. What seemed to be unfolding in near real time was a construc-

*Rain begins to fall in the Ninth Ward on Sunday, August 28, 2005 (*Trouble the Water, *frame capture).*

tion drawn from different temporalities. The discovery of Uncle Nat also reveals the film's manipulation of space, as he seems to be in two places at the same time.

Lessin and Deal manipulate time and space in order to demonstrate the cost of Katrina. Through the use of Roberts's footage, *Trouble the Water* shows the unfolding story before the storm and flood. Shaped by the filmmakers long after Katrina, this moment is also a farewell between Roberts and her uncle. When Lessin and Deal filmed Roberts returning to New Orleans after the storm, they show her discovering Uncle Nat's body in the home of a relative. He drowned in the floodwaters. All documentary, as all media, manipulates time and space to create unities, themes, arguments, and stories. Here, Lessin and Deal reveal something of that work to underscore how one man was killed by the floodwaters when the levees failed.

This third scene concludes with Roberts's camera looking out from her front porch, panning right and left to observe neighboring houses and trees blown by the wind.

> ROBERTS: They say on the news we should get out, but they got some people who just can't leave. Like me. Not that we didn't want to, but we couldn't afford the luxury.

This voice-over underscores the context for Roberts's video. She stayed and shot footage not because she was a journalist or filmmaker, but because she could not afford to evacuate, did not have a car, and was not provided with emergency transportation by the city. Lessin and Deal emphasize the human cost involved in the production of the footage. Roberts's record exists because she suffered and almost died in the flood.

WE GOING TO PLAN B HERE

One of the biggest problems with television news as the dominant source of imagery for almost all subsequent work on Katrina is that television news missed the opportunity to cover Katrina's landfall, the breaching of the levees, and the subsequent flooding of the City of New Orleans. As noted, television news picked up the story of the flooding late in the day on Monday, August 29, hours after floodwaters entered the city. Unlike professional media makers, Kimberly Roberts was in the Ninth Ward as Katrina made landfall and as the levees failed. For this reason, her footage is an extremely important contribution to the visual record of Katrina, providing access to events only described in other sources.

Working with Richman, Lessin and Deal shaped Roberts's footage into a series of short scenes depicting the approach and arrival of the storm and the impact of the flooding. A burn-in code reveals that the first footage was shot during the early morning hours on Monday, August 29, 2005. The image is dark, illuminated only by a flashlight. Roberts shoots from inside her front door, looking out at rain and wind.

ROBERTS: Golly, look at that fucking water, boy!

The image cuts as Roberts swings the camera to the right toward her neighbors' porch. The flashlight reveals several people also looking out into the darkness.

ROBERTS: Y'all roof leaking?

The image cuts away from the neighbors to frame Scott peering down with a flashlight. Moving into a close-up, the image looks down at the front steps to their house. Water has risen to the top (third) step.

SCOTT: We may have to poke holes in the roof, get in the attic.

With this, the image pans away from the front steps, left to right, revealing Roberts holding the front door.

*Water rising in the early morning on Monday, August 28, 2005 (*Trouble the Water, *frame capture).*

ROBERTS: Anything is better than drowning.

The humor and anticipation that connected members of their Ninth Ward community in Roberts's footage from Sunday here begins to give way to anxiety and recognition of mortal peril. Katrina has not yet made landfall, and the streets are already flooding, threatening houses. Importantly, through the pan shots, this scene establishes that Kimberly and Scott are not outliers, not alone. Other neighbors have stayed and are now threatened.

In the second scene during Katrina, the camera peers out of the back screen door. Low light is visible, heralding the dawn. The image looks around the door, finding water covering the entire backyard. In the left of the frame, a car is visible, water up to the windows.

SCOTT: You see how high this shit is?
ROBERTS: Holy Jesus!

The image cuts with the screen door shutting, next showing Roberts's face, wet with rain. She moves with the camera from the back to the front of the house, the camera tracking the jumping light from a flashlight. Roberts opens the front door, and the shot shows water covering the entire porch. Two bikes are submerged. The image pans from right to left, looking at the heavy wind and driving rain.

ROBERTS: We going to plan B here. Plan B is we might have to start stacking our furniture to get to the roof.

*Water rises onto Roberts's porch (*Trouble the Water, *frame capture).*

Even as they take steps to save their lives, Roberts continues to shoot and to document their experience. She continues to address an audience, recognizing that she is producing a record and communicating her perspective. The video camera becomes a response to the possibility of drowning and annihilation.

At this point, Lessin and Deal add an onscreen title—"the New Orleans levee system is failing"—recognizing their own audience, a national audience potentially lacking in detailed knowledge of events on the ground. Kimberly and Scott's actions speak more powerfully than the title about events and potential consequences.

With a cut, the scene jumps ahead. With more light coming in the window, the image shows Scott moving furniture. At this point, Roberts puts the camera on a table and jumps in to help with the furniture. The resulting shot is a striking departure from the relentless mobility of her amateur shooting style. For the first time, the frame is immobile. It is also oblique, as Kimberly and Scott can only be seen moving in the far background. This framing speaks to their desperation. Roberts does not have time at this juncture to find a framing. She does not even think to power down the camera, even though she is using up battery power. This shot reveals self-preservation overtaking self-documentation.

SCOTT: Wait, I'll help you get up first.

The image shows Roberts climbing up a pile of furniture. She has once again picked up the camera, and the image shakes as she climbs. Again,

Lessin and Deal have used a cut to advance time. As the image looks down from a high angle, water is visible inside the house, beneath the furniture.

SCOTT: Give me your foot.

The scene ends with a low-angle shoot looking up at the exposed beams of the roof.

The next scene begins with a pan across a space under the roof. The image shows light through cracks in the roof, rain dripping in, and wind audible. The image whips to show people, a cooler, and trash bags.

ROBERTS: So, me and my neighbors doing the best we can. Don't know how long we're gonna be up here.

The image pans, showing a woman, Scott, a boy, a little girl, and another woman.

ROBERTS: I got food, y'all. So, you're welcome to everything. There's ice, water, cold drinks. Mine is yours, until it's all gone.

Roberts is clearly performing to camera, addressing an audience beyond the attic space. While Lessin had argued that she and Deal had to construct Roberts as a character for their documentary, Roberts is also constructing herself in her footage. But, just as clearly, she is not just trying to appear beneficent. She and Scott have opened their home to their neighbors, offering shelter and sustenance, when the social contract eroded. As per Rebecca Solnit's argument in *A Paradise Built in Hell* (2010), Kimberly and Scott become their own first responders, saving themselves and their neighbors when the power of the state pulled back.

The fourth scene during Katrina begins with a pan over Scott, sitting on a roof board with his legs extended. The image cuts to a low angle up at Roberts's face, lit by a flashlight.

ROBERTS: It's 10-something. We still in the attic.

After showing the other people in the attic, the image looks down into the house. In the daylight, water can be seen flowing over the windowsill. The image shows their two dogs perched upon a mattress on top of the pile of furniture, above the water line. The image then tilts down dramatically, showing Roberts's bare feet as she walks across an attic beam toward a window.

*Roberts in the attic (*Trouble the Water, *frame capture).*

Once at the window, Roberts brings up the camera. The image cuts to a canted angle of water up to the top of a one-way sign. The image swings in a pan looking down the block, showing floodwaters up to eight feet. The images move right and then back again to the left, as if panning in disbelief. The sequence then cuts away from the attic to an image of President Bush smiling and tanned, addressing an audience in California.

The final scene during Katrina expands on the idea of citizen first responders. Roberts's camera continues to pan around, left-right-left, probing the images of water up to the top of a stop sign. The images frame Larry, their neighbor, floating into their house, holding onto a punching bag from World Sporting Goods, Mobile, AL.

> ROBERTS: It's like an ocean out there. Waves and shit. We be surfing and shit, you wanted to.

But, rather than surfing, Larry is using the punching bag to rescue neighbors who don't know how to swim, carrying them from one-story buildings to taller buildings, helping them through the water. Roberts had tried to shoot Larry during her bike tour of the neighborhood, but he was reluctant to appear on camera. Now, as she looks down with her camera from above, he reports on the status of their neighborhood.

> ROBERTS: Larry, how many people you see out there?
> LARRY: Just me. Myself. They bust the levee.
> ROBERTS: They bust the levee? You sure?

From the amount of water in the streets, Larry understands that the levees have failed. As with many residents of the Ninth Ward, remembering stories of intentional breaching of levees in 1927 to protect some parts of New Orleans from flooding, Larry attributes the breach to intention. Like a journalist, Roberts probes this story, seeking proof. However, even if the levee was not intentionally "busted," Larry can attest to the abandonment of his neighborhood. While police and rescue workers remained inside, protected from the storm, Larry swam out into the water to help fellow citizens. Naomi Klein argues that disaster capitalism has privatized

*Roberts shoots the street corner from her attic (*Trouble the Water, *frame capture).*

*Roberts films floodwaters from her attic (compare to figure on page 193) (*Trouble the Water, *frame capture).*

survival, forcing people to pay for private security to save them (2007). Larry offers evidence of Solnit's alternate vision of community as answer to the neoliberal state reneging upon the social contract.

To point up this contrast, Lessin and Deal include audio from recordings of 911 calls placed by New Orleans residents during Katrina. According to Lessin, they received access to the calls via a public records request. In a series of exchanges, residents call 911 to request assistance. In each case, the operator explains that citizens are on their own.

> OPERATOR: At this time, they're not rescuing.
> CITIZEN: I'm going to drown in my attic.

The bureaucratic responses are chilling, as operators express regret without emotion.

> CITIZEN: So, I'm going to die?

In contrast, the scene shows a high-angle long shot of Larry, swimming through water up to his neck. Another image shows Larry ferrying a child on the punching bag, and another shows a girl in an orange top clinging to Larry's back.

> LARRY: I'm standing up. Anybody who comes, I'm going to hold 'em. But you can't just panic.

These images of a citizen of the Ninth Ward rescuing other citizens are available to Lessin and Deal only because Roberts was present to shoot them. These images answer emphatically later arguments that New Orleans residents who stayed were foolish, lazy, or criminal. Using Roberts's footage of Larry's citizen response, Lessin and Deal argue that some New Orleanians were abandoned before the storm, due to failures in levee funding, construction, and maintenance; failures in evacuation planning and executing; and failures in providing for the safety of citizens. In response to the failures of the state, in an era of budget cutting and privatization of services, Lessin and Deal argue that citizens had no choice but to save each other.

WE ON THE LAKE

Kimberly and Scott and their neighbors were also rescued by Larry. *Trouble the Water* does not show footage of this rescue. Perhaps

Roberts had run out of battery power by this point. Perhaps her focus was solely on her safety and the safety of her husband and neighbors. Or, Lessin and Deal may have decided not to use this footage for technical or narrative reasons. Regardless, the next chronological image we see from Roberts is a shot of her house, taken from the building across the street, where her group sought refuge. This reverse shot provides a look back at the site of the previous scenes, scenes depicting the group's efforts to survive during the storm. In some ways, this reverse shot is closer to professional footage shot after Katrina had departed and after the levees had failed. Like CNN's Mark Biello, Roberts looks at a building from outside. The reverse reminds viewers of Roberts's unique perspective in the preceding scenes. Eventually, many camera people shot video looking at New Orleanians as they were pulled off rooftops or out of the water. Kimberly Roberts was one of the few citizens who showed the perspective of those left behind, shooting from the inside out.

Also, Roberts's reverse shot is a look back. The gaze in this shot is focalized with her experience, her history. Rather than trying to produce "exciting" images, Roberts is documenting her experience of survival. Typically, she does so with mordant humor.

ROBERTS: We on the lake.

The New Orleans Lakefront had long been a desirable and exclusive neighborhood. Lakefront residents enjoyed breezes off Lake Pontchartrain, and they built large homes in which to capture and enjoy the bounty of the lake. In contrast, the Ninth Ward is located between the Mississippi River and the MR-GO (Mississippi River Gulf Outlet) and is bisected by the aptly named Industrial Canal, which separates the Ninth Ward from the Lower Ninth Ward. Due to the breach in the 17th Street Canal, the Lakeview neighborhood also flooded. Looking through her camera out at the now calm expanse of water covering her neighborhood, Roberts compares the flooded Ninth Ward to the more affluent Lakeview by joking that she and Scott now live on the lake.

Roberts's footage from after the storm is increasingly pixilated, and Lessin and Deal chose to use very little of it. According to Lessin, when Roberts's battery ran out, she switched from her Sony High-8 camera to a still camera that could shoot MPEG video clips. These more compressed clips featured lower resolution than her earlier High-8 footage. As a result, Lessin, Deal, and Richman combined video from other sources with Roberts's video when constructing a scene that suggested Kimberly and Scott's escape from New Orleans in a borrowed truck. Roberts's footage of her neighbors and community before Katrina, and her footage during the storm and flood are used much more prominently by Lessin and Deal and offer much stronger contributions to the visual archive than do the limited shots created after the storm. Like Larry, but in her own way, with her camera, Roberts was performing an act of rescue and preservation of her community.

SOME PEOPLE I MET ARE DOING A DOCUMENTARY

In an interview for this book, Lessin emphasized the work involved in constructing Kimberly Roberts as a documentary character. As noted, Roberts's footage, edited and shaped by the professional filmmakers, only constitutes a small part of the film as a whole. *Trouble the Water* is not the story of Roberts's unique contribution to the visual archive of Katrina. It is the story of Roberts herself.

As Lessin indicated in an interview, on the basis of their initial encounter with Roberts, she and Deal agreed to bring Kimberly, Scott, and their friend Brian Nobles back to New Orleans to view their neighborhood and to check on their home. At this point, Lessin and Deal had not yet viewed Roberts's footage. They placed a cameraperson in an SUV with Kimberly, Scott, and Brian, and she shot them as they traveled back to New Orleans, discussing what they might see, calling relatives. In this footage, Roberts instructs Nobles on how to shoot with her Sony camera. Lessin and Deal use some of Nobles's footage of Kimberly and Scott, shot from the front passenger seat, in the final film, intercutting his footage, marked by overexposure, with the footage shot by their professional cameraperson. In a cell phone conversation with a relative, Roberts explains what they are doing.

> ROBERTS: Some people I met are doing a documentary, a real documentary . . . at the same time I am teaching Brian to be a director.

Lessin and Deal use this short scene, documenting the process of Kimberly and Scott's return to New Orleans, to reveal Roberts as a character. As her own footage of the aborted drug deal demonstrated, she and Scott were involved with crime and drugs before Katrina. At age thirteen, Roberts lost her mother to AIDS. She was raised by her grandmother and other relatives, but she also spent much time in the streets, pursuing pleasure and being pursued. Yet, as indicated in her own footage, she also

*Roberts shooting with her Sony Handycam during her first return to the Ninth Ward (*Trouble the Water, *frame capture).*

cared about her community. She checked on neighbors, showed interest in the perspectives of young girls, convinced her uncle to find a safe place to sleep off his drunkenness, and warned a young boy to avoid her uncle's fate. Most tellingly, during the storm, she rescued and fed her neighbors. She and Scott brought many of these neighbors out of the water to shelter in Alexandria. Brian Nobles was one of the people they collected. Kimberly and Scott did not know Nobles before Katrina, but after finding him floating in a tub, they brought him with them to Alexandria. After parting with the rest of their neighbors, Kimberly and Scott kept Nobles with them. A drug addict, in recovery before Katrina, Nobles is intelligent, but vulnerable. Roberts pays special attention to him, and Lessin and Deal use their relationship to define Roberts's compassion and concern for others. In the scene in the van, Roberts teaches Nobles how to use the High-8 camera, sharing her process with him and inviting him to collaborate with her in shooting footage. After creating such vitally important images of the storm and flood, Roberts easily surrenders the camera, seemingly knowing that Nobles needs a purpose and a way to process his experiences. In this scene, her documentary comes together with Lessin and Deal's "real documentary," and Roberts teaches Nobles to become a filmmaker.

In post-production, working with Richman and others, Lessin and Deal construct a story about Kimberly and Scott. This story begins with how they survived and documented the storm and flood. The story continues with how they helped others, including Nobles and Roberts's brother Wink, and how, in the process, they changed themselves. After Katrina, the story follows them as they seek a new life, first in Alexandria, then in

*Brian Nobles learning to shoot video (*Trouble the Water, *frame capture).*

Memphis. The story shows how Roberts found expression through music and how Scott found expression through working for a contractor to re-build his neighborhood. Throughout, as *Trouble the Water* tells their story, Kimberly and Scott speak out against injustice. The film concludes with Roberts participating in a protest rally at City Hall, where the Free Agents Brass Band plays "We Made It Through that Water."

In telling this story, Lessin and Deal do not bind themselves to chronology. *Trouble the Water* begins two weeks after Katrina, before returning to the day before the storm. The filmmakers intercut Roberts's footage with their own footage of Kimberly, Scott, and Brian's return to New Orleans. In so doing, they make the most of Roberts's footage, creating suspense and meaning from her images. They also suggest the working and structure of memory. As in other scenes of return, from the Blanchards in *When the Levees Broke* to Irving Trevigne in *Faubourg Treme* (2009), Kimberly, Scott, and Brian have difficulty reconciling their experience of seeing New Orleans after the floodwaters receded with their memories of their home. As with Terence and Wilhelmina Blanchard, Kimberly Roberts returns to New Orleans as part of a documentary film. Like Terence Blanchard, but unlike Trevigne, Roberts is a collaborator with filmmakers, helping them to make the documentary. Roberts works to invite Nobles into this process as well, understanding the importance of the documentary apparatus for providing shape to memory.

Kimberly and Scott lead Lessin, Deal, and crew through the Ninth Ward, explaining the significance of places and space. In these scenes, Kimberly and Scott perform what Peter Burke has described as a reconnaissance of the past (2001). In two instances, Kimberly and Scott use the presence of the documentary filmmakers as an opportunity to revisit and to investigate incidents that occurred in the immediate aftermath of the hurricane.

In the first case, Scott walks the documentary crew to the U.S. Naval Support Activity, a military installation in the Ninth Ward that did not flood after the levees failed. Two weeks before, after escaping with Larry to higher ground, Kimberly, Scott, Brian, and neighbors walked to the naval base to seek shelter. They were turned away at the gate by armed guards. In the documentary sequence, Scott's narrative is intercut with interviews with navy personnel. As with the NOPD's shift to focus on protecting property over search and rescue, the navy personnel prioritized the security of their base over the security of their people. An African American officer explained.

> NAVAL OFFICER: We had to do our job, protect the interest of the government.

In the second case, after being turned away from the naval base, Kimberly and Scott brought their group to Frederick Douglass High School. They were able to enter the building and find shelter in an unoccupied classroom. When Kimberly and Scott returned with Lessin and Deal, they found the school occupied by National Guard troops from Oregon. As Lessin and Deal observe, Kimberly and Scott are forced to seek permission from troops from the Pacific Northwest to enter a school in their own neighborhood. Nobles notes to one of the Guardsmen that he graduated from Frederick Douglass. Eventually, the group is admitted to the school, but they are closely monitored by the unit's press liaison. The clear implication is that without the documentary crew Kimberly and Scott would not have been given access to the school.

After shooting the classroom upstairs, they leave, walking past a group of Guardsmen playing cards on the steps of the school.

> ROBERTS: They are sitting on their asses waiting for a terrorist.

Once again, Roberts demonstrates both strong awareness and political critique. In K&M Super Market, Roberts confronted the owner who surveyed her, but objected to her filming him. Here, Roberts expresses a double critique: the executive branch of the federal government had been slow to deploy the National Guard to respond to the emergency in New Orleans and the Gulf Coast. Lessin and Deal had originally planned to make a documentary about the Louisiana National Guard, deployed to Iraq while their homes flooded. Roberts recognizes these failures. In her own footage, before the storm, she commented on military trucks moving through her neighborhood to higher ground. Outside the K&M, Roberts observed that NOPD would not focus on crime on the day before Katrina because they would be too busy worrying about their own safety. Lessin and Deal use the 911 audio to emphasize the cost of this decision.

Roberts also makes a second critique. Even after arriving in New Orleans, the National Guard troops focused their resources on the wrong problems. Rather than searching for the dead or missing, the National Guard focused on national security. The naval base was closed to American citizens in the name of security, just as the New Orleans Crescent City Connection bridge was barricaded by Gretna police so that American citizens could not cross to dry ground. Roberts's critique also suggests David Eggers's point in his nonfiction narrative, *Zeitoun* (2009), based on Syrian immigrant Ahmed Zeitoun's experiences in New Orleans after Katrina. A local businessman, Zeitoun spent the days after the storm helping others, until he was arrested and interred in a temporary prison facility constructed by the U.S. government in the Central Business District after Katrina. Rather than save drowning citizens, elements of the federal government created a scaled-down Guantanamo in which to imprison the populace. Roberts's critique picks up and amplifies the many ways in which the federal government failed its citizens during and after Katrina.

After looking and leaving with Lessin and Deal, Kimberly, Scott, and Brian returned to Roberts's uncle's house in Alexandria, Louisiana. The uncle's property was without running water. Lessin and Deal construct a scene in which a serviceman from the City of Pineville, Louisiana, shows up at the house and turns on the water. After showing the group enjoying the small joy of access to water, the filmmakers cut to the same serviceman returning to shut off the water once again. A title indicates that five minutes elapsed between the water being turned on and the water being shut off.

NOBLES: Katrina is still going on. She is still trying to do damage.

Nobles's observation encompasses not only the water situation, but also the navy's response to their need and the National Guard's treatment of them as potential hostiles in their own neighborhood. Brian reminds the viewer that injustice existed before Katrina and that it continues after Katrina. Katrina is just one of its names.

Even before picking up a video camera, Roberts had used performance to speak about injustice. As Lee and Pollard emphasized in *When the Levees Broke*, New Orleanians have long used the performance of culture as a way to document injustice and to articulate alternatives. Before Katrina, Roberts had self-produced a CD of original hip-hop. Performing as Black Kold Madina, Roberts wrote, performed, and recorded a self-financed CD, seeking to develop a new career as a rapper. Hip-hop became a significant musical form in New Orleans with the rise of Cash Money Records and No Limit Records in the late 1990s. Nationally known New Orleans rappers include Master P, Mistikal, Juvenile, and Lil Wayne. "Bounce," a significant regional hip-hop variant developed in New Orleans, involves queer and transgender performers, such as Big Freedia and Katy Red. Roberts was connecting to these developments and seeking to create an opportunity to become a professional culture producer instead of a part-time drug dealer.

Trouble the Water does not develop Kimberly as a rapper until late in the film. When Kimberly, Scott, and Brian relocate from Alexandria to Memphis, they stay with members of her extended family. A cousin drives up blasting hip-hop from his car. Lessin and Deal's cameras frame Roberts as she recognizes her CD playing from her cousin's car. Many culture producers in New Orleans lost all of their work in the flooding of the city. When his Mid-City home was flooded, filmmaker Stevenson Palfi lost all his footage from his documentary in progress on pianist Allen Toussaint. Palfi later committed suicide. Roberts believed that her music had been destroyed when her house flooded. Her cousin possessed the only existing copy of her CD. As she relates to camera, she intends to use it as her new master in order to start again to produce her music.

Having established the continuity of her music, Lessin and Deal build a scene in which Roberts performs her song "Amazing" along with the CD. The scene occurs inside her cousin's house, and Nobles is her primary on-screen audience. As noted, Nobles is a tertiary character, but one who provides significant insight ("Katrina is still going on"). Roberts takes a strong interest in Nobles, and her scenes with him reveal her compassion and concern for others. Lessin and Deal also use Nobles as a point of contrast to Kimberly and Scott. While they find ways to respond to Katrina and rebuild their lives, Nobles does not. Roberts has her video and her hip-hop, while Scott eventually finds a satisfying job with a local contractor. Lessin and Deal use Nobles to show how Katrina continued to grind down survivors, long after the floodwaters had subsided.

Nobles's status was contingent before the storm. Through titles, the filmmakers reveal that he was attempting to overcome addiction, living in a halfway house tied to a local church. Since he could not furnish proof of residency in his temporary quarters, Nobles was ineligible for aid from FEMA or other sources. Kimberly and Scott had to struggle to get support, but they finally received some funds from FEMA. Nobles had nothing. Lessin and Deal do not resolve Nobles's situation in the film. Apparently, he fell out of the project after Memphis, separating from Kimberly and Scott, possibly relapsing. Without footage of Nobles, Lessin and Deal maintain their focus on Roberts. The result is that Nobles disappears from the documentary. His unexplained absence suggests the continued costs of Katrina, as many survivors succumbed to depression, despair, or addiction. His disappearance stands in for the loss and absence of so many others. Katrina is still going on.

Nobles's subsequent absence from the film makes his final scene with Roberts more significant. Excited to share her music with her new friend, she plays the CD and begins to extemporaneously accompany herself. The song she performs combines self-assertion with defiance.

ROBERTS: I don't need no one to tell me I'm amazing!

Roberts's lyrics are frankly autobiographical. She describes her sadness and rage when her mother died of AIDS, a consequence of drug addiction. She admits to many of her own mistakes, including running the streets and selling drugs. She acknowledges that she was the target of predation, seemingly within and outside her family. She readily admits that she was "penitentiary prone," on a course to arrest or death. Yet, she emphasizes her efforts to respond, to change, to find ways to survive and to break from the cycle in which she was trapped. The song serves as personal history and self-therapy.

ROBERTS: I wrote that when I was depressed.

Roberts's performance of the song in the film demonstrates her effort to transcend her difficulties through performance and connection with other people. Lessin, Deal, and Richman alternate between shots of Roberts alone in the frame, two-shots with her and Nobles visible, and cutaways to Scott and her cousin listening and watching. Throughout *Trouble the Water*, Roberts has used the performance of self as a form of survival. Here, by rapping with her own recording voice, she makes explicit the vital importance of performance in her recovery and (re)construction of self. In writing "Amazing," Roberts used the form of the hip-hop song to retell her life story and to articulate her own understandings and meanings. In performing "Amazing" for Lessin and Deal's camera, Roberts concretizes her approach to the documentary process itself. Through Lessin and Deal's shaping intervention, she performs herself with herself, for a profilmic audience and for the eventual end-audience of the documentary.

More than any other, this scene reveals the work involved in constructing *Trouble the Water* and its meanings. *Trouble the Water* speaks so powerfully to Katrina, the flood, and survival because it is uniquely multi-voiced, built from the perspective of a survivor who is also an artist (an aspiring rapper and aspiring filmmaker), through the perspectives of filmmakers invested in making a film about the survivor as a character who is both representative and distinctive.

IT'S ME, KOLD MADINA

The significance of *Trouble the Water* is tied to the status of Roberts's footage and to her performance. *Trouble the Water* shows images, events, and (most importantly) perspectives that were not shown on television news or in other documentary films about Katrina. As noted, Kimberly Roberts's footage is unlike the first-person video curated into films like *Witness: Katrina* or posted directly to the web by amateur media makers. Roberts is plainly not a professional media maker. At times, she struggles with exposure, framing, and excessive camera movement. Yet, she also clearly has a strong sense of media conventions and has been a careful observer of media representations. In her footage, Roberts self-consciously plays with these conventions in order to capture voices, stories, and perspectives ignored in traditional, professional media sources. In this sense, her material is more than merely footage, images, and sounds collected by an amateur without a strong guiding perspective. Rather, Roberts's approach is marked by a strong and consistent intention. She shoots video in order to tell the story of her neighbors and neighborhood before, during, and after Katrina. She is self-aware enough to recognize her limitations as a videographer, and she responds with a strong sense of play.

For example, Roberts picks up and plays with the television news convention of addressing her audience via the camera, as a way of overwriting and commenting on her images. She adapts her hip-hop performance persona, Black Kold Madina, into her media performance persona, Kold Madina (perhaps eliding the "Black" in recognition of the potential value of her footage for an audience of "white folks"). Like Shepard Smith or Martin Savidge, Roberts introduces and signs off on each segment.

ROBERTS: Signing off, off top, it's me, Kold Madina. 'Til later.

More than her shooting, it is Roberts's address and her selection of interviews and places that mark her material as intentionally and meaningfully shaped. She understands that the dominant news media will not create stories about her neighborhood. Roberts sets out to create the stories missed by the dominant news media, and, in the process, she also critiques some of the limitations of news media formats. Pioneering a form of hip-hop newsmaking, Roberts draws on her song "Amazing" as a model, combining documentation and performance. However, rather than focusing on her own life and perspective, as she does in her hip-hop performance, Roberts uses her video camera to report on her neighbors.

In this sense, Roberts's video reportage challenges the claims of television news to provide national and international viewers with the truth of Katrina. Her citizen reporting reveals the gaps and absences in television news coverage of Katrina. While Carl Quintanilla and Shepard Smith reported from the French Quarter, interviewing tourists and property owners, Roberts reported from the Ninth Ward. CNN anchor Aaron Brown lamented the lack of a "wide angle" in the aftermath of Katrina, but Roberts's reporting argues that television news is intentionally narrow in its perspectives. With its strong conventions and practice of pre-production, television news tends to tell repeated versions of the same stories. Roberts's reporting sought the perspectives of young girls, mothers, men on the corner, perspectives missing from official news sources.

During the storm, as the levees failed and the city flooded, Roberts provided witness to the peril faced by those who stayed. While the television news networks looked down at flooded homes, zooming in from airplanes and helicopters, Roberts looked out from her back door, walked out onto her front porch as water rose to cover her steps. She interviewed her neighbors during the storm about the condition of their roof. She put down the camera in order to climb onto her roof to avoid the rapidly rising water. Yet, even in the face of drowning, Roberts maintained a sense of herself as citizen reporter. When Larry swam over to check on her, Roberts asked him about the status of other people. When he asserted that the levee had been blown, she pressed him for details. Kimberly Roberts's performance as reporter produced footage that revealed the experience of the storm and flood and its meaning for many of the citizens who were not able to evacuate New Orleans.

Roberts's video is marked by the intention to document and to report on life in the Ninth Ward and on the impact of Hurricane Katrina on the neighborhood. She addresses an intended audience by speaking into her camera mic while shooting footage. She selects and interviews members of her community. She visits and records footage of selected places in her community. She marks segments by introducing herself and by signing off as Kold Madina. She continues to shoot even as the storm and flood threaten her life and the lives of her family and friends. She shoots until she can no longer power her camera, then she shoots with a borrowed camera. Most significantly, she carried her footage with her when she evacuated, and she found a way to connect to and partner with professional film-makers in order to present her story to the wider world. Roberts's goal to address a wide audience is present from her first frames of video.

Of course, as noted, Lessin, Deal, and Richman had to do significant work on Roberts's footage in order to shape stories from it. According to Lessin, this work consisted of finding and refining moments incipient in Roberts's shooting. For all her effort to convey perspective to camera, Roberts did not have the tools or experience to edit her own footage. She was self-aware enough to recognize that she would need partners to bring her reporting to a wide audience. Thus, when Roberts met Lessin and Deal, the moment marked the coming together of two projects, from which emerged a new common project.

Lessin and Deal begin *Trouble the Water* with the scene in which Roberts meets the filmmakers. This decision is especially significant given the uniquely participatory nature of the common documentary project. Lessin and Deal understood the potential not only in Roberts's material but also in Roberts herself. *Trouble the Water* features citizen reporting on the impact of the flooding of New Orleans, but the film is about the citizen reporter herself, about how she used video as a way of responding to Katrina. The film is ultimately about how Roberts defined herself in response to the storm and flood. Her media making is an important part of this story, as is her rapping. In sum, *Trouble the Water* argues that Katrina presented Roberts with the challenge she needs to reshape her life through the use of media as a form of reporting and self-expression. Roberts doesn't need television news to tell her story. She tells a version of it herself, and Lessin and Deal shape this self-expression into a documentary feature film by observing Roberts's process of surviving and responding to the storm.

As a result, it is difficult to parse questions of authorship when considering *Trouble the Water*. Clearly, Roberts brings the strong perspective of an author to her video reporting and to her rapping. Her video is infused with her point of view, from her unusual formal choices (the bike perspective) to her interviews and observations. Also clearly, Roberts could not have made a film from her video without additional help. *Trouble the Water* is a professional feature documentary film. Lessin argues that, unlike the filmmakers, who drew on their experience as professional documentary media makers, Roberts would not have seen herself, or been able to construct herself as character. Indeed, it is the combination (if not collision) of the deeply located and personal perspective and the ambition by professional filmmakers to make a strong statement to national and international audiences that makes *Trouble the Water.*

Finally, through the joining of perspectives and approaches, *Trouble the Water* informs both history and memory of Katrina and the flooding of New Orleans. The film offers a counter-history to the record established by television news. Rather than look at flooded neighborhoods after the storm, *Trouble the Water* examines life in those neighborhoods on the cusp of the storm. It documents lives that were lost and a way of life that was imperiled. The film also provides images and perspectives on the flooding of the Ninth Ward. No other report, documentary, or fiction film about Katrina has provided this same access to images, voices, experiences, and perspectives. Like Pincus and Small, Lessin and Deal came to Katrina from the outside. Unlike Pincus and Small, Lessin and Deal worked with and developed the perspectives of a citizen survivor, a culture bearer, and a producer of new media. In *Trouble the Water,* the filmmakers participate with Roberts in the telling of her story. Through her story, they contribute to the visual history of Katrina. By challenging the conventions of television news, *Trouble the Water* offers a correction to the emerging collective, public memory of Katrina, changing how viewers see and understand the meaning and impact of Katrina. Per Brian Nobles, this work continues even as Katrina continues.

CHAPTER FOURTEEN

How Can Our Past Help Us to Survive This Time?

FAUBOURG TREME

*L*ESSIN AND DEAL'S *TROUBLE THE WATER* ADDED CITIzen reporting to the developing archive of images and sounds that currently constitute the historical record of Katrina. Kimberly Roberts's footage filled in gaps in the official visual record, first shaped by television news. By showing her neighbors before Katrina, during the storm, and after the flood, Roberts provided Lessin and Deal with an opportunity to correct and complicate the emerging record. *Trouble the Water* contributes to the present process of establishing what will become the history and fuel the collective memory of Katrina.

Dawn Logsdon and Lolis Elie's *Faubourg Treme: The Untold Story of Black New Orleans* (2009) is even more invested in history, both what is understood about the past and how those understandings are produced. Where *Trouble the Water* makes history, *Faubourg Treme* makes historiography. Elie himself is a key presence on camera in the film, and he voices *Faubourg Treme*'s central question, a question raised by Katrina and the flooding of New Orleans.

ELIE: How can our past help us to survive this time?

Elie and Logsdon are both New Orleans natives. Their own histories distinguish them from many of the most prominent documentarians of Katrina and link them to television news producer and New Orleans native Kim Bondy. For example, Lee and Pollard and Lessin and Deal are all New York–based filmmakers. S. Leo Chiang, director of *A Village Called Versailles* (2009), is based in Berkeley, California. Luisa Dantas co-produced *Wal-Mart: The High Cost of Low Price* (2005) with Robert Greenwald before moving to New Orleans to develop *Land of Opportunity* (2011). Katherine Cecil moved to New Orleans from the United Kingdom to continue her education, developing the research that became the basis of her film *Race* (2010). Logsdon's father was a historian at the University of New Orleans. She attended the University of California, Berkeley, and later became a prominent documentary editor based in San Francisco. Elie left New Orleans to earn degrees at Columbia University and the University of Virginia. He returned to become a reporter and a columnist for the *Times-Picayune* newspaper in New Orleans. On the basis of both his writing and his work in *Faubourg Treme*, Elie became a story consultant and eventually a writer for David Simon and Eric Overmyer's HBO series, *Treme*.

Logsdon and Elie's status as New Orleans natives is significant to their process of creating *Faubourg Treme*. Unlike Lee and Pollard or Lessin and Deal, Logsdon and Elie were not drawn to New Orleans by Katrina and its aftermath. Logsdon moved back to New Orleans in 1999 with the intention of beginning a project about New Orleans and its history. Elie explored Southern foodways and culture in the book *Smokestack Lightning: Adventures in the Heart of Barbecue Country* (1996, 2006), and he wrote and co-produced a documentary based on the book. When Logsdon and Elie decided to collaborate on a documentary film about New Orleans history, they chose to focus on the Treme neighborhood. Elie had recently purchased and had begun to restore a home there. Treme has a deep and vibrant history, having developed as an early extension of the original French settlement on the Mississippi River. It is also arguably the birthplace of jazz, as Louis Armstrong grew up and performed there. Throughout the twentieth century and into the twenty-first, Treme was ground for the production of much of the unique culture of New Orleans. Yet, the neighborhood was not well known outside New Orleans. Elie addresses this issue in voice-over during the opening scene of *Faubourg Treme*.

> ELIE: This is my neighborhood, Faubourg Treme. If you're not from New Orleans, you've probably never heard of it.

Today, many have heard of Treme from Simon and Overmyer's television series. The documentary *Faubourg Treme* is a significant intertext for the television series, inspiring not only the series' name and one of its locations, but also providing an orientation to the history of the politics of place.

Logsdon and Elie began production on *Faubourg Treme* in the years before Katrina, and they were in late post-production when the storm and flood devastated the city. In contrast to all other documentary films produced in response to Katrina, *Faubourg Treme* has a distinct identity separate from the storm and flood. Unlike Stevenson Palfi, Logsdon and Elie did not lose their footage, but they became concerned that their film would not find an audience if it did not engage Katrina. As a result, the filmmakers spent an additional eighteen months shooting new footage of Katrina's aftermath. They interviewed and observed their characters, tracking the impact of the flood on their lives. Ultimately, Logsdon and Elie became convinced of the relevance of their initial approach for understanding Katrina and subsequent events. Rather than abandon their initial focus on the importance of understanding the history of the Treme neighborhood, Logsdon and Elie determined that an understanding of Treme's history was necessary to the recovery of New Orleans.

If Brian Nobles is correct in his statement in *Trouble the Water* that "Katrina is still going on" weeks and months after the storm, Logsdon and Elie make a related argument that Katrina happened before August 2005. Nobles understands Katrina as another name for injustice. He believes that the storm and flood caused misery, but also revealed existing conditions. When Pineville turns on and then shuts off the water supply in five minutes, Nobles sees this prioritization of payment and process over human need as typical of other injustices in his life, including the destruction of his neighborhood when the federal levees failed. In *Faubourg Treme*, Logsdon and Elie argue that Katrina happened when the federal government removed protections at the end of Reconstruction in the late nineteenth century, allowing for white majorities to reassert control, reinstitute segregation, and deny African Americans the rights of citizenship. Katrina happened when the Supreme Court issued the *Plessy v. Ferguson* decision in 1895, making "separate but equal" the law of the land. Homer Plessy was a resident of Treme, and leaders based in Treme developed the legal challenge that would ultimately be refused by the Supreme Court. Logsdon and Elie argue that the challenges after Katrina were just like those after the Civil War: voting rights/agency, education, and reparation.

Logsdon and Elie draw on a more contemporary example to support their argument that Katrina must be understood within a much longer history of injustice and struggle. In the 1960s, using federal support, the City of New Orleans built the Interstate 10 Expressway over Claibourne Avenue, the main thoroughfare through the Treme neighborhood. *Faubourg Treme* argues that this site was chosen because of the lack of political power of the largely African American residents of Treme. The construction changed the neighborhood, perhaps more dramatically than did Katrina.

Faubourg Treme shares some approaches with Charles Burnett, Frank Christopher, and Kenneth Greenberg's film, *Nat Turner: A Troublesome Property* (2003). In *Nat Turner*, Burnett, Christopher, and Greenberg explore changes in understandings of Nat Turner over time and, in the process, how history and historical understandings are produced. The film investigates how historians, artists, activists, and Virginia residents have contested the meanings and status of Nat Turner. Some believe he perpetrated a massacre of local whites in Virginia in 1831, while others believe that he led a revolt or a struggle for liberation. *Nat Turner: A Troublesome Property* uses some of the traditional devices of historical documentary, including talking head interviews with academics and experts. The film also uses more radical and reflexive techniques, including re-creating and re-staging events from Turner's life, emphasizing the different interpretations of Turner offered from different perspectives. The filmmakers cast a different actor to represent Turner in each recreated sequence. For example, Carl Lumbly portrays Turner in a sequence re-creating the perspective on Turner offered by Thomas R. Gray in his *The Confessions of Nat Turner* (Tom Nowicki plays Gray in this sequence).

Faubourg Treme also uses experts including historians John Hope Franklin and Eric Foner, but otherwise eschews the conventional approaches of historical documentaries. Rather than focus on the interpretive power of experts, Logsdon and Elie emphasize the importance of community history and family memory. As noted, *Faubourg Treme* adopts some of the conventions of the essay film, featuring Elie sharing his impressions and interpretations to camera and in voice-over. The filmmakers use Elie's presence on screen to demonstrate the process of producing historical argument.

Faubourg Treme's central character is Irving Trevigne, a lifelong resident of Treme and a master carpenter. Elie meets Trevigne when he hires him to restore his home, and the filmmakers use the process of restoring the historic home as a symbol of the work required to preserve the material links to the past. Trevigne has lived in Treme for seven decades, and Logsdon and Elie draw on his lived experience to establish connections among the Reconstruction period, *Plessy v. Ferguson*, and the construction of the elevated Interstate 10 and the destruction of South Claiborne Avenue. The filmmakers use Irving Trevigne to introduce his ancestor, Paul Trevigne, a nineteenth-century resident of Treme, who published a newspaper and was a leading figure in Reconstruction and post-Reconstruction politics in New Orleans.

Logsdon and Elie explore Paul Trevigne's identity and significance in an extended sequence that poses the documentary's strongest historical and historiographic arguments. The sequence begins with an image of Irving, wearing blue overalls over a gingham shirt, working on Elie's French doors. The camera zooms out before dissolving to an image of Lenwood Sloan, an actor and a Treme resident, who leads a local group of historical reenactors called the Louisiana Living History Project. Sloan wears a tan top hat, a green coat, and a silver earring in his left ear. He stands outside St. Louis Cathedral, next to Jackson Square in the French Quarter. He tips his hat to a young white girl, a tourist dressed in a blue shirt and pink coat. This two-shot reveals the work of reenactment: Sloan's coat and hat, and his performance of courtesy, work to suggest the style and comportment of a nineteenth-century gentleman. The young girl's contemporary attire reminds the viewer that reenactment is a performance staged for the present in an attempt to suggest something about the past. Sloan is African American, and his performance and the girl's presence in the shot raise questions of race, class, and status, both for the past he attempts to suggest and for the present moment. To the girl, Sloan may only represent the past generally, not a specific history. New Orleans is packaged as a tourist destination that allows for visitors to play with the past without strong and specific engagement. Conscious of this tendency by the New Orleans tourist industry to exoticize and abstract the past, Sloan counters by anchoring his performance to a specific history.

SLOAN: Paul Trevigne at your service.

By dissolving from Irving to Sloan playing Paul Trevigne, Logsdon and Elie begin a sequence in which they seek to substantiate and explore the antecedents of the present, New Orleans in the twenty-first century, both pre- and post-Katrina. By cutting to the Sloan performance, the filmmakers begin to show the work involved in approaching the past. The connection via editing of living relative to reenactor lends weight to the performance of Paul Trevigne. The dark-skinned Sloan looks little like the light-skinned Irving Trevigne, but this difference raises questions about creolization, suggesting a history of intermarriage and racial and ethic intermixture. The racial difference between the actor and the girl suggests the different stakes involved in recovering aspects of the past.

SLOAN: I once published a newspaper here. I was baptized in this church. I decided to come back.

Lenwood Sloan, Louisiana Living History Project, performing as Paul Trevigne (Faubourg Treme, *frame capture*).

Sloan's performance references place, producing authenticity from proximity. As he mentions the cathedral, the camera moves to include the church in the frame, before cutting to a low-angle look up at the building's face. Sloan also attempts to place Paul Trevigne in relation to the familiar, connecting the known New Orleans frequented by tourists with the broader history of the city.

> SLOAN: I lived over there, in the neighborhood called Treme.

As with the previous shot of the cathedral, the filmmakers cut on Sloan's line, moving from St. Louis Cathedral to show another church, St. Augustine's, an anchor of the Treme neighborhood. Logsdon and Elie cut to a different audience for Paul Trevigne as resident of Treme. The white girl is replaced by a young African American girl, in braids, holding her mother's hand. These shots suggest the importance of recovering Paul Trevigne as a historical figure for all, but they also suggest special relevance for those wishing to understand the African American experience.

The sequence continues with a low-angle tracking shot of the Treme neighborhood. Elie, again in voice-over, reinforces the connection between Irving and Paul Trevigne, suggesting Paul's significance, both for the neighborhood and for the nation.

> ELIE: Mr. Trevigne told me that his ancestor started the first black daily newspaper right here in this neighborhood.

At this, the sequence shifts significantly, away from a contemporary representation of Treme's streetscape to an interior shot of a microfilm reader. As the camera tilts up to show a handwritten document in the reader, a black hand reaches into the frame to advance the reader. The next shot pans right to left, past the reader, to reveal Elie examining documents.

ELIE: I started searching for pictures of this Paul Trevigne.

Here, *Faubourg Treme* engages with the process of developing documentary evidence. The sequence begins with what Irving Trevigne had learned from relatives about his ancestor, as told to Elie, the documentary filmmaker. Familial and community memory offer important information for history as well as for documentary, but memory and family histories must be compared with other forms of historical documentation. By constructing a scene inside an archive, Logsdon and Elie reveal the work involved in recovering aspects of the past. They also reveal the importance of comparing various forms of documentary evidence.

Katrina challenged filmmakers because so much material was lost or destroyed by the flood. As noted in chapter 13, filmmaker Stevenson Palfi lost all his footage and material for a documentary about pianist Allen Toussaint when his Mid-City home flooded. Filmmakers interested in aspects of life in New Orleans before the storm and flood struggled to find missing documentation. As Logsdon and Elie discovered in making *Faubourg Treme*, the passage of time can be like a flood, washing away images and documents,

"I started searching for pictures of this Paul Trevigne" (Faubourg Treme, *frame capture*).

obscuring or erasing aspects of the past. Moreover, the policies of archives, museums, and libraries enshrine values and ideologies, protecting and preserving certain images and documents as important for history and rejecting or neglecting others. In "Artifacts of Disaster," David Shayt, a curator for the Smithsonian's National Museum of American History, discusses the process by which he traveled to New Orleans with colleagues to collect the material objects that would be used in future exhibits to represent the history of Katrina and the flooding of New Orleans. Shayt indicates that he was influenced by television news and other dominant representations and that much of what he collected was determined by what he had learned about Katrina from the first week of television news coverage. In this way, the selection and focus of television news shaped the selections by archivists that would in turn shape the possibilities for historical understanding of Katrina. Logsdon and Elie argue for the consequences of archival selection by building a scene in which Elie tries to find an image of Paul Trevigne.

The scene (within the sequence) begins by looking over Elie's right shoulder as he sits at a reader, scanning documents as they move across from right to left.

ELIE: But I wasn't able to find any (images of Trevigne).

The image cuts to an extreme close-up of the reader screen, as documents move across, from bottom to top. Elie sifts through the archive seeking visual evidence of the presence and significance of Paul Trevigne.

ELIE: Instead, I look at these anonymous portraits of black men from that period.

With Elie's voice-over, the scene cuts to an image of a man with a long face, deeply set eyes, and light skin. He wears a high white collar and has a mustache, and his hair is parted center left. The camera zooms on this image, allowing the viewer time to observe the visual details, before cutting again to the extreme close shot of documents moving swiftly past the reader's screening. The filmmakers use this recurring device to separate the portraits and to remind viewers of the work involved in finding the images.

The next portrait shows an older man, with a high forehead, curly hair brushed to his right, wearing a white bow tie and a black jacket. In the image, he looks directly at the camera, his mouth suggesting the hint of a smile. Logsdon and Elie zoom on his eyes.

"I look at these anonymous portraits of black men from that period" (Faubourg Treme, *frame capture*).

"Maybe this one is Paul" (Faubourg Treme, *frame capture*).

ELIE: Maybe this one is Paul.

After another extreme close-up of documents moving past the reader, another portrait shows a younger man, with darker skin, his hair parted on the far left. He wears a small dark bow tie and a black jacket over a white shirt. Again, Logsdon and Elie zoom into the portrait, observing details of the photograph.

ELIE: Maybe he's this one.

"Maybe he's this one" (Faubourg Treme, *frame capture*).

After another shot of the reader, another portrait shows a man with lighter skin, his hair swept back, with a mustache and beard. He wears a dark jacket over a waistcoat and a striped cravat. He is smiling at the camera. As the camera zooms slowly on this portrait, it becomes clear that the original image has become weathered, marked, faded. Even where photographic evidence was kept, visual information is imperiled by the vulnerabilities of the format to exposure to light and environment.

> ELIE: What I have found are the words that Paul Trevigne left
> behind.

Paul Trevigne is available to the filmmakers as a subject because of family memory and because he published a newspaper, some copies of which have been preserved and archived. Without these other forms of documentary evidence, Paul Trevigne would slip from history, losing his distinct, lived identity. Documentarians interested in history need images of the past in order to show past events and change over time. Logsdon and Elie encountered the challenge faced by many historians and documentarians before them, and they chose to represent this challenge, to show viewers some aspects of the work involved in visualizing the past.

In some cases, where neglect or ideology (class, race, political) have washed away visual evidence, filmmakers create new images to suggest what was not preserved. In this way, they draw on the tendency, incipient in documentary from the beginning, toward the "creative treatment of actuality" (as John Grierson described Robert Flaherty's 1926 film *Moana*). As noted, *Nat Turner: A Troublesome Property* included scripted scenes with different actors portraying different versions of the historical figure, Nat Turner. Burnett, Christopher, and Greenberg make the point that the paucity of visual evidence of Nat Turner is precisely what made him available for re-creation and appropriation over time. Like *Nat Turner: A Troublesome Property*, *Faubourg Treme* takes up the problem of representing Paul Trevigne by staging scenes to suggest what cannot be shown.

Having established Sloan's performance of Paul Trevigne as part of his Living History Project in the French Quarter at the beginning of the sequence, Logsdon and Elie employ Sloan to perform an editorial written by Trevigne for his newspaper, *L'Union*, in 1862. They frame Sloan in a medium shot, directly addressing the camera. Sloan is costumed in a red top hat, waistcoat, and a cravat, made to look like the third photographic portrait. The filmmakers draw on "maybe Paul" as visual inspiration for their representation of Sloan as Paul.

> SLOAN: The hour has sounded for the fight for greater humanitarian principles, against a vile and sordid interest. Men of my blood, shake off the contempt of your oppressors, defend yourselves against the barbarous spirit of slavery. You were born for liberty and happiness.

Set off by the direct address to camera, the framing of Sloan indicates that viewers are to understand this scene as a performance of Trevigne. By observing Sloan performing Trevigne in the earlier shot, Logsdon and Elie are able here to offer a degree of reflexivity, acknowledging their choices to animate Trevigne's spirit. These extra dimensions (framing, repetition of actor, address) render this moment a performance rather than a reenactment. The difference is that Logsdon, Elie, and Sloan show the work involved.

Logsdon and Elie chose this particular editorial in order to emphasize the role of Paul Trevigne and *L'Union* (first published entirely in French, but later published in an English language edition renamed the *Tribune*) in calls for civil and political rights for men of color. Launched during the Civil War, *L'Union* repeatedly made the case not only for the end of slavery but also for political and economic rights for freed slaves. The filmmakers use local historian Laura Rouzan to make this point. She appears first as a voice over images of actors performing as Trevigne and his staff preparing *L'Union* for publication before appearing in synch on camera.

> ROUZAN: They got together and decided somebody had to be a voice for black people . . . . So I see it as the beginning of the civil rights movement in the South.

Rouzan's claim is supported by Trevigne's words. As emphasized in the previous scene of Elie's search for an image of Paul Trevigne, the ideas of Paul Trevigne are preserved in the surviving pages of *L'Union* and the *Tribune*. To bring vitality to his words, Logsdon and Elie use Sloan to perform Trevigne's words. To further enliven their central claim about the importance of Trevigne and the newspaper, Logsdon and Elie also stage a scene in which an edition of *L'Union* is produced. By observing and engaging reenactors, and by staging stylized scenes of past events that were not recorded, *Faubourg Treme* argues that the past must be performed to be felt and understood.

Logsdon and Elie ultimately chose not to use most of their post-Katrina material in the final film. Instead, they emphasized the history and historiography of Treme, figuring Katrina as the latest in a long series of events affecting the neighborhood. Their first argument is that the Treme neighborhood was the birthplace of the civil rights movement in the United States, with Paul Trevigne's establishment of *L'Union* in the mid-nineteenth century, and that its status as key site for the civil rights struggle was cemented by Homer Plessy's testing the separate accommodations law in the 1890s. According to *Faubourg Treme*, Treme is one of the most important, if least appreciated, neighborhoods in America. Second, the film argues that the City of New Orleans (and the state of Louisiana and the federal government) failed to understand the neighborhood's importance when constructing the Interstate 10 overpass. The overpass construction destroyed much of the history and unique character of the neighborhood. Logsdon and Elie argue that Katrina poses a similar threat. The failure of the levees caused parts of Treme to flood, and floodwaters killed residents, destroyed homes, and imperiled memories. *Faubourg Treme* maintains that Katrina and the flooding of New Orleans not only threaten the city's present and future, but also its past.

However, *Faubourg Treme* argues that the history of the neighborhood also offers a model for responding to the crisis of Katrina. Paul Trevigne fought for the rights and opportunities afforded to his people by the end of the Civil War and by Reconstruction. But, as *Faubourg Treme* points out, the withdrawal of federal troops and the end of Reconstruction brought about the violent repression of many blacks and the stripping away of many civil rights. Subtler forms of re-segregation and abridgement of rights persisted throughout the twentieth century. Television news coverage suggested that Katrina revealed poverty and caused desperation, but poverty and desperation were dominant conditions in New Orleans long before Katrina and the flood. *Faubourg Treme* contends that many of the issues that animated Paul Trevigne remained insistent in 2005 and that citizens of New Orleans should adopt the techniques of Paul Trevigne in response to Katrina.

> IRVING TREVIGNE: Paul Trevigne organized the blacks in this city, man, to start fighting for the right to vote. They used to say that he was a radical, 'cause he bucked against the system. Going against the grain, going against what they wanted him to do.

For many, the expression "going against the grain" is just a metaphor. For Trevigne, who has spent his life working with wood to shape beautiful and useful structures, the expression holds deep resonance. Where Irving Trevigne has been trained to go with the grain, to keep to the nature and shape of things, his ancestor worked against the prevailing order to call for and to achieve freedom. *Faubourg Treme* argues that citizens threatened by floodwaters, neglected by government, and cheated by insurance companies must draw inspiration from past movements in order to go against the grain of the system to demand rights.

The one exception to the focus on pre-Katrina material was the scene of return to Irving Trevigne's house after the flood. As discussed, the scene of return is the most consistent trope in Katrina documentary. Unlike most Katrina documentaries, *Faubourg Treme* had followed its main characters well before Katrina. Because the film established Irving Trevigne as a main character before the storm, with scenes involving his work on Elie's house and his family memories of ancestor Paul Trevigne, the scene of Irving's return to his flooded home reveals more of what has been lost. Since the film established Irving before the storm, it is able to show the cost of the storm to him and his family and, by extension, to the Treme neighborhood and to the City of New Orleans.

The scene of Irving Trevigne's return to his home begins with a tight shot of a young African American man, with short dreadlocks and sunglasses, forcing his way through the front door to a home. As the young man kicks the door, the camera moves to a side view showing an older woman holding the screen door. As the move continues, the camera finds Irving, revealing the woman to be his wife Audrey and the young man to be a relative. Trevigne wears blue jeans and a dark polo. He wears glasses but no hat. After the previous scenes of Trevigne working on Elie's house, the viewer was familiar with his work attire of overalls and a ball cap. The absence of these elements here underscore that in this scene Trevigne is not working as a master carpenter, but examining his own home. Restoring Elie's home had been a professional challenge and opportunity. In this scene, Trevigne surveys the damage to his own home.

*Irving Trevigne returns to his flooded home after Katrina (*Faubourg Treme*, frame capture).*

AUDREY TREVIGNE: Oh, my God!

After looking in the door, she moves back, filling and then exiting the frame. The camera moves in, past Trevigne, through the door. The scene then cuts to Trevigne inside the front room of his house. He wears gloves and a mask and is pulling and sifting debris. The camera approaches him from behind, and he is heard on the soundtrack breathing heavily. The camera frames him closely as he lifts a broken coffee table. Trying to clear the couch, Trevigne accidentally hits the light fixture. He is struggling with the effort, his shirt stained dark with sweat. As he throws the table over the couch, he falls forward slightly, momentarily off balance. In the scenes before Katrina, Trevigne had been shown working with confidence, skill, and deep experience, in control of his tools and his movements. While working on Elie's home, Trevigne worked steadily, with deliberation. Sorting the debris in his home after the flood, Trevigne is halting and unsteady. His decades of experience seem undone by the floodwaters.

The scene cuts to a shot of mold spreading up a white wall, an image reused in the credits for Simon and Overmyer's *Treme*. The camera zooms out from the mold to reveal Trevigne moving past the couch, stopping in the doorway, holding onto the doorframe for support. The scene then cuts to a close-up shot of Trevigne's hands as he uses a flashlight to sort through debris on the floor of his home. He discovers a water-stained photograph.

TREVIGNE: That's my momma and daddy, man.

After showing the damaged photograph, the camera zooms out, showing the young man in the frame, working with Trevigne. Trevigne examines and discusses some additional family documents. After examining their work from a distance, the scene cuts to a shot of Trevigne back outside his home, on the porch. The camera observes him from a side angle as he struggles to articulate to Elie the impact of examining the flood damage to his home and possessions.

> TREVIGNE: All my tools . . . I don't know what to say, to be frank with you. It's a hard pill to swallow, I can tell you that.

Though speaking to the camera, prompted by the filmmakers, Trevigne does not look at the camera. He seems caught between the private experience of loss and his commitment to the filmmakers to share his experience. Over many decades, Trevigne had used his tools and experience to restore damaged and neglected homes. Where other residents might not have known where to start, Trevigne has the expertise to restore his home. As the scene indicates, he may not have the strength.

Trevigne cleans his hands and bows his head. Where in earlier scenes, Trevigne had seemed animated and experienced, here he seems old and defeated. Through this short scene of Irving Trevigne's return post-Katrina to his home in Treme, Logsdon and Elie show the human cost of the flooding, not only to individuals, but also to families, and through families to communities. *Faubourg Treme* constructs Irving Trevigne as a symbol of Treme, connecting closely to its past and committed to its future. With great econ-

*Irving Trevigne works inside his flooded home (*Faubourg Treme, *frame capture).*

omy, this scene shows the impact of Katrina on Treme and the threat posed by the flood to the neighborhood and its history. Logsdon and Elie use a title to reveal that Trevigne and Audrey evacuated to Vermont and that Irving died there eight months after Katrina.

Knowledge of the passing of Irving Trevigne reminds viewers of the absence of Paul Trevigne from visual representation. Earlier in the film, in a scene in the Tulane Library, Elie argues for the preciousness of the remaining archival material.

ELIE: Only a few of these newspapers have survived.

The camera observes Elie as he moves around library shelves, examining oversized volumes. The camera moves in as he takes down a volume of Paul Trevigne's *Tribune*, looking over his shoulder as he flips through the newspaper. The wider shots reveal that Elie is examining material stored in the library's basement, at risk to floodwaters. After examining Irving Trevigne's lost home, and after informing viewers of the loss of Trevigne himself, *Faubourg Treme* also suggests that Paul Trevigne is at risk. Irving kept Paul alive through family and community memory, passed from person to person. Tulane and other archives keep Paul alive through the preservation and maintenance of historically important primary documents. The same storm and flood that threatened Irving, threaten Paul. *Faubourg Treme* is unique among documentaries about Katrina in its deep insistence on the importance of history to understanding and to responding to the flood. The film also strongly argues that Katrina represents a threat to the raw material of history. Katrina threatens history even as its own history is contested.

CHAPTER FIFTEEN

We Were Not on the Map

A VILLAGE CALLED VERSAILLES

*I*N THE DAYS FOLLOWING LANDFALL, TELEVISION NEWS anchors and reporters loosely applied the term "refugees" to describe Americans forced to evacuate their homes in New Orleans due to the flooding of the city. This misapplication of the term "refugee" discursively stripped away rights from these citizens, making them seem stateless and without standing.

One group of New Orleans residents had been actual refugees, and they drew upon this experience to survive Katrina and the flooding of New Orleans. Between 1975 and 1978, hundreds of Vietnamese families moved into several neighborhoods in eastern New Orleans (known locally as New Orleans East). These immigrants had fled South Vietnam after North Vietnam took control in 1975, ending what Americans call the "Vietnam War" and what Vietnamese call the "American War." After time in refugee camps, such as Fort Chaffee, Arkansas, many Vietnamese immigrants were resettled along the U.S. Gulf Coast, where the environment and climate resemble that of Vietnam. Many of these immigrants had been fishermen and farmers in Vietnam, and the Gulf South provided them with opportunities to develop livelihoods. While the Catholic Church and other organizations supported these efforts, some local authorities and citizens responded with hostility, not seeing the Vietnamese immigrants as potential fellow citizens, but as aliens. The challenge of recognizing the Vietnamese Americans as fellow citizens persisted into the twenty-first century.

Television news struggled to cover the thousands of Vietnamese Americans in New Orleans East who were affected by Katrina. When television news reports considered race as a factor in the differential impact of Katrina and in the differential perception of responses to the flooding of New Orleans, it was framed through the black/white binary (for example,

229

the discursive controversy over the application of the term "looters" to photographs of African Americans carrying goods through floodwaters, and the term "foragers" applied to white citizens engaged in the same activity). The impact of Katrina on the Villa D'Este/Versailles community in New Orleans East was not widely covered by the national television news media. Vietnamese Americans were often not seen or recognized by television news reports. In the news footage used by Lee and Pollard in *If God Is Willing and Da Creek Don't Rise* to show Lt. General Russel Honoré's effort to relax the aggressive posture of the National Guard toward New Orleans residents, Vietnamese Americans are framed reacting, along with African Americans, cheering Honoré's efforts. Neither the original television news reporting nor the documentary film recognizes the presence of the Vietnamese Americans. They are invisible in plain sight.

Filmmaker S. Leo Chiang created *A Village Called Versailles* (2009) in response to this challenge to see and understand the response of the Vietnamese American community in New Orleans to Katrina. In the process, his film challenges the emerging consensus regarding the meanings and impact of Katrina on New Orleans. Chiang emigrated from Taiwan to the United States and studied film at the University of Southern California. He had previously made short documentaries, including *One + One* (2002) about couples with mixed HIV status, and feature documentaries, including *To You, Sweetheart, Aloha* (2006) about Bill Tapia, a Hawaiian jazz master reconnecting with his art in his late nineties. Chiang has also worked as a cinematographer and editor on other feature documentaries. The principal of Walking Iris Media, he is also part of the New Day Film Collective, a group of filmmakers focused on the social impact of documentary media who cooperate to distribute films to educational and consumer markets.

In an interview for this book, Chiang indicated that he first became aware of the Vietnamese American community in New Orleans through the research of Dr. Wei Li, a geographer at Arizona State University. After Katrina, Li and colleagues conducted a comparative analysis of community mobilization and access to relief by the Vietnamese American and African American communities in New Orleans East. Li's research found that Katrina had united the Vietnamese American community across generational lines and had prompted the community to participate more actively in New Orleans politics, developing stronger and more activist voices. *A Village Called Versailles* provides an important complement to Li's political geography, constructing visual understandings of the community and collecting and shaping the voices and perspectives of various members of the community. Chiang conceived of the film as having a dual address: to make the community visible to outside audiences and to show the community to itself.

Versailles opens with the sound of a helicopter over a black screen. This sound was overdetermined in American representations of the U.S. conflict in Vietnam. Television news reports showed "hunter killer" missions in which U.S. pilots flew helicopter missions to target North Vietnamese troops and the Vietcong on the ground below (Cook, 2001). American fictional films about the Vietnam War frequently emphasized the role of the military helicopter, both as a weapon and as a means of movement. Francis Ford Coppola's *Apocalypse Now* (1979) opens with a montage: Martin Sheen staring at a ceiling fan in a Saigon hotel intercut with spectacular widescreen images of a napalm bombing. Helicopters were also prominent in the imagery of the fall of Saigon to the North Vietnamese, as the last Americans and some of their allies were airlifted from the U.S. embassy by helicopter. By opening with the sound of a helicopter, Chiang references a familiar trope in American representation of Vietnam, quoting this sound, but also challenging its usual meaning and reference.

After a few beats, Chiang cuts from black to aerial footage of flooding homes, shot in a high angle from above. With this cut, Chiang links the helicopter from representations of the Vietnam War to the helicopter used in Katrina. In Katrina, helicopters were used by the Coast Guard to rescue civilians trapped in flooded homes. They were also used by television news to gather dramatic images of the devastated city. Unlike those used by the Coast Guard, television news helicopters observed suffering citizens without providing assistance. Chiang recognizes this complexity by heightening the sound of helicopters used over the footage.

The first voice heard in *A Village Called Versailles* is an African American woman. The African American female voice is prominently featured in documentary films about Katrina: Phyllis Montana-Leblanc provides one of the strongest and most indelible voices in *When the Levees Broke* and *If God Is Willing and Da Creek Don't Rise*; Kimberly Roberts is the key voice and the core of *Trouble the Water*; *Faubourg Treme* features the voices of historian Laura Rouzan, poet Brenda Marie Osby, and narrator JoNell Kennedy. While the woman in *Village* is not identified by title, Chiang confirmed that the voice belongs to New Orleans Councilwoman Cynthia Willard-Lewis. Chiang did not wish to identify Willard-Lewis or Fr. Vien Nguyen's voices at the outset of the film, preferring their perspectives to be less anchored and more open to viewers. Chiang returns to Willard-Lewis at the end of the film, featuring synch interview footage with her, providing perspective on the growth of advocacy in the Versailles community.

WILLARD-LEWIS: After Katrina, everything that you own is simply destroyed. What do you do when the walls are gone? You still must call something home.

Her voice appears over high-angle aerial footage of flooded homes and the damaged Causeway bridge across Lake Ponchartrain.

With the voice-over reference to "home," Chiang dissolves from the images of flooded homes to an exterior tracking shot of Mary Queen of Vietnam, a Catholic parish in the Versailles neighborhood. On the soundtrack, multiple voices can be heard in prayer. The church appears damaged, but the audio track suggests that it is still being used despite the damage. The initial voice-over by an unnamed African American woman is followed by the voice of a man, speaking English with a Vietnamese accent. Chiang soon reveals this second voice to be Fr. Vien Nguyen, pastor of Mary Queen of Vietnam and a key voice in the film.

NGUYEN: The Vietnamese community was always quiet. We were never on the map. Then came Katrina. This community was threatened, and we stepped forth.

Chiang selected these statements to articulate his key arguments that Katrina forced the Vietnamese American community in New Orleans to unite and to become more politically active. Accompanying Nguyen's voice, Chiang shows footage of community members leaving the church after the first post-Katrina celebration of mass. His camera frames several parishioners in close-up, emphasizing older residents. Then, Chiang cuts to a shot of young Vietnamese Americans protesting, holding signs, and chanting in objection to a landfill project. Finally, Chiang shows the community coming together at a celebration of Tet, the lunar New Year. Over these images, the viewer hears Fr. Nguyen.

NGUYEN: We had to fight because this is our land. We are connected to the land. New Orleans is our home.

With this articulation of "home," Chiang cuts to a tracking shot toward a two-story iron gate. The outline of the structure suggests Vietnamese architecture, and it is topped by a cross. As the main visual icon for the Versailles neighborhood, the gate gestures both backward and forward. Chiang uses this shot of the gate as a key image in the film, behind the film's title, in the DVD packaging, and on the film's website.

In this brief opening (1:52), Chiang addresses multiple audiences, seek-

*Versailles community in New Orleans East (*A Village Called Versailles, *frame capture).*

ing to connect the emerging consensus about Katrina to other understandings. By following the female voice with the voice of Fr. Nguyen, Chiang connects the impact of Katrina on the African American community to the impact on the Vietnamese American community. He also makes the case that the response of the Versailles community was unique. *A Village Called Versailles* argues that this response is important to understanding the fuller impact of Katrina on multiple communities living in proximity. For example, he shows Willard-Lewis working closely with the Versailles community to oppose the location of a massive landfill in New Orleans East as a dumping ground for Katrina debris from throughout New Orleans. The experiences of the two communities were not identical, but their responses to Katrina involved the building of a coalition to combine their voices to argue together for political change.

Chiang's own status is significant to the question of the film's address. As a Taiwanese American and professional filmmaker based in San Francisco, Chiang approached *Versailles* from the outside. He sought to make a documentary about a community of which he was not a part. However, as an Asian American, with grant funding for the project from the Center For Asian American Media, Chiang had an appreciation for the experience of a community that had immigrated to the United States from Southeast Asia.

The film's address is multiple and complicated. It speaks to a national audience that knows of Katrina primarily from television news and, as a consequence, knows nothing about the presence and experience of thousands of Vietnamese Americans living in New Orleans. Within that national audience, the film addresses a national Asian American audience in unique ways, suggesting connections between the distinct experiences of immigrant communities. The film also addresses an audience of New Orleanians, citizens who survived the storm and flood and who must struggle to reconstruct home. Within this local audience, the film addresses white, African American, and Vietnamese American communities, acknowledging difference, but also pointing toward connection and the possibility for coalition. Finally, the film addresses the Versailles community in order to make the argument that while Katrina devastated the community, it also provided a catalyst for youth leadership, an opportunity for cross-generational connection within the community, and a reason for youth to reinvest in the community, partially countering forces of assimilation and movement away from Versailles in search of opportunity.

REFUGEES (AGAIN)

Documentary is a mode of inquiry deeply invested in the past. Unlike television news, with its insistent focus on the present (the "live" story), documentary film often examines the present within the context of the past. Like *Faubourg Treme, A Village Called Versailles* is concerned with how past events provide perspective for Katrina. Specifically, it is concerned with the history of the migration of Vietnamese people to New Orleans East. Before the citizens of Versailles had to evacuate New Orleans East due to the flooding after the levees failed, the elders of the community had already endured two previous evacuations from earlier versions of home. Employing archival footage and found imagery, combined with interviews with Fr. Nguyen and Ngo Minh Khang, an elder in the Versailles community, Chiang documents the movement of Vietnamese Catholics from North Vietnam to South Vietnam after the Vietnamese defeat of the French and the post-colonial separation of French Indochina into Communist North Vietnam and (ostensibly) democratic South Vietnam (with a regime strongly supported by the United States). After the Vietnamese revolutionaries defeated the French at the battle of Dien Bien Phu in 1954, Catholics fled to the south, with the aid of the United States and France, fearing potential persecution by the Communist government of North Vietnam. They were forced to abandon their homes in the north and endure a difficult trip to the south, where they had to rebuild their lives.

In 1975, when the United States withdrew from South Vietnam, effectively conceding the war with North Vietnam, many Vietnamese in the south sought to leave Vietnam, fearing reprisals from the North Vietnamese troops. Once again, Vietnamese families were forced to abandon their homes and flee to another country. President Gerald Ford signed the Indochina Migration and Refugee Assistance Act in 1975, allowing approximately 130,000 South Vietnamese into the United States under special immigration status.

Fr. Nguyen and Ngo Minh Khang entered the United States at this time and were sent to a refugee camp at Fort Chaffee, Arkansas. As Nguyen relates to Chiang's camera, after Katrina, he was evacuated from Houston back to Fort Chaffee. Thirty years after entering the United States as a refugee, Fr. Nguyen, now a U.S. citizen, was sent back to a former refugee camp. Like Logsdon and Elie, Chiang seeks to understand the importance of knowledge of past struggles for surviving Katrina. *A Village Called Versailles* argues that the previous experiences of evacuation from north to south and from Vietnam to the United States prepared the community of Versailles to be able to survive the flooding of New Orleans East. Moreover, drawing on the lessons of the past experience of their own community, the people of Versailles were able to maintain community during evacuation and to provide aid and comfort to their own people and to others. The film also argues that the history of the Vietnamese Americans helped them to return and rebuild more swiftly than many other communities. *A Village Called Versailles* argues that the Vietnamese American community had survived previous Katrinas before Katrina happened.

As Fr. Nguyen argues in the opening of the film, Versailles was never on the map in New Orleans. The community in New Orleans East did not register strongly either within the city or in representations of New Orleans beyond the city. Chiang chose to open *A Village Called Versailles* with images of flooded homes, which were familiar from news and documentary representations, but still unusual to a national audience for the documentary. Significantly, Chiang focused on the image of the gate leading to the community of Versailles before cutting to imagery familiar to any tourist to New Orleans: a shot of the steamboat *Natchez* pulling away from the French Quarter and three shots of Mardi Gras parades. By ordering his images in this way, Chiang raises questions about the visual identity of New Orleans, questions that alter the viewers' approach to the trite images of tourist New Orleans. Chiang employs attorney Joel Waltzer, a white lawyer with an office in New Orleans East, to place Versailles within the normative white perspective of New Orleans, held both inside and outside the city.

> WALTZER: You have a tale of three cities. You have Uptown New
> Orleans, which didn't flood, almost coming back to normal life.

Chiang cuts to a shot of the French Quarter and a streetcar, confusing the geography of the city (he is showing the French Quarter and the Central Business District, not Uptown). Still, he conveys the sense of the so-called Isle of Denial, the oldest part of the City of New Orleans. On high ground closest to the Mississippi River, the Isle was not flooded after the failure of the levees. Waltzer's point is that some of the oldest and wealthiest areas did not flood. Chiang's additional point through this selection of images is that the part of the city that did not flood is the part most visually familiar to a national audience (of tourists or would-be tourists).

> WALTZER: Then you have maybe a thirty-mile stretch of block after
> block of flooded-out, gutted homes. Maybe 80 percent of the
> houses are still unoccupied. Just block after block after block of
> flooded, gutted homes. Just isolation and nothing really.

Under Waltzer's description, Chiang cuts to three images of flooded homes. The first shot shows a small, one-story white house in the left part of the frame, its door covered by plywood. The second shot shows two houses: the one in the left foreground has the siding stripped away, and the one in the right background has a listing front entrance. The third shot shows a one-story yellow-brick home with a damaged roof and a missing front window. The house is framed by two broken segments of chain-link fence. Over these images, the soundtrack features a guitar figure and the natural sound of insects. Chiang argues visually and aurally that Katrina has turned the city into the country. He has chosen images devoid of human beings to emphasize that Katrina and the flooding emptied most of New Orleans of its population.

> WALTZER: Then you go twenty miles out, and you come to the
> Vietnamese community.

Here, Chiang responds to the crisis of visibility of Vietnamese Americans by establishing visually the community of Versailles. In an establishing shot, Chiang shows a blue sign reading "Saigon Dr." in the upper-right portion of the frame. The sign sits on the neutral ground in the middle of a wide boulevard. Green trees are visible on the left and on the neutral ground behind the sign. Cars can be seen, both approaching the camera and driving away, out of the neighborhood. Across Chef Menteur Highway, perpendicular to the camera, a large oil and gas plant is visible. It appears operational. This first shot contrasts to the stillness in the three previous shots, suggesting that the "Vietnamese community," although suffering from Katrina, has come back to life while much of the rest of the city has not.

Chiang provides a sound bridge from this first shot into the second. The murmuring of a crowd is audible before the sequence cuts to a right-to-left pan across a nighttime festival. In sharp contrast to the shots of the unoccupied houses, this frame is crowded with people. As an amplified voice is heard over a microphone, the pan stops at an illuminated stage in a pavilion on the left side of the frame. The sequence then cuts to a medium close-up of Fr. Nguyen, dressed in a white shirt rather than a Roman clerical collar, cutting a red ribbon. He is framed by young women to his left and to his right. Several children are visible in the background in silk robes. Coinciding with the ribbon cutting, fireworks are lit and smoke billows on stage. The sequence cuts to a close-up of fireworks exploding brightly on the ground. Again, the movement, color, and action provide strong contrast to the stillness and quietness of the previous images, raising questions about the differences between this vibrant community and the devastation of the remainder of the city.

The next shot shows a crowd of young Vietnamese Americans, faces illuminated, looking up. This is followed by a side-view medium shot of a woman serving food. She smiles, acknowledging the camera, while holding a plate in her left hand. As Fr. Nguyen begins in voice-over to commemorate the Tet celebration, the sequence cuts to a close-up of Mary Tran, a young member of the community, smiling and laughing. The camera pulls back to reveal that she is holding a baby in her lap and sitting with others at a table under a tent.

> FR. NGUYEN: I know this sounds really strange, but, for us, in many ways Katrina was a good thing. It galvanized the people. We have a sense of who we are, or who we could be.

After the image of Mary and baby, the sequence cuts to Fr. Nguyen, completing his thought in synch, before cutting to an image of two nuns, one in white and the other in black, leading a group of very young children in a song about Vietnam. Without cutting, the camera pans right to left to show the rest of the group of schoolchildren, singing, several with their hands over their hearts. In the center of the frame, a young African American girl is visible, wearing a plaid dress like the Vietnamese American girls, more visual evidence of a connection between communities.

> FR. NGUYEN: We feel that we can now control our destiny. It has not always been that way.

Accompanying this voice-over, the camera zooms slightly on a boy in a blue, high-collared shirt and a blue silk hat, holding a yellow flag with three red stripes, the South Vietnamese flag. Thus far, the sequence has established Versailles as a vibrant community, active and alive, but also as a community apart from the rest of New Orleans. Other than the image of the African American girl, nothing in the sequence suggests that this community is a part of New Orleans. The voices in the observational footage speak in Vietnamese, the cultural celebration is Vietnamese, and the schoolchildren sing a Vietnamese anthem and carry the flag of South Vietnam.

Having raised the question of the relation of this community to New Orleans, Chiang locates Versailles by employing a graphic showing the map of New Orleans and surrounding areas. As the image zooms toward the east, first the French Quarter is illuminated in yellow, then the Lower Ninth Ward. Finally, Village de L'Est is identified in yellow, with a title indicating that this is the official name of Versailles.

> FR. NGUYEN: We are almost at the extreme eastern end of the City of New Orleans.

With this, Chiang dissolves to an image of the sun setting above water, with swamp trees and plants visible and insects audible. This shot is followed by a right-to-left pan over water to houses. Following the map, these shots emphasize that Versailles is intimately connected to the watery, swampy landscape of southern Louisiana. Employing another sound bridge featuring a crowd of voices, Chiang dissolves to an outdoor market in a parking lot. As the camera pans from left to right, a woman is visible in the background. She is wearing all black and a conical straw hat, recalling images produced by television news of the look of Vietnamese during the Vietnam War. But, Chiang's camera also captures a young woman, standing next to her in jeans and a tank top. Rather than suggesting that Versailles is like a transplanted Vietnamese village, Chiang suggests that the interrelations between Versailles and New Orleans, the past and the present, are more complicated. Because of this complication, Katrina both threatened and united the community. The final images of the sequence show a high-angle close-up of live catfish, Fr. Nguyen haggling with two women and then buying a catfish, a pan over a lush garden of greens, and a shot of a woman tending to her garden. These images suggest a closeness and harmony between the Vietnamese American community and the natural environment. Katrina imperiled their harmony by the failure of the built environment.

With this sequence, Chiang establishes a strong visual identity for Versailles as a vibrant community seemingly thriving again after Katrina. *A Village Called Versailles* answers the challenge to see the Vietnamese community and to place it on the map of New Orleans. The sequence also raises questions about Versailles. While dynamic, Chiang's portrait in this sequence suggests that the community is strongly invested in maintaining cultural and social traditions brought from Vietnam. The prominence of Vietnamese language, dress, song, food, and folklife in the sequence indicates that the community's separation from the rest of New Orleans may have been the product of insularity. In *The Accidental City: Improvising New Orleans* (2012), historian Lawrence Powell argues that the history of the city has always been marked by adaptation and improvisation. With each new group migrating to New Orleans, both that group and the city have changed. Powell focuses on creolization, the processes by which the offspring of immigrants, born in the new world, become strongly connected both to the old world and the new.

In the opening sequence of *A Village Called Versailles*, Chiang also begins to establish a difference between the older members of the community and young Vietnamese Americans. The sequence focuses on locating young people within the traditional milieu—such as in the shot of Mary Tran laughing in the tent during the Tet celebration—subtly suggesting a significant challenge facing immigrant communities: will new generations maintain traditions or adopt the new ways of the new place? As Fr. Nguyen notes, Katrina greatly challenged the Versailles community, but those challenges (evacuating, returning, rebuilding, resisting the location of a major landfill) forced the community to connect in new ways, both intergenerationally within the community and politically with allies in New Orleans East who had previously been located outside the boundaries of the community.

The opening sequence of the celebration of the Lunar New Year festival prompts another question. Given the successful restoration of Versailles, how badly affected was the community by Katrina and the flood? By representing a visual wholeness to the community after the flood, Chiang raises the possibility that Versailles was spared the worst of Katrina. Viewers might wonder if Versailles had avoided flooding, like the French Quarter or parts of Uptown New Orleans. *A Village Called Versailles* answers this question by representing the community's experience of the storm and flood. The film also represents the difficulties in returning and rebuilding. Ultimately, *A Village Called Versailles* argues that the closeness of the community, the qualities that separated it from New Orleans before Katrina, helped the community to survive Katrina and to rebuild.

Like Lessin and Deal, Chiang was able to secure footage from community members to represent the impact of Katrina and the flooding of New Orleans East. Much of New Orleans, including Versailles, was invisible to television news during and after Katrina. As a consequence, Chiang was not able to use television news footage to tell the story of the flooding of Versailles. While this absence of footage presented a production challenge, the lack of news footage also freed Chiang from the limitations of the visual perspectives of television news. Instead, he focuses on and benefits from the use of amateur footage to tell the story from the visual perspective of the residents themselves. In the process, Chiang contributes new images and new perspectives to the developing visual archive of Katrina, offering counter memories to complicate the dominant representations of television news.

Chiang contextualizes Katrina's impact by emphasizing the struggles of the immigrants over thirty years to establish themselves and build lives in New Orleans East.

> FR. NGUYEN: (They) have struggled for the last thirty years. First, to buy a car, and then to buy a house . . . then the church is built. If you can imagine people hunched over trying to do all that, finally they look up and say, "What's next?"

To show what happened next, Chiang opens with a mobile tracking shot of the exterior of the Mary Queen of Vietnam Church and School. Both show signs of moderate wind damage, but remain intact.

> FR. NGUYEN: We fared quite well through all of that.

Under Fr. Nguyen's voice, Chiang cuts to a mobile shot, through a car windshield, of tree branches in the street. The street appears wet, but not flooded. The next shot shows a tree, split by the wind. The camera pulls back to show a red brick house, seemingly intact. Chiang then cuts to a shot that zooms out from a white two-story house to reveal that the roof is heavily damaged. Smoke is emerging from a hole in the roof, and the camera zooms in on the smoke. The out-then-in movement is typical of amateur videography where the shooter is unsure of the importance of the visual information she or he is observing. By selecting footage formally marked as non-professional, Chiang seeks to suggest immediacy and connection between shooter and subject. The next shot zooms out to show water in the street, offering a wider perspective on the houses behind. For the first time, a figure is seen in the frame.

FR. NGUYEN: Then someone said, "Father, I think the water is rising."

Under Fr. Nguyen's voice, Chiang cuts to a tracking shot down an interior hallway, apparently in the church's rectory. The shot shows a few inches of water covering the floor of the hallway. The camera pans left to show some water accumulating in a kitchen. This shot dissolves into another tracking shot, down the same hallway, now showing a foot or more of dark water inside the building. The camera again pans left, showing the kitchen filling with water. In an interview, Fr. Nguyen explains the rapidity of the rising water, but these two shots show the impact of the flooding on a contained space. The temporal jump negotiated by the dissolve emphasizes the swiftness of the floodwater, and the tightness of the framing of the interior space creates a strong sense of the uncanny, as a familiar domestic space fills with dark water.

As with Kimberly Roberts's footage in *Trouble the Water*, looking down from the crawl space at water flooding over her windowsill, these images of the flooding of Mary Queen of Vietnam show the impact of the failed levees as it was happening. While television news gains authority from its claims to live-ness, ostensibly showing events as they happen, television news missed the story of the flood, instead doing stand-ups in front of minor damage in the French Quarter and declaring that New Orleans had "dodged a bullet." Although the footage of flooding in *A Village Called Versailles* reached audiences four years after Katrina, countless news cycles later, it maintains the immediacy produced by first-person observational documentary footage. The footage conveys a sense of the moment, when the levees failed and water swept into the city, flooding New Orleans East in minutes rather than hours. While not "live" in its presentation, this footage was live in its production. *A Village Called Versailles* benefits from this live-ness of observation to strongly convey the surprise and threat posed by the floodwaters.

As the sequence continues, Chiang intercuts some footage not specific to Versailles, including a high-angle zoom on a breached levee, shot from a helicopter (presumably news or freelance footage); house-level views of streets filled with eight feet of water; a canted view of water up to the eaves of a house; and interior shots of waves of waters washing into a house through a door and windows. These images are striking, but also familiar from other Katrina documentaries, and they serve the customary function of substantiating the breadth and intensity of the impact of the flooding.

For the remainder of the sequence, Chiang focuses visually on Versailles.

*Mary Queen of Vietnam Church, flooded after Katrina (*A Village Called Versailles, *frame capture).*

The next shot begins with an extreme close-up on the Saigon Dr. sign, already established by the post-Katrina footage of the community. Here, as the camera pulls back, the viewer sees the sign bent under a fallen tree. The camera pans right to show five feet of water in the street. The sequence then cuts to an exterior shot of Mary Queen of Vietnam Church surrounded by five feet of water. The next shot zooms out on a group of people on the second-floor balcony of the retail strip, shown earlier as the site of the open-air market in the post-Katrina sequence. By establishing these locations post-flood, Chiang is able to suggest the impact of the flooding to an audience unfamiliar with the neighborhood. Viewers are able to track and to process the damage wrought by the rising water.

Over images of water inside several homes, Fr. Nguyen relates that he and others drove around to pick up community members as the floodwaters rose. When the water became too high to drive through, the group used boats to collect people trapped in their homes. Having already established Vietnamese Americans as fishermen, comfortable with boats and on the water, Chiang is able to show how these traditions helped them survive the flooding of New Orleans East. The sequence cuts to an extreme long shot of two boats being paddled down the street, away from the camera. In the nearer boat, one man uses a paddle, while another uses a pole, to move the boat forward. Four people ride in the boat. The next shot observes a boat closely, tracking left to right, finding a woman in a floppy hat, crouching down in the boat and looking worried. The next shot shows two young Vietnamese men wading through the floodwaters. The contrast between the smooth movement of the boats and the struggle of the two men to advance through the water suggests the value of traditional cultural practices. As demonstrated in television news coverage and documentary film (see *When the Levees Broke*), many African American residents of Central City, Mid-City, and the Ninth Ward were forced to wade out of the floodwaters to seek higher ground. Many African American citizens in New Orleans did not know how to swim, and this lack of facility with water proved fatal for many. White Americans had referred to Vietnamese immigrants in the 1970s as "boat people," a derogatory reference to the use of boats to flee the fall of South Vietnam. Being boat people saved Vietnamese Americans during the flooding of New Orleans.

Like Larry in *Trouble the Water*, who used a punching bag as a float to carry neighbors out of the floodwaters, many Versailles residents responded to the flood by helping others. The sequence continues with a shot from inside a boat, over the shoulder of a man in a white shirt, poling toward a raised pavilion. Viewers recognize this pavilion as the site of the ribbon cutting in the opening scene. As the boat approaches, the camera shows people gathered on the raised platform. The final shot of the sequence is a handheld shot that zooms on the pavilion showing people organizing supplies and preparing food. The image shows the citizens of Versailles coming together and providing mutual aid and support even as the floodwaters continue to rise. Chiang uses this image, the punctuation of the sequence, to suggest that the television news focus on desperation and looting as the main responses to the flooding of New Orleans missed other important community responses and mischaracterized the response of New Orleans residents to the storm and flood.

*Versailles "boat people" escape floodwaters on August 29, 2005 (*A Village Called Versailles, *frame capture).*

A Village Called Versailles offers a short scene at the New Orleans Convention Center that provides a strong and clear alternative to the representations of New Orleans residents as dangerous and depraved after the flooding of their city. Television news contributed to elite panic by overemphasizing looting and crime by citizens and, for a time, under-reporting the threat to residents trapped in their homes and to citizens who lacked food, water, medicine, and shelter at the Convention Center. As analyzed in the section of this book on television news coverage of Katrina, NBC, CNN, and Fox portrayed New Orleans as a city out of control, but largely blamed that condition on the survivors of Katrina, not on the authorities who failed to uphold the social contract and to provide for their own citizens. As a consequence, television news demonized New Orleans residents, alternately blaming them for their suffering or criticizing them for taking goods. Television news reporting from the Convention Center emphasized human misery and desperation. *A Village Called Versailles* shows another view of how New Orleans residents provided for themselves when abandoned by their government.

Continuing the story of the evacuation of the Versailles community, Chiang uses video footage shot by independent filmmaker Neil Alexander (*An Eye in the Storm*, 2006) to create a scene showing a group from Versailles waiting at the Convention Center to be evacuated from the city. The scene begins with Vo Tran, a young male, directly addressing a video camera. The Convention Center is visible behind him.

> TRAN: I want to say roughly we have about 300-something people here. We've got them organized together and we slept together last night.

Importantly, Tran is speaking to a camera while at the Convention Center, not recalling events from memory in a documentary interview. Like the two shots of the water in the rectory hallway, this shot conveys a liveness of observation, as Tran relates things that are happening before the camera. The scene cuts to a slight high-angle shot of an older Vietnamese man, sitting outside the Convention Center in a chair and eating food from a plastic container, on a tray, with a fork. Two young girls sit next to him on a blanket, and a white woman sits next to them. In combination with Tran's calm and organized accounting of the group, the image of the man eating is starkly different from the images produced by television news of desperate, hungry citizens lacking any resources. Here, drawing from the community's own self-representation, Chiang shows a group of New Orleans residents who responded to the flood with organization and mutual care. Indeed, the presence of the white woman suggests that the Versailles group shared its resources with fellow citizens outside its own group.

> TRAN: We have a person who kept records of the names of the people in the group.

Tran speaks in present tense about events happening before the camera, creating a powerfully immediate document of the Convention Center that complicates and questions dominant representations. Where television news coverage represented chaos, Alexander's footage of the Versailles group emphasizes organization and cooperation.

> TRAN: So, that is one way that we band together. And we will stay together. We will wait until everybody leaves.

With this, the scene shows a slight high-angle shot of a group of Versailles residents, old and young, gathered together. Tran's role as leader and spokesman indicates that the younger generation of residents used their English language skills to negotiate and to speak for the group, even as the group drew upon the experiences of older residents, who had lived through previous evacuations. Chiang argues that Katrina served as a context for the strengthening of community ties across generations and for the assumption of greater ownership and leadership by the youth of Versailles.

Even as he constructs an alternate representation of survivors at the Convention Center, emphasizing community over chaos, Chiang is careful to emphasize that the Versailles group was not wholly exceptional. He avoids stoking division by suggesting that the Vietnamese Americans responded more effectively than other citizens. Chiang cuts to a close-up of an African American mother holding a baby. The camera pans right to left to show a second mother, bouncing another baby on her knee, patting the baby on the back. Chiang connects this shot to the previous shots via editing, suggesting a connection between the African American mothers and the Versailles community.

> TRAN: The conditions here are just unbearable. People here are desperate.

Tran suggests that the conditions were difficult for all, connecting the experience of the Versailles group to others who suffered at the Convention

Center. The disjunction between his description and the images selected by Chiang suggests that he may not be fully aware of the importance of the group's careful, organized response to alleviating further misery. The Versailles group had to be their own responders, providing mutual aid when authorities failed to provide help.

The next shot shows a white woman dabbing at her eyes, followed by an image of a Vietnamese man pushing a shopping cart neatly packed with luggage. The next image shows a younger Vietnamese American man, neatly attired in a ball cap and a backpack, and some young women recognizable from the post-Katrina Tet festival scene. The image then tracks along a line of citizens waiting patiently to be evacuated, a group containing both Vietnamese and African Americans.

> TRAN: I wouldn't say this is hell on earth, but I bet it is pretty close.

The difference between Tran's description and the images themselves suggests a duality. Rebecca Solnit argues in *A Paradise Built in Hell* (2010) that ordinary people usually respond to disaster and distress by pulling together, not by pulling apart. Solnit explores the concept and impact of elite panics and also the importance of community response and mutual aid as a counter to elite panics. Similarly, Chiang builds a scene demonstrating a very different representation of the Convention Center. Martin Savidge's NBC report from the Convention Center sought to show something of the hell on earth described by Tran. Like Solnit, Chiang is more interested in showing the paradise built from mutual aid despite the hellish conditions. In this way, *A Village Called Versailles* offers a strong counter-perspective to the dominant television news reporting, forging new ways to understand the meaning of surviving Katrina.

The efforts by the Versailles community to remain connected throughout the evacuation from New Orleans mitigated some of the negative impacts of the Katrina diaspora. In his film *Desert Bayou* (2007), Alex LeMay documents the dislocations felt by African American citizens from New Orleans who were evacuated without consent throughout the United States. LeMay focuses on a group of New Orleanians flown from New Orleans to Utah, their efforts to regain some control over their lives in a virtually all-white community in Utah, and their eventual struggle to return home to New Orleans. In *A Village Called Versailles*, Chiang shows community members evacuated to Houston, and he interviews Fr. Nguyen talking about being returned to Fort Chaffee. But, even as Vietnamese Americans were subjected to many of the same challenges as other New Orleans residents, their close community connections, and the community organizing by young leaders, helped the community to remain intact while dispersed and then to reform quickly in order to return to New Orleans East to rebuild Versailles.

Chiang documents the rebuilding efforts, showing families gutting their flooded homes down to the studs, disinfecting the foundation with bleach, and then rebuilding. Some families stayed with another Vietnamese American community in an unflooded part of Jefferson Parish, on the West Bank of the Mississippi, cutting down their commute to Versailles and allowing more time for rebuilding. Many of the homes in Versailles were rebuilt within six months after Katrina, long before other areas of New Orleans, especially in the eastern part of the city. Chiang creates a scene from the first mass celebrated at Mary Queen of Vietnam, emphasizing that, as the first church to open in New Orleans East, Mary Queen of Vietnam attracted African American neighbors. These scenes suggest an opening up of the community after Katrina and hint at the possibilities for building coalitions between Versailles and the neighboring community.

THIS IS NOT VIETNAMESE. THIS IS AMERICA.

After struggling to rebuild their flooded homes, the Versailles community faced a new challenge in early 2006 when Mayor Ray Nagin signed an executive order to open a landfill site bordering Chef Menteur Highway (Eaton, 2006). Hurricane Katrina produced an estimated 100 million cubic yards of debris. The flooding of 80 percent of New Orleans created an enormous amount of debris in the city, and the sheer volume of material impeded rebuilding efforts. Nagin decided to locate a new landfill near Versailles, even though New Orleans East was already the site of a disproportionate number of dump sites. The Versailles community concluded that the decision was related to their distance from the political process, and the Chef Menteur landfill became a flashpoint for Versailles post-Katrina. Chiang uses the fight against the landfill as the final act of *A Village Called Versailles*, using the story to demonstrate changes within and outside the community after Katrina.

Chiang builds a pivotal scene in which youth leaders join with elders and a coalition of African American and white allies to protest at the landfill site. The scene begins with a long shot looking at the protest from across the street, before zooming to find a middle-aged Vietnamese American man holding a sign reading "landfill" with a slash through the word. The next shot shows Mimi Nguyen, a Vietnamese American who helped the Versailles community in Houston and with rebuilding and activism, wear-

*Youth organizing a protest against the Chef Menteur landfill (*A Village Called Versailles, *frame capture).*

ing an orange T-shirt emblazoned with the word "ACT," speaking into a mic and gesturing to the protestors. The next shot shows a young man, with his shirt off and slung over his shoulders, walking past the camera holding two signs. The next shot shows a young woman, wearing a white T-shirt and a ball cap, being interviewed by local network WDSU. While the viewer cannot hear her words, the image emphasizes her composure and focus as she voices her community's perspective to the local television media. The fifth shot zooms on an older man, wearing a ball cap, leaning forward, among a group of residents five deep. This is followed by a medium shot of Minh Nguyen, a male leader of the youth group, wearing a yellow band around his arm, holding a mic and a sign. As the camera holds on Nguyen, an older man enters the frame, partially obscuring him. These shots begin to bring together visually younger and older members of the community in the same frame.

This is followed by a shot of the crowd, visually substantiating that the community is united in opposition to the landfill. From the crowd shot, the scene cuts to a tighter shot of an old woman holding a sign reading "no trash," moving from the lettering to a drawing of an unhappy face. The sign seems to have been written by a younger member of the community, but it is held by an elder, demonstrating cooperative action. The next two shots show a close-up on an older woman chanting, and then a zoom out to show a younger woman chanting and standing above a group of older women. The pace of the editing increases as the scene introduces more images from various parts of the protest. The next shot is held for a beat, as five young women, in white tanks, their hair in ponytails, chant,

"No justice, no peace. Save New Orleans East." The camera moves around behind them to observe their action and the crowd's reaction. The scene then cuts to Ngo Minh Khang, one of the elders of the community, speaking into the mic, standing in front of a youth holding a "no landfill" sign. The camera zooms on Khang as he speaks, showing for the first time one of the older generation leading the protest. In the next shot, the camera is located behind a young man in a tank top, holding a sign and shouting. The camera tracks up from the young man to observe a security guard, an African American woman in a black uniform, open the gate to the landfill in order to reach out to tear down a sign. This is the first image of conflict in the scene, and the aggressive act changes the stakes. The scene cuts from the security guard to a side view of an older woman, pressed against the fence, chanting. The next shot shows a second security guard, wearing a white uniform shirt and a headscarf, presenting a combination of authority and informality. She confronts the protesters verbally.

> SECURITY GUARD: Take all this down. Take it down. Take it down. Y'all cannot do this. This is not Vietnamese. This is America.

The elders begin to comply, undoing tape and ribbon from the fence, acceding to nominal authority. Mimi Nguyen is heard out of frame.

> NGUYEN: What about freedom of speech?
> GUARD: Yeah, it's free here . . . (trails off)
> NGUYEN: This is America!

Nguyen enters the frame, visible in her bright orange ACT T-shirt, and she gestures to the elders to leave the protest material as she confronts the private security guard about the group's legal right to protest. Chiang uses interview material with Nguyen over these images.

> NGUYEN: I was so upset, to the point where I was about to lose my cool. I was like, this is America. This is . . . to ask a citizen in America. You don't ask people to go home!

Midway through this reflection, Chiang cuts to synchronous interview footage of Nguyen. As she concludes, she smiles, tilts her head back, looking up out of the frame. Her gesture suggests the struggle faced by Vietnamese immigrants to exercise the rights promised by citizenship but challenged by the practices of authority and society.

This moment within the longer scene is representative of the challenges

*Guard at the landfill challenges protesters (*A Village Called Versailles, *frame capture).*

*Guard rejects citizens' right to protest in their own community (*A Village Called Versailles, *frame capture).*

faced by the Versailles community after Katrina. Even as the community came together, crossing generational divides that had weakened the group prior to the storm and had threatened the survival of the community before the flood, Vietnamese Americans still had to work to be seen and heard as American citizens. The security guard misreads the protesters as Vietnamese. Nguyen emphasizes that they are Americans. Like news anchors misusing the term "refugees," the security guard misunderstands the activists as foreign nationals without civil rights in the United States. Interestingly, given the pressures placed on civil rights by the vast increase in the security state post–September 11, and by the expansion of corporate rights and privileges, the security guard understands their nonviolent protest as "Vietnamese," not as American. In this scene, *A Village Called Versailles* argues that by coming together around their shared Vietnamese heritage, the community was finally able to exercise more fully their civil rights as Americans.

Katrina exacerbated inequality and threatened rights, but, more than this, the hurricane revealed pre-existing conditions of inequality and injustice. *A Village Called Versailles* focuses on a specific community of immigrant Americans, living for decades in New Orleans, who responded to Katrina by drawing on their particular history of forced migration and by responding to continued threats by coming together as a community. *A Village Called Versailles* is as much about finding and developing voice as a tool for advocating for rights as it is about wind, water, destruction, desperation, and misery.

Chiang ends the film with a scene showing a commemoration of the first anniversary of Katrina in the Versailles community. Chiang's camera emphasizes the Vietnamese aspects of this commemoration (for example, Minh Nguyen brushing steps with brushes and bells being rung during the ceremony), but also shows many white and black New Orleanians joining the group commemoration. Fr. Nguyen and Councilwoman Willard-Lewis appear in synch interviews emphasizing that the response of Versailles to Katrina, the rebuilding of the community, and the successful protest to close the landfill have located and established the community within the map of power relations in post-Katrina New Orleans.

Like the African American residents of Treme, the Vietnamese Americans of Versailles drew upon their history of combating injustice to survive Katrina and the flooding of New Orleans. But, in addition to reaching back toward the lessons drawn from forced migrations, the community had to change and to adapt to meet the challenges of Katrina as it "is still going on."

Chiang's documentary argues that the meanings of Katrina are not biracial, are not limited to the Ninth Ward, involve past events, and contribute to the future developments of the communities that together make up the City of New Orleans. Much as community groups fought the Green Space Plan that would have reconceived of New Orleans without the Ninth Ward or Versailles, independent documentary contests the efforts of television news to define the limits of the meanings of Katrina.

CHAPTER SIXTEEN

Our Mayor

RACE

PERHAPS THE ONLY OUTCOME IN POST–KATRINA POLI-
tics more surprising than Joe Cao's election to Congress (see
S. Leo Chiang's *Mr. Cao Goes to Washington*, 2012) was Ray Nagin's reelection
as mayor of New Orleans in 2006. Nagin was first elected mayor in 2002,
running as a businessman and a reform candidate, promising to break with
corruption and cronyism and to change politics as usual in New Orleans. He
had gained recognition in New Orleans as vice president and general manager of Cox Television, the local unit of the national cable conglomerate.
Credited with turning Cox New Orleans from a low-performing unit into
a profitable enterprise, Nagin received support for his candidacy from the
New Orleans business community. However, he was not embraced by African Americans, the majority population in the City of New Orleans. Nagin
was elected major, earning 58 percent of the vote, defeating Police Chief
Richard Pennington. In the 2002 mayoral election, Nagin received 86 percent of the white vote, but only 38 percent of the African American vote.

Many inside and outside New Orleans believe that Nagin did not prepare sufficiently for Hurricane Katrina or act effectively after the flooding
of the city (Leo, 2005; DuBos, 2013). While his administration had warned
residents to voluntarily evacuate on Friday, August 26, 2005, Nagin did not
issue a mandatory evacuation order until Sunday, August 28, fewer than
twenty-four hours before Katrina made landfall. In part, Nagin delayed because he did not believe that the city could afford to evacuate the approximately 134,000 New Orleans citizens who lacked personal transportation.
As a result, most New Orleanians with means and access to transportation
left the city by car. The majority of those who stayed lacked the means to
evacuate: they did not have private automobiles, and/or they lacked cash
in advance of paychecks or Social Security payments, which would arrive

during the first week of September. Nagin issued the mandatory evacuation, but his administration did not provide the means to evacuate all of the remaining citizens. He opened the Superdome as a shelter of last resort, but did not adequately supply the facility with food and water. When the storm struck and when the levees failed, police and other responders were ordered to take shelter for their own safety, leaving residents trapped in their rapidly flooding homes without aid. City school buses that might have been used to evacuate citizens after the storm were stored in low-lying areas and were flooded. After the storm, the city's emergency communication system failed, and police and rescue workers were unable to communicate with leadership or with each other.

In this climate, Nagin and Police Chief Eddie Compass accepted and endorsed rumors, engaging in what Rebecca Solnit describes as elite panic (2010). Unable to provide for their own citizens, having lost communications and (seemingly) control, Nagin, Compass, and other authorities began to express fear of their own citizens. Residents who saved themselves from floodwaters went to the New Orleans Convention Center, seeking emergency aid and evacuation. However, since Nagin had not designated the Convention Center as an official shelter of last resort, the site was considered insecure, and authorities decided they could not offer aid or supplies to their citizens, who were left on their own until evacuation by bus began days later. Two blocks from the Convention Center, at Harrah's Casino, city and state employees, along with National Guard troops and media, received food and water. As residents attempted to evacuate New Orleans via the Crescent City Connection twin span bridge over the Mississippi River, they were blocked from crossing the bridge to the largely unflooded West Bank by armed police from the City of Gretna and from Jefferson Parish. Nagin and officials from New Orleans did not negotiate access to West Bank via the bridge. Indeed, West Bank police barricaded the bridge due to fears of looting, fears exacerbated by Nagin's and Compass's remarks to the press linking property damage to fears of rampant violence, which, for the most part, never happened (see Thevenot and Russell, 2005). Eventually, in a WWL radio interview with newsman Garland Robinette, Nagin expressed anger at the delays in state and federal aid. His comments were picked up and amplified by national media, turning Nagin briefly into a Katrina celebrity who spoke truth to power. Lost in this story was Nagin's own ineffectiveness before, during, and after the storm.

Yet, despite his performance during and after Katrina, Nagin was re-elected mayor of New Orleans in 2006. He narrowly defeated challenger Louisiana Lieutenant Governor Mitch Landrieu. Landrieu's father, Maurice "Moon" Landrieu, had been mayor of New Orleans from 1970 to 1978, and his sister Mary Landrieu (D) is the senior U.S. senator from Louisiana. The mayoral election was held in May 2006, nine months after Katrina, despite the fact that more than half of the population of New Orleans had not yet returned after evacuation. Nagin earned 53 percent of the vote to Landrieu's 47 percent. Most surprisingly, Nagin won reelection in 2006 by capturing nearly 80 percent of the African American vote, while only receiving about 20 percent of the white vote. Between 2002 and 2006, Nagin's political support had flipped.

In the documentary *Race* (2010), filmmaker Katherine Cecil examines the role of race in Nagin's 2006 reelection and, more broadly, in post-Katrina politics. Her central question is how Nagin could have managed to survive the political fallout from Katrina and completely shift his base of support from middle- and upper-class whites to a majority of the African Americans who had returned to New Orleans after Katrina. Originally from England, Cecil had moved to New Orleans in 2001. She worked as a field and an associate producer in documentary and news programming, while also pursuing graduate education in New Orleans. *Race* is her first film as producer and director. Drawing on her documentary interviews as research, Cecil also produced a master's thesis, titled "Race, Representation, and Recovery: Documenting the 2006 New Orleans Mayoral Elections" (2009).

Cecil uses two moments early in *Race* to articulate the political stakes in New Orleans after Katrina. Recognizing Nagin's vulnerability, twenty-two challengers entered the 2006 mayoral race. Cecil selects a moment from an early candidate forum featuring Peggy Wilson, a white Republican and a former New Orleans city council member, to reveal the racial stakes involved in the recovery of the city. In response to a question about the "right to return" for those who had been evacuated after Katrina, Wilson proposes instead to prevent certain residents from returning.

> WILSON: When you come back to New Orleans, we don't want you here if you are a crack dealer, if you are a member of a gang, if you are a welfare queen . . .

By linking New Orleans residents to drug crime and gang violence, Wilson picks up and extends the elite panic engaged in by Nagin, Compass, and television news in the first week after Katrina. Wilson stokes elite panic by portraying fellow citizens as dangerous criminals. Without evidence, she and her audience are unable to make meaningful distinctions between law abiders and criminals. In the absence of meaningful distinction, Wilson proposes to substitute racial difference. Her "we" assumes

"We don't want you here if you are a crack dealer, if you are a member of a gang, if you are a welfare queen . . ." (Race, frame capture).

racial and class coherence. According to Wilson, wealthy white New Orleanians could take advantage of Katrina as an opportunity to exclude some citizens from returning to the city. Her linkage of phantom crime with poverty is especially insidious, equating welfare recipients with criminals. Employing the Reagan-era code language of "welfare queen," Wilson proposes to use Katrina as an excuse to change the racial and political composition of New Orleans. Her use of "welfare queen" evinces the same logic that led Nagin and the city council to join with the Department of Housing and Urban Development to push through the demolition of undamaged public housing after Katrina. Cecil understands Wilson to offer the political equivalent of what Naomi Klein calls "disaster capitalism." As presented by Cecil, Wilson advocates unapologetically for using Katrina as an opportunity to enact ethnic and racial cleansing, to use race as a key factor in deciding who gets to be a New Orleanian after Katrina.

Cecil uses the Wilson clip to make visible in her film an attitude that was otherwise hidden and closely guarded. In contrast to Wilson's appeal to racial division, spatial and political apartheid, Cecil selects a second moment, an interview with the Reverend Leonard Lucas, pastor of the Light City Church, to articulate the dilemma facing African American voters. Where Wilson speaks in code, Lucas reflects openly on the difficult choices afforded by the 2006 election.

> LUCAS: Blacks have a tough choice. Do we put a man back in power who has neglected us for the last four years? Or, do we open the door for the white community to come back and control the city and neglect us for the next forty years?

But, as Cecil makes clear in *Race*, after a primary election cleared the field, the choice was not between Nagin and Wilson or Ron Forman, but between Nagin and Landrieu. While stopping short of endorsing either candidate, Cecil constructs a scene that contrasts each man's immediate response to Katrina. The scene ultimately reveals her point of view regarding the choices posed by Nagin and by Landrieu in the 2006 election.

The scene opens with an interview of Nagin in his office in City Hall. The scene begins with a medium shot of Nagin, before moving to observe a framed photograph of him and his daughter, and then a painted portrait of Nagin. As Cecil's camera zooms in on Nagin's portrait, focusing on his signature smile, he offers self-justification in voice-over.

> NAGIN: You know being the only person who has been the mayor pre-Katrina, during Katrina, and post-Katrina, I have a pretty unique aspect. Pre-Katrina, it was pretty unique, because I don't come from a political family, or a political organization, so I was like Sisyphus pushing a rock up the hill. Then Katrina hit, and the rock became a boulder.

Nagin's remarks combine several narratives. First, he argues that no one can judge his performance because no one else has experienced his unique circumstance as mayor during Katrina. By this formula, Nagin seeks to disqualify any criticism of his actions during and after Katrina. Second, he works to construct himself as an underdog and a maverick. His use of "political family" is a shorthand reference to the Landrieu family's long (and distinguished) history in Louisiana politics. Despite being backed by the Business Council of Greater New Orleans and other white elites in 2002, and despite having run the city for four years, Nagin sought to portray himself as an outsider during his reelection, an incumbent somehow running against the political establishment. Cecil's focus on the official portrait of Nagin under his remarks, and her move forward on his smile, underscore that he is trying to repaint his political portrait and to rewrite his recent history.

As Nagin likens himself to Sisyphus, Cecil cuts to a still image of homes flooded to the eaves with the New Orleans skyline visible in the background. This reminds viewers that many citizens who were not evacuated by the city drowned in their flooded homes. Nagin's reference to Sisyphus also contains multiple meanings. He intends the reference to demonstrate the enormity of the challenges he faced with Katrina, but Sisyphus is a figure of futility and failure, doomed to push the rock (or boulder) up the hill, only for it to repeatedly fall back. Nagin may wish to argue that Katrina was too big for anyone to respond effectively, but in so doing he leaves the impression that his approach was insufficient from the start.

Here, Cecil cuts to journalist Warren Bell Jr., interviewed on top of the *Times-Picayune* building with the city skyline visible behind him. Cecil uses Bell throughout the film to provide perspective on and analysis of the mayoral race, both as a professional journalist and as an African American citizen of New Orleans.

> BELL: Crisis either brings out the best in someone or the worst. I didn't see the best of someone right after Katrina coming out of our mayor's office.

Under this observation, Cecil cuts to a still image of Nagin, framed in close-up. Her camera tilts up to observe him, wearing a tight, white T-shirt that says "This is no place for trash." Nagin is indoors, seemingly in a hotel lobby. His shoulders are thrown back, as if he were leaning against a railing. The effect of the image is that Nagin looks strong, but haggard. The T-shirt slogan, combined with the interior location of the photo, seems to support Bell's argument that Nagin separated himself from his citizens after Katrina.

> BELL (continuing): I couldn't understand how the mayor could be locked up in a hotel room next to the Superdome where his people brought thousands of his citizens.

Cecil dissolves to a still photo of a group of more than two hundred citizens, almost all African American, crowding a dry evacuation spot on the neutral ground of a major street, clustered around a large oak tree, with water visible around them. Four white National Guardsmen are visible in the foreground, holding back the crowd and gesturing out of the frame. Cecil cuts back to Bell, interviewed in synch.

> BELL: And he doesn't even have the *cojones* to walk over to that Superdome the way any of his predecessors would have done and say, "I'm here with you, I'm feeling this with you, and we are waiting to get you help."

Cecil cuts to a still photo of the Superdome, her camera tilting down from the dome to frame thousands of citizens filling the walkways used to approach the structure. She then cuts to a still image of five African American men and women and one white woman, waiting at the Superdome. Cecil's camera zooms in on the central figure, an African American man, with gray hair and a mustache, leaning back with his left arm behind his head. His glasses are tucked into the neck of his gray T-shirt and a black ball cap rests on his stomach. As the camera moves in, the viewer is drawn to his eyes, which stare intently at the camera, conveying pain and a challenge to the photographer. The next shot pans from left to right across a still image of hundreds of African Americans crowded against barricades. On the right side of the frame, twenty white National Guard troops, in camouflage uniforms with machine guns visible, hold back the much larger group of survivors, keeping them corralled on the other side of the barrier.

> BELL: They did nothing. They just let them sit there and fester. I'm sorry, even if you don't have a solution, if you're the mayor, if you are the shepherd of your people, you should be out there.

Having used Bell to voice a critique of Nagin's actions after Katrina, Cecil shifts the scene, cutting to an interview with Landrieu at his campaign headquarters.

> LANDRIEU: My first instinct was to get down here.

The scene shifts again to a still image of a skiff, with two white men and an African American passenger, moving down a flooded street filled with ten feet of water.

> LANDRIEU: And we got in skiffs and we started going down St. Claude Avenue, just rescuing people.

Cecil cuts to another still image, beginning on two white men in a boat, shown from behind, before tilting up to frame a middle-aged African American man in a gingham shirt and jeans, sitting on his roof, next to a hole through which he had escaped his attic. From this image, Cecil cuts to a group of African American women and children in a boat. The camera zooms on a young girl (about seven years old) wearing a denim jumper. The girl looks directly at the camera as she scratches her face with her right hand. Her face is tightly drawn, her brow low, conveying anxiety and confusion. Cecil dissolves from the girl to a zoom on a still image of a street sign for St. Claude Avenue. Where the still images accompanying Bell's critique of Nagin stressed stasis and neglect, citizens stuck and forced to wait for help, the images in this sequence convey action and movement, even as the image of the girl reminds viewers of the consequences of the flood.

Cecil concludes the scene by cutting from the still image of the St. Claude Avenue sign to video of the avenue in 2006. As the camera pans left to right across the street, the soundtrack features a siren in the distance. The image shows New Orleans after the floodwaters receded. While there is no water, trash is visible, especially a bag that blows through the frame. The pan ends on a long shot of a billboard advertising the Nagin reelection campaign. The shot cuts to a close-up on the billboard, still panning left to right, over the words "Our Mayor," surrounding Nagin's face, a smile visible. Beneath Nagin's image, a secondary slogan reads, "Reunite Our City."

> LANDRIEU: I want people to know where I was. It's important from my perspective for people to understand that leaders do what they are supposed to do, when they're supposed to do it.

In this scene, Cecil draws her most explicit distinction between Nagin and Landrieu. She refutes Nagin's argument that Katrina defied meaningful action (too big to move, according to Nagin's Sisyphus analogy) with Landrieu's account of his efforts to provide direct assistance to the people of New Orleans. The still photos selected by Cecil suggest Landrieu's direct action without representing it (the white male rescuers are shown from a distance and from behind, allowing them to stand in for Landrieu as he recounts his actions). In his short documentary, *An Eye in the Storm* (2006), Neil Alexander uses his camera to observe New Orleans in the immediate aftermath of Katrina. A professional filmmaker who remained in New Orleans, Alexander shot video footage of Landrieu performing search-and-rescue operations. Even without this visual evidence, Cecil constructs a strong contrast between Nagin's disconnection and paralysis and Landrieu's immediate and direct action.

Cecil concludes the scene with the image of Nagin's billboard in order to probe the key claims of his campaign. At first glance, the billboard seems to propose Nagin as a unifying force for the City of New Orleans. However, the billboard's language addresses different audiences in different ways. When Wilson used "we" in her remarks during the campaign forum, she was not speaking for all New Orleanians, but for a smaller, specific population of white, Republican, wealthy New Orleanians who desired to remake the city by restricting the return of some citizens and by shrinking the city's footprint by not rebuilding certain neighborhoods. Wilson's "we" was addressed to a specific audience, despite its seeming inclusiveness.

*Ray Nagin reelection billboard (*Race*, frame capture).*

Similarly, Cecil argues, the description of Nagin as "Our Mayor" addresses African American citizens, rather than all New Orleanians. Having won election in 2002 with a majority of the white vote, Nagin reversed course after Katrina and courted African Americans by suggesting that Landrieu was aligned with Wilson, despite their real political differences, because both are white.

By contrasting Nagin's and Landrieu's responses to Katrina, Cecil argues that Landrieu had served African American citizens more effectively than had Nagin. During his tenure as mayor in the 1970s, Moon Landrieu had prioritized civil rights and opened up civil service jobs in city government to African Americans. As Reverend Lucas and Warren Bell Jr. emphasize in interviews, Nagin did not have a strong relationship with African American voters prior to Katrina. In order to neutralize the Landrieu family's long history of strong support for the African American community, Nagin had to run a campaign based on racial division. In order to win over African American voters, Nagin asked voters to choose him because of his race, regardless of his policies or actions.

To convince African American voters that he best represented their interests, Nagin had to downplay his record and to disavow any responsibility for the city's failed planning and response to Katrina. Guided by Jim Carvin, his campaign manager in 2002 and a fixture in mayoral politics in New Orleans, Nagin cynically played on racial fears by promising to restore African Americans to majority status in post-Katrina New Orleans. In so doing, he offered a vision strikingly similar to that of Wilson, only inverted. Cecil shows a clip from an interview in which Nagin ostensibly speaks off the cuff.

NAGIN: I don't care about what people are saying Uptown or wherever they are. This city will be a Chocolate City at the end of the day.

In an interview with Cecil, Carvin disavows that Nagin's "Chocolate City" remark was strategic. However, while the comment was widely criticized nationally, it resonated with African Americans in New Orleans fearful that the rebuilding of the city would lead to a permanent white majority. The Green Space Plan, supported by the Business Council and offered by Nagin's own Bring New Orleans Back Commission, had recommended that some low-lying neighborhoods not be rebuilt, but instead be converted into green spaces and urban gardens. As Cecil demonstrates, Nagin was for the Green Space Plan before he was against it. After the plan met with loud and sustained protest from many New Orleans residents, Nagin reversed course and lifted the moratorium on building permits in the Ninth Ward and other parts of the city that had flooded. In an act of political calculation, seeking to appeal to African American voters, Nagin rejected the plans he had commissioned and instead shifted to support a "right to return" for all.

THE BRIDGE

Cecil examines Nagin's political transformation through constructing a sequence focused on the March 21, 2006, mass march across the Crescent City Connection bridge to promote voting and civil rights and to protest injustice during Katrina. Cecil locates the sequence near the middle of her film, structurally positioning the scene to represent a turning point in the campaign. Cecil sets up the scene by showing Reverends Al Sharpton and Jesse Jackson arriving in New Orleans to announce the march, spurred by concerns that the diaspora of New Orleans residents after Katrina would disenfranchise many unable to return to the city to vote. Cecil selects a shot from a nighttime press conference showing Sharpton and Jackson, holding brass instruments, posing with New Orleans musicians Glen David Andrews and Troy "Trombone Shorty" Andrews. This image cuts to a daytime image of Glen David Andrews singing "Jesus on the Main Line" with the Treme Brass Band. Sharpton and Jackson are in the background, smiling and singing along. The march is launched with a New Orleans brass band performance, transforming a street parade into a protest march.

Cecil uses Andrews's voice and the noise of the crowd as a sound bridge to the next image, a high-angle long shot, panning from left to right, following several thousand marchers up an on-ramp toward the Crescent City Connection. A title reads, "The Following Day." The long shot is followed by a closer stationary shot, still from a high angle, of the marchers, who fill the screen, spilling out of the frame. This shot recalls images from the days after the levees failed, when television news cameras observed hundreds of citizens crowded together at the Convention Center or along the I-10 Expressway. Cecil uses natural sound to capture the many voices, and a marching band can be heard amid the marchers. As Sharpton begins to address the crowd, the scene cuts to a medium shot of a group of marchers holding a banner reading "NAACP" in blue letters over a yellow background. The scene cuts to Sharpton at the podium. A sign on the podium reads: "Right to Return; A Protected Vote; & Reconstruction."

> SHARPTON: We are here today, just like we gathered forty-one years ago in Selma. We are here prepared to go across another bridge. A bridge that they stopped us on the night that Katrina hit.

At the first reference to the bridge, Cecil cuts away to a shot of Nagin, from the side, posing for a photograph with a man and a woman. Through editing, Cecil places Nagin at the march, although he has not yet been shown in the frame in any of the images at the march. After the second reference to the bridge, Cecil cuts to an interview with a male marcher, who recounts his attempt to cross the bridge after Katrina. As he continues in voice-over, the scene cuts to a low-angle still photo of the twin span bridge. Cecil's camera zooms on the photo, suggesting movement across the bridge. Interestingly, the original photograph was taken from the West Bank side, looking across at the Central Business District of New Orleans. Even though the voice-over shares the testimony of a resident who tried to cross the bridge to safety, the image and the camera provide a perspective from the West Bank, perhaps focalized from the point of view of the Gretna police. Regardless of intention, this juxtaposition creates tension between sound and image, suggesting something of the conflict between citizens that played out on the bridge.

> MALE MARCHER: They denied us, this is a federal bridge, they denied us to come across this bridge. That's why I'm here today.

Under the marcher's testimony, Cecil cuts to a still image of a policeman with a shotgun raised in the air, confronting a crowd. However, as the camera tilts up, the image is revealed to be in front of the Superdome, not on the bridge. This image is suggestive of the barricade on the Crescent City

Connection bridge, as it represents another example of a threat of violence by authorities directed toward fellow citizens, but it does not show the events themselves.

As Sharpton continues, the scene cuts to images of crowd reactions, focusing on three women, two of them capturing the event with cameras. Then, Cecil cuts to a synch interview with Nagin.

> NAGIN: The thing I'm trying to do here today is to make sure there is as much awareness about voting as possible and how to do it.

Despite Nagin's professed focus on the civic process, Cecil's editing of the scene suggests that he has come seeking credibility by association with national civil rights leaders (Sharpton, Jackson, and Bruce Gordon, head of the NAACP) and celebrities (Bill Cosby). Later in the sequence, as Jackson addresses the crowd about stakes, Cecil frames a marcher holding up a Nagin campaign sign reading "Re-elect Our Mayor, Ray Nagin." She follows this image with an interview with historian Douglas Brinkley, who makes clear the transformation attempted by Nagin.

> BRINKLEY: Traditionally, the Landrieus are considered the great civil rights family. They are almost civil rights royalty in the United States.

Under Brinkley, Cecil cuts to an image of Landrieu at the march, surrounded by African Americans, including a tall woman in a white shirt. He is smiling and shaking hands.

> BRINKLEY (continuing): So when Jackson entered and started shaking hands with Ray Nagin, that was a very powerful commentary that Jackson was making. Once you had Jackson strongly on Nagin's side, it was very apparent the direction of the Nagin campaign.

Under Brinkley's analysis, Cecil shows a high-angle shot of the mass of marchers advancing across the bridge. She then cuts to a medium-long shot, facing the front of the march, framing the leaders as they advance over the bridge. Congressman Bill Jefferson, Jesse Jackson, and Al Sharpton stand at the front of the march. Ray Nagin stands in the next row, over Jefferson's right shoulder. As the frame holds steady, Jackson reaches back with his right hand to grasp Nagin's right hand. They hold the shake for a moment, and Nagin smiles broadly. Following Brinkley, this moment gen-

Nagin with Jesse Jackson at the March 21, 2006, voting rights march across the Crescent City Connection bridge (Race, frame capture).

erated significant political capital for Nagin in the African American community. Cecil cuts to an interview with journalist Warren Bell Jr., amplifying Brinkley's point.

> BELL: It was the first time you saw lots of black folks with Nagin shirts on. That to me was the beginning of the shift from things being very anti-Nagin in the black community, to things [*sic*] suddenly Nagin became the symbol for people concerned about issues of importance to black people.

Under Bell, Cecil cuts to a slight low angle on the crowd, showing both NAACP and Nagin campaign signs in the same frame. She then cuts to a slight high angle looking down at two women wearing white Nagin campaign shirts. The taller woman looks directly at the camera, with her head up, seemingly representing her allegiance for the camera. Cecil cuts to a wider shot of four older men and women, also wearing "Our Mayor" shirts, climbing the ramp onto the bridge.

Earlier in the film, Bell had described Nagin's attempt to perform blackness in order to attract support from the African American community, labeling this performance as "Brother Ray Ray." Here, Bell recognizes the effectiveness of Nagin's association with key civil rights leaders. As Brinkley and Bell suggest, Nagin's image as Black Mayor (defender of Chocolate City) trumped both his own previous history as a pro-business candidate and Landrieu's actual legacy in civil rights.

In order to associate himself with civil rights leaders, Nagin had to dissociate himself from his past as a business executive, denying and downplaying his own history. Similarly, in order to run as a candidate who could promote justice after Katrina, Nagin had to dissociate himself from his own record as mayor during the storm. Cecil demonstrates that Nagin was able to distance himself from responsibility for Katrina with complete cynicism.

> NAGIN: This march was about the voting issue, but it was also symbolic in that we were also busting through the barrier that people who were suffering could not bust through.

Nagin's revision of history denies that he had agency to alleviate the suffering of his citizens. Discursively, he locates himself on the bridge with the citizens seeking safety on the West Bank, when, in actuality, he did not set foot on the bridge. Instead, Nagin worked out of a hotel room on the twenty-seventh floor of the Hyatt Regency Hotel, next to the Superdome, but high above it. In *Katrina's Secrets*, his self-published account of his actions during Katrina, Nagin makes the assertion that the attempt to evacuate via the bridge to the West Bank was his idea. No independent sources support his contention. Rather, his claim seems influenced by the success of his experience participating in the march across the bridge on March 21, 2006. Having benefitted from placing himself on the bridge, next to Jackson and Sharpton, Nagin sought to place himself on the bridge on September 1, 2005.

Cecil concludes this long sequence with a selection from an interview with Nagin, shot on the day of the march. In this shot, after having claimed

*Nagin supporters at the voting rights march (*Race*, frame capture).*

*Nagin reelected (*Race, *frame capture).*

that he could not be held responsible for the failed local response to Katrina, Nagin asserts that his experience as mayor during Katrina would benefit his community in the event of another hurricane and flood.

> NAGIN: What I try to tell voters is that they have a very important election decision to make. June 1st hurricane season starts. Do you want a rookie running this city with the start of hurricane season and the city still recovering? My bet is they are going to say "No."

In *Race*, Cecil seeks to dissect the process by which Nagin and Carvin were able to convince voters to ignore Nagin's actual record and instead to vote out of racial solidarity and out of fear of a white takeover of New Orleans. Cecil argues that Landrieu offered inclusiveness and accountability and that he had a stronger record than Nagin on the key issues for the African American community. However, Cecil argues that racial perception trumped history and policy and that a majority of voters chose Nagin because of his race rather than because of his record. After Nagin's cynical argument that his failures in Katrina would be more beneficial for his city in the event of another hurricane than Landrieu's ideas and planning, Cecil fades out on Nagin's smile. The image recalls her attention to his official portrait in the mayor's office. At the end of the interview, Nagin's smile seems to acknowledge his performance, a small reflexive gesture signaling his political agency.

Cecil's film concludes with Nagin's reelection in 2006. She released the film in 2009. Nagin completed his second term in 2010, unable to run again due to term limits. Landrieu easily defeated businessman Troy Henry to become mayor. After leaving office, Nagin was investigated by the Justice Department and the FBI for accepting bribes and kickbacks from city vendors, before and after Katrina. Nagin's chief technology officer Gregory Meffert pleaded guilty in 2010 to bribery charges, raising suspicion that he was cooperating with federal authorities by providing incriminating information about Nagin. In 2013, Nagin faced trial on twenty-one criminal counts of bribery, money laundering, defrauding the public, and filing false tax returns. In February 2014, he was found guilty of twenty of the corruption charges. Subsequent events have underscored Cecil's main argument: that voters elected the wrong candidate for the wrong reasons, elevating racial identity above all other factors in the mayoral race. *Race* demonstrates the corrosive influence of racial politics in New Orleans after Katrina. Even after many African Americans and poor white residents suffered in the aftermath of Katrina due to neglect and prejudice related to racial and class perception, these citizens were not able to bracket their own racial perception during the 2006 New Orleans mayoral election.

CHAPTER SEVENTEEN

Re-Occupying New Orleans

LAND OF OPPORTUNITY

K ATHERINE CECIL STRUCTURED *RACE* TO EXAMINE THE political equivalent of disaster capitalism, and her film documents the political expediency employed by Ray Nagin, Peggy Wilson, and others who sought to use Katrina to increase their political fortunes and advance their political agendas. In *Land of Opportunity*, filmmaker Luisa Dantas examines disaster capitalism in the aftermath of Katrina by focusing on housing, land use, and redevelopment in the aftermath of the flooding of New Orleans. The failure of the federally constructed and maintained levee system resulted in the flooding of 80 percent of the City of New Orleans and the destruction of most of the city's housing stock. Katrina produced a housing crisis as those who lost their homes struggled to find affordable places to live as they worked to rebuild flooded homes and restart disrupted lives.

Dantas's truth claim in *Land of Opportunity* is based on the lives and experiences of average citizens of New Orleans. Rather than employ extensive interviews with experts or create arguments from found footage, Dantas and her collaborators, Rebecca Snedeker (producer) and Michael Boedigheimer (cinematographer), employed an observational approach to focus on the lives and perspectives of eight characters. By focusing on a large number of characters, Dantas was able to create a mosaic of voices, representing both common and distinctive experiences of the storm and flood. *Land of Opportunity* demonstrates the power of individual and collective testimony as a source of truth about traumatic experience. Where Cecil makes a persuasive argument about the impact of Katrina and racial division on the politics of New Orleans, her frame and focus are intentionally delimited. Her *Race* contributes to the archive of collected memory about Katrina by reinterpreting the meaning of a significant political outcome. Dantas's *Land of Opportunity* contributes to this archive by bringing to screen the experiences and perspectives of a diverse group of citizens engaged in the work of rebuilding, reconstructing, and reoccupying New Orleans.

Luisa Dantas has lived and worked between Brazil and the United States. She earned a BA in English and Latin American Studies at Brown University and an MFA in film from Columbia University. Dantas wrote and directed a fictional short film *Bolo* (2001) that was produced and distributed in Brazil. She co-produced *Wal-Mart: The High Cost of Low Price* (2005) with Robert Greenwald. Working with Greenwald, she began to develop her approach to documentary for social advocacy. Drawing on the model of Greenwald's Brave New Films, which produces progressive, activist media in multiple formats, she developed her own grassroots distribution and social action plan for *Land of Opportunity*. In 2005, Dantas moved to Los Angeles to write for the animated television show *Go, Diego, Go!* While in Los Angeles, she followed closely the impact of Katrina on New Orleans. In January 2006, five months after the hurricane, she relocated to New Orleans in order to begin developing documentary content about the efforts of New Orleans citizens to recover and rebuild their lives after Katrina.

Unlike many other filmmakers who sought to document Katrina and its aftermath, Dantas emphasized duration. In an interview, she indicated that she and Boedigheimer began in early 2006 to shoot footage of community events throughout New Orleans, with special focus on the Ninth Ward and the Treme neighborhoods. At this early stage, Dantas knew that she wanted the project to document and to affect local efforts to respond to Katrina. Dantas and Boedigheimer shot for more than five years. In the process, they amassed an archive of more than fifteen hundred hours of footage. On a Kickstarter page for the project, Dantas posted a photo of their data storage regime, a "tera-army" of fourteen 1-terabyte storage drives.

As a recent arrival to the city, Dantas recognized that she needed to learn about New Orleans from longtime residents. She committed to an extended production process in order both to fully understand the situation on the ground and to develop sufficient material to tell a complex and nuanced story from multiple perspectives. Through *Land of Opportunity*, Dantas demonstrates the power of documentary media making as a research tool for developing qualitative and humanistic data.

Dantas worked closely with local advocacy groups to shape her short content and to develop her archive of documentary material. In an interview, she indicated that the videos were produced and distributed in conjunction with local groups working on specific post-Katrina issues and campaigns. For example, the videos "Sectioned Off" and "Deep Sixed" were produced with the New Orleans Fair Housing Action Council for their Four Years on the Road to Housing Justice campaign around the fourth anniversary of Katrina.

By working closely with local groups like the New Orleans Fair Housing Action Council, Dantas embraced a participatory mode of documentary production, de-centering her own authority as controlling voice in order to create a documentary of many voices. Her decision to partner with local groups and to be open to local perspectives distinguishes her documentary from films like *The Axe in the Attic*. Rather than impose her perspectives onto New Orleans, or make a film about her struggles as a filmmaker to understand Katrina, Dantas listened to local advocates, learned from them, and developed content to convey their perspectives and concerns to audiences outside New Orleans.

Dantas decided to produce both short- and long-form media from her growing archive of footage. Like Annabel Park and Eric Byler's approach with *9500 Liberty* (2009), where the filmmakers created a website on which to post short work and through which to create a commons for discussion about the treatment of immigrants in Prince William County, Virginia, Dantas decided to create and share shorter pieces focused on specific issues and specific characters. She produced a series of intermediate products, short-format stories distributed through her own website (landof opportunitymovie.com), beginning August 29, 2010, the fifth anniversary of Katrina's landfall. Like Brave New Films or *9500 Liberty*, *Land of Opportunity* exists as a multi-format, multi-platform documentary project. Dantas and collaborators produced the short videos between 2006 and 2010, and they originally distributed the videos individually via YouTube. With the launch of the website, Dantas organized the discrete videos by character and by social issues, suggesting linkages that she would also make in the feature documentary. Moreover, she continues to add video content. In 2011, on the sixth anniversary of Katrina, she added a short video on Tr'Vel Lyons, a teenager who moved with his mother from New Orleans to Los Angeles after Katrina. The site currently features sixteen videos. One of these shorts, entitled *St. Joe* (2009), was entered in festivals and won Best Short at the Patois New Orleans International Human Rights Film Festival. In 2010, to coincide with the five-year anniversary of Katrina, Dantas created a television edit of *Land of Opportunity* that aired on Arte, a European cable television channel. In 2011, she completed a theatrical edit and screened the feature version at film festivals throughout the world. After the festival circuit screenings, she joined the New Day Film Collective in order to distribute the feature version via DVD to universities and libraries.

In 2012, Dantas received grant funding to develop *Land of Opportunity* into an interactive web-based video player, which launched in fall 2013. She uses the interactive player to invite viewers/players to engage with her documentary material as participants. Dantas plans for the interactive player to be used as a tool for exploring challenges and responses common to many cities. Through the transmedia project, she hopes that her stories about the recovery and rebuilding of New Orleans after Katrina can spark dialogue and action in other cities facing versions of the same challenges. In July 2013, when the City of Detroit declared bankruptcy, law professor Peter Hammer described Detroit as a "five-decade Katrina" (Fletcher, 2013). Through her multi-year, multi-format, multi-platform documentary project, Dantas explores the challenges of rebuilding New Orleans in order to contribute to the crucial dialogue about the future of cities like Detroit.

Early in her project, Dantas identified housing, land use, and redevelopment as key issues in the recovery and rebuilding of New Orleans. As noted, a majority of the more than one hundred thousand New Orleans residents who remained in the city at Katrina's landfall lacked the means to evacuate. Many of these citizens lived in public housing, including several large projects built during the late 1930s and early 1940s. The St. Bernard Housing Project in the Seventh Ward contained fifteen hundred apartment units. Many residents from St. Bernard and other public housing sought shelter from Katrina in the Superdome. Others went to the Convention Center seeking evacuation. By Saturday, September 3, 2005, the sixth day after landfall, residents were completely evacuated from the Superdome and from the Convention Center, sent by bus and plane around the United States. Many did not have any choice in their destination. While FEMA and the National Guard facilitated their evacuation, provisions were not made for helping these citizens return. Complicating the return process for residents of public housing, the City of New Orleans closed St. Bernard and other housing projects after Katrina, despite the fact that St. Bernard had not flooded and did not suffer structural damage. While middle- and upper-class citizens were eventually allowed to return to their homes to perform a "look and leave," public housing residents were not allowed access to their apartments in St. Bernard. With full support from the Department of Housing and Urban Development (HUD), the Housing Authority of New Orleans (HANO) planned to demolish St. Bernard, using FEMA money earmarked for demolition of public buildings damaged by Katrina.

Residents and housing advocates argued that St. Bernard and other public housing should be reopened. While public housing had long been neglected by federal, state, and local policy, and housing projects had become sites for violent crime and drug dealing, many residents of public housing were hard-working citizens. With the loss of 80 percent of housing stock in the flood, New Orleans housing costs skyrocketed. Without access to public housing, many residents evacuated from New Orleans by the federal government could not afford to return.

Following HUD policy, HANO proposed to replace St. Bernard and other housing projects with new construction, less dense, mixed-income housing. The problem with the proposal was that the new mixed-income housing would contain only a small number of subsidized units for the very poor. In the case of St. Bernard, 1,500 subsidized units would be "replaced" by 150 subsidized units in the new construction. HUD and HANO did not make provisions for the other 90 percent of St. Bernard residents.

HOUSING IS A HUMAN RIGHT

Dantas and collaborators had been following these developments, and the community effort to resist the demolition of St. Bernard became a major focus in *Land of Opportunity*. As they continued to shape the feature film, Dantas and Boedigheimer produced *St. Joe* (2009), a short film focused on the demolition of the St. Bernard Housing Project. The film runs 10:26 and contains no dialogue, only the wild sounds of wind and birds, and eventually, the sounds of cranes and bulldozers. The film uses 102 shots to create a portrait of the St. Bernard Housing Project and to document its demolition.

St. Joe opens with a series of perspectives on the buildings of St. Bernard. The first twenty shots examine the exterior of the buildings. The footage was shot on a bright, clear day, and the filmmakers frame details of the red brick buildings and wrought iron porches and railings against the blue sky. The overall impression is of a solid, well-built complex. Other than the iron work, the design is utilitarian, but in a series of close-ups and creative framings of architectural details (roof lines, corners, windows), Dantas and Boedigheimer find beauty and visual interest in a place that had been widely considered ugly and run-down by those outside St. Bernard.

The next eighteen shots look inside at the interior of apartments in St. Bernard. One shot looks down from a slight high angle on dishes left by a sink. Another shot finds a wedding dress hanging in a closet, and another examines in close-up the August 16, 2005, front page of the *Times-Picayune*. These shots and others create a strong sense of lives interrupted. As with the exterior shots, the interior shots do not show any people. The dress, the plates, and the newspaper stand in for the residents. The interior shots convey absence, but in the case of St. Bernard, the loss is not directly attrib-

*St. Bernard Housing Project (*Land of Opportunity, *frame capture).*

utable to Katrina. Unlike Terence and Wilhelmina Blanchard's return in *When the Levees Broke* or Irving Trevigne's return in *Faubourg Treme*, Dantas and Boedigheimer return in place of the residents who have been denied access, trespassing in order to shoot their footage. Unlike the films featuring scenes of return to homes destroyed by flooding, *St. Joe* suggests that life could resume in these spaces if policy allowed. Like Katrina itself, public policy has consequences. In the thirty-seventh shot of the sequence, the filmmakers show the decomposed body of a cat, a domestic pet left behind that starved behind the chain-link fences surrounding St. Bernard. The cat's skeleton serves as a symbol of the loss of lives in Katrina, not only from drowning, but also from the disruptions of evacuation and diaspora.

Near the middle of the film, Dantas and Boedigheimer show a sign identifying the complex as the St. Bernard Housing Development. The sign is framed by a chain-link fence. Shots of the moon behind clouds convey the passage of time. After a fade to black, the second half of the film begins with a daytime, side view of a brick building. As the filmmakers hold the shot, a large metal claw enters the frame, emerging from around the corner. Paired with the opening exterior shots, this sequence captures the demolition of St. Bernard by large equipment. Cranes and claws tear at roofs and walls, causing bricks to break and cascade. The fifty-third shot is a close-up of a single, undamaged brick reading "St. Joe." The brick was produced by St. Joe's Brickworks in Pearl River, Louisiana. Founded in 1891, St. Joe's continues to supply bricks to construction projects throughout the United States. Dantas and Boedigheimer use the St. Joe's brick to reference the history and solid construction of St. Bernard, emphasizing the waste and loss represented by the demolition.

Later in the sequence, the filmmakers create a moment of suspense from a series of quick edits alternating between shots of a crane swiping downward violently and the interior of an apartment in the building being demolished. The camera can see into the apartment because the exterior wall has already been destroyed. As the crane slashes down, the exposed apartment shakes, unsettling a sofa. After six frames, the sofa falls. In the seventy-sixth shot, the camera zooms into a close-up on a mirrored vanity. The double mirrors of the vanity reflect the crane destroying the building. As in the shots of clothes and plates left behind during evacuation, these shots use the sofa and the vanity to suggest the people who used them.

Toward the end of the film, Dantas and Boedigheimer include a shot that unambiguously expresses their argument in the film. In a wide, long shot, they frame a half-demolished building on the right and a sign on the lower left. The sign is written on a sheet, attached to the fence surrounding St. Bernard, and it reads, "Housing Is a Human Right." As the filmmakers hold the shot, a crane topples the upper part of the structure.

In the remaining shots, the camera finds and observes family photos among the debris. The first shot, observed from above, shows a high school graduation photo of a young African American male. He wears a white cap and gown and clutches his diploma. The next shots show groups of male and female friends. Together, these shots argue against common, discursive understandings of public housing as sites of criminality and deviance. The photos emphasize the importance of St. Bernard as home to families and friends, a place where graduations and parties were celebrated, where people lived ordinary lives.

Demolition of the St. Bernard Housing Project by the Housing Authority of New Orleans. (St. Joe, frame capture).

Wide shot of the demolition of the St. Bernard Housing Project (St. Joe, *frame capture*).

Formally and thematically, *St. Joe* resembles the city symphony film, a hybrid approach to representing modernity, combining elements of documentation and experimentation. In *Manhatta* (1922), Charles Sheeler and Paul Strand edited an array of perspectives on New York City, shot from different heights and employing different angles and framing, to create a composite portrait of the city. In *Man with a Movie Camera* (1929), Dziga Vertov went further, exploring the formal possibilities of film as a tool for creating modernist visual perspective. Vertov did not only want to convey multiple perspectives on St. Petersburg, but also to explore how the camera apparatus can be used to create *kino pravda*, cinematic truth. Decades later, Jean Rouch and Edgar Morin referenced Vertov in creating *Chronicle of a Summer* (1960), developing what would be known as cinema verité. *St. Joe* uses images poetically to suggest the history of St. Bernard and the cost to its residents of its destruction.

In 2009, Broderick Webb and Ed Holub released a short called *Cut Off* that explored housing rights in New Orleans. The film contains footage of the destruction of public housing. The short references music video and agit prop as well as documentary, employing music, quick cutting, found material, and titles on screen. Where *St. Joe* employs the visual poetics of the city symphony film, *Cut Off* is more aggressive, more explicitly critical of HANO, HUD, and the federal Hope Six Program that seeks to replace large, mid-century public housing with less dense, mixed-income housing. In the process, the inventory of affordable units for the very poor is greatly reduced.

In *St. Joe*, Dantas creates a strong and direct visual representation of oppression. The first half of the short argues that St. Bernard was intact and available after Katrina to house evacuated citizens. Moreover, Dantas and Boedigheimer show St. Bernard to be a place of beauty, a place where generations of New Orleans citizens had lived their lives. They argue that, though St. Bernard was the site of drug dealing and violence, it provided an essential condition for self-development. In the second half, the filmmakers show the destruction of the complex as an attack on the lived history of residents of St. Bernard and as an attack on the possibilities for future development. By showing the destruction of interior as well as exterior spaces, they convey the act of demolition as a form of oppression. HANO did not only demolish structures; it also destroyed homes, memories, and opportunities. In this way, the short documentary suggests the softer, less visually apparent forms of oppression, such as the reduction of affordable housing.

Land of Opportunity employs two core strategies to explore issues of social justice raised by Katrina and its aftermath: visualizing oppression and documenting community agency. First, the film seeks to visualize the forces and forms of oppression. In a discussion of social justice theory and pedagogy, Lee Anne Bell defines oppression as the forces that inhibit self-development and self-determination (2010). Bell understands self-development to include all opportunities for the individual and the community to learn, grow, and prosper. Safe, affordable housing is crucial to self-development, as the individual cannot grow personally, or support the development of others, without shelter and security.

Where *St. Joe* only suggests people through visual poetics, *Land of Opportunity* focuses on people, their faces, bodies, voices, testimonies, and actions. In the feature documentary, Dantas employs observational approaches, drawing on the traditions associated with Direct Cinema more than the reflexivity of cinema verité. In *Land of Opportunity*, the frame is crowded with bodies, movement, and activity. Dantas does not include expert testimony or graphic representations of data. She does not formally interview her subjects, abstracting them from their lives by creating special visual scenarios for sit-down interviews. Instead, Dantas follows people, observes them, and listens carefully to what they have to say.

Drawing from her archive of more than fifteen hundred hours of original video, Dantas could develop multiple documentary characters and story lines. In the theatrical feature version, she interweaves these characters and stories, seeking to construct a broader mosaic and a wider view of the impact of Katrina and the flood on housing and development. As a result, *Land of Opportunity* features a polyphony of voices. While this choice creates a more complex representation, the number of voices and lives makes *Land of Opportunity* less coherent and focused in argument than documentaries focused on fewer characters, like *Trouble the Water* or *Faubourg Treme*.

To develop her second strategy of community development and advocacy, Dantas introduces Vanessa Gueringer, a resident of the Ninth Ward who becomes an activist and a community organizer after Katrina. Like the Versailles community in New Orleans East, the Ninth Ward community had to fight for self-determination after Katrina. As *Race* demonstrated, the initial planning process for rebuilding New Orleans was dominated by business interests and proposed not to rebuild the Ninth Ward. Through Vanessa, Dantas depicts the efforts by Ninth Ward residents to have a strong voice in the rebuilding or their community and city.

To investigate affordable housing and housing as a right, the filmmaker tells the stories of Kawana and Sharon Jasper, former residents of the St. Bernard Housing Project who become public housing activists after Katrina. Sharon is a grandmother and a lifelong resident of St. Bernard. After returning to New Orleans, she protests HANO's plan to demolish St. Bernard and to replace it with mixed-income housing. Even as Sharon struggles to gain a low-income spot in the new development, she protests the dramatic reduction in housing for the working poor. Her daughter Kawana, a single mother, had moved out of St. Bernard before Katrina, hoping to increase opportunities for her children. After Katrina, Kawanna recognizes the importance of St. Bernard as a housing option, and she fights against the demolition.

To demonstrate the challenges of the Katrina diaspora, Dantas follows Tr'Vel Lyons, a young man who evacuated with his mother from New Orleans East to Los Angeles. Unlike Gueringer or the Jaspers, Tr'Vel does not move back to New Orleans. Instead, he remains in California, taking advantage of the educational opportunities in Los Angeles, graduating from high school and earning a Gates Millennium scholarship to UCLA. Dantas shows the young man returning to New Orleans to visit his father, emphasizing what Tr'Vel has lost as well as what he has gained by the move to Los Angeles.

To explore the issue of development and rebuilding, Dantas introduces Andrés Duany and Al Aubry. Duany is an architect and urban planner based in Miami, Florida. As a planner and developer, he co-founded the New Urbanism movement. His firm, Duany Plater-Zyberk (DPZ), developed Seaside, Florida, and Kentlands, Maryland. Like many other prominent urban planners, Duany was attracted to the challenge of rebuilding New

Orleans, seeing the city as a canvas for his creative projection. In the film, he seems surprised when local community members do not immediately embrace his vision. While Duany is not able to accomplish his larger proposals, he does design and build four units of affordable housing in the Bywater neighborhood, proposing these as a new model for the construction of affordable housing without public subsidy. Unlike Duany, Aubry is a lifelong resident of New Orleans. Dantas finds him living with his wife and two children in a Katrina trailer parked next to his destroyed home. As Aubry waits for permission from the city to demolish his house and to begin to rebuild, he meets Duany, who suggests that he start a community garden. Embracing the idea, Aubry grows a large garden, providing him with an escape from the confines of the trailer and providing his family with fresh produce.

Dantas chose to title her film *Land of Opportunity* to suggest the American promise as a place for people to pursue self-development and self-determination. Dantas recognizes not only the importance of realizing opportunity for all citizens (social justice), but also the real forces preventing many citizens from enjoying opportunity (oppression). While focused on the social challenges after Katrina, *Land of Opportunity* also explores the antecedents of injustice. By using found footage of home movies shot in St. Bernard, Dantas argues that public housing has been important for poor families but has never been fully adequate to their needs. Her title also critiques disaster capitalism, the understanding that disaster and suffering might also provide corporations and wealthy individuals with opportunities to make a profit from catastrophes suffered by others. *Land of Opportunity* critiques the confluence of public policy and disaster capitalism that led to the demolition of St. Bernard and its replacement by the Columbia Parc development. As noted, St. Bernard was constructed from bricks produced by St. Joe, bricks that had weathered more than half a century. Dantas's camera shows Columbia Parc to be made from cheaper, less substantial material in order to provide greater profits for the developer. Dantas questions whether Columbia Parc will last a fraction of the time St. Bernard survived. As she makes clear, policy destroyed St. Bernard, not Katrina.

In *Land of Opportunity*, Dantas also focuses on the role of immigrant labor in rebuilding New Orleans. Due to the diaspora, the city experienced a labor shortage after Katrina. In hopes of earning good wages in construction and rebuilding, immigrants (many undocumented) headed to New Orleans. Like the Vietnamese who migrated to New Orleans East in the 1970s, many of the Central and Latin American immigrants who moved to New Orleans after Katrina experienced hostility from residents, themselves the products of earlier moments of migration. Dantas explores the realities faced by undocumented immigrant labor by observing two characters, Elza F. and Marcio P. Elza, the mother of three young daughters, enters the United States from Brazil in hopes of earning good wages by participating in the rebuilding of New Orleans. Instead, as Dantas documents, she finds good work difficult to find and wages lower than she had hoped. Dantas shows Elza cleaning toilets in the Superdome and vacuuming the clubhouse of a country club. Marcio is also from Brazil, where he left a white-collar job in hopes of earning more money in construction in New Orleans. Unlike Elza, Marcio eventually leaves New Orleans when the rebuilding boom does not materialize and returns to Brazil. While *A Village Called Versailles* addresses a history of immigration, *Land of Opportunity* focuses on post-Katrina immigration to New Orleans and, in the process, tells the stories of people occupying the social margins of a devastated city, largely invisible to national awareness.

In *Land of Opportunity*, Dantas seeks to contrast injustice with individual and community agency. Television news coverage of Katrina repeatedly represented the surviving citizens of New Orleans as powerless. Long and wide images of the Convention Center and the Superdome, often shot from long distance using zoom lenses, showed crowds of citizens, waiting for aid. In *Land of Opportunity*, Dantas repeatedly builds representations of her characters acting.

In the film's third scene, she shows Vanessa Gueringer as she goes door-to-door in the Ninth Ward seeking signatures on a petition to oppose the Green Space Plan, which would have prohibited rebuilding in the Ninth Ward, turning the neighborhood into a "green zone." As Dantas and Boedigheimer shoot from over Gueringer's shoulder, she engages her neighbors, discussing their shared stakes and the threat posed by a planning process moving forward without their involvement. Dantas represents community organizing at the ground level. Later in the film, she shows Gueringer meeting with Mayor Nagin, who assures her that he (now) opposes the smaller footprint plan. Having learned about political promises, Gueringer promises to watch Nagin carefully to ensure that he keeps his word. In another scene, she meets Senator Barack Obama, then a presidential candidate. Gueringer presses Candidate Obama on what he would do for New Orleans if elected. Obama promises to appoint a czar to oversee federal efforts to support rebuilding, a promise he failed to keep.

Dantas shows Sharon Jasper testifying about the importance of public housing at the city council meeting to determine whether the city will demolish St. Bernard. As Dantas makes clear, the city council sought to restrict access by citizens to the meeting. After Jasper testifies, security guards use tasers to shock into submission a young male protestor. Amidst the chaos, proximate to the act of repression, Dantas's camera finds Jasper, standing her ground and insisting on exercising her rights.

In an earlier scene, Dantas and Boedigheimer accompany Kawana Jasper into St. Bernard. HANO had surrounded the housing development with fences and posted signs threatening trespassers. Having been prohibited from returning to her mother's apartment, Kawana returns with Dantas to reclaim the space of St. Bernard. Many of New Orleans's cultural traditions involve carnivalesque inversion and the use of the parade, second line, stepping club, or march as an act of retaking space through presence, movement, and creativity. Dantas follows Jasper as she strolls her daughter through St. Bernard, taking back the space by showing and narrating it to the documentary camera.

Dantas also builds scenes around other expressions of agency. She shows Al Aubry as he learns to garden. Aubry is a very large man, both tall and wide, and Dantas's camera contrasts the image of him in the confining spaces of the family's trailer, where he fills the frame, with wider framing of his work in the garden under open sky, framing him amid leafy green plants. Dantas makes clear that growing, harvesting, and sharing vegetables with neighbors is an act of resistance against the constraints of insufficient support and an uncaring, incompetent system. In a small moment, Aubry cooks a ratatouille, using fresh vegetables from this garden, briefly transforming the trailer into a space of delicious smells and fresh flavors.

Dantas shows Tr'Vel Lyons struggling to adjust to life in Los Angeles, far away from his father and his childhood home. The young man applies himself, does well in middle school, and gets into a good high school. Dantas

*Aubry describes his garden (*Land of Opportunity, *frame capture).*

*Aubry's garden amid the devastation in Gentilly (*Land of Opportunity, *frame capture).*

concludes Tr'Vel's story line with the news that he has won a Gates Millennium scholarship. *Land of Opportunity* shows Tr'Vel exerting agency in his own life, becoming a dedicated student, and developing his own way. Dantas also suggests that Tr'Vel's success in Los Angeles is a loss to New Orleans, an example of indigenous brain drain, not fully offset by the influx of bright young people into New Orleans after Katrina. Even with her most constrained characters, Elza and Marcio, Dantas is able to show them each exerting some agency. While lacking free choice of employment, and unable to determine their wage rates, they nevertheless use their labor to benefit their families back in Brazil. Elza and Marcio have each chosen to come to New Orleans, to contribute to the rebuilding of the city, and to earn money to support their families.

In *Land of Opportunity*, Dantas shows oppression at work, but she also shows citizens demonstrating agency, organizing, protecting, protesting, growing, supporting each other. In *When the Levees Broke*, Lee and Pollard argue that culture is the answer to injustice created, or made worse, by Katrina. Dantas argues that self-determination is the answer. Following social justice theory, both culture as a form of self- and community development and agency as a form of self-determination are necessary conditions for justice in New Orleans after Katrina.

CHAPTER EIGHTEEN

Disappeared People

LAW & DISORDER

*I*N AUGUST 2005, AT THE TIME OF KATRINA'S LANDFALL
and the flooding of New Orleans, independent investigative
journalist A. C. Thompson was in the Bay Area working on a story about
the U.S. government's practice of torture post-September 11. Thompson
remembers watching television news coverage of the flooding of New
Orleans. He noted two dominant story lines at the time. Readable in some
of the footage aired by the television news networks, and expressed by
Kanye West while appearing on camera with comedian Mike Myers during a fund-raising broadcast across NBC's networks, one story line argued
that the state had neglected its people, leaving them to drown in the floodwaters. The second story line argued that New Orleans residents had gone
crazy—especially African Americans, who had descended into chaos and
banditry. Thompson remembers feeling shame over the neglect, even as
television news shifted to stress the second story line, blaming surviving
citizens for their own plight. Since Thompson was fully engaged in reporting his story on torture, he did not immediately ask deeper questions
about what was happening in New Orleans. Like the majority of Americans, he watched the news, felt sorrow, shame, and anger, and went back
to his normal life.

Unlike the majority of Americans, though, Thompson eventually returned to his original questions about Katrina. In reporting "The Uses of
Disaster" for *Harpers*, Rebecca Solnit had come across stories about white
citizens shooting and killing African Americans in the days and weeks after
Katrina (2005). When Solnit had been unable to substantiate these stories,
she proposed to Thompson that he investigate. These accounts seemed to
offer another story line, distinct from the dominant media accounts of

neglect by the state and anarchy by the people. Thompson learned about Henry Glover, a thirty-one-year-old African American resident of the Algiers neighborhood on the West Bank of New Orleans. Glover had been shot from a distance, by a rifle, on Friday, September 2, 2005. Seeking medical attention for Glover, his brother Ed King and a stranger named Will Tanner brought him to Habans Elementary School in Algiers, a temporary outpost for the New Orleans Police Department. According to King and Tanner, they were taken from Tanner's car by police, handcuffed, and beaten. Neither man knew what had happened to Glover or to Tanner's car.

For Thompson, the story of Glover's wounding and disappearance raised echoes of the disappearance of political dissidents in Chile and Argentina. Glover's disappearance also reminded Thompson of the practice of extra-legal rendition used by the CIA and non-agency contractors after September 11, 2001. Having recently finished his investigation of black sites and torture as techniques used by the United States in the "War on Terror," Thompson was struck by the mystery of Glover's disappearance, by the treatment of King and Tanner by police, and by the lack of an official investigation into Glover's shooting and disappearance.

In investigating Glover's disappearance, and other shootings after Katrina, Thompson used a process that resembled the work of documentary media makers. He sought and received grant support from the Nation Institute, the Center for Creative Reporting, New American Media, and ProPublica. This funding and the lack of a hard deadline gave Thompson the time to accumulate and evaluate information. In addition to acquiring and analyzing documents, he collected oral histories. By interviewing a wide range of citizens with direct connections to events, Thompson was able to build alternative evidence, especially crucial in the absence of records or a paper trail. For example, King was able to take Thompson to the spot where Glover was initially shot. Tanner corroborated details provided by King. From these two accounts, Thompson determined that Glover had likely been shot from the second floor of an adjacent strip mall. Thompson found that a New Orleans Police Department (NOPD) substation had occupied a storefront on the second floor. Through interviews, he was able to collect specific memories from which to build arguments about events. These collected memories countered official accounts (or non-accounts) by NOPD and helped to identify gaps in record keeping by the police and by the New Orleans coroner's office, led by Dr. Frank Minyard.

After a year and a half of reporting, Thompson published two long reports on ProPublica's website, "Post-Katrina, White Vigilantes Shot African Americans With Impunity" and "Body of Evidence" (both December 19, 2008). Both articles were also published in hard copy in the *Nation*. In

"White Vigilantes," Thompson countered the impression, stoked by local and state authorities and widely circulated by television news, that the African American citizens of New Orleans had turned lawless and violent after Katrina. While Brian Thevenot and others had reported that the claims of rape and murder by New Orleans citizens at the Superdome and at the Convention Center were greatly distorted and exaggerated, Thompson determined that a group of twenty to thirty white men in Algiers had carried on an organized campaign of vigilante violence directed against African American men. He reported that white vigilantes shot and killed unarmed African Americans, some residents of the same neighborhood. In "Body of Evidence," Thompson focused on Henry Glover, reporting that Glover had been shot by forty-two-year-old rookie policeman David Warren. Further, Thompson had determined that while King and Tanner were detained and beaten by police, other officers removed Tanner's car, with Glover in the backseat. The incinerated car was later discovered at the levee nearby with Glover's remains inside. Thompson argues that Glover was killed by police, that the car was burned to hide evidence, and that police conspired to avoid investigating Glover's death and disappearance. Glover's skull was removed from the burned car, but was never admitted into evidence. It disappeared, much as he had.

Thompson's long-duration, long-form investigations point the way toward the future of journalism, a future in which journalism and documentary media will increasingly share approaches and outcomes. In a personal interview in 2013, Thompson related that his method requires years of investigation. As a consequence, he must find stories with significant stakes, both to sustain his own interest in exposing injustice and promoting action and to attract the foundation and grant support necessary to fund years of full-time investigation and writing, his version of documentary production and post-production.

Thompson's journalism thus requires partners, both citizens who share their lived experiences and multiple media outlets to support and distribute the work. Thompson and ProPublica partnered with the New Orleans *Times-Picayune* and PBS's *Frontline* to investigate police and vigilante violence in the aftermath of Katrina. This partnership involved joint investigation and collaborative reporting. It also involved the production of documentary media, both short videos for the web and eventually an hour-long *Frontline* episode entitled *Law & Disorder* that first aired on PBS on August 25, 2010. In an interview for this book, Thompson argued that journalists, like filmmakers, must develop partnerships and multiple platforms for their work. Thus, during his own investigation, Thompson worked with Laura Maggi and Brendan McCarthy of the *Times-Picayune* and Tom Jennings of *Frontline*. For Thompson, *Law & Disorder* was another platform for the presentation of the discoveries of his investigation.

PBS initially broadcast *Law & Disorder* just before the fifth anniversary of Katrina's landfall. In final form, the episode features Thompson himself as the structuring element. The documentary follows him as he retraces aspects of his reporting, especially his reporting on "Body of Evidence." Thompson narrates the program, advancing the story via voice-over: "I had my own theory . . ." In this way, *Law & Disorder* resembles Thompson's own print journalism. He regularly uses the first person to share his own process of unraveling the stories he investigates. For example, in "White Vigilantes," Thompson writes, "After hearing of these gruesome stories, I wonder if any of the militia figures I've interviewed were involved in the shootings of Herrington and company" (Donnell Herrington, the young African American male who was shot in the Algiers Point neighborhood while trying to evacuate). Reminiscent of New Journalists from Tom Wolfe to Michael Herr, Thompson makes his own process part of his stories. In the *Frontline* documentary, Thompson as character leads the viewers to the sites crucial to his reporting, introducing Ed King and Will Tanner to camera.

In "Body of Evidence," Thompson describes amateur video footage of Glover's remains in Tanner's burned-out 2001 Chevrolet Malibu. *Law & Disorder* shows viewers selections from the footage. Shot by Istvan Balogh, a former corrections officer from Pennsylvania, who, with a friend, spent two weeks in New Orleans after Katrina as a "security consultant," the footage shows the burned remains of a formerly white car. As Balogh moves in closer, the camera reveals the partial remains of a human skull. Other bone fragments are visible inside the car. Balogh had heard about the car and the remains and had gone to see for himself. The result is a visual record at odds with the eventual official report by the coroner. Minyard claimed not to have received or examined the skull, and he failed to determine a cause of death, consigning the Glover case to unresolved and uninvestigated status.

In addition to providing a visual tour of Thompson's reporting, *Law & Disorder* also reviews Maggi's reporting on the NOPD shooting of unarmed civilians on the Danziger Bridge on Sunday, September 4, 2005. Collectively, Maggi, McCarthy, and Thompson, working with *Frontline*, seek to understand how rumors of violence by citizens could lead to fatal shootings of citizens by police and to shootings of civilians by white vigilantes in Algiers. Using footage from *Frontline*'s previous news documentary "The Storm," broadcast in November 2005, in the near aftermath of the storm and flood, *Law & Disorder* implicates NOPD leadership in the shooting of Henry Glover and in the subsequent cover-up. In footage from "The Storm," Lt. Dwayne Shurmann, second in command of the NOPD SWAT team, is described as a hero for his efforts to rescue survivors from flooded homes during the flood. Thompson also concludes that Shurmann was in charge when King and Tanner were beaten and when Glover was murdered and his body burned. With the footage of Glover's remains, the discrepancy between the images of Shurmann saving lives and the argument that he oversaw the murder and disappearance of an unarmed citizen powerfully argues for the need to reevaluate the production and meaning of images and memories from the storm. Shurmann is not reducible: he is both first responder and, by the documentary's argument, responsible for Glover's disappearance.

Law & Disorder uses Balogh's footage as a visual counter to the much more familiar television news reports about violence by citizens against NOPD officers. Christopher Lawrence's CNN September 2, 2005, reports about "Fort Apache" focused entirely on the perspectives of a small group of heavily armed police officers who felt besieged by an unseen populace (see chapter 7). Lawrence's camera operator recorded images of police firing weapons into the dark night. The television news report served as a screen for the panicked projections of the police, who processed their own anxiety about the collapse of communications and command and control by figuring their fellow citizens as threatening enemies. Rather than protect and serve citizens, the NOPD officers in the Lawrence report create a fortified position ("Fort Apache") from which to protect themselves from those they were duty bound to serve. Against these reports, *Frontline* positions a counter-image, the burned and fractured skull of Henry Glover. Where the police in the Lawrence report, or the tourists in a September 1, 2005, report by Carl Quintanilla on NBC (see chapter 6), could not see those they feared, since their fears were more projected than actual, *Frontline* shows the actual cost of police panic. Balogh's footage is crucial as evidence for Thompson's reporting and as evidence for grand jury consideration.

Law & Disorder concludes that the killings were produced by a context created by NOPD leadership. As police and official communications failed on Tuesday, August 30, 2005, city leaders, including Mayor Ray Nagin and Chief of Police Eddie Compass, began to demonstrate signs of elite panic. In the absence of fact, Nagin and Compass acted on the basis of rumors and extended the potency of rumors by repeating and further exaggerating them. As a consequence of Compass's claims that babies were being raped in the Superdome and his own claims that snipers were shooting at police, Nagin ordered Compass to divert resources from search and rescue toward security and suppression of the surviving citizens. *Frontline* shows Governor Kathleen Blanco's press conference encouraging the National Guard and police to use deadly force. *Law & Disorder* includes original interviews with Nagin, Compass, and Deputy Chief Warren Riley. These interviews suggest a failure of command and control by NOPD after the circulation of an order to revoke the usual rules of engagement. Police could normally use deadly force only to protect a life, but, in the days after Katrina, as Thompson reports on *Frontline*, NOPD leadership, egged on by Blanco and Nagin, encouraged the police to use deadly force against their own citizens in cases of looting or perceived disorder. *Law & Disorder* directly contradicts much of the television news coverage during the first week after Katrina, arguing that the NOPD was itself the source of the most deadly violence.

David Simon and Eric Overmyer asked Thompson to serve as a consultant for the third season of *Treme* so that the fictional HBO series could dramatize Thompson's discovery of the revocation of the rules of engagement by the NOPD after the flooding of New Orleans. Simon and Overmyer eventually decided to create a fictional character, L. P. Everette (Chris Coy), based closely on Thompson. In Season 3, Everette conducts a version of Thompson's actual investigation, including scenes in which the fictional character meets with actors playing King and Tanner. In an interview for this book, Thompson indicated that he went along with Simon and Overmyer's plan to fictionalize his actual investigation because he saw the potential in *Treme*'s documentary fiction for creating a new platform for his actual reporting. In the final section of this book, I examine the potential of fiction to shape knowledge and memory of the real events of Katrina. I propose that fiction offers a crucial opportunity for viewers to develop understanding and empathy for those who suffered most during the flood.

Part Three

FICTION

CHAPTER NINETEEN

My Fiction Seems a Bit Inconsequential to Me Now

TREME'S TRUTH CLAIM

IN "THE FOOT OF CANAL STREET," THE FOURTH EPISODE of *Treme*'s first season, Creighton Bernette (John Goodman), a professor of literature and creative writing at Tulane University, struggles to write. Creighton has been working on a novel about the 1927 Mississippi River flood, in which authorities dynamited sections of the levees, flooding some areas in order to save parts of New Orleans. Creighton's book is based on John Barry's 1998 nonfiction book, *Rising Tide: The Great Mississippi Flood of 1927 and How It Changed America* (Creighton can be seen reading Barry's book during Season 1). His manuscript is long overdue to his publisher, and *Treme* suggests that he had difficulty writing before Katrina. Rather than acknowledge these struggles, Creighton blames Katrina for rendering the act of fiction writing unimportant.

> CREIGHTON: My fiction seems a bit inconsequential to me now.

This comment raises an important question for *Treme*, which plays out both inside and outside the show's diegesis: what is the value of fiction for understanding disaster or crisis? Theodor Adorno answered a version of this question in his 1951 essay "Cultural Criticism and Society" by arguing that "to write a poem after Auschwitz is barbaric." Adorno contended that to impose artistic coherence on atrocity would be inherently false.

In contrast, sociologist H. G. Adler argued that all forms and modes must be used in order to illuminate in as many ways as possible the experiences of the Holocaust (Franklin, 2011). Adler was himself sent from Prague to Theresienstadt, then, after several years, to Auschwitz. From there, he was eventually sent to a work camp near Buchenwald, from which he was liberated in 1945. For Adler, Auschwitz was not an abstraction but a place he had survived and a source of memories. As Ruth Franklin notes, society expects survivors of disaster or human-created atrocity to be witnesses, not artists. But, as Kelly Oliver argues, witnessing has a dual dimension (2001). The first dimension of witnessing is to experience, to see. The second dimension is to share or convey. After surviving the death camps, Adler decided that he must use all available means to convey the experiences of the camps. Franklin cites an interview with Adler conducted in 1980: "'If I survive, then I will describe it . . . by setting down the facts of my individual experience, as well as to somehow describe it artistically . . .'" (74). Adler's use of the present tense reveals an important aspect of survival and witness: trauma is always experienced in the present tense. It is a somatic memory, playing out again on and through the body. For Adler, scholarship and narrative fiction served as necessary and complementary ways to remember and to process experience. As Franklin notes, Adler considered his writing to constitute his "self-liberation." Moreover, fiction served as an important avenue for Oliver's second dimension of witnessing: sharing or conveying experience. Through fiction, Adler could liberate himself and help to liberate others.

In response to atrocity, Adler produced *Theresienstadt, 1941-1945* (1947), a nine-hundred-page study and analysis of the details of the organization and operation of the camp. His goal was to record, preserve, and analyze, working from his direct observation and surviving records. He also wrote a series of five novels between 1948 and 1955, including *The Journey* (2008, English language translation) and *Panorama* (2011, English language translation). Franklin describes *The Journey* as "neither a novel, exactly, nor reportage"; rather, she understands the book as a "discomfiting, in-between form" (78). Adler's method was to investigate the camps, testing his memories against records and against the memories of others. He then worked to contextualize his findings within human experience, to engage what James Agee described in *Let Us Now Praise Famous Men* as the challenge of rendering another human life. Adler understood literature to be the process through which experience was transformed and shared. He understood fiction to be as legitimate and as important a method for conveying witness to the Holocaust as his sociological scholarship.

Katrina was not Auschwitz. But, like Auschwitz, Katrina was not a wholly exceptional event. As I have argued, we must understand the term "Katrina" to condense not only the hurricane as a form of natural disaster, but also the systemic and man-made failure of the federal levees and the continued atrocity of a failed social contract that left citizens to drown in their attics and die of heat and exposure at the New Orleans Convention

Center. As Brian Nobles states in *Trouble The Water*, "Katrina is still going on," and thus the term "Katrina" also condenses the continued injustice of FEMA response, insurance fraud, and bureaucratic mismanagement of the Road Home Program. In this broader sense, Katrina was not an exception, but was connected to past injustices and contributed to future suffering. Per Adler, fiction must be used as a tool to convey witness and to render the experience of Katrina, if the lived impact of the storm and flood are to be understood and remembered. While it should not replace other forms of witnessing or remembering, fiction remains extremely consequential for Katrina.

Franklin's description of Adler's *The Journey* could also describe David Simon and Eric Overmyer's *Treme*: "neither a novel, exactly, nor reportage." *Treme* has not enjoyed universal critical praise or been embraced by a mass audience because it too is a "discomfiting, in-between form." The series resembles a novel in its scope and in its transformation of factual detail into fictional story. In an interview for this book, Simon argued that the true text of *Treme* was not an episode or even a season but the full run of the show, more than 36 hours, more than 2,160 minutes. As a former reporter, he approached the creation of *Treme* as an investigative project. Like Adler, Simon and Overmyer conducted extensive research before working to transform that research into character and story. Just as Adler hoped his fiction would complement his mammoth scholarly investigation of Theresienstadt, Simon and Overmyer intend their extensive and elaborate fiction to complement the historical record, the work of other representations (such as documentary), and the developing collective memory of Katrina.

Another way to understand the value and limitations of fiction for conveying important knowledge about Katrina is to consider how *Treme* is like and unlike Dawn Logsdon and Lolis Elie's documentary, *Faubourg Treme* (2009). Both media texts seek to understand and convey the unique culture and history of the Treme neighborhood in New Orleans. Both the television series and the documentary seek to understand and convey the impact of Katrina on the neighborhood and community. *Faubourg Treme* uses many of the formal conventions of documentary: interviews, observational footage, and found footage. At times, it is expository: the documentary employs two narrators (Elie, who is seen on camera in the film, and JoNell Kennedy, a traditional narrator) to explain aspects of Treme's history and experience to viewers. *Faubourg Treme* also includes aspects of the participatory and performative modes of documentary, as when Lenwood Sloan of the Louisiana Living History Project performs as Paul Trevigne in

Jackson Square. The documentary observes rather than stages Sloan's performance as he interacts with groups of tourists and locals.

Treme also employs many of the formal conventions of its genre, fictional television drama: characters, scenes, sequences, cross-cutting, and point-of-view shooting and editing. Simon and Overmyer created characters, imagined backstories, cast actors to perform as these characters, and scripted scenes and scenarios to create dramatic tension, character development, and (at times) relief and release. *Treme* manipulates time and space to focus on meaningful moments and to build story.

On its face, *Faubourg Treme* seems to offer a much stronger connection to the real world than *Treme*. The subjects in the documentary are real people who exist independent of the film. The film observes lives before and after Katrina. The documentary represents afilmic events, such as Irving Trevigne's return to his flooded home.

However, upon closer examination, the contrast between documentary and fiction begins to break down, and it is no longer clear which text is better able to help viewers understand Katrina. As in any film, *Faubourg Treme* also manipulates time and space for emphasis and argument. The documentary originally focused on the history of the birth of the American civil rights movement in the Treme neighborhood. The storm became a frame for this story, allowing the filmmakers to argue that knowledge of Treme's past as a center for social activism and community action will help the community to survive the flood and the rigors of a new form of reconstruction. Logsdon and Elie created the shape of their film in order to make a historical argument. Rather than "capture" reality, they constructed an argument.

Like *Treme*, *Faubourg Treme* includes actors and performance. *Faubourg Treme* includes a reenactment of Paul Trevigne and colleagues producing the newspaper the *Tribune*. Logsdon and Elie recreate this scene because no other representations exist of Paul Trevigne. As discussed elsewhere in this book, Logsdon and Elie set up the recreation with a reflexive scene in which Elie searches in the Tulane University archive for an image of Trevigne. The filmmakers make explicit their reasons for constructing scenes with an actor performing Paul Trevigne: without the recreation, they could not bring Paul Trevigne into their film visually. In "Public Memory and Its Discontents," Geoffrey Hartman argues that the imagination is "traditionally defined as a power that restores a kind of presence to absent things" (1994, 24). As documentary filmmakers, Logsdon and Elie use imagination to recreate a scene with Paul Trevigne precisely to restore Trevigne to presence, both in their film and for history. Ultimately, in *Faubourg Treme*, Logsdon and Elie concluded that the power of fiction to make present people and events absent from representation was an essential tool for conveying their truth about Treme and Katrina.

If both documentary and fictional television series employ actors and stage scenes, why does documentary enjoy a privileged relation to the real? In "How Real Is the Reality in Documentary Film?," filmmaker, theorist, and teacher Jill Godmillow proposes a broad and inclusive definition of documentary that would exclude only "scripted dramas" (1997). Godmillow argues that documentaries are films that make some kind of claim to represent a real world, contain performances by social actors (rather than professional actors), and claim to edify, to persuade, or to raise awareness. By offering this definition, Godmillow seeks to complicate the easy association of documentary film with the real. *Faubourg Treme* corresponds to Godmillow's formulation for documentary: it claims to represent the real world and it features social actors. *Faubourg Treme* also intends to raise awareness of the history of the Treme neighborhood and to reframe Katrina in terms of this history.

Treme also seems to fit into Godmillow's definition of documentary. Like *Faubourg Treme*, *Treme* claims to represent important information about the real world. Simon and Overmyer do not offer *Treme* as an allegory of Katrina (as Behn Zeitlan does in his 2012 feature film, *Beasts of the Southern Wild*). *Treme* is offered to viewers as a carefully constructed version of real events, transformed, as per Adler, through fiction into stories about the real world. Like *Faubourg Treme*, *Treme* contains performances by social actors: New Orleans residents appear in the show as themselves. Some, like musicians Kermit Ruffins and Donald Harrison Jr., appear multiple times each season. *Treme* includes documentary moments within its fiction when it represents live musical performance. In such moments, it represents and conveys an aflimic reality. For example, when Kermit Ruffins performs "Basin Street Blues" in Vaughn's Lounge, he and his band are playing the song. Even if the cameras and mics stopped recording, the performance would exist as an act of culture.

However, as a scripted drama, *Treme* would not fit Godmillow's definition of documentary. *Treme* features professional actors, including Wendell Pierce and Rob Brown, who perform as musicians alongside actual musicians, complicating any easy understanding of the profilmic real. But, as noted, *Faubourg Treme* also includes professional actors within scripted scenes of re-creation. Both the documentary and the television series hope to edify audiences. By Godmillow's formulation, both *Faubourg Treme* and *Treme* have strong and significant relations to the reality of Katrina. If *Treme* is clearly not a documentary, as usually defined, the question remains: what is *Treme*'s status in relation to the real?

Godmillow also raises questions of documentary that closely mirror the arguments Simon offers regarding *Treme*'s truth claim.

> Is telling the truth to tell everything? Or simply not to lie? Or not to get something wrong? Or to find a form that illuminates the material, making possible a clearer or entirely new understanding, by use of analysis, or paradigmatic shape, or through self-reflexive presentation? (1997, 80)

As Godmillow continues to refine her question, she suggests that the goal of all media invested in the real world is to "find a form that illuminates the material, making possible a clearer or entirely new understanding." Godmillow is suspicious of the primacy of realism over fiction, skeptical that documentary as a mode is intrinsically closer to truth than fiction. In her film *Far from Poland* (1984), Godmillow explores the potential of "self-reflexive presentation," creating fictional scenes to represent images to which she could not gain access with her documentary camera. Following Godmillow, Simon and Overmyer's reflexive use of fiction provides the potential for illuminating Katrina, for making new understandings of the failure of the levees, the flooding of the city, and the neglect and oppression of the people of New Orleans.

MAGIC HUBIG'S PIE

In *Documentary: A Very Short Introduction*, Patricia Aufderheide offers the following definition: "a documentary film tells a story about real life with claims to truthfulness" (2007, 2). Aufderheide argues that documentary films are usually distinguished from fiction by their strong truth claims. In *Representing Reality*, Bill Nichols links the truth claim in documentary to the indexical relation between documentary footage and the profilmic real (1992). Like Godmillow, Aufderheide is less concerned with indexical links than with audience reception. For her, the truth claim of documentary rests in the film's (and filmmaker's) relation with her or his audience. According to Aufderheide, audiences of documentary film understand the film's truth claim as a form of contract between the film and its viewers. Thus, viewers of *Land of Opportunity* understand that Luisa Dantas promises to represent the reality of the struggles for housing after Katrina to the best of her ability without intentional deception. As Aufderheide makes clear, however, the contract between film and audience does not (cannot) promise literal truth. Rather, filmmakers use the full range of formal and rhetorical techniques to craft a story about reality.

Treme is a story about real life with claims to truthfulness, though it does not claim to be a documentary. Jonathan Lisco (executive producer and creator) and Kevin Dowling (producing director) did not make a claim that *K-Ville* (Fox 2007) offered stories about real life. Rather, they offered a cop show set in post-Katrina New Orleans, with greater investment in genre than in truth. Similarly, in a 2012 interview for this book, Overmyer joked that *CSI: Crime Scene Investigation* (CBS) did not have to make explicit its truth claims to viewers. Simon and Overmyer have made explicit truth claims for *Treme*, an extremely unusual decision for the show runners of a fictional television drama. In particular, Simon has used interviews and an editorial in the New Orleans *Times-Picayune* to lay out a contract between *Treme* and its viewers.

On April 11, 2010, the airdate for *Treme*'s pilot episode, the *Times-Picayune* published an editorial written by Simon, "HBO's 'Treme' Creator David Simon Explains It All for You." In the editorial, Simon uses the figure of a Hubig's pie (a fried pie produced in New Orleans and sold throughout the city) to explicate *Treme*'s truth claim. In the pilot episode, Creighton and Toni Bernette (Melissa Leo) dine at Janette Desautel's (Kim Dickens) restaurant. When Creighton refuses gelato for dessert (preferring to wait until Angelo Brocato's on Carrollton Avenue reopens), Janette produces a Hubig's pie from her purse and serves it to him with crème fraîche. In his editorial, Simon describes the dessert as a "Magic Hubig's," making clear that he and Overmyer recognized that the bakery Hubig's Pies in the Marigny neighborhood had not yet resumed producing pies in November 2006. In reality, then, Janette would not have had a Hubig's pie in her purse in November 2006. In the fictional story, Simon and Overmyer put the pie in her purse to offer a moment of light comedy, revealing Janette's character traits of informality and creativity.

Simon employs a wry tone in the editorial, setting up as a straw man "fact-minded literalists" who might object to the provenance of the pie. While ostensibly offering self-critique, admitting to an inaccuracy, Simon chose an inconsequential example in order to establish terms with his audience. His editorial seeks to anticipate the grounds for critique and to propose rules of engagement by viewers with his television show. Simon goes to unusual lengths to explain his and Overmyer's intentions and approaches in creating *Treme*.

Simon undertakes this highly unusual form of direct address to his audience because he recognizes the stakes involved.

Our television drama is taking liberties with a profound, unforgettable period in this city's history. It depicts day-to-day life in New Orleans in the aftermath of Katrina, referencing certain real events, real people and places, real cultural reference points known to many, if not most of those who call this city home.

Unlike Lisco and Dowling (of *K-Ville*), Simon could not simply take the "liberties" with the real traditionally afforded fiction. Because *Treme* focuses on the lives of New Orleans residents in the immediate aftermath of Katrina, creating characters based on careful research about lived experience, rather than on fictional cops pursuing fictional criminals, Simon feels not only that he should justify his transformation of the real, but also that to fail to do so would be perceived as a violation of his contract with his viewers.

While the editorial was picked up and circulated by the national media, Simon published the piece in the *Times-Picayune*, rather than the *New York Times*. Simon's choice reveals New Orleanians as his key audience.

> Beginning tonight, you are the ultimate arbiters — the only ones we really care about — on the question of whether our storytelling alchemy has managed to make anything precious or worthy from the baser elements of fact.

Simon has often insisted that his goal with *Treme* (as with *The Wire*) was not to reach and maintain a mass audience. In an interview for this book, Simon stated, "I am the worst fucking show runner. My numbers are terrible." He offered a story in which Simon Cellan Jones (director of "Smoke My Peace Pipe," Episode 7, Season 1, and "On Your Way Down," Episode 3, Season 2) joked that the only audience Simon cared about were the "five hundred people on Frenchman every night." (Frenchman Street is in the Marigny, just outside the French Quarter, and is home to a concentration of bars, clubs, and restaurants. *Treme* has frequently shot on location on Frenchman Street at d.b.a., the Apple Barrel, the Spotted Cat, the Blue Nile, and Café Rose Nicaud.) In his editorial, Simon makes clear that the "ultimate arbiters" of *Treme* are the citizens of New Orleans who lived through Katrina. While Simon cannot be wholly disinterested in a national, mass audience and maintain the patronage of HBO, a division of Time-Warner, he is primarily focused on a sub-audience, the hundreds of thousands of New Orleanians who survived Katrina, rather than on the majority of the 30 million HBO subscribers who lack such direct connection.

Your sensibilities matter to us because we have tried to be honest with that extraordinary time—not journalistically true, but thematically so. We have depicted certain things that happened, and others that didn't happen, and then still others that didn't happen but truly should have happened.

Given the stakes, Simon begins to stipulate aspects of his contract with his viewers. In a highly unusual move for the creator and show runner of a television drama, Simon promises to be "honest" and "true" to the experiences of his viewers during "that extraordinary time." As noted in a previous section of this book, television news also offers a strong truth claim, implicitly promising to provide truthful and accurate information about the most important events in the world. As I have argued, television news selects, shapes, and invests the stories it tells with particular values and perspectives. The truth claim of television news remains implicit, subsumed into the history of the formal choices that distinguish television news from other forms of media (live-ness, authoritative discourse by anchor and reporter). Unlike television news, fictional drama cannot assume an understanding with its audience. Thus, Simon has to explain the grounds for his commitment to present "true" and "honest" representations of Katrina. Simon's distinction between thematic and journalistic truth suggests a further distinction between the implicit claims of fiction and of television news. Simon suggests that fictional drama does not claim to represent the real world but can do so if undertaken with great care. Similarly, while television news assumes its truth claim, its representations might include distortions or inaccuracies given status by their formal properties (they look and sound like what viewers have conventionally come to know as television truth).

As a former journalist, Simon remains committed to an approach to fiction that involves observation, research, and verification. His thematic truth is dressed as fiction but maintains much of the commitment to accuracy that marked his journalism and long-form nonfiction, *Homicide* (1991) and *The Corner* (1997): "referencing certain real events, real people and places, real cultural reference points." Fiction enjoys an advantage over journalism or some forms of documentary in that it can use imagination to reveal hidden events absent from visual or aural documentation. Fiction allows Simon and Overmyer to depict things that "didn't happen," as well as things that "truly should have happened." Simon's category of "should have happened" resembles critic James Woods's concept of "plausibly hypothetical." In "Invitation to a Beheading," his review of Hilary

Mantel's *Wolf Hall* and *Bring Up the Bodies*, Woods argues that while historians strive to describe what happened, poets may show what might have happened or what might yet happen. Woods argues that "authenticity" is more about performance than about accuracy. While the usual move in historical fiction is to simulate historical authenticity, Woods identifies Mantel as seeking animate details in order to "inhabit the movement of vitality." Woods argues that Mantel seeks the "reachably real" (2012, 74).

In *Treme*, Simon and Overmyer create "plausibly hypothetical" situations in order to show events that did not happen but should have. For example, in "Smoke My Peace Pipe" (Episode 7, Season 1), Albert Lambreaux (Clarke Peters) occupies the B. W. Cooper Apartments, better known in New Orleans as the Calliope Project, in an act of protest. In reality, two white activists, Jamie Loughner and Curtis Rumrill, occupied an apartment in the St. Bernard Housing Development in January 2007. However, neither Loughner nor Rumrill were from New Orleans. They had not lived in public housing in the city. Rather, they were public housing activists who traveled to New Orleans in order to be arrested and draw attention to public housing issues nationally. In "Smoke My Peace Pipe," Albert is arrested and removed from Calliope. During his arrest, he is beaten by NOPD officers, who have targeted him not only as a housing activist, but also as a Mardi Gras Indian Big Chief. Moreover, the beating is shot in part with a handheld camera in order to reference the video footage of the beating of retired teacher Robert Davis, who was beaten by two white NOPD officers in the French Quarter in October 2005. Albert Lambreaux does not exist, and he did not occupy an apartment in the Calliope. He was not arrested and beaten by New Orleans police. But, Simon and Overmyer create this "plausibly hypothetical" scenario in order to convey the agency of local New Orleanians who protested the demolition of public housing by HANO and HUD after Katrina. Simon and Overmyer establish Albert as a stubborn man of conviction, so his decision to occupy public housing and to defy the city is read as "reachably real."

> By referencing what is real, or historical, a fictional narrative can speak in a powerful, full-throated way to the problems and issues of our time. And a wholly imagined tale, set amid the intricate and accurate details of a real place and time, can resonate with readers in profound ways. In short, drama is its own argument. (Simon, 2010)

In *Jail Sentences: Representing Prison in Twentieth-Century French Fiction*, Andrew Sobanet introduces the concept of "documentary fiction" to describe the writings of Jean Genet, Victor Serge, Albertine Sarrazin, and

François Bon. Sobanet argues that these authors, each of whom experienced imprisonment, use fiction as a documentary tool, writing prison novels as a form of testimonial literature. By building upon their own experiences, they employ documentary detail in fictional stories. "Prison novelists benefit from 'the documentary effect' created by certain textual and paratextual markers, and, at the same time, can creatively alter their stories to render them more compelling" (Sobanet, 2008, 185).

Simon also proposes to combine "intricate and actual details of a real place and time" with things "that didn't happen." *Treme* builds a "documentary effect" through textual markers such as carefully constructed composite characters. For example, Toni Bernette is based in part on series consultant Mary Howell, a well-known civil rights lawyer in New Orleans. Janette Desautel is based in part on series consultant Susan Spicer, the chef of Bayona, Herbsaint, and other restaurants. *Treme* also employs paratextual markers such as location shooting. In Season 3, L. P. Everette (Chris Coy) visits Habans Elementary School in Algiers. During Katrina, Habans served as a site for a temporary NOPD station. Investigative journalist A. C. Thompson (the model for the Everette character) determined that Algiers resident Henry Glover had been brought to Habans by his cousin and a Good Samaritan after being shot by a police sniper at a nearby strip mall. Weeks later, parts of Glover's body were found in the burned-out remnants of a car, which had been dumped on the batture by the Mississippi River not far from Habans. By shooting a scene at Habans for *Treme*, Simon and Overmyer make paratextual reference to these real events, which exist both within *Treme*'s fiction (Everette follows Thompson's actual investigative process) and afilmically in the real world.

In the "Magic Hubig's" piece, Simon indicates that his reason for employing what Genet called "referential and verifiable detail" was to provide his fiction with power and impact (Sobanet, 2008, 25). Simon argues that "what is real, or historical" can provide his fictional narrative with the power to address "the problems and issues of our time" in "a full-throated way." Similarly, Sobanet argues that "referentiality gives fiction ideological currency and urgency" (18). Thus, through fictional characters like Toni Bernette and L. P. Everette, Simon and Overmyer are able to use fiction to expose real injustice. In an interview for this book, A. C. Thompson indicated that he decided to collaborate with Simon and Overmyer on a character based on his reporting because he understood the *Treme* story line to be another platform for disseminating his investigative journalism. Simon and Overmyer cloak Thompson in the fictional character of Everette in order to provide testimony to the murder of Henry Glover by NOPD officers. Even as viewership of *Treme* declined to around five hundred thousand viewers in Season 3, *Treme*'s audience represented a larger group than the readership of *ProPublica* or the *Nation*. Thus, for Thompson, as for Simon and Overmyer, *Treme* provided another forum for sharing the facts about Henry Glover's murder.

In this sense, *Treme* is a testimonial narrative, like the novels of Genet. Sobanet suggests that "a fundamental aim of testimonial narratives is to impart the telling of an individual or group experience to an audience that is ostensibly unfamiliar with what is recounted" (19). *Treme* testifies through stories about the investigation into Henry Glover's murder (in Season 3) and through the dramatization of the murders of Dinneral Shavers and Helen Hill and the reenactment of the Stop the Violence March on January 11, 2007 (both in Season 2). By blurring the lines between fiction and nonfiction, *Treme* infuses its social criticism with the flexibility of fiction and the immediacy of referentiality.

> With *The Wire*, we tried our best to be responsible, of course—to choose carefully where we would cheat and where we would not. . . . If we are true to ourselves as dramatists, we will cheat and lie and pile one fraud upon the next, given that with every scene, we make fictional characters say and do things that were never said and done. And yet, if we are respectful of the historical reality of post-Katrina New Orleans, there are facts that must be referenced accurately as well. Some things, you just don't make up. (Simon, 2010)

Simon's use of the term "cheat" recalls the story line in Season 5 of *The Wire* in which an ambitious reporter for the *Baltimore Sun* (played by writer and director Tom McCarthy) "cheats" his story about Baltimore's homeless in order to court national prizes, encouraged in the focus on awards by the paper's publisher. In writing for the *Sun*'s City Desk from 1982 to 1995, Simon insisted on not cheating a story by distorting details or omitting important information in the interest of generating sentiment. In an interview with Cynthia Rose in 1999, Simon indicated that he had adapted his approach to journalism to writing for *Homicide: Life on the Street* and to preparing *The Corner* for HBO: "Now, all I want is to bring the best story to the campfire. To make it something people want to hear, and not to cheat it" (Rose, 1999). Simon's approach to *Treme* is built upon his approach to reporting.

Part of what makes the prison novels of Genet, Serge, Sarrazin, and Bon "documentary" is their contract with their readers. Like Aufderheide, Sobanet argues that documentary is distinguished by the relationship of text to audience: "prison novels propose a contract between text and reader"

(15). Simon also proposes a contract with the viewers of *Treme*: he and his collaborators will be "respectful of the historical reality of post-Katrina New Orleans." But, Simon also makes clear that *Treme* will "cheat and lie and pile one fraud upon the next." As with prison novels, *Treme* can have it both ways, as long as Simon is transparent and reflexive. Sobanet argues, "fiction allows writers to manipulate source material without a breach of contract between text and reader" (15). Simon wrote the *Times-Picayune* editorial in order to stipulate the nature of his truth claims and his contract with his viewers. Simon will "manipulate source material," intentionally and consistently, but he will be careful to cheat only when to do so would not do fundamental violence to "historical reality."

Sobanet argues for the importance of reflexivity in the contract proposed by documentary fiction. He cites James Frey as an example of an author who violated his contract with his audience. Frey claimed that his book, *A Million Little Pieces*, was an accurate account of his life, when, in fact, it contained made-up scenes and composite characters. Unlike Frey, Simon uses the "Magic Hubig's" piece to set up favorable terms with his audience before the pilot episode of *Treme* aired. By claiming not to have invented any detail, Frey was unable to use fictional forms to shape and tell his story. By admitting to having cheated and lied in the making of *Treme*, but by also indicating that "some things, you just don't make up," Simon offers his viewers a contract that allows him flexibility and the power of referentiality.

STANDING

On August 27, 2011, a year after the publication of his "Magic Hubig's" piece, David Simon served as a keynote speaker for the sixth annual Rising Tide Conference. Held that year at Xavier University in New Orleans, Rising Tide convenes a yearly conversation on the recovery and future of New Orleans after Katrina. Bloggers are the primary audience for Rising Tide, and the event and organization seek to use new media to promote community organizing and recovery activity. Simon used his keynote speech to renegotiate his contract with *Treme*'s audience. In his editorial, Simon had emphasized the care the show runners would exercise when using fiction to transform real events into character and story. In his remarks at Rising Tide, he sought to recover more latitude and to argue that local sensibilities were not the only important consideration in determining how to tell stories of the recovery of New Orleans after Katrina.

At Rising Tide, Simon responded to online criticism of Season 1 of *Treme* by attacking the concept of "standing." According to Simon in an interview for this book, the standing argument posited that he could not effectively tell stories of the recovery because he did not live in New Orleans, had not experienced the flood directly, and had not lost a home or had to fight the FEMA bureaucracy. Simon countered that this argument was too limiting, that creators must be given the freedom to imagine what they had not themselves experienced. In support of his counterargument, he cited examples from Gustave Flaubert to David Mills. Simon argued that if male authors could not write women characters because they lacked gender standing, *Madame Bovary* would not exist. Looking to his own writing staff, Simon argued that David Mills (who passed away while helping produce Season 1) had been able to effectively build character and create dialogue for the character of Andy Sipowicz (Dennis Franz) as a writer on *NYPD Blue* (NBC 1993–2005). Simon argued that Mills's status as African American did not prevent him from writing in the voice of white characters. Novelist George Pelecanos, a writer and producer on both *The Wire* and *Treme*, and a Greek-American from Silver Spring, Maryland, has written in the voice of African American characters in a series of well-reviewed novels, including *Soul Circus* (2003) and *The Night Gardener* (2006).

Beyond his rejection of essentialism, Simon articulated new terms in his agreement with his audience. Before the first season of *Treme* aired, Simon emphasized that he would take great care to get things right, to strive for accuracy in detail and authenticity in tone. After the first season, at Rising Tide, Simon argued for the importance of distance as counter and complement to closeness in representing Katrina. Simon is able to reject the litmus of standing because he has moved away from his initial position that accuracy was more important than invention in the telling of *Treme*. He argued that standing or direct experience could be limiting as well as enabling. In an interview for this book, Simon argued for the fragmentary and incomplete nature of memory. As an example, he cited a conversation with political consultant Jacques Morial, son and brother of two former mayors of New Orleans, in which Morial asked Simon why *Treme*'s pilot episode did not feature more discarded refrigerators. Because New Orleans was without power for weeks after Katrina, even citizens whose homes were not flooded still had to deal with ruined refrigerators filled with spoiled food. Morial remembered the "dead" refrigerators lining curbs throughout the city in November 2005. However, Simon's research showed that almost all of the refrigerators had been collected by the end of October 2005. Thus, set in November 2005, *Treme*'s pilot featured only one dead fridge.

Simon re-defines his truth claim by arguing that research, professional experience, and critical perspective are as important to the representation of Katrina as lived experience or autobiographical memory (Maurice Halb-wachs's term). In the "Magic Hubig's" piece, Simon had also proposed a bal-ance of outside and inside, but there he had sought to focus on the impor-tance of inside experience, of getting things right. After *Treme* was greenlit by HBO for a second season, Simon sought to renegotiate his contract with his viewers by emphasizing the importance of outside. He seemed to draw on his experience as a journalist as a model for the production of a fictional television show about New Orleans after Katrina. In his past role covering the police beat for the *Baltimore Sun*, Simon cultivated sources throughout the city, gaining access to those with direct experience. He also spent time on the drug corners in West Baltimore so that he could observe the people and practices of the drug trade. Like an ethnographer or an observational documentarian, he positioned himself inside the cultures he was covering, but maintained his professional distance and critical perspective, so that he could see, analyze, and share perspective on drug dealing and policing in Baltimore. While situated, Simon's position was not the same as that of a cop or a dealer.

In a 2011 interview with filmmaker Michael Dunaway, Simon described his approach to making *Treme*. Employing the analogy of a traveler, Simon proposed a model of immersion and close analysis.

> Then there's the kind of trip where you get to these places and actu-ally get off the bus and wander into a bar, or tavern, or bistro, and sit in a corner, and sit there long enough to interact with the locals, and to experience life in these places as it actually is. I guarantee you won't get everything, particularly if the language is not your lan-guage. You won't get everything when you need it, and you'll be confused. But the next day, you'll come back, and you'll be a little less confused. And by about the third day certain patterns will start to reveal themselves as far as social interaction. And you stay there for a month or two and the place gets in your blood.

Substitute a Baltimore drug corner for the "bistro," and you have Simon's journalistic practice, honed via beat reporting and long-form nonfiction writing, as a model for fictional television production. Like ethnography, he proposes immersion and observation as key to critical insight. With time and focus, "certain patterns will start to reveal themselves." At Rising Tide, Simon clarified an important dimension of his approach in *Treme*. The show could claim to represent truths of Katrina because it was pro-duced through a combination of outside perspective and expertise applied to deep research and immersive observation. *Treme*'s truth claim makes it unlike other fictional television dramas. Rather than to entertain, its primary goal is to testify to lived experience.

In his comments to Dunaway, Simon also provides his viewers with a schema for approaching and interpreting the show. Simon and Overmyer chose in *Treme* not to explain New Orleans but to immerse viewers in various experiences of the city. The opening scene of the pilot episode begins with extreme close-ups of instruments, feathered costumes, alcohol being poured and consumed. Unless viewers are familiar with New Orleans cultural tradition, they will not understand that these small details convey preparation for a second line in honor of chef Austin Leslie, who passed away after Katrina. Instead of offering an establishing shot or dialogue to explain the significance of these details, Simon and Overmyer ask viewers to "sit in a corner," processing details and waiting for a pattern to emerge. Also in the pilot episode, the scene in which Albert Lambreaux (Clarke Peters) emerges from the darkness in his Big Chief suit also requires viewers to work toward understanding by processing details without prior explanation. Viewers of *Treme* learn about Mardi Gras Indian traditions by watching Albert perform and interact. As a complex narrative form that attempts to engage the lived experience of recovery from an actual disaster, *Treme* requires viewers to commit to an extended experience that moves from confusion, to curiosity, to understanding. Simon asks his viewers to get off the bus of traditional television spectatorship, as marked by distraction, partial engagement, and strong narrative and formal cues.

A SHALLOW POOL OF IMAGES

While Simon argued for the benefits of fiction as an approach to representation, Eric Overmyer argued against the limitations of documentary. The production approaches of television news shaped the footage created during and after landfall of the storm and the footage of the flooding of the city. Documentary filmmakers wishing to bring visual representation of the storm and flood into films had to use television news footage as the largest available source of images and audio. Some filmmakers (Tia Lessin and Carl Deal in *Trouble the Water*) focused on amateur footage to create visual perspectives different from those of television news, and other documentarians (Spike Lee and Sam Pollard in *When the Levees Broke*) licensed footage from the networks, bringing footage already coded by the approaches and values of network news into their films.

In an interview for this book, Overmyer proposed that the relatively small pool of available footage of Katrina constrained the possibilities of documentary to examine the truth of Katrina and the flooding of New Orleans. Overmyer found Katrina documentaries looped the same footage over and over, exhausting the power of these images to provoke insight or understanding. To Overmyer's point, many Katrina documentaries create a visual echo chamber of representation. Rather than remain constrained to the available "real" images, strongly shaped by television and other sources, Overmyer argued that fiction provided a necessary opportunity to re-create and restage that which was not or could not be captured by cameras and mics. Overmyer makes a version of Godmillow's argument in *Far from Poland* that the search for truth and understanding cannot be limited to images coded as real due to their production via documentary conventions. Though lacking the critical reflexivity of Godmillow, Overmyer and Simon reach a similar conclusion that fiction can be as effective as documentary in framing and responding to the real.

CHAPTER TWENTY

In the David Simon Business

TREME'S MODE OF PRODUCTION

*D*AVID SIMON BEGAN HIS TRANSITION FROM JOURNAL-
ist to long-form nonfiction author to television writer to
producer and show runner by taking a leave of absence in 1988 from the
Baltimore Sun to research his first book, *Homicide: A Year on the Killing Streets*
(1991). Having been actively involved in a strike by the *Sun* writers in 1987,
seeking to prevent cuts in benefits, Simon was angry with the paper and
wanted a change. Rather than quit, he proposed a yearlong "internship"
with the Baltimore Homicide Unit. Building on his experience as a police
reporter for the *Sun*, Simon spent a year inside the Baltimore Homicide
Unit, observing, interacting, and eventually writing about what he saw
and heard. He started with his usual journalistic approaches and adapted
these to the much longer time frame inside the Homicide Unit. In an interview with Cynthia Rose, Simon discussed the challenge of adapting his approach: "In the unit, I filled a notebook every day. But I needed time to let
it settle, understand it. I was trained to write fifteen inches in an hour. So,
it was unnerving; it was actually hard to do" (Rose, 1999). Through journalism, Simon had learned to become a trained professional observer. In
shifting from daily journalism to long-form writing, he had to develop
greater patience in order to process and understand the increased complexity of the cultures and systems he observed. By, as he put it, "seeming
like furniture," Simon could be in a position to observe and to learn (just
as he would later advise viewers of *Treme* to do).

After *Homicide* was published to significant acclaim, Simon went back
to reporting for the *Sun*. Barry Levinson optioned the book and developed it into a fictional television series, *Homicide: Life on the Street*, for NBC
(1992–1999). Simon declined to write the series pilot, citing inexperience
as a television writer. He and David Mills, a *Washington Post* reporter and

Simon's friend from the University of Maryland, co-wrote "Bop Gun," the first episode of *Homicide*'s second season. Simon left the *Sun* in 1995 to join *Homicide* as a writer for the fourth season. He was story editor on Season 5 and became a producer on Seasons 6 and 7.

Simon met Eric Overmyer on the writing staff for Season 4 of *Homicide*. They collaborated on the teleplay "Self Defense" for Season 7. Overmyer is a playwright who became a television writer and producer in the 1980s, writing for *St. Elsewhere* (NBC 1982–1988) and writing and producing for *The Days and Nights of Molly Dodd* (NBC 1987–1988, Lifetime 1988–1991), among other programs. Overmyer grew up in Seattle, but began a lifelong interest in New Orleans when his father, who worked for Boeing, brought home an Oscar "Papa" Celestin record from a trip to New Orleans in 1959. In an interview for this book, Overmyer indicated that he developed a strong imaginary relationship with New Orleans by repeatedly listening to the jazz record. He began to visit New Orleans as an adult in the mid-1970s. In 1989, after enjoying early success as a television writer, Overmyer purchased a house in New Orleans. Eventually, he and his family would split time between a home in the Marigny neighborhood and an apartment in New York City. Overmyer holds a Louisiana driver's license and votes in New Orleans.

While working together on *Homicide*, Simon and Overmyer discovered their shared interest in New Orleans. In 1995, ten years before Katrina, they discussed the idea of creating a television drama set in New Orleans. Both Simon and Overmyer understood the challenge to be to "get New Orleans right." They critiqued the 1980s films that had failed to convey the complexity of New Orleans—*No Mercy* (Tri-Star 1986), *Angel Heart* (Tri-Star 1987), and *The Big Easy* (Columbia 1987)—and considered how a television show could avoid similar mistakes. Ironically, after his initial discussion with Simon, Overmyer gained direct experience with the difficulties in representing New Orleans by writing for the second season of the television adaptation of *The Big Easy* (USA Network 1996–1997). The television version of *The Big Easy* was a crime drama, loosely based on the feature film, featuring what Simon described to Michael Dunaway as "all the lame tropes of television" (2011). In the 1990s, Simon and Overmyer could not figure out an approach to doing a show about New Orleans that would be salable but also "truthful."

In 1993, Simon took a second leave from the *Sun* to collaborate with Ed Burns, a former Baltimore homicide detective, on a study of a single drug corner in West Baltimore. As with *Homicide*, Simon's approach was to spend significant time observing and learning about the people who lived at the corner of West Fayette and North Monroe Streets in Baltimore. In 1997, *The Corner: A Year in the Life of an Inner-City Neighborhood* was published.

Simon and Burns received critical praise for the detail of their observation. Some critics raised concerns about point of view, as *The Corner* is written in a third-person omniscient perspective (as was *Homicide*). In his interview with Rose, Simon argued for the importance of de-centering the author, of not making a book about life on the corner in inner-city Baltimore about the author. Further, Simon stated that he was drawing upon devices familiar from fiction (condensation, changes in chronology and structure, narrative omniscience) in order to shape the most compelling stories about life on the corner. As Simon moved away from journalism toward storytelling in long-form print and on television, he began to blend nonfiction with fictional approaches and to redefine his understanding of truth. With *Homicide* and *The Corner*, Simon was beginning to work in the realm of "thematic truth" rather than from the verifiable truth of journalism.

After *Homicide: Life on the Street* ended its run in 1999, Simon worked with David Mills to adapt *The Corner* into a miniseries for HBO. Nina Kostroff Noble, who would go on to work with Simon on *The Wire* and *Treme*, produced the six-episode series. *The Corner* won three Emmy Awards, including a writing award for Simon and Mills.

Following *The Corner*, Simon and Burns collaborated to develop *The Wire* (HBO 2002–2008), based in part on Simon's reporting for *Homicide: A Year on the Killing Streets* and in part on Burns's experience using wiretapping to investigate drug cases in Baltimore. While pleased by the critical response to *The Corner*, HBO was initially reluctant to green-light *The Wire*. In the 1990s, HBO had built its brand by differentiating its programming from network television, using the tagline "It's not television. It's HBO." The premium cable network was at first hesitant to approve a police procedural show. Simon was able to convince Carolyn Strauss, the president of HBO Entertainment, that to do a police procedural in a way network television could not (including language, violence, nudity, situations that could not be included in broadcast television) would be subversive and in keeping with HBO's goal to change television programming. In addition to working with Burns, Noble, and producer Robert Colesberry, Simon recruited crime fiction authors—including Richard Price, Dennis Lehane, and George Pelecanos—to write for *The Wire*. In 2005, when Pelecanos left *The Wire* after the third season to research and write his next novel, *The Night Gardener* (2006), Simon brought in Overmyer as a writer and consulting producer.

While working together on Season 4 of *The Wire*, Simon and Overmyer restarted their discussion of a show set in New Orleans. Both were acutely aware of the challenges to representing that city, having swapped critiques of representations focused on "ceiling fans and people sweating." According to Overmyer in an interview for this book, to get New Orleans "right," the show must "be about the light, the smells, the talk." Overmyer indicated that Les Blank's *Always For Pleasure* (1978) and Stevenson Palfi's *Piano Players Rarely Ever Play Together* (1982) were key intertexts for the idea that would become *Treme*. While agreeing on the importance of mise-en-scène and textural detail, Simon and Overmyer struggled to develop a compelling story. Since working on *Homicide*, Overmyer had written and produced for *Law & Order*, *Law & Order: SVU*, and *Law & Order: Criminal Intent* (NBC 1990–present). After *The Wire*, Simon did not want to do another "cop show." He and Overmyer decided to focus on the people who make culture in New Orleans, the Papa Celestins of the twenty-first century. When they proposed to create a show about New Orleans musicians, the networks expressed no interest.

When Katrina made landfall on Monday, August 29, 2005, Overmyer was in Baltimore working on Season 4 of *The Wire*. His family had been in New Orleans and had to evacuate to North Carolina. He followed television news coverage of the storm and flood and used Google's newly released mapping software to determine that his own home had not flooded. Like all other viewers, both New Orleanians and those without any ties to the city, Overmyer was limited to the coverage offered by the broadcast and cable news networks. He felt that television news simplified and reduced the complexity of events, seeking to provide simple, compelling narratives about the storm and the flood. In an interview for this book, Overmyer described media coverage of Katrina as "an echo chamber that reinforced itself about what happened." He felt that the stories initially misunderstood the scope of the damage and then overcompensated by focusing almost exclusively on the Ninth Ward and the suffering of residents left stranded at the Convention Center. Once again, national media had failed to understand New Orleans and to "get it right."

After dissecting national news coverage, Simon and Overmyer saw an opportunity to shape a more complex accounting of the storm and flood, using fiction to tell stories missed by television news. They felt that fiction would afford a larger canvas than news or documentary, allowing them to explore and connect multiple points of view and feature multiple voices. They also each acknowledged that Katrina provided them with the missing frame they needed for their New Orleans narrative. Before Katrina, they had struggled to interest networks in their show idea because the stories of culture bearers lacked obvious stakes (network executives were unmoved by the impact of the tourist economy on local wages or the effect of a failed school system on public education). Katrina provided the missing hook: would the musicians, chefs, writers, and artists of New Orleans survive the aftermath of the flood? Would New Orleans itself survive? Simon and Overmyer acknowledge that Katrina gave new vitality to their ideas for a television drama about New Orleans culture.

According to Simon, he and Overmyer soon began to revise their concept for *Treme*, and they pitched the show in Los Angeles in October 2005, a month after Katrina hit land. According to Simon, he wanted to take advantage of the moment when the networks might be open to programming about New Orleans. Fox was developing *K-Ville*, and NBC was in talks with Spike Lee about developing a series (he eventually partnered instead with HBO to produce *When the Levees Broke* and *If God Is Willing and Da Creek Don't Rise*). Simon and Overmyer pitched *Treme* to Michael Lombardo, president of programming at HBO, Carolyn Strauss, and Chris Albrecht, chairman and CEO of the network.

Simon maintains that HBO bought the pitch because of national interest in Katrina. Overmyer argues that HBO responded favorably because of *The Wire* and their relationship with Simon. According to Overmyer, he and Simon described their idea for *Treme* to Strauss, talking about Mardi Gras Indians and street parades. Strauss responded, "I don't know what you're talking about, but go write the pilot because I am in the David Simon business." Albrecht and Strauss had been Simon's patrons at HBO, supporting his development of *The Corner* and *The Wire*. Despite relatively low audience numbers for most of *The Wire* (Simon describes the network as threatening to cancel the show after each season due to low numbers), the HBO leadership was thrilled by the buzz enjoyed by the show at the end of its five-season run (and thereafter). In 2006, Jacob Weisberg of *Slate* asserted, "*The Wire*, which has just begun its fourth season on HBO, is surely the best TV show ever broadcast in America," and in July 2013, *Entertainment Weekly* voted *The Wire* as the all-time greatest show in the history of television.

Simon used his capital at HBO to secure a green light for the pilot of *Treme* without a script. According to Overmyer, the process was "atypical," even for HBO, and he made the point that *Treme* might only have been approved by HBO, given its investment in auteur show runners, artistic freedom, and the importance of critical praise and buzz to its brand. Simon and Overmyer secured approval to move forward on *Treme* without scripts or a season outline. Simon sent two memos to Lombardo and Strauss, and he and Overmyer wrote the pilot (based on a preliminary draft by Simon). Once Strauss and Lombardo read the script, they approved the budget to shoot the pilot in New Orleans, and after reviewing the completed pilot, they approved the first season of *Treme*. It is arguable that during its run on HBO, *Treme* was subsidized by the success of Alan Ball's vampire drama, *True Blood* (2008–2014). But even if *True Blood* allowed for *Treme* to function as a loss leader for HBO, *Treme* would not have been possible without the creative capital amassed by Simon as a result of the critical success of *The Wire*.

According to Simon, he and Overmyer pitched *Treme* as the story of the near-death of an American city. The flooding of New Orleans offered the jeopardy missing from their previous pitches for a show about New Orleans culture creators. Simon stressed that *Treme* would be about stories of individual, familial, and community recovery. Further, he argued that African American music in general, and New Orleans jazz in specific, was the greatest American art form. Simon wanted to make a television drama about the effort to create that art amid the challenges posed by recovery after the flood.

Simon was clear-eyed about the problems in New Orleans that predated Katrina. Like Baltimore, New Orleans had long been plagued by substandard public education, poverty, lack of opportunity, crime, political corruption, and police brutality. Yet, New Orleans was also the home to Mardi Gras, the Jazz and Heritage Festival, Super Sunday, and other ecstatic traditions of public performance. Simon and Overmyer were struck by the contrast between the problems in New Orleans and the promise of its culture. From the pitch phase, Simon and Overmyer had already imagined scenes like the one in which Albert Lambreaux emerges from the darkness of a Central City street, his brilliant, handmade costume contrasting with the devastated landscape. Where *The Wire* was driven by crime and punishment (and corruption and survival), *Treme* would be driven by the performance of culture as the answer to death and disaster. Rather than another police procedural, *Treme* would be, in part, a musical, or at least a document of the performance of culture, like Blank's *Always for Pleasure*.

Simon and Overmyer chose the title *Treme* for its mystery, hoping it would pique the curiosity of viewers, but HBO executives must have found the choice obscure. HBO had to provide pronunciation guides to the press to educate critics and viewers to pronounce the name "trah-MAY." Simon and Overmyer liked the location of the Treme neighborhood as the backstage of the tourist French Quarter, close to well-known landmarks, but unknown to most outside—and many in—New Orleans. The fact that Simon and Overmyer hired Lolis Elie as a consultant, and eventually as a writer and story editor, suggests that they drew upon Elie and Logsdon's documentary *Faubourg Treme* as an important intertext. *Faubourg Treme* argues that Treme was the oldest African American neighborhood in America, a neighborhood populated by free(d) men and women of color who had gained freedom from slavery through various forms of manumission. As Logsdon and Elie argue, Treme can also be understood as the birthplace of the modern civil rights movement in the United States. Simon and Overmyer found these historical arguments important as backstory to their contemporary focus post-Katrina, believing that setting stories of contemporary oppression and agency in a place where Paul Trevigne and others fought against oppression after Reconstruction would add relevance to their fiction.

Perhaps most important to Simon and Overmyer was the argument that, as home to innovative coronetist Buddy Bolden, Treme was the birthplace of jazz.

Simon and Overmyer made these arguments to Lombardo and Strauss, during their pitch and in subsequent memos. Simon saw *Treme* as related to *The Wire* in that both shows engaged the crises facing cities in America. Simon maintained that *Treme* was not just about New Orleans, but also about the stakes for America in the fate of New Orleans. He contended that the fate of New Orleans was related to the fate of St. Louis, of Detroit, of Baltimore (an argument echoed by Luisa Dantas in the *Land of Opportunity* transmedia platform). Moreover, he saw in New Orleans a model for the coexistence, connection, and improvisation that, he believed, were essential to the viability of cities in twenty-first-century America. As these arguments make clear, Simon's vision of New Orleans was as much shaped by values and ideology as was television news reporting. Simon and Overmyer designed a production method for *Treme* that involved careful research and observation and the identification and use of actual references. These details and documents, however, were used in service of a vision and an argument. They were not in any way mainline truth. Thus, in determining the significance of *Treme* for collective and public understandings of Katrina, it is important to analyze the choices made in the creation of this particular version of New Orleans post-Katrina.

With the support of HBO, Simon took his first research trip to New Orleans in November 2005. He spent days with New Orleans musicians Kermit Ruffins and Donald Harrison Jr. *Treme*'s first season begins in November 2005. The Atlantic hurricane season forced production on *Treme* in New Orleans into the window from November through May. Even given this production context, the coincidence of *Treme*'s temporal setting and Simon's first research visit suggests the importance Simon placed in his direct observations. Like Dziga Vertov's argument about *kino pravda* (cinematic truth), Simon asserts that his powers of perception (his outsider perspective), channeled through the apparatus of television and reinforced by the contributions of collaborators, can yield a unique form of truth about the flooding of New Orleans.

In an interview for this book, Overmyer argued that *Treme* was the product of a dialectic between the sensibilities and approaches of the two show runners. He indicated that before each season of the show, they would build a time line for the actual events that happened in New Orleans during the period in which that season was set. The show runners would lead the writing staff in a discussion of the events they wanted to reference or represent in a given season. For example, they determined early in the process of planning Season 2 that they wanted to address the murders of Dinneral Shavers in December 2006 and Helen Hill in January 2007. They decided to cast an actor to play Shavers, but not to represent Hill before her death.

According to Overmyer, Simon was chiefly concerned with argument and theme, while Overmyer was most interested in character and motivation. As a journalist and nonfiction writer, Simon was invested in thematic ground, while, as a playwright, Overmyer focused on rendering dimensional human characters. Overmyer sees their working relationship as tied to *Treme*'s dialectic between fact and fiction, to the ongoing debate between accuracy and invention. He acknowledges that each co-creator also flipped at times throughout the show, as he became focused more on argument and Simon focused more on character. Simon also cautioned that viewer assumptions about voice and authorship were sometimes mistaken. According to Simon, Overmyer wrote the rant Creighton delivers while being interviewed by the British news crew in the first episode. While critics have cited this scene as evidence of Simon's use of characters to ventriloquize his own arguments, Simon points out the Overmeyer shaped this initial "soliloquy," not him.

Simon and Overmyer alternated producing episodes during the first season. In Season 2, Jim Yoshimura, a veteran television writer and producer with whom they had worked on *Homicide*, acted as third producer, and in Season 3, Pelecanos filled that role. According to Overmyer, Simon liked to seed the writing staff with non-television writers. Having come to television after journalism and long-form nonfiction, Simon was skeptical of television writers as wedded to formula and shorthand. On *Homicide*, Simon was junior colleague to both Overmyer and Yoshimura, each of whom had considerably more experience in television. As a non-television writer, he respected their craft, but he also found ways to turn his inexperience into virtue, arguing against the "usual tropes" of television. When Simon became a full-fledged show runner on *The Wire*, he cultivated writers from outside television (Price, Lehane, and Pelecanos). On *Treme*, Simon and Overmyer hired as writers the journalist and filmmaker Lolis Elie, essayist and novelist Tom Piazza, activist Jordan Hirsh, chef and food personality Anthony Bourdain, and journalist Chris Rose. In order to manage the new writers, Simon and Overmyer turned to veteran television writers and frequent collaborators, including David Mills and Yoshimura. The show runners oversaw the work of the other writers, and each would take responsibility for rewriting certain scripts, even those of the most experienced writers (Simon would rewrite David Mills, while Overmyer would rewrite Tom Piazza). As Overmyer put it, only the two show runners could channel the voice of the series. Simon and Overmyer rewrote scripts from their writing staff to ensure continuity of approach and vision, a vision that began in the early 1990s, but was given its final form after Katrina and *The Wire*.

2,160 MINUTES

Treme (2010–2014) is the most significant and influential media text to represent Katrina and the flooding of New Orleans, distinguished from other representations by its form and length. Spike Lee and Sam Pollard's documentaries *When the Levees Broke* (2006) and *If God Is Willing and Da Creek Don't Rise* (2010) can be understood as a two-part documentary project totaling more than eight hours of programming, aired by HBO over four nights in August 2006 and August 2010, respectively. Lee and Pollard's documentary project is by far the largest documentary text to seek to represent Katrina. Yet, *Treme* dwarfs *Levees*.

As a television series on HBO, *Treme* conformed to the network's template for dramatic narrative. Broadcast in hour-long episodes on Sunday evenings, it premiered on April 11, 2010, with the pilot episode, "Do You Know What It Means?" Because HBO's economic model is based on premium subscriptions, with cable customers paying seventeen to twenty dollars per month to add access to the network, HBO does not air commercials. As a result, it has greater freedom over programming since they do not have to guarantee commercial play within specific programming blocks. HBO uses this freedom to allow the total running time of certain episodes to exceed the usual fifty-eight-minute HBO "hour." *Treme*'s first season consisted of ten episodes, which aired from April to June 2010. *Treme*'s second season consisted of eleven episodes, which aired from April to July 2011, and its third season consisted of ten episodes, airing from September to November 2012. *Treme* concluded with a five-episode fourth season (December 1–December 31, 2013).

In total, as a supertext, *Treme* consists of more than thirty-six hours of narrative. Its total running time exceeds 2,160 minutes. At this length, *Treme* is the most extensive and sustained representation of Katrina across all media, modes, and formats. Even CNN's *NewsNight with Aaron Brown*, which aired for two hours per night for the first seven nights of Katrina and the flood, generated only 840 minutes of representation. Recalling Paula Rabinowitz's concept of a "house of representation," *Treme* occupies significant space in the house of representation of Katrina, more space than any other single representation or group of representations (1994, 218).

Of course, total running time is not in itself any guarantor of audience engagement or impact. *Treme* has been well received by some critics (see Nussbaum), but it has not been as well reviewed as *The Wire*. While Weisberg called *The Wire* the best show in the history of television, *Treme* has enjoyed minimal "buzz," the metric that HBO executives Richard Plepler and Michael Lombardo use to assess public awareness of and subscriber interest in an HBO show, and which is measured in part by digital discussion across entertainment media and fan blogs. Alan Ball's *True Blood*, David Benioff and D. B. Weiss's *Game of Thrones*, and even Lena Dunham's *Girls*—which has attracted smaller audiences than *Treme*, averaging fewer than five hundred thousand viewers during its first season—have generated significantly more buzz for HBO. Due to mixed critical reaction and minimal buzz—except in New Orleans, where coverage by Dave Walker of the *Times-Picayune* has been extensive—*Treme* is perceived as a boutique cable drama viewed by a small audience.

However, when compared with other examples of Katrina media, *Treme* has been seen by more viewers than any documentary representation. According to Walker, *Treme* averaged 3.2 million cumulative weekly viewers during its first season (August 14, 2011). HBO determines cumulative viewers by combining the initial Sunday night audience with viewers of repeats, DVR time-shifts, and video on-demand (via HBOGO). By comparison, *When the Levees Broke* had 1.7 million cumulative viewers during its initial broadcast in 2006 (O'Connell, 2013). Thus, the most watched documentary about Katrina drew 1.5 million fewer viewers than a weekly episode of *Treme* during its first season.

Each episode of that first season was also seen by more viewers than viewed either Fox or CNN during an evening of prime-time coverage of Katrina and the flooding of New Orleans during the first week after the storm. According to the Pew Research Center, Fox attracted 2.8 million viewers per night during prime-time coverage of Katrina, up 35 percent from August 2005 viewership. CNN averaged 1.9 million viewers, up 168 percent from August. As I have noted previously, many more viewers watched television news coverage than any other form of representation of Katrina and the flooding of New Orleans. For example, Pew's research shows that 100 million unique viewers watched CNN during Katrina, across all programming and platforms (2006). Broadcast network news also attracted large numbers of viewers. For example, NBC *Nightly*

News with Brian Williams averaged 10.8 million viewers during the first week of the storm and flood. NBC *Nightly News*'s numbers approached the weekly cumulative viewership for HBO's popular *True Blood* (13 million for Season 3) and exceeded the first season of *Game of Thrones* (9.2 million for Season 1). For this reason, television news coverage dominates the memory project of Katrina. Having established the ground floor of the house of representations, television news serves as both source for many other Katrina representations and schema through which viewers interpret, understand, and remember Katrina and the flooding of New Orleans. Yet, even though many more viewers watched television news than documentary, millions of viewers also watched *Treme* on HBO, making it an extremely significant text for understanding representation and memory of Katrina. *Treme* demonstrates that fiction can be an important corrective to contributions of TV news to collective memory.

Where viewership numbers have climbed for *True Blood* and *Game of Thrones*, *Treme*'s numbers have decreased with each season. *Treme* went from 3.2 million cumulative weekly viewers in Season 1 down to 2.2 million in Season 2. Overmyer argued that the first season numbers included viewers attracted to *Treme* by their interest in *The Wire*. He understood this audience to be (slightly) inflated and the second year audience to be the "true audience." According to Overmyer, that true audience consisted of viewers with interest and connection to New Orleans, whether through direct experience, through the music and culture, or through having watched mediations of Katrina on television news and documentaries. In an August 14, 2011, article for the *Times-Picayune*, Walker reported that numbers for Season 3 had dropped even more, down to five hundred thousand for some early episodes (similar to the first season numbers for *Girls*).

In an interview for this book, Simon claimed not to be interested in a mass audience. He argued that he had failed to attract large audiences to *The Wire*, but that audiences had "found it late," and embraced it as a five-season text on DVD. Simon noted that his HBO miniseries *Generation Kill* (2008) was selling more than 160,000 DVD copies per year in 2009 and 2010, and he argued that *Treme* should be judged by the quality of its representation of recovery from Katrina, not by raw numbers. Fox's *K-Ville* had earned as many as 9 million viewers for its first few episodes, reinforcing the difference in scale between broadcast and premium pay cable. Simon has proposed that a larger audience will find *Treme* when its run is complete, consuming the series as a 36-episode, 2,160-minute text.

HBO's 30 million subscribers (or 28.77 million, according to *Variety*, see Wallenstein, 2013) pay an average monthly premium of $17.99 per month in addition to the cost of a basic cable package. This additional fee places

HBO out of reach of some customers, including many of the viewers Simon claimed to be targeting. Overmyer noted in an interview for this book that many residents of the Treme neighborhood in New Orleans were not able to afford HBO and thus were unable to view the dramatic series about their own community in their own homes. In response, local bars and other venues, including the Charbonnet Funeral Home, hosted Sunday evening screenings of *Treme* (Laborde, 2011). These public screenings created unique forms of exhibition and reception, taking cable television out of the home and into commercial and community spaces. This engagement with television in public suggests a participatory dimension to *Treme* and recalls the earliest days of the television medium, when viewers would gather in bars, at neighbors' homes, and in front of store windows to watch television programming together. These screenings also underscore the ways in which *Treme* was received differently in New Orleans than elsewhere.

As a cable television drama series, *Treme* is organized into seasons made up of weekly episodes. Unlike television news, which is viewed nightly (on broadcast networks like NBC) or on a 24-hour cycle (like Fox and CNN), *Treme* could only be viewed weekly. Viewers had to wait for the next episode in order to continue to follow the stories and characters. Yet, unlike discrete documentary films or short or feature fiction films, which resolve within a limited time frame, *Treme* continued to unfold according to the narrative structure of the series, where stories develop over months and years. While other television series, such as *K-Ville* (Fox aired eleven episodes in 2007), also were distributed weekly, *Treme* has been the longest running fictional television series about Katrina. *Treme*'s recurrent and progressive narrative structure contributes to the show's impact on the memory project of Katrina.

Whereas TV news responded immediately to Katrina, rushing reports to air even before the scope and specificity of the storm and flood were understood, *Treme* took years to develop and did not begin airing until almost five years after Katrina. This additional time allowed for more research and perspective on the significance of events over time, but it required the trade-off of less immediacy and connection to the flood. Moreover, *Treme* sets its stories in the recent past, creating a complicated temporality of not-present, but also not-long-past. This temporality presents a challenge for viewers who must understand not only what is going on, but also when the events are taking place. *Treme*'s first season is set from November 2005 to May 2006. Subsequent seasons follow this pattern, beginning in fall and ending in spring: Season 2 runs from November 2006 until May 2007; Season 3, November 2007 until May 2008; and Season 4, November 2008 until 2009.

This temporal structure was influenced by the exigencies of production. In order to shoot on location in New Orleans, Simon and Overmyer had to shoot outside the Atlantic hurricane season, which extends from June through November. Shooting during hurricane season would be too expensive and risky, and insurance companies did not want to underwrite production under the threat of hurricanes. Working within these constraints, Simon and Overmyer set each season of the show during the time of year in which they were shooting, although each season was set several years earlier. Few other television dramas attempt to fictionalize real events set in the recent past (Aaron Sorkin's *The Newsroom*, also produced for HBO, attempts a similar temporal structure).

Treme is also the most expensive media representation of Katrina yet produced. In a May 13, 2011, article, Walker reports that HBO budgeted *Treme* at $30–40 million per season ($3–4 million per episode) for the first three seasons (HBO provided Simon and Overmyer with an undisclosed lump sum budget with which to execute the show's final shortened season; based on previous budgets, the budget for Season 4 was $15–20 million). To put this budget in perspective, HBO had budgeted Season 2 of *Game of Thrones* at $80 million, more than twice the cost of *Treme*, and budgeted *When the Levees Broke* at $2 million for four hours of programming. *Treme* had significantly larger resources than other productions, and the show used these resources to shoot on location, to record original musical performances with actual New Orleans musicians, and to employ a large and diverse cast. The series used HBO's resources to render New Orleans after Katrina with an attention to detail and reference missing from fictional narrative representations of New Orleans before Katrina.

Simon and Overmyer indicated that the production shot extensively on location (for example, shooting at Patois Restaurant as a stand-in for Desautel's or shooting outside St. Augustine Church in Treme) and that less than 15 percent of footage was shot on a soundstage constructed across the Mississippi River in Algiers. The soundstage was used to construct interiors, including that for the apartment of Albert Lambreaux's son Delmond (Rob Brown) in New York City. The production schedule usually provided for one day of preparation and eleven days of shooting per episode, with one or two days set aside for shooting on the soundstage. The production shot six scenes per day at four or five locations throughout the city, resulting in nearly forty locations per episode (many more than the norm for television series production). Daily production would usually last twelve to fifteen hours. Musical performance scenes would take longer to shoot.

Simon has long used music as another reference point in his fiction. Blake Leyh was music supervisor for both *The Wire* and *Treme*. In an interview for this book, Leyh discussed Simon's dislike for nondiegetic music. *The Wire* used Tom Waits's "Way Down in the Hole" over its opening credits, and an original composition by Leyh called "The Fall" over its closing credits. Leyh suggested starting "The Fall" while the character D'Angelo Barksdale (Larry Gilliard Jr.) walked away from a shooting at the end of the pilot for *The Wire*. Simon refused, not wanting the non-diegetic music to compromise his realism. In another scene in Season 1 of *The Wire*, Leyh tried to use a Treme Brass Band song coming out of a low-rise apartment in Baltimore. Leyh related that Simon noticed the music: "He was like, well that works really well, that's great, but you would never hear that coming out of a project in Baltimore. So we can't use it."

Simon would allow sound design in *The Wire*, but only when it heightened realism. Leyh cited the example of a scene during Season 4 in which a school kid is in the school office asking about his dying grandmother. Leyh recorded two other actors screaming at each other in the next room to play under the conversation about the grandmother. According to Leyh, he and Simon sought to create observational moments like those in the films—for example, *High School* (1968)—of documentarian Fred Wiseman.

According to Leyh, Simon knew what he wanted on *The Wire* and in *Treme*, but not how to produce it. Leyh noted that Simon would often demand, "I want it to feel real," but, as a writer not strongly versed in video production, he would leave it up to his director, music supervisors, and others to work out the approach required to simulate the real. With *Treme*, they decided to forgo playback tracks when recording musical performance. In television and film, when musical performance is created, it is usually a simulation. Musicians lay down a track, which is then played back as they are shot pretending to play the track. With *Treme*'s focus on the creation of music, Simon, Overmyer, and Leyh decided that they needed to record performances live, without playback. To accomplish this, they had to develop a style of multi-camera and mic shooting. Since the musicians were playing live, they might inadvertently change the tempo of their playing in retakes. To avoid this problem, multiple cameras and mics were used to record one performance from multiple perspectives. According to Leyh, this approach worked because the New Orleans musicians appearing on the show knew the same repertoire of standard material and did not need to be rehearsed significantly.

While musicians playing themselves present a production challenge, non-musician actors performing as musicians present a greater challenge, both to production and to the verisimilitude of the scenes. Leyh could ask Kermit Ruffins to show up at Vaughn's Bar and start playing "Basin Street Blues" without rehearsal, but actor Wendell Pierce would need hours of rehearsal in order to learn to execute fingering and breathing. Actors like Pierce or Rob Brown could not improvise, contra the essence of jazz. Instead, they would work out every note in advance and rehearse the exact performance in order for the actors to successfully simulate musicians. According to Leyh, Pierce proposed passing the "Delfayo Marsalis Test" as his goal. If Pierce could convince jazz trombonist Delfayo Marsalis (brother of Wynton and Branford) that he was really playing, then he would have succeeded. According to Leyh, Pierce never came close. Leyh noted that Rob Brown looked great playing the trumpet, but that he always screwed up his face in a show of intensity, even in moments when a real trumpeter would be relaxed. Thus, *Treme* contained moments of documentary in representations of actual performance by New Orleans musicians, but it also had numerous moments where actors performing as musicians would simulate performance.

Finally, according to Leyh, Simon was always concerned with point of view and narrative. Thus, instead of structuring musical performance–like numbers in a musical film, where narrative would stop and give way to performance and spectacle, Simon insisted that narrative had to advance during musical performance. Although *Treme* pioneered approaches to the recording of live performance, both Simon and Overmyer, in interviews for this book, indicated that they felt that musical performance had to be connected to (at times, interrupted by) narrative. Simon and Overmyer, working with editors Alex Hall and Kate Sanford, frequently employ cross-cutting between scenes to create counterpoint and connection, and within scenes, especially within scenes of performance. For example, their approach to shooting and editing Kermit Ruffins's performance at Vaughn's in the pilot episode established an approach to which they return repeatedly in the series. After observing Ruffins blowing his horn, the camera finds Davis McAlary (Steve Zahn). As the scene continues, attention cuts from Ruffins's performance to a small comic moment in which Davis tries to approach and speak with Elvis Costello, who is in New Orleans to record the *River in Reverse* album with Allen Toussaint. While the scene produces a partial document of an actual profilmic performance by Ruffins, it also constructs business for two fictional characters, Antoine (Pierce simulating playing the trombone with Ruffins) and Davis (Zahn hovering around Costello). Simon and Overmyer depart from the typical structure of musical genre, with its alternation of narrative and number. Performance scenes usually intercut thirty seconds of performance with a shot of main character, either performing or listening to the music. In this way, Simon used the documentary performance to give heightened realism to his fictional moments.

CHAPTER TWENTY-ONE

The Continuance of Culture

*I*N ORDER TO UNDERSTAND HOW *TREME* SPECIFICALLY RE-
members and forgets Katrina, it is necessary to examine closely
the textually inscribed rhetorics by which the series builds its representations. As with television news or documentary, it is necessary to move beyond broad claims and summaries to investigate how *Treme* shaped stories
about New Orleans after Katrina. If fiction can provide important information about the storm and flood, information unavailable through news
or documentary, that information must be decoded, its form and structure
examined. Since meaning in media is never self-evident, but always historical and structural, analysis of the history of *Treme*'s mode of production is complemented by analysis of additional scenes and moments from
the show's run.

WON'T BOW DOWN

The key scene and image for the first season of *Treme* (HBO 2010–
2014) occurs late in the pilot episode, "Do You Know What It Means?,"
written by Simon and Overmyer and directed by Polish filmmaker Ag-
nieszka Holland (airdate April 11, 2010). The scene begins with a slight
high-angle shot as a hand reaches down into the frame to carefully lay
down a garment bag. The shot is dark, as the only illumination seems to be
natural light coming from outside the frame. The next shot reframes the
figure, revealing a man in a blue shirt, unzipping the bag. The camera pans
around to the right to observe his movement. The scene cuts to a close-up
of the man's hands on the zipper, before pulling back, as he opens the bag,
to reveal yellow feathers, shining dully in the darkness. The next shot re-

*Albert Lambreaux (Clarke Peters) opens a garment bag (*Treme, *frame capture).*

*Shot of the feathered costume in the bag (*Treme, *frame capture).*

veals the figure to be Albert Lambreaux (Clarke Peters). The camera frames him in a slight high angle as he examines the feathered suit, before tracking down his arm into a close-up on the feathers. Briefly, the scene cuts away to Vaughn's, a bar in the Treme neighborhood, where Kermit Ruffins and his band perform on Thursday nights. Antoine Batiste (Wendell Pierce) is sitting in with the band, and Davis McAlary (Steve Zahn) is in the audience with friends.

Using Ruffins's trumpet as an audio bridge, the scene cuts from Vaughn's to an exterior wide and long shot of the Crescent City Connection bridge, lit up at night. As Ruffins's trumpet begins to fade out, the soundtrack brings up the sound of a single tambourine, and the camera pans from right to left from the bridges to a dark neighborhood. The stillness and darkness of the frame contrast with the noise and activity of Vaughn's, marking a shift in tone and meaning. At first, nothing is visible. As the shot continues, sparkles begin to flicker in the darkness, suggesting movement and approach. Someone begins to chant, "Injuns!" With his call, the scene cuts to a side-view shot of a porch, suggesting the point of view of the figure and his possible destination. The scene cuts back to a straight-on wide shot, as a figure begins to emerge from the darkness. As the shot continues, feathers become visible, slightly haloed by a light source behind the figure, revealing him to be wearing a large elaborate feathered outfit. As the figure chants, "Injuns," he opens his arms wide, a gesture of calling together a group, and then brings his hands together to beat the tambourine. The figure resolves into Albert, dressed in a large and elaborate yellow suit, with beads and yellow feathers catching the light. He spins clockwise, chanting, "I'm Big Chief!" The scene cuts back to the side-view of the porch as a door opens and Albert's neighbor Robinette (Davi Jay) emerges, pulling on a shirt. The camera tracks with him as he moves out onto the porch to see who is calling out in the dark neighborhood. The scene reverses to show Chief Albert, more distinctly visible, spinning 180 degrees, displaying his suit, and continuing to chant.

CHIEF ALBERT: I'm Big Chief, Guardians of the Flame!

Robinette enters the frame, approaching Chief Albert, creating a two-shot, contrasting Robinette's subdued, workingman's clothes with the brilliance of Albert's suit. The scene cuts to a close-up on Albert, his face framed by a beaded and feathered headdress and braids. Within the flam-

Big Chief Lambreaux dancing in the darkness (Treme, *frame capture*).

boyant suit, Albert appears focused and passionate. The next shot moves behind Albert to show Robinette's reaction, as he begins to smile. The scene cuts back to show Albert in a tight close-up, smiling in response to Robinette, stepping out of character for a moment to acknowledge his audience and his performance. Robinette nods in response. The camera cuts back to a tight close-up on Albert as he continues to chant.

>CHIEF ALBERT: I'll wake up the dead and make 'em bow!

At this, the scene cuts to a wide shot, providing full perspective on Albert in his suit, dancing and chanting in the darkness on a nearly empty street, in the devastated Central City neighborhood. Albert stops chanting and the scene is suddenly silent, with only a lone dog barking. This shift creates contrast between the visual noise of the Big Chief's suit and the absence of light and sound in the neighborhood. The scene cuts to Albert's perspective on Robinette and his wife, who had joined the two men in the street. Then, the shot reverses to show Robinette's view of Albert.

>ROBINETTE: Oh, Chief. That's pretty. That's real pretty. I wondered
>if I was ever going to see something like that again.

The shot reverses again to frame Chief Albert, over the shoulders of Robinette and his wife.

>CHIEF ALBERT: I'm looking for the Trail Chief, got a heart of steel.

The reverse finds Robinette and his wife, shaking their heads in amazement, smiling at Albert's performance, drawn into the ritual he performs. From Robinette's perspective, the shot frames Albert as he spins clockwise, dancing in the street.

>ROBINETTE: Might not be a Mardi Gras this year. St. Joseph's
>neither.

At this, the shot frames Albert in close-up, determined and defiant.

>CHIEF ALBERT: Won't bow. Don't know how.

In many ways, the scene has built to this line, a powerful, ritual proclamation used by Mardi Gras Indians to signal strength and defiance. In this

"Won't bow. Don't know how" (Treme, *frame capture*).

moment, Simon and Overmyer connect to the deep traditions of performance by Mardi Gras Indian tribes in New Orleans, but they also advance
their construction of Albert's character as especially intractable.

> ROBINETTE: Ain't nobody home. Ain't nobody thinking about no
> needle and thread.

In response, Albert continues to spin and dance. Then the shot frames him
in another close-up as he enunciates each word.

> CHIEF ALBERT: Won't bow. Don't know how.

After another series of reverses, as he continues to watch Albert dance,
Robinette gives in, agreeing to serve as Trail Chief and to help Albert constitute a gang.

> ROBINETTE: All right, put your suit away, Chief. I'll be round by
> the bar tomorrow afternoon.

In close-up, Albert nods three times. Robinette and his wife exit, leaving
Albert again in a wide shot, surrounded by darkness. He turns slowly, first
clockwise, then counterclockwise. After executing two full spins, he begins to dance back up the street, into the darkness. The soundtrack emphasizes his breathing, his concentration and exertion, suggesting finally the
effort involved in wearing and performing in a costume that can weigh up

*Robinette and wife as audience for the continuation of culture (*Treme, *frame capture).*

to 150 pounds, the work involved in creating the performance. As he moves away from the camera and its light source, Albert and his suit become less and less distinct, finally fading into black.

DON'T KNOW HOW

Simon and Overmyer's approach to Chief Lambreaux's performance in the dark streets of Central City demonstrates their strategy for representing New Orleans and its culture in the broader series. Simon and Overmyer choose to place their viewer into a specific place and cultural context, often without establishing or explaining that context. In this scene, viewers must first work to make out the figure in the darkness and then must work to read and interpret the figure's costume and performance. For viewers unfamiliar with New Orleans cultural traditions, the sight of Clarke Peters in an elaborate costume of feathers and beads, emerging from the darkness in an area of New Orleans submerged by the flood, might be baffling. Why is this man dressed in this way? Why is he singing and dancing alone in a dark street? Simon and Overmyer do not explain his appearance or actions. Rather, as the scene plays out, viewers attentive to details of performance, framing, and editing begin to understand his pride and defiance through his actions and interactions with Robinette and his wife.

Viewers familiar with Mardi Gras Indian traditions recognize that the character of Albert Lambreaux is meant to represent a Big Chief, the leader of a Mardi Gras Indian tribe. Simon and Overmyer engaged modern jazz musician Donald Harrison Jr. as a consultant on *Treme* in order to bene-fit from his knowledge of Mardi Gras Indians. Harrison Jr. is Big Chief of the Congo Square Nation, and his father, Donald Sr., was Big Chief of the Guardians of the Flame. Simon and Overmyer drew on aspects of both Harrisons to create the character of Albert Lambreaux, and they drew heavily on Harrison Jr.'s career as a jazz musician, steeped in both modern jazz and traditional New Orleans music, to create the character of Del-mond Lambreaux (Rob Brown), Albert's son. Like Harrison Sr., Albert is Big Chief of the Guardians of the Flame. The tribe's name suggests Albert's mission to keep alive cultural traditions. Moreover, the scene constructs Big Chief Albert as himself a flame, a light in the darkness of streets with-out power after Katrina, streets that lacked opportunity before Katrina. As he emerges from the darkness, the Big Chief sparks and shimmers like a flame about to gutter out. The scene uses space and mise-en-scène to sug-gest both the Big Chief's passion and the pervasive threat to the continu-ance of his culture.

In *Cities of the Dead* (1996), Joseph Roach argues for the significance of Mardi Gras Indians as performers of memory. He suggests that in the twen-tieth century the production of memory shifted from traditions of perfor-mance into "places of memory," like museums and memorials. For Roach, by singing, dancing, and parading, Mardi Gras Indians perform remem-brance of the histories of slavery and oppression and of the traditions of free black communities in New Orleans. bell hooks understands Mardi Gras Indians to be performing resistance by marching in the streets, their parades retaking contested space and their rituals and narratives recalling previous resistance to white control, enacting continued resistance against white society and oppression by the New Orleans Police Department (NOPD), which often acts as an agent of forces of gentrification (1992).

American Studies scholar George Lipsitz understands the appearance of the Mardi Gras Indians to convey historical argument and interpreta-tion. "The Indian image calls attention to the initial genocide upon which American 'civilization' rests. It challenges the core dualism of American racism that defines people as either white or black" (1988, 120). For Lip-sitz, the act of sewing and creating the suits worn on Mardi Gras and on St. Joseph's Day each year is an act of material memory and of critical reading. He also makes clear that Mardi Gras Indians are themselves fic-tional constructs, not "Indians," but African Americans participating in a century-long adaptation of signifiers of "Indian-ness" to perform publicly remembrance and social criticism. "Drawing upon the tools available to them—music, costumes, speech, and dance—they fashion a fictive iden-tity that gives voice to their deepest values and beliefs" (1988, 102). Mardi

Gras Indians use imagination and performance to convey the truth of their lived experience ("their deepest values and beliefs") via fictive identities.

Similarly, *Treme* deploys fictional characters with the goal of conveying truths about lived experience. In this scene, Peters performs a fictional character wearing a Big Chief costume to express something of the experience of culture bearers in November 2005. Within the story, Chief Albert parades alone—without his tribe and without an audience—in order to draw out other survivors and to call them to join in the production and renewal of culture.

Simon and Overmyer construct the scene as a potent visual argument for the continuance of culture. Big Chief Albert conveys an image of beauty and defiance amid destruction and loss. Isolated against the darkness of the rest of the frame, his beauty and heat seem fragile, easily snuffed by the surrounding forces. Albert stands in the darkness as the last of the Big Chiefs, a poetic figure for all cultural traditions imperiled as much by diaspora as by storm and flood. Simon and Overmyer understand the truth of New Orleans to lie in its cultural traditions: if the city is to survive, it must do so through the renewal of the production of culture.

In the tenth and final episode of the first season, "I'll Fly Away," Albert's assertion of the continuance of the Guardians of the Flame is realized. In contrast to the scene in the first episode, where Albert emerges from the darkness in costume to perform a parade as a lone guardian of tradition, in the final episode, he parades as Big Chief with other members of the renewed Guardians in full daylight on St. Joseph's Day (March 19, 2006). The St. Joseph's Day scene begins with a close-up on a snare drum, cuts to a small group (Delmond, his sister Davina, Albert's lady, and her son) keeping the beat, before moving inside the doorway to Poke's Bar, framing the emergence of the Spyboy from his perspective. A quick cut shifts back outside of Poke's to frame the Spyboy, wearing purple and red feathers, dancing through the doorframe and moving toward the camera. After he enters the street, the scene cuts back to a handheld shot from inside Poke's. The Spyboy approaches the camera, inviting the Flagboy, clad in orange feathers, out into the street. The two then position themselves in front of the door, shielding camera and viewer from seeing the Big Chief until they move apart to reveal Big Chief Albert in a new suit of red and purple feathers. This scene provides a privileged point of view on the performance of Mardi Gras Indian ritual, showing the view from the Indians' perspective, out onto the street. In contrast to the scene in the first episode, the Big Chief's emergence is heralded by the Spyboy and Flagboy and met by an appreciative community. By resisting loss, inertia, depression, and diaspora, Albert has willed his community to come together through the continuance of culture. As the Big Chief steps out into the street, he bears his cultural tradition in his costume, his stance, and his movement. Simon and Overmyer offer him as a figure of cultural renewal and of the continued viability of New Orleans.

DO WHATCHA WANNA

Like Mardi Gras Indians parading, the second line is a vital form of cultural performance in New Orleans. In *When the Levees Broke*, Lee and Pollard stage a one-man second line in which trumpeter and composer Terence Blanchard performs "Just a Closer Walk with Thee" to camera while walking through the devastated Gentilly Woods neighborhood.

Treme also structures representations of second lines at key moments over its multi-season run. In Season 1, the pilot episode opens with a representation of one of the first second lines to be performed in the city after Katrina. In Episode 5 of Season 1, *Treme* represents the much larger "All Star Second Line" that took place on January 15, 2006. In the first episode of Season 3, *Treme* represents a memorial second line for New Birth Brass Band member Kerwin James that was broken up by the NOPD. By analyzing these three scenes, it is possible to identify shifts in the series' formal approach to shooting and recording live performance. *Treme* figures the second line as a crucial form of remembrance and resistance.

The pilot episode begins with a representation of a second line parade. The opening scene, preceding the title credit sequence, recreates an actual second line held on October 9, 2005, for chef Austin Leslie. Leslie was well known in New Orleans as the former chef of Chez Helene, a creole and soul food restaurant on North Robertson that was the basis for the television show *Frank's Place* (CBS 1987). Leslie was seventy-two years old when Katrina hit, and he was trapped in his attic by floodwaters. Before he was rescued, temperatures in his attic exceeded 120 degrees. Leslie became ill and died in October 2005, another casualty of Katrina and another example of Katrina's impact on the elderly. Unlike Lee and Pollard, who created their own second line equivalent, Simon and Overmyer were careful to base their second lines on actual, verifiable memorials and parades. The goal of the opening sequence of the *Treme* pilot is to place the viewer inside the preparations for the second line in honor of Leslie. With the formal choices in the opening scene of the series, *Treme* forced viewers who did not know much about New Orleans, the culture of the second line, or the impact of Katrina to learn and to make sense of culture and history from the inside.

Season 1, Episode 1 opens with the titles "New Orleans, LA" and "Three Months After" on separate cards over black screen. *Treme* begins by assuming certain knowledge: that "three months after" means after Katrina, and, since Katrina hit land on the morning on Monday, August 29, 2005, "three months after" means late November 2005. From the jump, Simon and Overmyer are "cheating," exercising the power of television to shape time and space by placing an event that happened in early October in reality in late November in the fiction.

Over black screen, the audio track features voices, as if of a crowd of people. From black, the sequence cuts to an extreme close-up of the mouth of a young African American man. He is unshaven, and he bites down on a Popsicle stick. The next image is an extreme close-up of a clarinet, as a hand reaches into the frame to adjust part of the instrument. The next shot shows a hand adjusting a trumpet and fingers applying a lubricant. The next shot shows an African American man's forearm with a trombone tattoo, then cuts to an extreme close-up on a white feather. The following shot shows a memorial card for Chef Leslie, attached to a straw fan, being shaken. The memorial card is evidence of the real event that the scene recreates, but the shot length is so short that most viewers could not process the information, even if they had a context in which to do so. The next shot begins with an extreme close-up on fingers on the keys of a sax, before tilting up the instrument as it begins to be played. Matching the upward motion, the next image tilts up a bottle of Old New Orleans Rum, a locally distilled spirit, as a hand reaches into the frame to grab the bottle. This is followed by an extreme close-up of green fabric, piled into ribbons. The camera tilts down to reveal buttons and a green shirtsleeve, then continues downward, finding a black-gloved hand smoking a cigarette. In the next shot, the focus shifts from a brass instrument in the foreground to an African American NOPD officer in the background. This is the first full-body shot in the sequence. Placed in deeper space, the officer looks at the instrument, and the camera, from a distance, outside. The sequence has brought the viewer inside the preparation, separate from the police, linked to the event's unfolding.

As the sequence continues, camera placement, framing, and movement continue to reveal small, intimate details: a man plays a trumpet, warming up; more drinks are poured and passed around; two women talk while fanning themselves; two young men light and smoke a joint; and an older man bounces up and down and takes a swig from a beer bottle. A young boy and a girl walk past the camera, then crouch down and attempt dance moves. Thus far, every person represented in whole or in part has been African

American. As such, *Treme*'s opening is highly unusual for a television show, as television historically constructs a world in which whiteness is the default dominant experience. In this way, *Treme* makes a significant break from what Simon described as "the lame tropes of television."

The sequence is constructed to explore the centrality of African American culture in New Orleans. It also foreshadows conflicts that will be represented later in the series. A shot tilts up through a group of people, all African American, in the foreground to find a white member of the National Guard, before panning left to bring a second white National Guard soldier into the frame. Unlike high-concept television news, *Treme* does not figure the Guardsmen as saviors but as heavily armed outsiders. Like the NOPD officer, they are placed deeper in the frame, away from and outside the main event. In another shot, hinting at conflict to come in the series, the camera looks through the window of an SUV, past two young African American men, at the African American NOPD officer. As hip-hop plays in the truck, the camera holds on the passengers and the cop, each giving the other hard looks. These two shots suggest that New Orleans is being occupied by troops, that conflict and tension exist between groups, and that citizens must struggle with authority in order to create and perform culture.

The sequence thus far has constructed a sense of larger cultural activity, without yet revealing the wide, explanatory shot. The sequence defers meaning, requiring viewers to continue watching, to work to interpret what they are seeing. Simon, Overmyer, and Holland's approach resembles that of Dziga Vertov, a televisual version of Vertov's use of cinematic detail and perspective. The sequence constructs a collage of details, building toward a whole.

In *Treme*, while constructing or capturing performance, Simon and Overmyer typically shift to a second (or third) track to bring in more narrative details and create opportunities for cross-cutting across stories and events. In this sequence, they cut from the street to the inside of a club. Members of several Social Aid and Pleasure Clubs and marching groups are negotiating with the leader of the Rebirth Brass Band over the band's fee. Gralen Banks, a New Orleans resident and non-actor, interviewed by Lee and Pollard in *When the Levees Broke* and *If God Is Willing and Da Creek Don't Rise*, plays the leader of the Black Men of Labor, an actual Social Aid and Pleasure Club, started by Fred Johnson (among others) in 1994 to honor the death of jazz musician Danny Barker (the inspiration for Deacon John Moore's character, Danny Nelson). Banks argues with the band's snare drummer over the band's compensation.

BANKS: $1,200 was for 8 pieces. Ya'll said you was gonna have Shorty kicking it with ya'll.

DRUMMER: Shorty gonna be here.

BANKS: Well, he ain't here now. See ya'll only got the one bone out there. . . . Seem to me 7 get you 10.

The scene plays out in the darkened interior of the bar, illuminated by natural light though the windows. Banks wears a headscarf and glasses and carries a fedora. The men around him wear the colors and symbols of other clubs. After the storm and flood, with the diaspora of New Orleans residents, Social Aid and Pleasure Clubs and brass bands lacked the critical mass to parade as per tradition. Thus, groups had to join together in order to continue the second line tradition in the immediate aftermath of Katrina.

DRUMMER: How much water ya'll get up in here?

BANKS: Shit. You see that line over my head? 6, 6½ feet.

The drummer capitulates, in part in recognition of the struggle of the clubs to sponsor the second line. With the narrative business complete, the sequence again picks up pace. The drummer exits the bar, enters a wide shot, explaining the resolution to his musicians. The image reverses, showing the musicians picking up instruments, getting ready. None of the musicians wears a uniform. The image cuts to a wide shot of the band, "Rebirth Brass Band" visible on the tuba. A woman walks in front of the camera, simulating the informality of documentary representation, even though this opening sequence is clearly structured with performances blocked for the camera. The shot cuts back inside the bar, as the club members put on fedoras and pick up umbrellas. The camera tracks from the back of the bar to the door as the men exit. The sequence cuts back outside.

With this, the second line begins. The band strikes up the song "Do Whatcha Wanna," as the camera dips down to frame the feet of a man in a canary yellow suit, dancing with a large feathered fan. The camera pans right to frame a second man. The sequence cuts to a high angle looking down at a man in two-tone shoes dancing. The next image shows Banks from a low angle, wearing his fedora, smoking a cigar, and dancing. As he moves forward, the camera tracks back, keeping him framed up. The image then cuts to another club member, wearing a dark hat, dancing with a fan. The next image is a tight shot of the crowd, with brass band members visible. The camera pans left to right with a light-skinned man in a bandana, before moving into a high angle to observe the lower bodies of dancers moving and swaying to the music. The camera finds a man in a wheelchair (again raising the suggestion of gun violence), moving his wheels to the music.

The sequence continues with more images of dancers, the main line of the parade—usually the marshals, steppers, and the band—blending with the second line, suggesting a loosening of tradition required by the circumstances. In the fifty-fifth shot of the sequence, the camera cuts to a wide shot, ahead of the second line. As the camera tracks slowly backward, the parade advances. A man leads the parade, carrying a Black Men Of Labor banner (yellow over black). As the parade approaches, the camera frames a ruined refrigerator and a microwave in the foreground of the shot. To this point, Simon, Overmyer, and Holland had resisted providing an establishing shot. Instead, they forced viewers into intimate connection with details of the parade, placing viewers inside in order to convey a sense of the feeling of parading. Simon and Overmyer employ a similar strategy throughout the series, expecting viewers to interpret details and events from the inside out. In this way, they activate viewers, provoking deeper connection through the necessity of engagement with the text.

Treme's opening sequence concludes with another narrative interlude. As with the negotiation in the club, the sequence cuts away from detailed observation of the performance in order to introduce information and establish character. The scene shows trombonist Antoine Batiste (Wendell Pierce) arguing with a cab driver about his fare. Throughout *Treme*, Antoine is always late and always short of money. Having lost his house and his car during the flood, Antoine is living in New Orleans East with Desiree (Phyllis Montana-Leblanc) and their infant daughter. Given the lack of public transportation in New Orleans, a pre-Katrina challenge to the city's poorest residents, Antoine is forced to use cabs to get to gigs throughout the city. Each time, Antoine argues with the cabbie about his choice of route in a ploy to reduce his fare.

The camera tracks behind Antoine as he runs down the street to catch up with the second line. As he runs, he plays a few notes to announce his presence, causing heads to turn up the street. The sequence reverses as the camera moves ahead of Antoine as he runs. After cutting to the band hearing him, the sequence cuts behind Antoine as he approaches, then moves into a side view. As the camera tracks beside Antoine, Pierce works to simulate playing the trombone. In his first scene, he fails the Delfayo Marsalis Test. Pierce appears too stiff, too studied, his preparation and rehearsal apparent in his performance. Where the actual members of the Rebirth and Treme Brass Bands playing in the second line move fluidly, in the moment but easy in their playing, Pierce cannot mask the anxiety of his performance. This sense of disjunction continues throughout the series when Pierce simulates playing the trombone. (Simon and Overmyer may have responded to this problem by creating more opportunities for Pierce to sing in Season 2 as front man for the Soul Apostles.)

The sequence ends with a dialogue reference and an elaborate camera move. Referencing Kermit Ruffins, founding trumpeter for Rebirth Brass Band, Antoine exhorts the band, reminding them that playing music is both culture and work for musicians.

ANTOINE: Play for that money, boys. Play for that fucking money.

After Antoine's exhortation, the shot begins in front of him and the band, centering him, before tracking counterclockwise toward the right, moving up and around the players, flying past Antoine. The camera continues around, past the trumpeter, and back to find Antoine. According to Blake Leyh, Simon ruled out crane shots or other spectacular visual moves when the *Treme* team recorded performances. Leyh indicated that Simon wanted *Treme* to avoid the "Top of the Pops" approach to performance that features sweeping crane and dolly shots. At the beginning of the series, Simon and Overmyer were still experimenting with their formal approach. In several instances in *Treme*'s first season, Simon and Overmyer departed from the realism that typified *The Wire*. LaDonna's nightmare in Episode 5 and the flashback in Episode 10 are anti-realist, using the formal possibilities of television to offer subjective perspectives and to explore alternative temporalities and possibilities. With the 360-degree tracking shot, *Treme* explores the power of television to offer perspectives impossible in the real

Antoine Batiste (Wendell Pierce) joins the second line for Austin Leslie (Treme, frame capture).

*Antoine sings with the brass band (*Treme, *frame capture).*

world. Simon and Overmyer argue that realism is too limiting of a mode to account for the affective truths of Katrina or performance in the face of Katrina. Compared to this elaborate shot, the final shot of the sequence is prosaic, a close-up on Antoine as he sings with the band, "I Feel Like Funkin' It Up." Antoine moves forward with the second line, the camera moving to keep him in frame, until the shot fades to black. It is as if *Treme* retreats from the ecstatic exploration of perspective on performance back to the straight-ahead possibilities of basic realism.

THE SECOND SECOND LINE

The next representation of a second line is in *Treme*'s fifth episode. According to Leyh, the *Treme* team rethought their approach to shooting second lines after the pilot episode. The pilot uses formal choices to present a series of perspectives on a second line possible only through television (or cinema). Like Vertov's *kino pravda*, Simon, Overmyer, and Holland seek a form of televisual truth, representing the cultural performance via the power of camera and nonlinear editing, a truth only available through mediation. When they approached filming the second second line, Simon and Overmyer consulted with Leyh and veteran television director Christine Moore to devise a different approach. Rather than block out every camera move and shoot multiple takes, they decided to deploy multiple cameras and mics to capture various moments within a larger performance. The team would employ a similar approach to shooting performance elsewhere during *Treme*'s run.

Like the first, the second second line represents an actual event, the All Star Second Line, which took place on January 15, 2006. This second line was hosted by the Social Aid and Pleasure Club Task Force, an organization formed to advocate for parade culture against efforts by the City of New Orleans to require new, prohibitively expensive permits to approve what had always been local, community practice. The first second line honored Chef Leslie, but it was also an assertion of identity and tradition. Like Albert donning his Big Chief suit and parading in the darkened street, the first second line was a performance against disappearance and against forgetting. For *Treme* viewers, it was a performance intended to confound and intrigue, calling viewers to work toward an understanding of unfamiliar iconography and ritual. Like most second line parades in New Orleans, *Treme* argued, it was possible for anyone to fall in line and dance along, picking up cues along the way.

The second second line was a call for those who had left New Orleans to return from diaspora. The parade featured thirty-two Social Aid and Pleasure Clubs marching with banners, flags, fans, and feathers. It also featured three brass bands. The memorial second line for Chef Leslie attracted dozens of marchers. Hundreds marched in the All Star Second Line. The parade also had an explicit political message. Participants wore T-shirts bearing the slogan "RENew Orleans" and called for city government to move on the needs of returning residents for housing, jobs, and health insurance (Reckdahl, 2006).

Unlike the re-creation of the parade for Chef Leslie, *Treme*'s second second line begins with the parade in full swing. The sequence begins with a high-angle shot that tilts down to find a large banner proclaiming "RENew Orleans" along with smaller banners for many Social Aid and Pleasure Clubs, including Nine Times and the Treme Sidewalk Steppers. The sequence cuts closer to the action, showing a brass band, with five musicians in the frame. They wear hoodies against the cold, and the camera tracks back as the band and marchers pass. The sequence then cuts to another high-angle shot looking down at the tops of marchers' heads, a New Orleans Bayou Steppers banner, and the shining bell of a tuba. The next image is a side shot of a group of female steppers, wearing black shirts with red sleeves, red bandanas, and black fedoras. The sequence cuts to its first close-up of a large African American man in glasses, a cap, and a puffy vest, dancing to the band. The sequence then looks up from a low angle at two guys, dancing in tandem across the peak of a roof. The first man squats as the second places his hands on the first man's hips. They then hop forward across the roof, presumably transported by the music into a seemingly dangerous display. High above the parade, they seem literally carried away by the music and dancing.

The sequence next moves into a close-up on a woman in a RENeW Orleans shirt, dancing among other women, all of them African American. The second line route seems to be following North Claiborne Street through the *Treme* neighborhood and the crowd is predominantly African American. The sequence cuts to show a wider, side view of three kids, standing on a stoop in front of a barred door, watching the parade move past. The sequence then cuts behind a group of marchers, showing their T-shirts listing all thirty-two participating Social Aid and Pleasure Clubs. One woman in the group spins around. The sequence shows a side view of the band playing, then a 45 percent angle on the marchers, one of whom is Jordan Hirsh, consultant and writer for the show. With the twelfth shot, the sequence shows Davis McAlary (Steve Zahn) and friends, including local filmmaker Henry Griffin, staggering along in an exaggerated dance. The camera tracks with Zahn, keeping him in the frame. A woman turns to check him out, breaking the fictional wall and suggesting that the cast had been mixed among a large group of actual club members and local extras.

Unlike the first second line, the second contains no extreme close-ups. Rather than beginning inside before moving out, the sequence begins with a wide and long shot, locating the march in space, before moving into tighter shots. Because they decided to use multiple cameras to re-create the All Star Second Line, the *Treme* team finds, rather than constructs, moments. Their approach has shifted from formalism to observation. The resulting images feel more organic, their naturalism supporting a sense that what the viewer is seeing is the actual January 15, 2006, second line.

As with the first second line, the introduction of fictional characters shifts the focus of the sequence from documentary observation to narrative building. Davis and friends demonstrate their solidarity and interest in second line tradition, even though they are not members of a Social Aid and Pleasure club. Recent arrivals to New Orleans, Sonny (Michiel Huisman) and Annie (Lucia Micarelli) join the fringe of the parade with Arnie (Jeffrey Carisalez), the roadhouse bouncer Sonny brought back from Texas. Later in the sequence, Antoine and Desiree are seen walking with their baby daughter.

Like the first second line, Simon and Overmyer interrupt the documentary observation with narrative business. Sonny admonishes Arnie (and the viewer) to "just watch and learn." The sequence leaves the parade entirely and moves inside the Mother-in-Law Lounge, Ernie and Antoinette K-Doe's club, for a meeting of the captains of the Krewe de Vieux, including Creighton Bernette. Creighton suggests a pause in their business to go watch the parade, and Toni runs from the crowd to embrace him, excited by the number of people who have returned for the second line. She is participating as a volunteer observer, to intervene with the NOPD if necessary.

Treme functions as documentary fiction because of its use of referentiality to convey the power of the real to fictional narrative. *Treme*'s status as documentary fiction enables the show to convey important understandings about Katrina and its aftermath. Forty-six shots into the sequence, a low-angle shot looks up at an African American woman, her hair in braids, dancing to the brass bands and whipping a bandana around. Viewers of Tia Lessin and Carl Deal's *Trouble the Water* will recognize the woman as Kimberly Rivers Roberts, whose amateur footage and story of recovery are the core of Lessin and Deal's documentary. Simon and Overmyer use subjects from Katrina documentaries throughout *Treme*'s run. They cast Phyllis Montana-Leblanc, the Kim Roberts of *When the Levees Broke*, as Desiree, the mother of Albert's baby daughter. Montana-Leblanc plays a character, not herself, on the show, but, like Felicia Pearson in *The Wire*, her presence, her way of speaking, and her very embodiment convey a reality that eludes the professional performers. Simon's populating of fiction with real residents, like the practice of *typage* in Soviet cinema, alters the impact of his narrative.

The sequence cuts from Kimberly to show Albert's daughter Davina (Edwina Findley) dancing. As the shot continues, she looks out of frame right, spots Roberts, and screams "Kim!" The shot then reverses as Roberts sees Davina and yells. The sequence cuts back to Davina, in close-up, as she starts crying and runs toward Roberts, the camera moving with her in order to keep her in frame as she and Kim embrace. The sequence cuts to a high angle, showing the women embracing, before cutting to a close-up on Roberts's face. Unlike Davina, who jumps and emotes, Roberts is more restrained, as if some part of her cannot let go of the fact that she is embracing a fictional friend. Simon and Overmyer use intertextual reference to connect *Treme*'s fiction to *Trouble the Water*'s documentary story about loss and recovery. In Episode 7 of Season 3, in one of Simon's "moments of unrestrained meta," Kimberly gives Davina and Delmond a DVD of *Trouble the Water*, and Delmond and Albert watch the film at Albert's house. The scene does not show real friends finding each other for the first time after the storm, but it does convey what it must have felt like to find a friend, alive and well, five months after so many others drowned and died of exposure. Simon and Overmyer use intextuality and referentiality not to claim for *Treme* the status of documentary but to use documentary to convey emotional truth via fiction. As Alison Landsberg has argued, emotional truth is central to memory formation (2004).

The second second line passes Roberts and Davina and continues. Simon and Overmyer leave the parade a final time for a scene between LaDonna Batiste (Khandi Alexander) and Marcus, a drug dealer recently returned to New Orleans after the flood. LaDonna spies Marcus off to the side of the second line, and she leaves her husband, Larry Williams (Lance E. Nichols), and her boys to ask Marcus about her brother Daymo. LaDonna wants to know whether Daymo is again using drugs. Marcus relates that Daymo had not bought drugs from him, a non-answer that does not reassure La-Donna. The strong implication of this short scene is that after a respite of a few months, crime and violence have returned to New Orleans.

As the second line (and the sequence) ends, Simon and Overmyer actualize the threat implicit in the scene with Marcus. As the parade breaks up, the sequence shows an inebriated Sonny lighting a cigarette and stumbling along beside Annie and Arnie.

ARNIE: Well, that was different.

As soon as Arnie speaks, gunshots are heard on the audio track, and the crowd starts to move. The next shot shows a young African American in khakis and a striped shirt struck in the leg by a bullet. Drunk and disoriented, Sonny falls to the ground. The next shot shows a girl hit in the shoulder, spun to the ground. In the next shot, Arnie grabs Annie and hustles her away. The sequence then cuts to a close-up on a hand holding a gun, down next to the legs of blue jeans, as the shooter calmly walks through the crowd. Next, the image shifts from a high-angle shot showing the first shooting victim, writhing in pain, to a whip pan, left to right, over the panicked crowd. The scene is focalized through Sonny's perspective as he foggily tries to decide what to do. The girl shot in the shoulder cries out. Roberts and Davina crouch behind a car. The sequence ends with a tight 180-degree shot of Sonny, as he calls out to Annie and stumbles over people crouching in fear.

The eruption of violence at a second line parade is not an invention for television. On May 12, 2013, Mother's Day, a second line parade sponsored by the Original Big 7 Social Aid and Pleasure Club was shattered by gunfire. A gunman shot into the parade, his target unclear, wounding nineteen marchers, including women and two children. African American Studies scholar Laura Murphy, who was at the second line, has written about the lack of national media coverage or interest in the shooting, in contrast to coverage of other acts of mass violence (2013).

On January 15, 2006, a shooting occurred on Broad Street, after the All Star Second Line. Simon and Overmyer shift the shooting to the conclusion of the parade to make a point about violence as an insistent and oppressive challenge to recovery and life in New Orleans. The conclusion of the sequence shows the encroachment of violence on celebration. The shooting at the second line suggests the limits of culture as answer to systemic injustice, desperation, anger, and violence. Culture can bring people together. It can commemorate shared experience. Culture can advocate for justice, as the All Star Second Line did, but it cannot itself achieve justice.

Like Lee and Pollard, Simon and Overmyer are drawn to the power of traditional cultural performance in New Orleans. They use the second line and Mardi Gras Indian traditions as symbols of resistance against neglect, injustice, and oppression. In his interview with Michael Dunaway, Simon argued that "the city's only reason for being right now is its culture" (2011). But, Lee and Pollard, Simon and Overmyer, and Behn Zeitlan in *Glory At Sea* (2008) and *Beasts of the Southern Wild* (2012) all overstate the power of cultural performance. The second line is potent performance, but it is not in itself the answer to the most serious problems facing the citizens of New Orleans. The shooting scene at the end of the All Star Second Line reminds viewers of the limits of the second line. Culture helps New Orleanians survive and provides them with strength, but an overinvestment in culture as solution can reduce commitment to policy work, to action, and to systemic change. Like *When the Levees Broke*, *Treme* argues that culture sustains New Orleans. The shooting scene suggests that culture may distract as well as sustain.

PUNCHING DAVIS

After the sequence depicting the January 15, 2006, All Star Second Line, Davis ends up drinking with musician Bunchy Johnson and another African American friend in a bar in Treme. Davis is drunk and expresses surprise and disappointment at a news report on the shooting after the second line. Due to his impaired judgment, but consistent with his character's assumptions about his own liminality, Davis comments on the shootings, quoting Antoine Batiste and employing the epithet "nigger."

> DAVIS: I can only quote Antoine Batiste, New Orleans niggers will fuck up a wet dream.

As a white man enamored of African American music and tradition, and steeped in Bounce and other forms of rap and hip-hop, Davis uses the epithet casually, revealing his assumption that he too may (re)appropriate the term. A clean-cut young African American man sitting nearby takes offense at the remark and asks Davis to repeat himself, to take ownership of his casual usage. Steve Zahn performs Davis as beginning to recognize through his fog that he has crossed a line. He does not repeat the term, but instead of apologizing, he offers his credentials: he lives nearby. Unmoved, the other patron punches him in the face. Davis reacts with pain, confusion, and anger, yelling at his friends and the patrons and stumbling out of the bar. In this moment, Davis must come to terms with the distance between his self-perception and how others see him. He must acknowledge the limits of his mobility and privilege.

In an interview for this book, Simon indicated that he considered Davis to be like an "unreliable narrator" in literature. Viewers and critics struggled to find perspective on the character. *Time* television critic James Poniewozik labeled Davis "the Jar-Jar Binks of *Treme*" (2010). In a representative blog post, Aymar Jean Christian, an assistant professor of Communications at Northwestern, asks, "Why Do I Hate Steve Zahn's Davis in *Treme*?" Christian's reasons include Davis's unconsciousness toward his own privilege, his obsession with authenticity, and his bigotry toward his gay neighbors, whom he considers gentrifiers for moving into Treme. Yet, Davis's disconnection from his own choices and beliefs opens up space for viewers to recognize his assumptions.

Simon and Overmyer use Davis as an emissary into the cultures they wish to explore in *Treme* (Antoine Batiste serves a similar purpose as a musician playing gigs all over town). Davis functions in *Treme* as an outsider/insider, participating in second lines and going to clubs, without completely belonging to the worlds in which he travels.

As Simon indicated in an interview for this book, he intended *Treme* to offer a model of racial and cultural interconnection necessary to the future of cities. In the scene of Davis getting punched, Simon and Overmyer face their own conceits, acknowledging that cities are not only full of progressive possibility but also histories of racial antagonism and uneven access to power and status. By labeling Davis as an "unreliable narrator," Simon reveals the instability of narration and representation itself. Like Davis, *Treme* is the product of deep enthusiasm for African American culture in New Orleans and an assumption that that culture is available for mass representation. As the character of Davis makes clear, that work of connection is ongoing and fraught with the real histories of privilege, opportunity, and oppression.

Simon and Overmyer feature a third second line re-creation to start the third season of *Treme*. As with the first two, the third second line is based on an actual event. On Monday, October 7, 2007, New Orleans musicians Phil and Keith Frazier led a second line in memory of their brother Kerwin James, who died of complications from a stroke. James's family considered him to be a casualty of Katrina. Like Austin Leslie, James suffered during the flood, and his health declined over the next two years. Simon and Overmyer re-created the first second line in the pilot to show the performance of culture as an essential step in the return to life after Katrina. They used the second second line in the fifth episode to show the performance of culture as a galvanizing force for return, attracting a large and diverse group of New Orleanians, calling on the city and state to fulfill the social contract. The shootings at the end of the second second line show the limits of culture as answer to desperation and violence. With the third second line, in the premiere episode of Season 3, Simon and Overmyer show how authority itself can oppress culture, transforming it into a more explicitly political act.

Season 3 begins like the first two seasons with two title cards on black screen announcing "New Orleans, Louisiana" and "Twenty-five months after." The first nine shots involve a piece of character business. As in the series pilot, Antoine is late for the second line and short of money. The episode opens with Antoine arguing with a cab driver over his fare. As Antoine emerges from the cab, the camera backs away as he moves forward, tracking backward to keep him in the frame. The sounds of brass instruments and singing become more prominent. The sequence reverses to look from behind Antoine as he walks up to a large group of musicians and singers. Then the camera swings counterclockwise, first framing Glen David Andrews singing "I'll Fly Away," before continuing around to find Antoine. The next shot shows Keith Frazier, playing the tuba, just as he did for his brother's actual memorial. By visually referencing Kerwin James's family, *Treme* gains power for its fiction. Antoine gains status from his visual association with real musicians, investing his perspective, central to scene, with authority. The next shot looks down from a high angle at the group, finding Glen David Andrews and Phil Frazier, finally ending with a framing showing the group from behind Antoine. As Glen David Andrews plays a trombone, pointing it up to the sky, and Pierce performs as if he were playing, pointing down to the ground, the audio track brings up the sound of police sirens. Flashing lights are reflected on the wall behind Antoine.

The group continues playing, even as the sirens grow louder, until an authoritarian voice interjects.

> POLICEMAN: That's it. Stop the music!

The sequence cuts to a wide shot of the players and the crowd, as a policeman enters the frame, waving his arms, signaling the group to stop. The sequence cuts to a handheld shot of the policeman, with Glen David Andrews in the shot. From Andrews, the sequence cuts to Phil Frazier.

> PHIL FRAZIER: It's a memorial for my little brother. Come on
> now!
> POLICEMAN: We've got noise complaints.
> GLEN DAVID ANDREWS: This a memorial for Kerwin James, man!

Simon and Overmyer are re-creating in 2012 a version of an actual incident that had occurred five years earlier. The NOPD responded to noise complaints from unnamed citizens and stopped a second line in honor of James taking place in the Treme neighborhood. As Simon and Overmyer reconstruct the scene, seeding it with actual participants, they create a convincing interpretation of the showdown. This reading of the confrontation argues that the NOPD harassed and oppressed the performance of culture in a moment when cultural performance was one of the few options left for citizens to respond to the neglect and destruction of their city and their lives. The logic of the sequence contends that the police were insensitive and excessively confrontational, too eager to enforce the complaints of gentrifiers and too antagonistic to traditional cultural forms.

> ANTOINE: Any people complaining about music in Treme, they in
> the wrong place altogether.

Yet, in the re-creation, the police give more credence to the complainants than to the community members performing a ritual of remembrance. Simon and Overmyer suggest that both the police and new property owners fail to understand Treme.

As the sequence continues, the camera frames Antoine from the perspective of an African American NOPD officer.

> ANTOINE: Come on man! We're here out of respect.
> POLICEMAN: I'm telling you, clear the street.

Antoine glares at the officer, but ultimately complies. Framed in a wider shot, over the policeman's shoulder and through his perspective, Antoine walks away. Midway across the street, however, he raises his right arm and extends his middle finger. He walks away, humming "I'll Fly Away." After a few beats, just as the viewers begin to think Antoine got away with his small gesture of diminished agency, the sequence suddenly shifts to a shot from inside a police car, looking past two policemen, to find Antoine frozen in the headlights in front of a fence. The African American policeman gets out of his car, and the sequence shifts to a close-up on Antoine. Having been assaulted by NOPD officers in Episode 3 of Season 1 for drunkenly stumbling into their squad car with his trombone, Antoine tenses, anticipating a beating.

POLICEMAN: Respect, huh?

The first policeman's partner enters the frame, cuffing Antoine. The sequence then fades to black.

Simon and Overmyer combine elements of their two previous approaches to re-creating second lines to represent the Kerwin James second line. As with the All Star Second Line, they employ wide framings and handheld shots to represent performance by showing the relations between bodies in space. Like the Austin Leslie second line, they carefully storyboard and block shots to construct a tight sequence. As a result, the Kerwin James second line has some of the organic quality of the All Star Second Line, but also the tight control of the Austin Leslie second line. The third second line conveys performance but also narrative.

Unlike the first and second second lines, the third re-creation explicitly frames the performance of the parade as a form of resistance to social control. The community demonstrates a form of cultural authority, and *Treme* figures this authority as more legitimate than the legal authority of the police. By showing the NOPD's antipathy, *Treme* emphasizes that the stakes involved are significant. Second lines are about more than just singing and dancing. As Lipsitz and hooks have argued, the New Orleans second line enacts a critique against historic injustice and stands as a challenge to contemporary powers. After being ordered to stop playing, the community members shifted to an a cappella rendition of "I'll Fly Away," demonstrating creative resistance. This performance of culture as resistance is more powerful than Antoine's tossed-off disrespect to the police. He shows his displeasure, but does not fully own his critique, turning his back and walking away. In contrast, by singing when told to stop playing, the community performs an alternative in response to social control. *Treme* understands the second line to be a performance of politics as well as culture. When Lee and Pollard re-create second lines, their scenes are symbolic and associative. By re-creating three historical second lines, by using the power of the television apparatus to structure perspective, *Treme* is able to place viewers inside community performance, providing them with points of view from which to experience culture as agency.

CHAPTER TWENTY-TWO

All These Trucks Got Bodies?

DRAMATIZING INJUSTICE

*A*FTER KATRINA, FEMA CREATED A DISASTER MORTU-ary Operational Response Team (D-Mort) facility in Car-ville, Louisiana, a "state-of-the-art morgue built to handle the victims of Hurricane Katrina." FEMA spent $17 million to build a 70,000-square-foot facility to handle up to 5,000 bodies. New Orleans coroner Dr. Frank Min-yard, who declined to categorize Henry Glover's killing as murder, and who resisted A. C. Thompson's efforts to investigate violence by police and white vigilantes after Katrina, called D-Mort "the Taj Mahal of forensic science. It is a beautiful place." D-Mort in Carville closed in February 2006, ten weeks after opening, having examined approximately 900 bodies. Built to process 150 bodies per day, D-Mort had received only a single body per day by February 2006. FEMA had overestimated the casualties of Katrina. The facility, built on private land owned by Bear Industries, a construc-tion supply company, was decommissioned and abandoned (Dewan, 2006).

In Season 1, Episode 7 of *Treme*, "Smoke My Peace Pipe," David Simon and Eric Overmyer set a scene at D-Mort, Minyard's "beautiful place," to reveal the injustices involved in the treatment of prisoners and in the han-dling and disposition of the bodies of the people who died in the flood. At the start of Season 1, LaDonna Batiste (Khandi Alexander) enlists the help of Toni Bernette (Melisso Leo) in locating her missing brother, Daymo. They discover that he had been arrested on Sunday, August 28, the day be-fore Katrina made landfall, after a traffic violation.

For the first ten hours of its first season, *Treme* avoided representation of Katrina, focusing instead on the challenge of living in its aftermath. At the end of "I'll Fly Away," the tenth and final episode of the first season, Simon and Overmyer present a scene that flashes back in time to Sun-day, August 28, 2005, the day before Katrina made landfall. The flashback

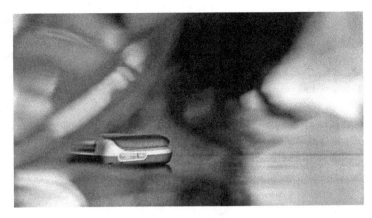

*Flashback to Sunday, August 28, 2005, the day before Katrina makes landfall. Daymo's phone ringing (*Treme, *frame capture).*

sequence is bracketed by the funeral for David Maurice "Daymo" Brooks (Daryl Williams), LaDonna's younger brother. In an exterior shot on the St. Louis Cemetery No. 1, as a female singer performs "Just a Closer Walk with Thee," the camera zooms on LaDonna. As the camera frames her in an extreme close-up, the soundtrack features the sound of a phone ringing. Using the ringing as a bridge, the image begins to dissolve as the camera tracks to the right. The next shot matches this move, tracking to the right to find a cell phone. Daymo reaches into the frame, answering the phone. As he steps back, the camera reframes him in a medium shot, revealing the setting to be the interior of his mother's house. Anticipating the loss of power, Janette's sous chef, Jacques (Ntare Guma Mbaho Mwine), has called to ask Daymo if he could empty the fridge at Desautel's, where Daymo works as a busboy.

DAYMO: Tell the boss lady not to worry. I got this.

Daymo grabs his keys and heads toward the door.

By beginning on LaDonna and moving into an extreme close-up on her face, the shot signals that the flashback is initially focalized through LaDonna's perspective. As she buries her brother, she is thinking back to the chain of events that led to his death. Since LaDonna was not present to see her brother leave for Desautel's, the shot focuses on her face, rather than constructs her cinematic point of view. The viewer sees LaDonna rather than sees as LaDonna.

Later, the scene cuts back to LaDonna, during her evacuation from New Orleans. In an exterior, high-angle crane shot, the camera quickly tracks down on LaDonna, her husband Larry, her mother, and her boys in Larry's Land Rover, waiting in a long line at a gas station, jammed with evacuees. The camera frames LaDonna as she gets out, looks around, hot, flustered, and annoyed. In a series of reverses, LaDonna and her mother discuss Daymo. LaDonna tries to call him, but the circuits are busy.

The scene then cuts back to Daymo, driving to Desautel's. The camera frames a cross hanging from his rearview mirror in close-up, approximating Daymo's point of view. Reversing, the shot looks at him through the windshield, before cutting to a shot over his shoulder, out through the windshield. A red light is visible. Singing along to a rap song, Daymo runs the light. The shot reverses again, looking at Daymo through the wind-

*LaDonna at Daymo's funeral (*Treme, *frame capture).*

*LaDonna and family stop for gas while evacuating to Baton Rouge (*Treme, *frame capture).*

*Daymo (Daryl Williams) runs a stoplight (*Treme*, frame capture).*

shield as a police car, lights and siren on, comes around the corner and enters the shot. The camera reverses to show him looking in the rearview, seeing the cop. He pulls around the corner to a stop, watching the policeman approach in his side mirror.

The sequence cuts back to the policeman, framing him in a side view, as he gets into his car, checking Daymo's information. The camera cuts to a shot through the windshield of the police car, showing Daymo in the backseat in handcuffs. He argues with the policeman that the bench warrant for his arrest was a mistake. Daymo asks the policeman to give him a ticket.

POLICEMAN: Sorry. It's a bench warrant. Got no choice.

The final view of Daymo is a high-angle shot, framing the Tchoupitoulas Street sign as the police car drives away. Beads hang down from the sign into the frame, as the camera holds a beat on Daymo's car (where Toni will locate it months later). The reveal of Daymo in the backseat is structured to shock the viewer with the recognition that a traffic stop would become a death sentence. Because of a traffic infraction and bad record keeping by the New Orleans courts, Daymo was arrested for a bench warrant he had already resolved.

GET ME OUT OF HERE, SIS!

Treme's fifth episode, "Shame, Shame, Shame," opens with a dream sequence in which LaDonna imagines Daymo locked in an Orleans Parish Prison (OPP) cell. Like the flashback at the end of the final episode of Sea-

*Daymo arrested on an erroneous bench warrant (*Treme, *frame capture).*

*In a dream sequence, LaDonna (Khandi Alexander) visits prison (*Treme, *frame capture).*

son 1, the dream sequence is focalized through LaDonna's perspective and motivated by her concern about the fate of her brother. These are the only two scenes in Season 1 of *Treme* to break with the realist style employed by Simon on *The Wire*. The scene begins with a shot of an iron jail door being opened. The camera pans left to find Toni Bernette, smiling and nodding at the camera. In the first four episodes of the first season, LaDonna had sought Toni's help to find her brother.

The camera pans back and to the right to follow over a prison guard's shoulder, as he leads LaDonna down a cellblock. The shot then reverses, showing a front view of an African American male guard leading LaDonna down a prison hallway. In the dream, LaDonna wears a bright red dress, and she draws the attention of the men in the cells as she and the guard pass. The camera shows her perspective on the men pressing against small glass windows to see her. The camera reverses to look at LaDonna, tightening into a close-up as she becomes upset. The camera cuts from LaDonna to a cell door being opened to reveal Daymo. The camera tracks into the cell as he rises from the lower bunk. He looks at the camera and says, "Finally!" There is movement in the upper bunk behind him. The shot reverses to show Daymo's perspective on his older sister. The cell door closes behind her. A series of reverses show the siblings talking. She accuses him of "messing around with that dope." At this, the figure in the top bunk begins to laugh, and the camera pans right to frame the figure, his face turned toward the wall, away from the camera. As the camera frames Daymo from LaDonna's perspective, the figure rises from the top bunk, and the camera tilts up to find Keevon White (Anwan "Big G" Glover). In Episode 4 of Season 1, "At the Foot of Canal Street," Toni and LaDonna had met White, who had assumed Daymo's identity in an attempt to gain release after the storm. White had shared a cell with Daymo, but claimed not to know what had happened to him. In the dream sequence, LaDonna reacts to White with horror, the camera looking down at her from a high angle. The camera cuts to a low angle, looking up at White, then tilts down to Daymo.

DAYMO: Get me out of here, Sis!

The camera cuts back to LaDonna's perspective, as she begins to hear the sound of water. She looks down and sees water entering the frame and covering her feet. Daymo pleads for her help. When she looks down

*Daymo appeals to LaDonna to get him out of prison (*Treme, *frame capture).*

*Keevon White (Anwan Glover) in the bunk above Daymo (*Treme*, frame capture).*

again, the camera observes muddy water now up to her ankles. White continues to laugh. The camera cuts to a long shot on Daymo standing in his cell, with White looming over him, his left leg dangling by Daymo. Water covers the floor of the cell. As the water sound continues, LaDonna wakes up, breathing heavily. She wears a red nightgown and is with Larry in her bedroom in Baton Rouge. As she sits up, the shot fades to black.

The dream sequence recalls Werner Herzog's *Bad Lieutenant: Port of Call New Orleans* (2009). In a scene early in the film, Nicholas Cage, playing a corrupt cop, discovers prisoners abandoned to drown by their guards. In a brief moment of morality, Cage jumps into the water to free the prisoners. Characteristic of Herzog's vision of human morality, the film frames the decision as a mistake. Cage hurts his back diving into the water, forcing him to take painkillers and launching his descent into corruption, dissipation, and murder.

In August 2006, the American Civil Liberties Union published "Abandoned & Abused: Orleans Parish Prisoners in the Wake of Hurricane Katrina." This ACLU report found that the Orleans Parish Prison system abandoned sixty-five hundred inmates during and after the storm. Rather than evacuate the prisoners in advance of Katrina's landfall, Sheriff Marlin Gusman decided to leave them "where they belonged." As a consequence, thousands of prisoners were left locked in facilities that flooded: "As floodwaters rose in the OPP buildings, power was lost, and entire buildings were plunged into darkness. Deputies left their posts wholesale, leaving behind prisoners in locked cells, some standing in sewage-tainted water up to their chests."

The dream sequence and flashback are paired, linked by LaDonna's perspective and by shared formal techniques, including audio bridges and point-of-view shots. The flashback shot shows how Daymo was brought into the Orleans Parish Prison on the day before Katrina's landfall, and the dream sequence suggests the peril he faced in OPP, both from floodwaters and from his fellow inmates. Together, these scenes offer pointed criticism of the treatment of prisoners in New Orleans before and after the storm. As per Sobanet's argument about French prison novels, in these scenes, *Treme* references actual events in order to use fiction to advance social critique (2008).

Through their private investigation, Toni and Ladonna confirm that Daymo had been in the Orleans Parish Prison when the levees failed and

*LaDonna's point of view down as water rushes into the cell (*Treme, *frame capture).*

*Water fills the cell (*Treme, *frame capture).*

*Daymo trapped in a flooded cell with White (*Treme, *frame capture).*

the city flooded. Like other OPP prisoners, Daymo was initially abandoned, left locked up in facilities that began to flood. Eventually, he was brought out with other prisoners, forced to spend days without shelter or adequate food, and then eventually shipped to a prison in St. Gabriel, Louisiana, in Iberville Parish (parishes received FEMA funds for holding OPP prisoners, creating an incentive for holding prisoners in the system). Their search eventually revealed that Daymo had switched identification with another prisoner, Keevon White, and later assumed the identity of a cousin who did not have a criminal record. When Toni and LaDonna discover the cousin's name on a list of bodies being held at D-Mort, they drive to Carville to view the body.

Following the scene of Danny's (Deacon John Moore) funeral, the D-Mort sequence begins with a high-angle shot that tilts up as a dark car drives into an industrial site. As the car approaches, a black hearse emerges from deeper in the facility. The sequence cuts inside the car, looking past Toni and LaDonna in the front seat, as the black hearse moves past them on the left side of the frame. The shot then reverses, showing Toni through the windshield, looking at the hearse, before panning over to LaDonna, looking out at the facility and a large asphalt area crowded with eighteen-wheel refrigeration trucks. The sequence cuts to an exterior long shot as they emerge from the car. A white female staff member emerges from between two large trucks. The camera zooms on LaDonna and Toni as they follow the D-Mort staffer. The tighter framing closes down the space around LaDonna, trapping her as she begins to understand the scope of the facility.

LADONNA: All these trucks got bodies?

From this point, the sequence is increasingly focalized through La-Donna. As the women walk past the camera, it pans to follow them, again framing LaDonna, as the staff member leads them to a truck and up a ramp. The shot focuses on LaDonna standing before the truck. When the noise of the door opening is heard offscreen, LaDonna jumps at the sharp sound. After Toni reassures her, the sequence cuts inside the truck's cargo trailer, a new visual perspective from which to see the impact of D-Mort on La-Donna. The shot is black at first, before the door opens at the far end of the trailer, admitting light and revealing bodies in black bags laid out on the left and right sides. The three women enter, with the image cutting to a tighter framing, as LaDonna walks past the bags into a close-up, reveal-ing her apprehension. The D-Mort staff member identifies and begins to unzip a body bag. The camera shifts behind LaDonna to convey her per-spective down on the bag as it opens to reveal Daymo's body, discolored by the draining of fluids and scarred from the autopsy. The sequence shows LaDonna in a low-angle close-up as she covers her face and sinks to her knees. As Toni reaches out to her, LaDonna runs toward the opening, out of the shot. The sequence cuts outside the truck to see LaDonna emerge into the light.

Back inside the trailer, Toni identifies the body as David Maurice Brooks and examines the death certificate.

> TONI: Cause of death, cerebral hemorrhage. Manner of death, acci-dent. Fall from top bunk!

The implication is that another inmate or a guard killed Daymo at some point during the five months he was imprisoned for a mistaken arrest. Fur-ther, Toni believes that his murder was covered up as an accident and that the cover-up was blessed by D-Mort, which did not even attempt to deter-mine his real identity. Daymo did not receive due process, was not allowed to contact his family or a lawyer, and died in custody without a credible investigation or notification to his family. Through the Daymo plotline, *Treme* argues that governmental authority (at the city, state, and federal levels) committed injustice both through neglect and through commis-sion. *Treme* argues that prisoners suffered more than most because of lack of access to representation, advocacy, or communication. When the so-cial contract was abandoned after Katrina, surviving New Orleanians were treated as "refugees," non-citizens. Surviving prisoners, like Daymo, were treated as non-persons.

Outside the trailer, the camera observes LaDonna's reaction to finding

Daymo's body. Beginning with a close-up on LaDonna, trying to find some comfort in a cigarette, the camera pans around her, moving counterclockwise to show the array of trucks, ultimately panning 180 degrees to frame the open door to the trailer behind her. The next shot directly conveys LaDonna's visual perspective through a clockwise pan looking at the trucks. The sequence then cuts to a stationary shot of LaDonna, slowly turning her head in the same clockwise motion, confirming the previous shot as from her perspective. A long, wide shot shows more than thirteen large trucks arrayed across the asphalt. The audio track amplifies the sound of the refrigeration units on the trucks, bringing up a loud buzzing sound, indirectly suggesting LaDonna's perspective. After holding this shot for several beats, the camera shows LaDonna, keeping her in frame as she bends over, as the buzzing noise gets louder. In this moment, she connects Daymo's death and her own loss to the deaths of the other nine hundred people examined at D-Mort.

Through these final shots of the D-Mort sequence, *Treme* offers its strongest critique of the response of authorities before, during, and after Katrina. Through framing, camera angle, and sound design, these shots demonstrate LaDonna's movement from grief to consciousness of the scale of the injustice. The buzzing noise is amplified by her perspective, not by diegetic or afilmic reality, as she fully processes and understands what D-Mort represents. Using the full formal potential of the televisual apparatus, Simon and Overmyer provide their viewers with the opportunity to understand more fully the loss of life during and after the flooding of New Orleans and the consequences for those who survived.

PEOPLE WANT TO SEE WHAT HAPPENED

In Episode 2 of Season 1, Albert and Lorenzo (Ameer Baraka) discover the body of Jesse, Lorenzo's father and Albert's Wild Man in the Guardians of the Flame. Jesse had drowned at his home in the lower Ninth Ward, but search-and-rescue teams missed his body, which Albert and Lorenzo find beneath an overturned boat. In "Right Place, Wrong Time," Episode 3 of the first season, written by David Mills and directed by Ernest Dickerson, Albert and Lorenzo gather together members of the Guardians and representatives of other tribes at Jesse's house to give him an Indian send-off.

The group consists of professional actors (Clarke Peters, Ameer Baraka, Davi Jay), Mardi Gras Indians (Big Chief Monk Boudreaux of the Golden Eagles, Darryl Montana of the Yellow Pocahontas, and Otto DeJean of the

Hard Head Hunters), and other locals. Fred Johnson, co-founder of the Black Men of Labor Social Aid and Pleasure Club, who was interviewed by Lee in *When the Levees Broke*, is also part of the group. By placing actors in the frame with actual Mardi Gras Indians, *Treme* uses referentiality to give the fictional scene strong resonance.

Simon, Overmyer, Mills, and Dickerson stage a performance of "Indian Red," featuring individual voices and group chanting, with percussion via drums and tambourines. They employ here the same approach worked out by Blake Leyh for recording other forms of live musical performance. They use multiple cameras and mics, placed both inside and outside the circle, to create a range of perspectives on the performance, providing episode editor Alex Hall with a range of shot options.

After Boudreaux arrives, Albert thanks those assembled and then launches into "Indian Red." As Peters sings, the scene begins with a close-up on him before cutting to a wide shot outside the circle, as the group responds with the refrain, "Injun red, Injun red." The image tracks around past Boudreaux to Albert before framing Johnson, as he takes a verse of the song. As the group continues to sing, Hall structures a series of reverses, revealing several perspectives on the circle, alternating from inside and outside, and from left and right. The editing creates a visual dynamic to match the performance as the group pushes the song's tempo.

With the fifty-sixth shot in the scene, a tight shot over Johnson's shoulder at the group, the audio track includes a noise from offscreen. As the scene cuts to a wider shot of the group, the noise becomes louder, interfering with the singing. In a close-up, Albert looks out of frame left, seeking the source of the noise. With a reverse, the scene reveals the source to be a tour bus driving up the street toward the group. A sign on the bus reads "Katrina Tour." The group stops singing, looking out of the frame toward the sound of the bus. Reversing again, the scene shows a high-angle shot, panning from the "Tour" sign to frame the white bus driver. The windows of the bus are darkened, so that the occupants can see out but not be seen clearly from the street, like the one-directional look at the television screen. The shot frames the bus, as flashes become visible through the dark glass. The tour-goers are taking photos of the group memorializing Jesse.

The camera looks down on Albert from a high angle as he stares hard at the driver, his head back.

DRIVER: How you doing, sir? What's this about?

The shot reverses, as Albert looks up at the driver and the group gathers around the bus.

*Katrina Tour bus interrupts the memorial for Wild Man Jesse (*Treme, *frame capture).*

ALBERT: You tell me what this here is about?

DRIVER: Well, people want to see what happened. Say, is that your house?

BOUDREAUX: Drive away from here.

The driver struggles to explain their purpose.

DRIVER: No. We were just tryin' . . .

Albert and Chief DeJean face down the driver.

ALBERT: Just drive away.

DRIVER: I'm sorry. You're right. I'm sorry.

The driver fires up the engine and drives away down the street and out of the frame. In a high-angle shot, the group gathers in the street watching the bus depart. The final shot is over the shoulder of a man holding a spear with a blue feather. The camera looks past the feather as the bus drives away and the image fades to black.

The scene of Wild Man Jesse's memorial is a pivotal scene for understanding *Treme* and what and how it can tell viewers about Katrina. The scene begins with and prioritizes the performance of Mardi Gras Indian ritual. The scene begins with Albert and the group and focuses visually and aurally on their singing and playing in honor of a friend who was drowned when the levees failed. The bus arrives from outside, out of the frame, intruding and interrupting the ceremony. In contrast to the Indians, the bus is inauthentic, commercial. The tour commodifies the suffering caused by the flood, charging a fee to show passengers the Lower Ninth Ward. While television news coverage initially missed the story of the flooding of the Ninth Ward (just as television news missed the flooding of New Orleans East and St. Bernard), eventually national broadcast and cable television news established "the Ninth Ward" as a crucial site of impact by the flood.

In an interview for this book, Simon criticized the fetishization of the Ninth Ward in media coverage of Katrina. He argued that to focus exclusively on the Ninth Ward, or the idea of the Ninth Ward, was to neglect the impact of the flood on the other devastated neighborhoods: Central City, Mid-City, Lakeview, Gentilly, Broadmoor, and Treme, among many others. One reason he set his television show in Treme rather than in the Ninth Ward was to avoid this tendency. The Katrina Tour bus represents this national fascination and investment in the construct of "the Ninth Ward." The Wild Man Jesse scene argues against this fetishization and the transactional tourist economy it fueled.

In a sense, viewers watch *Treme* for some of the same reasons they might take a disaster tour: they too "want to see what happened." Simon and Overmyer and collaborators work hard to create referential fiction that dramatizes the suffering and recovery of residents of New Orleans with respect for the historical record, for what really happened. *Treme* is deeply invested in portraying the dignity of characters such as Albert Lambreaux and LaDonna Batiste-Williams. In these ways, the series is distinctly different from a disaster tour. Yet, viewers are drawn to *Treme* by a desire to see the impact of Katrina on the lives of New Orleanians. While the impulse may be similar, the structure of the television series is different from the narrative structured by the disaster tour. The disaster tour point of view looks at survivors of Katrina from a distance without consciousness of the significance of the separation. In contrast, *Treme* positions viewers inside the lives of its characters, enabling viewers to see their pain, suffering, and resilience.

Geoffrey Hartman has argued that television news structures two positions: those who suffer and those who watch the suffering of others (1994, 2000). Like viewers of television news, *Treme*'s viewers watch the suffering of a group of carefully drawn characters. Like the tour bus passengers, looking out from behind darkened windows, television viewers look at the screen, but are not subjected to a returned gaze. Albert and Big Chief Boudreaux confront the bus driver because he is visible through his open window. He is subject to their gaze, as they are to his. The passengers, however, are not visible during the scene. Like television viewers, they look without being seen.

Paula Rabinowitz has argued that documentary addresses its audience differently from television news (1994). Sturken and Fleetwood argued that television news constitutes viewers as weather citizens, members joined by their fascination with disaster without implication. Like Sturken (2007) and Fleetwood (2006), Hartman critiques the one-directional dynamic of television news. Rabinowitz understands documentary to propose a two-directional dynamic, whereby viewers of documentary are implicated and called to engage and act. Documentary addresses its audience as citizens, people who not only watch suffering but also are called to act in relation to suffering. As documentary fiction, *Treme* wants this same relation with its audience. But unlike documentary, *Treme* can create points of view that allow viewers to occupy the positions of characters, seeing Katrina from the inside rather than staring through darkened glass.

As per Simon, *Treme* asks its viewers to get off the bus, to spend time listening to and learning from New Orleanians. In the Wild Man Jesse scene, viewers are already inside the circle of friends performing a memorial. The logic and structure of the scene separate *Treme*'s viewers from the unseen tourists paying to see suffering. The viewer is witness to authentic performance. *Treme* positions its viewer to resent the arrival of the bus, as do the characters. These fictional characters serve as hosts for viewers in two senses. First, they welcome viewers, bringing them along to enjoy privileged perspectives on cultural performance. Second, these fictional characters also serve as positions for viewers to occupy, as host bodies that bring viewers into perspectives on Katrina unavailable through television news or documentary film.

Jill Godmillow has cautioned against the "pornography of the real" (2002). Like Hartman, Godmillow is suspicious of a one-directional gaze that allows viewers to look at the suffering of others without implication. In her own work, Godmillow has increasingly turned to reflexivity and fictionalization to force her viewers to engage their own status in relation to the real. Thus, in *Far from Poland* (1984), Godmillow creates a documentary from performances and re-enactments of events she could not capture with her documentary camera.

Like Godmillow in *Far from Poland*, *Treme* re-creates "real" events with actors, referencing the real, but also benefitting from the flexibility of fiction to construct dynamic perspectives, to show things that television news or documentary cannot. The second line for Kerwin James actually occurred on October 7, 2007, and was stopped by the NOPD, who arrested several musicians, including Glen David Andrews. When *Treme* re-created the real event, the televisual representation was able to show something of Andrews's perspective, as he exercised agency by singing "I'll Fly Away."

By adding the presence and perspective of a fictional character, Antoine Batiste, who stands next to Andrews and is also arrested, *Treme* transforms the reality of the second line into a scene intended to show viewers the dynamic of oppression and resistance from the inside. By using fiction to structure point of view on real events, *Treme* is able to bear witness to things it never saw.

The difference between the Wild Man Jesse scene and the scene of Big Chief Albert dancing in the darkness is who is seeing and who is being seen. Big Chief Albert put on his Indian suit as a performance, to be seen. Simon and Overmyer construct the scene so that *Treme*'s viewers are the audience for Big Chief Albert's display. Before he arrives at Robinette's house and calls him out, the viewer has already watched him emerge from the darkness. *Treme* creates a special place from which its viewers may see the re-creation of local performance and ritual. In the memorial for Wild Man Jesse, the performance is created by camera and editing for the viewer. But, when diegetic viewers arrive, the group objects. They have been on display, just not for disaster tourists. The disaster tour perpetuates and extends viewing without context, generating misunderstanding. *Treme* provides viewers with situated perspectives in order to counter erasure and forgetting.

As noted earlier in this book, Alison Landsberg has argued for the potential of mass media, including television, to produce memories that viewers could adapt and adopt (2004). This allows people to combine lived memory—what Halbwachs called "autobiographical memory" (1992)—with prosthetic memory. Landsberg argues that prosthetic memory is crucially important as the ground for empathy and connection. Like Godmillow, she suggests that fiction can speak powerfully about the real world. For Landsberg, empathy is the product of a dual understanding of connection to and distance from another's experience. Landsberg distinguishes empathy from sympathy, the weaker sense of affective connection without the critical perspective necessary for implication. She argues that media can create possibilities for empathy and connection. In this way, she calls for multi-directional relations among viewers, texts, and reality. Landsberg seeks to theorize a third position beyond Hartman's looking or being looked at. This third position, what I would call looking with, is what allows *Treme*, a fictional narrative television series created and aired by a premium cable network, to show things about Katrina that are crucial for viewers to understand, to know, and to remember.

Desitively Katrina

*I*N 1974, DR. JOHN RELEASED THE ALBUM *DESITIVELY BON-naroo* (ATCO Records), a follow-up to his hit *In the Right Place* (ATCO Records, 1973). Mac Rebennack, who performs as Dr. John, culti-vates a unique patois, ostensibly derived from New Orleans street slang, but augmented by Rebennack's own linguistic inventions. "Desitively" is a portmanteau combining "definitely" with "positively." Rebennack claims that the term originated in the Ninth Ward.

What would constitute Desitively Katrina? How may we know the truth of Katrina? For those who did not experience the storm and flood directly, a flood of images and sounds provided a surplus of representation. As Geoffrey Hartman (1994) has cautioned, television news shapes experi-ence into stories, erasing as much as illuminating. As Aric Mayer (2008) and Diane Negra (2010) argue, television news coverage of Katrina *was* Katrina for most Americans. The shared experience of viewing news stories about Katrina created a powerful collective memory, but one shaped by the con-ventions of television news production and the values of producers, net-works, and parent corporations. Undoubtedly, television news provided the ground for collective memory of Katrina. Because of the significance of television news in shaping these memories, I have sought to analyze the specific visual rhetorics employed to represent and remember Katrina. In this book, I have examined both the specific strategies and the overall process of television news coverage in order to understand the nature of the dominant representations of Katrina, representations that continue to overdetermine collective and national memory.

As Hartman has argued, collected memory offers an alternative to col-lective memory. In *Flood of Images*, I offer an alternative archive of Katrina media, contextualizing specific broadcasts, documentaries, and television programs. I have sought to read across different forms and modes of media in order to understand how viewers encountered representations of Katrina. In particular, documentary film offers an array of voices and perspectives missing from television news coverage. Documentaries about Katrina come closest to realizing Hartman's goal of collected memory, but documentary is also produced within conventions and shaped by perspectives and values. For this reason, I have analyzed documentary film in order to understand how documentary has constructed Katrina.

Both television news and documentary film make claims to represent the truth of Katrina. David Simon and Eric Overmyer's fictional television series *Treme* also explicitly claims to represent the truth of Katrina, if not always all the realities of recovery. Like the prison fiction of Jean Genet, Simon and Overmyer's *Treme* is an example of documentary fiction, a form of culture that uses reference to the real to invest fiction with power and possibility for social criticism. Alison Landsberg has argued for the potential of mass media, especially fictional narrative, to provide "prosthetic memory," or the opportunity for viewers to experience something of the lived experience of trauma or disaster via media (2004). Following Landsberg, *Treme*'s fictional characters provide viewers with opportunities to experience a powerful, if indirect, form of memory. In the scene at D-Mort, where LaDonna sees her brother Daymo's dead body, *Treme* affords access to the experience of loss and injustice through framing, editing, and Khandi Alexander's performance. This scene creates the grounds for empathy, as viewers understand, perhaps even feel, a version of LaDonna's pain, loss, and outrage, across the distance of mediation and the difference in circumstances between those who suffer and those who watch.

Landsberg's concept of prosthetic memory shares with Andrew Sobanet's "documentary fiction" the premise that reference to the real transforms the possibilities of fiction (2008). In *Treme*, Simon and Overmyer cast Kermit Ruffins, Donald Harrison, Susan Spicer, and former City Councilman Oliver Thomas to play themselves. When fictional characters connect with real New Orleanians, *Treme* gains power for its representations of Katrina. Landsberg argues that much the same happens in the final scene of Steven Spielberg's *Schindler's List* (1993), where actual surviving "Schindler" Jews are filmed with actors from the film. "As the authentic touches the inauthentic, survivor touches actor, the possibility emerges for memory to be transferred across temporal and geographic chasms" (111). Where disaster tours present a form of Godmillow's "pornography of the real," enacting Hartman's division into those who look at the suffering of others, Landsberg's prosthetic memory holds out the promise of connection and understanding. As she argues, thinking ethically means thinking beyond the self

(149). The representations of Katrina in television news, documentary film, and fictional television offer both the lure of sympathy and the promise of empathy. The work involved in the memory project of Katrina is to negotiate the difference in order to work toward understanding.

IN HIS MEMORY AND OUTSIDE OF IT

In his "Magic Hubig's" editorial in the New Orleans *Times-Picayune*, David Simon promised that *Treme* would feature moments of "galloping, unrestrained meta." One such moment was featured in Episode 4 of Season 3, "The Greatest Love." In this episode, Simon and Overmeyer and team re-create the performance of Samuel Beckett's *Waiting for Godot* that was staged outdoors in the Lower Ninth Ward. In 2006, Christopher McElroen directed a production of Beckett's play for the Classical Theater of Harlem, featuring Wendell Pierce in the role of Vladimir. McElroen staged the performance on a rooftop in Harlem, inside a fifteen-thousand-gallon pool, meant to suggest the representation of the Lower Ninth Ward seen on television news. Inspired by this production, visual artist Paul Chan partnered with McElroen and Pierce to develop a staging of the play in New Orleans. Chan's project was financed by Creative Time, the cultural investment company that funded the projection of ghostly beams of light in place of the missing World Trade Center towers. Produced by Chan and directed by McElroen, the production featured Pierce and J. Kyle Manzay as Estragon. *Waiting for Godot* was performed in New Orleans, in the Lower Ninth Ward, on the corner of Forstall and North Roman Streets, on November 2 and 3, 2007. On November 9 and 10, the production was staged in Gentilly, at the corner of Pratt Drive and Robert E. Lee Boulevard.

In Episode 4 of Season 3, Simon and Overmyer include a scene recreating the performance of *Waiting for Godot* in the Lower Ninth Ward. In *Treme*'s version, Manzay plays Estragon, but Anthony Anderson, who played Marlin Boulet in Fox's *K-Ville*, plays Vladimir. In the television show, Antoine Batiste, played by Pierce, attends the performance. In an interview for this book, Simon indicated that this moment was challenging for Pierce, who was performing a character watching a show in which he had himself performed, staged in the same exact location at Forstall and North Roman. In the process, he had to watch Anderson playing Pierce playing Vladimir. Simon described Pierce as being "in his memory and outside of it" at the same time.

Pierce's experience in "The Greatest Love" episode is a particular version of a more common phenomenon with *Treme* and memory. Because

Treme invested such great care in referencing the real and in avoiding unintentional mistakes, the television series created moments in which viewers experienced a collision between prosthetic memory and autobiographical memory. Like Pierce, viewers found themselves both in their memories and outside of them. Writing in the *Times-Picayune*, Alison Fensterstock described this phenomenon as "*Treme*-ja vu," which she defined as "those disconcerting moments when things in New Orleans remind you of the show rather than of your actual life." In Fensterstock's version, "*Treme*-ja vu" describes an overwriting of actual experience by carefully constructed fiction resulting in confusion between reality and fiction. In an interview for this book, co-creator Eric Overmyer explained "*Treme*-ja vu" as the experience of viewers who recognized an event on the show that they had experienced in real life. Pierce's experience of the restaging of *Waiting for Godot* was Overmyer's version of "*Treme*-ja vu." Rather than implanting a false memory, or replacing autobiographical memory with prosthetic memory, Overmyer argues that *Treme* could reference individual, lived memory in order to make a stronger impact and provoke deeper understandings.

Like other forms of Katrina media, *Treme* both references and incites memory. In order to understand the collective memory of Katrina, one must engage the versions of representation, comparing and contrasting media texts with memories. Landsberg reminds us of Freud's arguments about "screen memories": memories transform actual events (15). Memories are composite and synthetic, texts not facts. Thus, to understand what Katrina means and how it is remembered, one must analyze what *Treme* reveals about memory and what memory reveals about *Treme*.

KATRINA IS STILL GOING ON(LINE)

Between 2006 and 2010, Luisa Dantas and her collaborators produced short films on aspects of the recovery of New Orleans with community partners such as the New Orleans Fair Housing Action Council. Dantas posted short videos, including "Sectioned Off" and "Deep Sixed," individually on sites including YouTube (which launched in 2005) and Vimeo (which launched in 2004). In 2010, Dantas released a feature version of her project, titled *Land of Opportunity*, for European cable network Arte, and she launched a website for *Land of Opportunity*, featuring short video content amplifying and extending the arguments of the feature documentary. In 2011, Dantas released a longer feature version of *Land of Opportunity* at festivals and conferences in the United States.

After completing her feature documentary about housing, development, and community agency in New Orleans after Katrina, Dantas sought grant funding from the Ford Foundation's Metropolitan Opportunity Division and BlackPublicMedia.org to create a new interactive website drawing from and extending her documentary material and connecting this material to media from other filmmakers about crises in other American cities. Her new interactive site, launched in fall 2013, provides visitors with opportunities to view rich media content about the impact of the flooding of New Orleans on housing and development, the impact of Hurricane Sandy on the New York and New Jersey coast, the impact of gentrification and development on Brooklyn, and the consequences of the city's bankruptcy for citizens of Detroit. For example, visitors can explore Kelly Anderson's short documentary "My Brooklyn," considering connections between the development of Brooklyn and efforts to develop a new New Orleans after the flooding of the city. While watching videos, visitors can click on embedded triggers to view and explore stories, maps, and data that amplify the documentary content. Visitors can also move between the cities and stories, forging their own points of connection and building their own arguments.

Through the interactive *Land of Opportunity* website (http://landof opportunityinteractive.com), Dantas is making Katrina present and relevant, providing visitors with opportunities to test Brian Nobles's contention that Katrina keeps going on. Her web project reaches back to her own past material and to representations consigned to history and collective memory in order to recover these images and sounds for new consideration, comparison, and connection. Through the creation of a transmedia project, Dantas and collaborators have converted their documentary material into an opportunity for experiential learning about Katrina.

Like Dantas's interactive web project, I have intended this book to be an intervention into the memory project of Katrina. Since Katrina keeps going on, both in New Orleans and elsewhere, scholarship must continue to analyze representations of the storm and flood, comparing and contrasting histories of production and textual rhetorics. As Landsberg argues, the urgency of memory projects in the modern era is about acting in the present more than authenticating the past. *Flood of Images* is situated scholarship intended to act in the present by examining representations and memories of the past.

Katrina media require a response. At the end of the credits for *Trouble the Water*, Tia Lessin and Carl Deal include a title card reading "do something." This book responds to Katrina media by intervening in the ongoing efforts to remember what happened, what it means, and what we must do now.

Bibliography

Abrams, Floyd. *Speaking Freely: Trials of the First Amendment.* New York: Penguin Books, 2006.

Adler, H. G. *The Journey.* New York: Modern Library, 2008. First published in 1950.

———. *Panorama.* New York: Modern Library, 2011. First published in 1968.

———. *Theresienstadt: das Antlitz einer Zwangsgemeinschaft,* 2nd ed. Göttengen: Wallstein Verlag GmbH, 1960. First published in 1947.

Adorno, Theodore. "Commitment." In *The Essential Frankfurt School Reader,* ed. Andrew Arato and Eike Gebhart. New York: Continuum, 1982.

Agee, James, and Walker Evans. *Let Us Now Praise Famous Men.* Boston: Mariner Books, 2001.

American Civil Liberties Union. "Abandoned & Abused: Orleans Parish Prisoners in the Wake of Hurricane Katrina." August 10, 2006.

Associated Press. "New Orleans Since Katrina: Before and After." August 27, 2012.

Assmann, Jan. *Moses the Egyptian: The Memory of Egypt in Western Monotheism.* Cambridge, MA: Harvard University Press, 1997.

Aufderheide, Patricia. *Documentary: A Very Short Introduction.* New York: Oxford University Press, 2007.

Barry, John. *Rising Tide: The Great Mississippi Flood of 1927 and How It Changed America.* New York: Simon and Schuster, 1998.

Baughman, James L. *The Republic of Mass Culture: Journalism, Filmmaking and Broadcasting in America Since 1942.* Baltimore: Johns Hopkins University Press, 2006.

Bell, Lee Anne. *Storytelling for Social Justice.* London: Routledge, 2010.

Bennett, Jill. *Empathic Vision.* Palo Alto: Stanford University Press, 2005.

Berger, Aimee, and Kate Cochran. "Covering (Up?) Katrina: Discursive Ambivalence in Coverage of Hurricane Katrina." *CEA Forum* 36, no. 1 (January 2007).

Birnbaum, Michael. "Stumbling Stones Show Path of Holocaust." *Washington Post,* December 16, 2012.

Bondy, Kim. Interview. March 14, 2011.

Bordwell, David. "Showing What Can't Be Filmed." *Observations on Film Art.* March 4, 2009. Accessed January 31, 2011. www.davidbordwell.net/blog/.

Brock, David, and Ari Rabin-Havt. *The Fox Effect.* New York: Anchor Books, 2012.

Brown, Matthew. "Bridge Exposes Racial Divide." *Times-Picayune*, September 22, 2005.

Brunkhard, Joan, Gonza Namulanda, and Raoult Ratard. "Hurricane Katrina Deaths, Louisiana, 2005." *Disaster Medicine and Public Health Preparedness.* American Medical Association, August 28, 2008.

Buck, Michelle Mahl. *The St. Bernard Fire Department in Hurricane Katrina.* Gretna, LA: Pelican Publishing, 2008.

Buirski, Nancy. Interview. June 16, 2011.

Burke, Peter. *Eyewitnessing: The Uses of Images as Historical Evidence.* London: Reaktion Books, 2001.

Campanella, Richard. *Bienville's Dilemma: A Historical Geography of New Orleans.* Baton Rouge: University of Louisiana Press, 2008.

Cecil, Catherine. "Race, Representation, and Recovery: Documenting the 2006 New Orleans Mayoral Elections." Master's thesis, University of New Orleans, 2009.

Chiang, S. Leo. Interview. March 21, 2011.

Chanan, Michael. *The Politics of Documentary.* London: British Film Institute, 2007.

Christian, Aymar Jean. "Why Do I Hate Steve Zahn's Davis in 'Treme'?" *Televisual* (April 26, 2010).

Cook, Bernie. "Over My Dead Body: The Ideological Use of Dead Bodies in Network News Coverage of Vietnam." *Quarterly Review of Film and Video* 18, no. 2 (2001): 203–216.

———, ed. *Thelma & Louise Live! The Cultural Afterlife of an American Film.* Austin, TX: University of Texas Press, 2007.

Cooper, Christopher, and Robert Block. *Disaster: Hurricane Katrina and the Failure of Homeland Security.* New York: Henry Holt and Company, 2006.

Cuthbert, David. "Artist Paul Chan Brings His 'Godot' to a Waiting City." *Times-Picayune*, November 2, 2007.

Dantas, Luisa. Interview. April 28, 2012.

DeBarry, Jarvis. "'Mr. Cao Goes To Washington' and Gets Sent Back Home." *Times-Picayune*, October 11, 2012.

Dewan, Shaila. "'Taj Mahal' of Morgues Closes as Pace Slows in New Orleans." *Times-Picayune*, February 15, 2006.

DuBos, Clancy. "Tipping Points." *Gambit Weekly*, January 29, 2013.

Dunaway, Michael. "A New Orleans Documentarian Talks to the City's New Storyteller." *Paste*, June 29, 2011.

Durham, Frank. "Media Ritual in Catastrophic Time: The Populist Turn in Television Coverage of Hurricane Katrina." *Journalism* 9, no. 1 (2009): 95–116.

Eaton, Leslie. "A New Landfill in New Orleans Sets Off a Battle." *New York Times*, May 8, 2006.

————. "Study Sees Increase in Illegal Hispanic Workers in New Orleans." *New York Times*, June 8, 2006.

Eggers, Dave. *Zeitoun*. New York: Vintage, 2009.

Elie, Lolis. Interview. February 28, 2011.

————. *Smokestack Lightning: Adventures in the Heart of Barbecue Country*. Berkeley, CA: Ten Speed Press, 2006. First published in 1996.

Ewing, Heidi. Interview. April 17, 2013.

Fensterstock, Allison. "Find Local Bars as Seen on HBO's *Treme*." *Times-Picayune*, July 21, 2010.

Flaherty, Jordan. *Floodlines: Community and Resistance from Katrina to the Jena Six*. Chicago: Haymarket Books, 2010.

Fleetwood, Nicole. "Failing Narrative, Initiating Technologies: Hurricane Katrina and the Production of a Weather Media Event." *American Quarterly* 56, no. 3 (September 2006).

Fletcher, Michael A. "As Detroit Teeters on Bankruptcy, Creditors Are Left Holding the Bag." *Washington Post*, July 9, 2013.

Franklin, Ruth. "The Long View." *New Yorker*, January 31, 2011.

Giralt, Gabriel. "Realism and Realistic Representation in the Digital Age." *Journal of Film and Video* 62, no. 3 (Fall 2010).

Giroux, Henry. "Reading Hurricane Katrina: Race, Class, and the Biopolitics of Disposability." *College Literature* 33, no. 3 (2006): 171–196.

————. *Stormy Weather: Katrina and the Politics of Disposability*. Boulder, CO: Paradigm Publishers, 2006.

Godmillow, Jill. "How Real Is the Reality in Documentary Film? Jill Godmillow, in Conversation with Ann-Louise Shapiro." *History and Theory* 36, no. 4 (1997).

————. "Killing the Documentary as We Know It." *Journal of Film and Video*, 54 (Summer/Fall 2002): 2–3.

Grossman, David. *On Killing*. Boston: Back Bay Books, 1995.

Halbwachs, Maurice. *On Collective Memory*, trans. and ed. Lewis A. Coser. Chicago: University of Chicago Press, 1992.

Hartman, Geoffrey. "Public Memory and Its Discontents." *Raritan* 13, no. 4 (Spring 1994): 24–40.

————. "Telesuffering and Testimony in the Dotcom Era." In *Visual Culture and the Holocaust*, ed. Barbie Zeiler. New Brunswick: Rutgers University Press, 2000.

Hartnell, Anna. "Katrina Tourism and a Tale of Two Cities: Visualizing Race and Class in New Orleans." *American Quarterly* 61, no. 3 (September 2009): 723–748.

Hirsch, Anna, and Claire Dixon. "Katrina Narratives: What Creative Writers Can Teach Us about Oral History." *Oral History Review* 35, no. 2 (2008): 187–195.

Hoefer, Anthony Dyer. "A Re-Vision of the Record: The Demands of Reading Josh Neufeld's A.D." In *Comics and the U.S. South*, ed. Brannon Costello and Qiana J. Whitted. Oxford: University Press of Mississippi, 2012.

Holden, Stephen. "'When the Levees Broke': Spike Lee's Tales from a Broken City." *New York Times*, August 2, 2006.

hooks, bell. *Black Looks: Race and Representation*. Boston, MA: South End Press, 1992.

Hornaday, Ann. "The Man in the Monument." *Washington Post*, November 9, 2012.

Horne, Jed. *Breach of Faith: Hurricane Katrina and the Near Death of a Great American City*. New York: Random House, 2006.

Hurricane Digital Memory Bank. Preserving the Stories of Katrina and Rita. Roy Rosenzweig Center for History and New Media, 2005–2012. www.hurricane archive.org.

"Hurricane Katrina Devastation Makes Ratings Rocket." *Entertainment Sun Journal*, September 8, 2005.

Jameson, Frederic. *Postmodernism, or the Cultural Logic of Late Capitalism*. London: Verso, 1991.

Jaramillo, Deborah L. "The Family Racket: AOL Time Warner, HBO, The Sopranos, and the Construction of a Quality Brand." *Journal of Communication Inquiry* 26, no. 1 (January 2002): 59–75.

———. *Ugly War, Pretty Package: How CNN and Fox News Made the Invasion of Iraq High Concept*. Bloomington: University of Indiana Press, 2009.

Jones, Jeffrey P. "Fox News and the Performance of Ideology." *Cinema Journal* 51, no. 4 (2012): 178–185.

Kennicott, Philip. "A War of All Heroes and No Villains." *Washington Post*, April 12, 2011.

King, Stephen. *Under the Dome*. New York: Scribner, 2009.

Kirshenblatt-Gimblett, Barbara. *Destination Culture: Tourism, Museums, and Heritage*. Berkeley: University of California Press, 1998.

Klein, Naomi. *Shock Doctrine: The Rise of Disaster Capitalism*. New York: Henry Holt, 2007.

Krupa, Michelle. "Ray Nagin Casts Himself as Hero of Katrina in Memoir." *Times-Picayune*, June 26, 2011.

Kunzelman, Michael. "Katrina Victims Hope to Avoid Repaying FEMA." *Washington Post*, January 2, 2012.

Laborde, Lauren. "Where To Watch 'Treme.'" *Gambit*, April 22, 2011.

Landsberg, Alison. *Prosthetic Memory: The Transformation of Public Memory in the Age of Mass Culture*. New York: Columbia University Press, 2004.

Leo, John. "Ray Nagin, the Error-Prone Mayor." *U.S. News & World Report*. September 21, 2005.

Lessin, Tia. Interview. February 23, 2011.

Leyh, Blake. Interview. August 16, 2012.

Li, W., C. Airriess, A. Chia-Chen Chen, K. Leong, and V. Keith. "Katrina and Migration: Evacuation and Return in an Eastern New Orleans Suburb by African Americans and Vietnamese Americans." *Professional Geographer* 62, no. 1 (2010): 103–118.

Li, W., C. Airriess, A. Chia-Chen Chen, K. Leong, V. Keith, and K. Adams. "Surviving Katrina and its Aftermath: A Comparative Analysis of Community Mobilization and Access to Emergency Relief by Vietnamese Americans and African Americans in an Eastern New Orleans Suburb." *Journal of Cultural Geography* 25, no. 3 (2008): 263–286.

Lindahl, Carl. "Publishing Up A Storm." *Callaloo* 29, no. 4 (2007): 1543–1548.

Lipsitz, George. "Mardi Gras Indians: Carnival and Counter-Narrative in Black New Orleans." *Cultural Critique* 10 (1988): 99–121.

———. *Time Passages: Collective Memory and American Popular Culture*. Minneapolis: University of Minnesota Press, 2001.

Logsdon, Dawn. Interview. February 22, 2011.

Lowenthal, David. *The Past is a Foreign Country*. Cambridge, UK: Cambridge University Press, 1985.

Macherey, Pierre. *A Theory of Literary Production*. Boston: Routledge & Kegan Paul, 1978.

Maggi, Laura. "Danziger Bridge Gunfire Was Caught on Video by NBC News Crew on Nearby I-10 Bridge." NOLA.com/ *Times-Picayune*, July 24, 2011. www .nola.com/crime/index.ssf/2011/07/danziger_bridge_gunfire_was_ca.html (accessed March 7, 2013).

Maggi, Laura, and Brendan McCarthy. "2 New Orleans Cops Convicted in Beating Death of Treme Man." *Times-Picayune*, April 13, 2011.

Maklansky, Steven. *Katrina Exposed: A Photographic Reckoning*. New Orleans: New Orleans Museum of Art, 2006. (Catalog for exhibit, *Katrina Exposed: A Community of Photographs*, NOMA, May 20–September 17, 2006.)

Maloney, Ann. "For New Orleanians, 'Waiting For Godot' Hits the Spot." *Times-Picayune*, November 2, 2007.

Mason, Wyatt. "The HBO Auteur." *New York Times Magazine*, March 17, 2010.

Mayer, Aric. "Aesthetics of Catastrophe." *Public Culture* 20, no. 2 (Spring 2008).

Mayer-Schonberger, Viktor. "Can We Forgive If We Can't Forget?" *Washington Post*, November 25, 2012.

Mbembe, Achille. "Necropolitics." *Public Culture* 15, no. 1 (2003).

McCarthy, Brendan. "Federal Lawsuit in Beating of Man by Police in French Quarter after Katrina Settled by City." *Times-Picayune*, August 7, 2009.

Morris, Errol. *Believing Is Seeing: Observations on the Mysteries of Photography*. London: Penguin Press, 2011.

Murphy, Laura. "Shots Not Heard Round the World in NOLA." *The Root*, May 16, 2013. www.theroot.com/articles/culture/2013/05/new_orleans_mothers _day_shooting_not_just_street_violence.html.

Nagin, C. Ray. *Katrina's Secrets: The Storm After the Storm*. New Orleans: CreateSpace Independent Publishing Platform, 2011.

National Public Radio. "Spike Lee On Race, Politics, and Broken Levees." *All Things Considered*, August 13, 2006.

Negra, Diane. *Old and New Media After Katrina*. New York: Palgrave MacMillan, 2010.

Nichols, Bill. *Representing Reality: Issues and Concepts in Documentary*. Bloomington: Indiana University Press, 1992.

NOLA.com/*Times-Picayune*. "Police Shot 10 People in the Aftermath of Hurricane Katrina." http://media.nola.com/law_and_disorder/other/NOPD-Katrina-Incidents2.pdf (accessed March 7, 2013).

Nora, Pierre. "Between Memory and History: Les Lieux de Memoire." *Representations* 26 (Spring 1989): 7–25.

Nussbaum, Emily. "Roux with a View." *New Yorker*, October 1, 2012.

O'Brien, Miles. Interview. February 1, 2011.

O'Connell, Michael. "TV Ratings: Dueling Beyonce Specials Bring Big Numbers to HBO and OWN." *Hollywood Reporter*, February 19, 2013.

Olick, Jeffrey K., and Joyce Robbins. "Social Memory Studies: From Collective Memory to the Historical Sociology of Mnemonic Practice." *Annual Review of Sociology* 24 (1998): 105–140.

Oliver, Kelly. *Witnessing: Beyond Recognition*. Minneapolis: University of Minnesota Press, 2001.

Overmyer, Eric. Interview. July 13, 2012.

Pareles, Jon. "Bonnaroo Journal." *New York Times*. www.nytimes.com/ref/arts/music/bonnaroo-journal.html (accessed August 26, 2013).

Pew Research Center's Project for Excellence in Journalism. "Cable TV Audience: 2006 Report. Fox News vs. CNN." Journalism.org., March 13, 2006 (accessed August 11, 2013).

Poniewozik, James. "Treme Watch: New Orleans Is Coming Home." *Time*, May 10, 2010.

Powell, Laurence. *The Accidental City: Improvising New Orleans*. Cambridge, MA: Harvard University Press, 2012.

Rabinowitz, Paula. *They Must Be Represented: The Politics of Documentary*. New York: Verso, 1994.

Reckdahl, Katy. "Culture, Change Collide in Treme." *Times-Picayune*, October 7, 2007.

———. "The Price of Parading." *OffBeat*, November 1, 2006.

Richman, Alan. "Yes, We're Open." *GQ*, November 2006.

Rivlin, Gary. "A Mogul Who Would Rebuild New Orleans." *New York Times*, September 29, 2005.

Roach, Joseph. *Cities of the Dead: Circum-Atlantic Performance*. New York: Columbia University Press, 1996.

Robinson, Sue. "A Chronicle of Chaos: Tracking the New Story of Hurricane Katrina from the *Times-Picayune* on Its Website." *Journalism* 10, no. 4 (2009): 431–450.

———. "'If You Had Been with Us': Mainstream Press and Citizen Journalists Jockey for Authority Over the Collective Memory of Hurricane Katrina." *New Media Society* 11, no. 5 (2009): 795–814.

Rodgers, John. "Memories Of Holocaust Preserved, in 3-D." *Washington Post*, February 3, 2013.

Rojecki, Andrew. "Political Culture and Disaster Response: The Great Floods of 1927 and 2005." *Media, Culture and Society* 31, no. 6 (2009): 957–976.

Rose, Cynthia. "The Originator of TV's 'Homicide' Remains Close to His Police-Reporter Roots." *Seattle Times*, February 18, 1999.

Rosenblatt, Susannah, and James Rainey. "Katrina Takes Toll on Truth, News Accuracy." *Los Angeles Times*, September 27, 2005.

Rothman, Adam. "Hurricane Katrina and the Burdens of History." *History Compass* 4, no. 2 (2006): 368–372.

Salaam, Kalamu Ya. "New Orleans Mardi Gras Indians and Tootie Montana." In *He's the Prettiest: A Tribute to Big Chief Allison "Tootie" Montana's 50 Years Of Mardi Gras Indian Suiting* (virtual book). Louisiana's Living Traditions. Louisiana Folklife: A Guide to the State. www.Louisianafolklife.org.

Sallit, Dan. "Bazin on Documentaries, Real and Imaginary." *Sallit.Blogspot.com*, January 31, 2011.

Scott, Rebecca. *Degrees of Freedom: Louisiana and Cuba After Slavery*. Cambridge, MA: Harvard University Press, 2005.

Select Bipartisan Committee to Investigate Preparation and Response to Hurricane Katrina. "A Failure Of Initiative," July 27, 2007.

Shankman, Sabrina, Tom Jennings, Brendan McCarthy, Laura Maggi, and A. C. Thompson. "After Katrina, New Orleans Cops Were Told They Could Shoot Looters." *ProPublica*, July 24, 2012. www.propublica.org/nola/story/nopd-order-to-shoot-looters-hurricane-katrina (accessed March 7, 2013).

Shayt, David. "Artifacts of Disaster: Creating the Smithsonian's Katrina Collection." *Technology and Culture* 47, no. 2. (April 2006).

Simon, David. "HBO's 'Treme' Creator David Simon Explains It All for You." *Times-Picayune*, April 11, 2010.

———. *Homicide: A Year On The Killing Streets*. New York: Houghton Mifflin, 1991.

Simon, David. Interview. June 21, 2012.

Simon, David, and Ed Burns. *The Corner: A Year in the Life of an Inner-City Neighborhood*. New York: Broadway Books, 1997.

Skoller, Jeffrey. *Shadows, Specters, Shards: Making History in Avant-Garde Film*. Minneapolis: University of Minnesota Press, 2005.

Sloan, Stephen. "Oral History and Hurricane Katrina: Reflections on Shouts and Silences." *Oral History Review* 35, no. 2 (2008): 176–186.

Snedeker, Rebecca. Interview. March 24, 2011.

Sobanet, Andrew. *Jail Sentences: Representing Prison in Twentieth-Century French Fiction*. Lincoln: University of Nebraska Press, 2008.

Sobchack, Vivian. "Inscribing Ethical Space—Ten Propositions on Death, Representation, and Documentary." *Quarterly Review of Film and Video* 9, no. 4 (1984): 283–300.

———. "Toward a Phenomenology of Non-Fictional Experience." In *Collecting Visible Evidence*, ed. Michael Renov and Jane Gaines. Minneapolis: University of Minnesota Press, 1999, 241–254.

Solnit, Rebecca. *A Paradise Built in Hell: The Extraordinary Communities that Arise in Disaster*. New York: Penguin, 2010.

———. "The Uses of Disaster." *Harpers* (October 2005): 31–37.

Stam, Robert. "Beyond Fidelity: The Dialogics of Adaptation." In *Film Adaptation*, ed. James Narremore. London: Athlone Press, 2000.

Sturken, Marita. "Desiring the Weather: El Niño, the Media, and California Identity." *Public Culture* 13, no. 2 (Spring 2001): 161–189.

———. *Tourists of History: Memory, Kitsch, and Consumerism from Oklahoma City to Ground Zero*. Durham: Duke University Press, 2007.

Sturken, Marita, and Lisa Cartwright. *Practices of Looking*. Oxford: Oxford University Press, 2009.

Swenson, Dan. "Flash Flood: Hurricane Katrina's Inundation of New Orleans, August 29th, 2005." NOLA.com/*Times-Picayune*, May 14, 2006. www.nola.com/katrina/graphics/flashflood.swf (accessed June 7, 2013).

Swenson, Dan. "What Happened That Day on the Danziger Bridge." NOLA.com/*Times-Picayune*, June 19, 2011. www.nola.com/crime/index.ssf/2011/06/what_happened_on_the_danziger.html (accessed, March 7, 2013).

Thevenot, Brian, and Gordon Russell. "Rape. Murder. Gunfights." *Times-Picayune*, September 26, 2005.

Thomas, Lynnell. "Roots Run Deep Here." *American Quarterly* 61, no. 3 (September 2009): 749–761.

Thompson, A. C. "Body of Evidence." *Nation*, January 5, 2009.

———. Interview. April 11, 2013.

———. "Katrina's Hidden Race War." *Nation*, December 17, 2008.

———. "New Evidence Surfaces in Post-Katrina Crimes." *Nation*, July 20, 2009.

———. "Post-Katrina, White Vigilantes Shot African Americans with Impunity." ProPublica, December 18, 2008.

Thompson, A. C., and Brendan McCarthy. "Feds Exploring Claims of Racial Vigilantism in Algiers Point in Days After Hurricane Katrina." *Times-Picayune*, April 12, 2010.

Troncale, Terri. Interview. May 1, 2013.

Vallely, Richard M. "What's Gone Right in the Study of What's Gone Wrong." *Chronicle of Higher Education* 50, no. 32 (April 16, 2004): B6.

Vollen, Lola, and Chris Ying. *Voices From the Storm: The People of New Orleans on Hurricane Katrina and Its Aftermath*. San Francisco: McSweeney's, 2006.

Walker, Dave. "HBO Renews 'Treme' for a Third Season." *Times-Picayune*, May 13, 2011.

———. "LSU's Mari Kornhauser Joins 'Treme' Writing Staff." *Times-Picayune*, May 22, 2011.

———. "On The 'Treme' Trail: HBO Series Co-Creator Eric Overmeyer Defends Fox's 'K-Ville.'" *Times-Picayune*, May 5, 2009.

———. "The Story Behind 'Treme's' Second Season Opening Credits Sequence." *Times-Picayune*, April 24, 2011.

———. "'Treme' Explained." *Times-Picayune*, April 11, 2010.

———. "Wendell Pierce Explains 'Waiting for Godot.'" *Times-Picayune*, October 14, 2012.

———. "With 'Treme' Renewed for a Third Season, Its Writers Focus on Stories Left to Tell." *Times-Picayune*, August 14, 2011.

Walker, Janet. "Rights and Return: The Perils of Situated Testimony after Katrina." In *Documentary Testimonies: Global Archives of Suffering*, ed. Bhaskar Sarkar and Janet Walker. London and New York: Routledge/AFI Film Readers, 2010.

Wallenstein, Andrew. "Netflix Keeps Its Lead over HBO in U.S. Subscriber Count." *Variety*, June 11, 2013.

Warner, Coleman. "Where They Died." *Times-Picayune*, October 23, 2005.

Weisberg, Jacob. "'The Wire' on Fire." *Slate*, September 13, 2006.

Weisel, Elie. "The Holocaust as Literary Inspiration." In *Dimensions of the Holocaust*, ed. Elliot Lefkowitz. Evanston, IL: Northwestern University Press, 1977: 5–19.

White, Ryan. "Reed College Grad Is 'Treme's' Real Davis McAlery [*sic*]." *Oregonian*, June 7, 2011.

Winter, Jay. *Remembering War: The Great War Between Memory and History in the Twentieth Century*. New Haven, CT: Yale University Press, 2006.

Wolf, Daniel. *The Fight for Home: How (Parts of) New Orleans Came Back*. New York: Bloomsbury USA, 2012.

Woods, Clyde. "Katrina's World: Blues, Bourbon, and the Return to Source." *American Quarterly* 61, no. 3 (September 2009): 427–453.

Woods, James. "Invitation to a Beheading." *New Yorker*, May 7, 2012.

Films and Media

1968

The Cradle Is Rocking. Dir. Frank DeCola. Cinematographer: Tom Davenport. U.S. Information Agency. USA.

1978

Always for Pleasure. Dir. Les Blank. Flower Films. USA.

2003

All on a Mardi Gras Day. Dir. Royce Osborn and Jerry Brock. SpyBoy Pictures. USA.
Nat Turner: A Troublesome Property. Dir. Charles Burnett. Produced by Frank Christopher and Kenneth Greenberg. Subpix. USA.

2005

Desire. Dir. Julie Gustafson. Women Make Movies. USA. 84 min.
An Eye in the Storm. Dir. Neil Alexander. Full Frame/IndiePix. USA. 20 min.
Hurricane Katrina. Dir. Peter Doyle. PBS: NOVA. USA. 12 min.
Skeleton Key. Dir. Iain Softley. Universal Pictures. USA. 104 min.
The Storm. Dir. Martin Smith. PBS: Frontline. USA. 60 min.

After Katrina: Rebuilding St. Bernard. Dir. Adam Finberg. FF/IndiePix. USA. 21 min.
Bayou Landfall: The Houma Nation vs. The Hurricanes. Dir. Leslye Abbey. USA. 18 min.
By Invitation Only. Dir. Rebecca Snedeker. Palmetto Pictures. USA. 57 min.
Déjà Vu. Dir. Tony Scott. Scott Free Productions. USA. 126 min.
God Provides. Dir. Brian Cassidy and Melanie Shatzky. Pigeon Projects. USA. 9 min.
Hatchet. Dir. Adam Green. Anchor Bay Entertainment. USA. 93 min.
Hexing the Hurricane. Dir. Jeremy Campbell. Ten18films. USA. 45 min.
Hurricane on the Bayou. Dir. Greg MacGillivray and Glen Pitre. MacGillivray/Freeman Films. USA. 43 min.
New Orleans Furlough. Dir. Amir Bar-Lev. Full Frame/IndiePix. USA. 10 min.
Tim's Island. Dir. Laszlo Fulop and Wickes Helmboldt. Full Frame/IndiePix. USA. 86 min.
When the Levees Broke: A Requiem in Four Acts. Dir. Spike Lee. HBO. USA.

2007

American Experience: New Orleans. Dir. Stephen Ives. Insignia Films. USA.
The Axe in the Attic. Dir. Ed Pincus and Lucia Small. The Axe in the Attic LLC. USA. 110 min.
Forgotten on the Bayou: Rockey's Mission to the White House. Dir. Steven Scaffidi. Ghost Rider Pictures. USA. 84 min.
K-Ville. Created by Jonathan Lisco. Fox. USA, 2007–2008.
Kamp Katrina. Dir. Ashley Saban and David Redmon. Carnivalesque Films. USA. 75 min.
Low and Behold. Dir. Zach Godshall. Sidetrack Films. USA. 96 min.
New Orleans Musicians in Exile. Dir. Robert Mugge. Full Frame/IndiePix. USA. 115 min.
The Reaping. Dir. Stephen Hopkins. Village Roadshow Pictures. USA. 99 min.
Shake the Devil Off. Dir. Peter Entell. Show and Tell Films. USA. 99 min.
Still Standing. Dir. Paula Mendoza. Full Frame/IndiePix. USA. 7 min.
Ya Heard Me. Dir. Matt Miller and Steven Thomas. Catch in the Wall Productions. USA.

2008

Circles of Confusion. Dir. Phoebe Tooke. USA. 11 min.
The Curious Case of Benjamin Button. Dir. David Fincher. Paramount Pictures. USA. 165 min.
Cut Off. Dir. Broderick Webb and Ed Holub. USA. 45 min.
Desert Bayou. Dir. Alex LeMay. Cinema Libre. USA. 92 min.

From the Mouthpiece on Back. Dir. Jason de Silva and Colleen O'Halloran. USA. 56 min.

The Fullness of Time. Dir. Cauleen Smith. Creative Time. USA.

Glory at Sea. Dir. Bhen Zietlan. Court 13 Pictures. USA. 25 min.

Katrina's Children. Dir. Laura Belsey. Shadow Pictures. USA. 83 min.

Left Behind: The Story of the New Orleans Public Schools. Dir. Jason Berry and Vince Borelli. MedArt Productions. USA. 97 min.

Member of the Club. Dir. Phoebe Ferguson and Fernanda Rossi. Bayou and Me Productions. USA. 70 min.

New Orleans for Sale. 2-Cent Media Collective. USA.

New Orleans, Mon Amour. Dir. Michael Almereyda. Voodoo Production Services. USA. 77 min.

102 Minutes That Changed America. Siskel/Jacobs Productions. A&E Television. USA. 102 min.

The Second Line. Dir. John Magary. MFA thesis, Columbia University. USA. 20 min.

Trouble the Water. Dir. Tia Lessin and Carl Deal. Zeitgeist Films. USA. 96 min.

Wade in the Water, Children. Dir. Elizabeth Wood and Gabriel Nussbaum. Bank Street Films. USA. 76 min.

2009

Bad Lieutenant: Port of Call New Orleans. Dir. Werner Herzog. Millennium Films. USA. 122 min.

Faubourg Treme: The Untold Story of Black New Orleans. Dir. Dawn Logsdon and Lolis Elie. Serendipity Films. USA. 68 min.

The Human Cost. Dir. Ed Holub and Christian Roselund. USA. 8:02 min.

Mine. Dir. Geralyn Pezanoski. Film Movement. USA. 80 min.

St. Joe. Dir. Luisa Dantas and Michael Boedigheimer. USA. 10:26 min.

Tootie's Last Suit. Dir. Lisa Katzman. Pomegranate Productions. USA. 97 min.

A Village Called Versailles. Dir. S. Leo Chiang. Walking Iris Films. USA. 67 min.

2010

The Big Uneasy. Dir. Harry Shearer. USA. 98 min.

Bury the Hatchet. Dir. Aaron Walker. Cine-Marais Altaire Productions. USA. 86 min.

Hurricane Season. Dir. Tim Story. Weinstein Company. USA. 102 min.

If God Is Willing and Da Creek Don't Rise. Dir. Spike Lee. HBO. USA.

Law & Disorder. PBS: Frontline. USA. 60 min.

Race. Dir. Katherine Cecil. CecilFilm Productions. USA. 59 min.

The Sunken City. Dir. Marline Otte and Laszlo Fulop. New Orleans Tea Party. USA. 53 min.

Treme. Created by David Simon and Eric Overmyer. HBO. USA, 2010–2013.

Witness: Katrina. Dir. Greg Jacobs and Jon Siskel. National Geographic Television. USA. 90 min.

2011

Land of Opportunity. Dir. Luisa Dantas. USA.
Keeper of the Flame. Dir. Brian Nelson. USA. 32 min.

2012

Beasts of the Southern Wild. Dir. Behn Zeitlin. Journeyman Pictures. USA. 93 min.
Detropia. Dir. Heidi Ewing and Rachel Grady. Loki Films. USA.
I'm Carolyn Parker. Dir. Jonathan Demme. POV/American Documentary. USA.
Mr. Cao Goes to Washington. Dir. S. Leo Chiang. Center for Asian American Media
    USA. 72 min.
My Louisiana Love. Dir. Sharon Linezo Hong and Monique Verdin. USA. 64 min.

2013

Getting Back to Abnormal. Dir. Louis Alvarez, Andrew Kolker, Peter Odabashian, and
    Paul Stekler. Center for New American Media. USA. 92 min.
The Whole Gritty City. Dir. Richard Barber and Andre Lambertson. USA.

Index

Page numbers in italics indicate frame captures.

Bondy, Kim, 12, 20, 26–27, 122, 213
Boudreaux, Big Chief Monk, 358
Bourbon Street, New Orleans, 21
Bourdain, Anthony, 315
Bowl Championship Series of college
football, 21
Bowling for Columbine (Moore, 2002), 175
brass bands, 150, 163, 168, 261, 334, 338; in
funeral first line, 151; in *Treme*, 331–
340, 344. *See also specific bands*
Brave New Films, 269, 270
Breach of Faith (Horne, 2006), 14, 51, 85, 92
Bring New Orleans Back Commission,
261
Brinkley, Douglas, 263
Brisette, James, 112
British Petroleum oil spill, 171
Broadmoor (New Orleans neighbor-
hood), 361
Brock, David, 62
Brown, Aaron, 5, 11, 13, 14–15, 21, 22,
45–46, 93, 99; and Jeanne Meserve's
"breaking news" reporting, 27–31, 32,
127; presenting footage from Con-
vention Center strongly overwritten
with his perspective, 82–84; and the
"wide shot," 3–4, 41–43, 53–55, 210
Brown, Campbell, 103
Brown, Michael, xxi, 93, 110, 170
Brown, Rob, 295, 320, 322, 329
Brunkhard, Joan, 144, 150
Buck, Michelle Mahl, 92
Burke, Peter, xv, 204
Burnett, Charles, 216, 222–223
Burns, Ed, 309–310
Bush, George W., 93, 110, 121, 170, 198.
See also Bush administration
Bush administration: argument of, that
no one could have anticipated or pre-
pared for Katrina, 21, 73; argument
of, that a smaller government cannot
uphold the social contract, 68; failure
of, to respond quickly to Katrina, 157,
170; and necropolitics, 56; and politi-

cization of federal aid, 157; and September 11 as justification for domestic
surveillance and "homeland security,"
91; and wars in the Middle East, 176
Business Council of Greater New
Orleans, 256, 261
Byler, Eric, 270
Bywater (New Orleans neighborhood),
x, 278

Cage, Nicholas, 354
Calliope Project, 300
Canal Street, New Orleans, 43, 44
Cao, Joe, 252
Carisalez, Jeffrey, 339
Cartwright, Lisa, xx
Carvin, Jim, 260–261, 266
Cash Money Records, 207
Catholicism/Catholic Church, 152–153;
in the Vietnamese community in
New Orleans, 229, 232, 234
Causeway (man-made bridge leading
across Lake Pontchartrain), 169, 232
CBD. *See* Central Business District, New
Orleans
Cecil, Katherine, 214, 254–267, 268
Celestin, Oscar "Papa," 309, 311
Center for Creative Reporting, 284
Central Business District (CBD), New
Orleans, 12, 98, 105, 139, 146, 147, 236,
262; familiar to television viewers,
21; flooding in, 52; human and tech-
nological resources located in, post-
Katrina, xiii, 11; looting in, 39, 45;
temporary prison facility in, 206
Central City (New Orleans neighbor-
hood), 4, 243, 326, 361
Chalmette, 85, 86
Chan, Paul, 367
Charity Hospital, New Orleans, 51,
98–100, *101*
Chef Menteur Highway, 114, 236, 247
Chef Menteur landfill, 247

ders of Helen Hill and Dinneral Shavers, 165–166; perceived, in New Orleans during Katrina, 16–18, 39–49, 80–98, 171, 244; perpetrated by police against unarmed civilians, 86, 112, 171; police encouraged to use deadly force to combat, 39, 145, 288; in public housing, 271–272, 274; and shooting after All Star Second Line, 341–342. *See also* Danziger Bridge incident; looting/looters, in New Orleans post-Katrina; violence, New Orleans

Cronkite, Walter, 63

culture, performance of. *See* performance of culture

Cut Off (Webb and Holub, 2009), 275

Dantas, Luisa: and *Go, Diego, Go!*, 269; and *Land of Opportunity* (2011), 214, 268–274, 276–282, 296, 314, 368–369; and *St. Joe* (2009), 270, 272–275, 276; and *Wal-Mart: The High Cost of Low Price* (2005), 213, 269

Danziger Bridge incident, 86, 103, 112–118, *115, 117*, 286

Davis, Cindy, 74–75

Davis, Robert, 300

Deal, Carl: and feature film about National Guard troops, 176, 205; and *Trouble the Water* (2008), 173–176, 178–189, 191–194, 196–197, 200–209, 211–212, 306, 340, 369

DeBoisblanc, Ben, 99

DeJean, Otto, 358

DeLange, Eddie, 135–136

Department of Housing and Urban Development (HUD), 255, 271–272, 275, 300

Desert Bayou (LeMay, 2007), 246

Detroit, Michigan, 167, 271, 314, 369

Detropia (Ewing and Grady, 2012), 167

Dhue, Laurie, 16, 56, 62, 104–105

Dickens, Kim, 297

Dickerson, Ernest, 358, 359

diegetic vs. non-diegetic sound, 151, 321, 358, 363

Direct Cinema, 148, 276

disaster capitalism, 199–200, 255, 268, 278

Disaster Mortuary Operational Response Team (D-Mort), 348, 356, 357, 358, 366

D-Mort. *See* Disaster Mortuary Operational Response Team

documentary film: as compared to fiction, 293–295, 301, 306–307; as compared to television news, xviii, 37–38, 53, 54–55, 126–129, 133, 138, 362, 366; conventions of, 293–294; and creation of the grounds for empathy, xxiii, 367; and the "creative treatment of actuality," 222–223; definitions of, 295, 296; focus of, on the past, 234; funding of, 126–127; Grierson's concept of, as creative treatment of actuality, xix, 162; and the importance to, of evidence such as photographs and historical papers, 219–222; long-form vs. short-form, 127; openness of, to changing circumstances, 176; and relationship of text to audience, 302–303; techniques of, 37; television news archive as source of footage for, xvii, 180–181, 306; trope of return in, 158–163, 225. *See also specific documentaries*

Douglas, Alice, 158–160

Dowling, Kevin, 297, 298

Dr. John, 365

drug(s): addiction to, 203, 208; crime, and elite panic, 254; dealing, 185, 202, 207, 208, 276, 341; death from overdose of, 119; and public housing, 271, 276; David Simon's research into (and use of in *Treme*), 305, 309, 310, 341

Duany, Andrés, 277–278

Dumesnil, Emile, 146

Dunaway, Michael, 305–306, 309, 342

Dunham, Lena, 317

MR-GO. *See* Mississippi River Gulf Outlet (MR-GO) Canal

Mt. Carmel Church, 154

murders. *See* violence, New Orleans

Murphy, Laura, 341

music, New Orleans. *See* brass bands; gospel music; hip-hop; jazz; jazz funerals; second lines; *and specific bands and musicians*

Mwine, Ntare Guma Mbaho, 349

Myers, Mike, 283

My Father, the Genius (Small, 2002), 180

NAACP, 262, 263, 264

Nagin, Ray, *260, 264*, 266, 268, 280; and "Chocolate City" remark, 261, 264; delay of, in issuing mandatory evacuation order, 99, 184–185, 252; election of, in 2002, 252; found guilty of corruption charges, 267; ineffectiveness of, during Katrina, 252–253; role of race in 2006 reelection of, 253–266; shifting of blame by, and shifting of focus from rescue to property protection, 8, 145, 287–288; signing of executive order to build landfill in New Orleans East, 247; in *When the Levees Broke*, 141, 170

Namulanda, Gonza, 144, 150

Natchez (steamboat), 235

National Football League, 21

National Guard, 17, 45, 99, 165, 178, 184, 253, 257, 258, 333; Bar-Lev's documentary about, 177; at the Convention Center, 120, 137, 271; deployment of, to New Orleans post-Katrina (and arrival of, depicted as high concept by television news), 14, 17, 104–108; encouraged to use deadly force against citizens, 39, 145, 288; focus of, on security and protecting property rather than search and rescue, 40, 206; Honoré tries to relax ag-

gressive posture of, 178, 230; in Iraq, 61, 176, 178, 205; Lessin and Deal's planned documentary about, 176–178, 205; safety of, prioritized, 51; at the Superdome, 52, 119, 120, 169, 271

National Hurricane Center, 9

Nation Institute, 284

Nat Turner: A Troublesome Property (Burnett, 2003), 216, 222–223

NBC, 18, 21, 41, 105, 121, 138; advertising on, 24; high-concept approach of, 79, 92; and *Homicide: Life on the Street*, 308; and the "hurricane playbook," 20; and Katrina fundraiser (with Kanye West), 170, 283; story format of, xvii, 127; why author focuses on, xvii. *See also* NBC Nightly News

NBC *Nightly News*, 3, 4, 20–21, 25, 71, *72, 75, 77, 80, 115, 117*; blaming New Orleans residents for "failing" to evacuate, 15; on conditions at the Convention Center, 137; and coverage of the dead/dying, 64, 68–73, 84, 141; Danziger Bridge incident filmed by, 112–118; emphasis on looting and crime on, post-Katrina, 41, 244; images of rescue and mutual aid on, 34, 70–72, 74, 77; and length of broadcast, xvii, 122, 131; report of, on public health post-Katrina, 98, 100–103; reports of human casualties on, 68–73; stories about public health on, 100–103; story about "imperiled" tourists on, 79–81, 287; timeline of discovery of, 5; use of the term "refugees" on, 52; viewership of, xvii, 317–318. *See also* Williams, Brian

necropolitics, xviii, 56, 60, 69, 75, 86, 102, 150, 186

Negra, Diane, 5; and *Old and New Media After Katrina* (2010), xiv, xv, 365

neoliberalism, 56, 68, 110, 200

Nevins, Sheila, 132

New American Media, 284

New Birth Brass Band, 331

New Day Film Collective, 230, 270

Newman, Paul, 94, 96

New Orleans, *135*, 319; brain drain in, 281; diaspora created by Katrina in, 150, 165, 246, 261, 273, 277, 279, 330, 334, 338; drainage of, x, xxi; evacuation of, prior to Katrina, 7, 22, 50, 99, 163, 167, 184, 252–253, 254; and the Green Space Plan, 251, 261, 279; and immigration, 171, 279; politics of race in, 252–267; rebuilding of, 68, 97, 150, 157, 159, 161, 166, 171, 204, 235, 239, 247, 251, 259, 261, 268–269, 271, 277–281. *See also* crime/criminality, in New Orleans; education, public, in New Orleans; food and foodways, New Orleans; hospitals, in New Orleans; housing, New Orleans; Mardi Gras; Mardi Gras Indians; music, New Orleans; poverty, in New Orleans; race, in New Orleans; religion, in New Orleans; second lines; Social Aid and Pleasure Clubs; violence, New Orleans

New Orleans (musical), 136

New Orleans Bayou Steppers (a Social Aid and Pleasure Club), 338

New Orleans East, 277, 335; and the Danziger Bridge incident, 112; flooding and desperate conditions in, 4, 29, 43, 81, 361; landfill project in, 232, 233, 239, 247–251; and necropolitics, 56; Vietnamese immigrants in, 229–251, *233*, 279. *See also* Villa D'Este/Versailles community

New Orleans Fair Housing Action Council, 270, 368

New Orleans Furlough (Bar-Lev, 2006), 176–177

New Orleans Lakefront, 201

New Orleans Police Department. *See* NOPD

New Orleans Saints, 171

New Orleans *Times-Picayune*, 214, 257, 272; coverage of *Treme* in, 317, 318, 368; on police and vigilante violence post-Katrina, 112–113, 118, 146, 285; on rumors of rape and murder at the Superdome and Convention Center, 83, 119; David Simon editorial in, on *Treme*, 297–299, 301–303, 367

NewsNight with Aaron Brown, xvi, xvii, 3, 5, 8, *14*, *16*, 22–24, *24*, *30*, *34*, *36*, *37*, *38*, *94*, *95*, *98*, *100*; "Fort Apache" story on, 93–98, 287; images of rescue and mutual aid on, 33–34, 74; and length of broadcast, 122, 127, 316; Meserve and Biello's story of flooding on, 13–16, 27–31, 32–41, 43, 44, 64, 81; on post-Katrina looting and crime in New Orleans, 41–46, 82–84; reporting from the Convention Center, strongly overwritten with anchor's perspective, 82–84; reporting of, before the storm, 21–24; reporting of, on public health post-Katrina, 98–100; reporting rumors without corroboration, 8; use of term "refugees" on, 52

New Urbanism movement, 277

Nguyen, Fr. Vien, 231, 233–235, 237, 239, 240–242, 246, 251

Nguyen, Mimi, 247–248, 249

Nguyen, Minh, 248, 251

Nichols, Bill, 296

Nichols, Lance E., 341

911 calls, 200, 206

Nine Times (a Social Aid and Pleasure Club), 338

9500 Liberty (Park and Byler), 270

Ninth Ward, xiii, 33, 34, 57, *131*, 155, 180, 187, 189, *193*, 199, 201, 251, 269, 277, 279, 365, 367; community, in *Trouble the Water*, 175, 176, 179, 181, 183, 185, 186, 187–191, 195, 200, 204, 210–211, 212; and first-person perspectives of residents of, 146, 155, 164, 165; and

Hurricane Betsy, 40; Jeanne Meserve and Mark Biello's reporting and footage from, 64, 81, 127; Lower, x, *14*, *30*, 131, *136*, 141, 155, *156*, *157*, *166*, 201, 238, 359, 361, 367; moratorium on building permits in, 261; naval base in, 205; and necropolitics, 56; post-Katrina flooding and desperate conditions in, x, 4, 13–16, 27–31, 33, 34–35, 43, 50, 81, 127, 139, 176, 179, 181, 186, 212, 243, 361; television news focused almost exclusively on, 311; in *When the Levees Broke*, 131, 141, 155–156, 164, 165

Noble, Nina Kostroff, 310

Nobles, Brian, 182, 202, 203, 204, *204*, 205, 208, 212, 369; and his line "Katrina is still going on," 167, 206–207, 215, 251, 293

No Limit Records, 207

NOPD (New Orleans Police Department, *95*, *98*, 148, 301, 329, 332, 333, 340, 346; beatings and shootings of unarmed civilians by, 112–118, 171, 300; bunker mentality of, and concern for their own safety ("Fort Apache"), 45, 88, 93–98, 145, 206, 287; encouraged to use deadly force against citizens, 39, 118, 288; and failure of disaster communications during Katrina, 7, 35, 145; focus of, on protecting property over search and rescue, 205; and Henry Glover's murder, 284–287, 301–302, 348; stopped second line in Treme in 2012, 331, 345, 362; television news aligning with perspective of, 82–84. *See also* police; SWAT teams

North Vietnam, 229, 231, 234

Nowicki, Tom, 216

Nussbaum, Emily, 317

Obama, Barack, 280

O'Brien, Miles, xv, 9, 20

Oliver, Kelly, 292

On Collective Memory (Halbwachs, 1992), xix, xx, 305, 363

102 Minutes That Changed America (Siskel and Jacobs, 2008), 181

"Operation Air Care," 108–111

OPP. *See* Orleans Parish Prison (OPP) System

Original Big 7 (a Social Aid and Pleasure Club), 341

Orleans Avenue Canal, x

Orleans Parish, x

Orleans Parish Prison (OPP) system, 351, 354–356

Orleans Parish schools, 171

Osby, Brenda Marie, 231

Overmyer, Eric, 166, 214, 288, 320, 323, 345, 348, 358, 363, 366; arguing against the constraints of documentary, 306–307; and development of *Treme*, 311–316; and memory, 368; and music in *Treme*, xii, 320–321, 322; pre-*Treme* collaborations of, with David Simon, 309–311; representing New Orleans culture, including second lines and Mardi Gras Indians, in *Treme*, 328, 330, 332, 333, 335–337, 339, 341–343, 344, 346, 359, 367; and research for *Treme*, 293; and truth vs. fiction in *Treme*, xix, 294–302, 306–307; and use of intertextuality and referentiality, 340, 359, 361; viewership of *Treme*, 318–319

Palfi, Stevenson, 207, 215, 219, 311

Paradise Built in Hell, A (Solnit, 2010), 7, 75, 197, 246, 253

Park, Annabel, 270

Patois New Orleans International Human Rights Film Festival, 270

Pelecanos, George, 304, 310, 315

Pennebaker, D. A., 148

Pennington, Richard, 252